Left of Center

Adolf Sturmthal

LEFT OF
CENTER

European Labor
since World War II

229264

HD
6657
·S85
1983

UNIVERSITY OF ILLINOIS PRESS

Urbana   Chicago   London

Library of Congress Cataloging in Publication Data

Sturmthal, Adolf Fox.
   Left of center.

   Includes index.
   1. Trade-unions—Europe—History.   2. Socialist
parties—Europe—History.   3. Industrial relations—
Europe—History.   I. Title.
HD6657.S85   1983   331.88′094   82-11022
ISBN 0-252-01008-6

Contents

Preface

THIS WORK IS in some respects, but by no means in all, a sequel to my earlier book, *The Tragedy of European Labor, 1918–1939*. Addressed to readers not familiar with the main facts in the evolution of the non-Communist left and its labor allies in Western Europe since the end of World War II, it starts out with a study of the international background, followed by a series of factual reports on the life of European trade unions and non-Communist parties associated with labor. The third part discusses the main events in international and intra-European trade union and political organizations. The last part is essentially analytical. It presents some of the main problems and issues confronting the groups referred to above in all or most of the countries of Western Europe. It is this part that I believe to be the core of my discussion and for that reason the mere factual chapters, important as they are, have been kept as short as possible.

The mixture of trade union and party in the collective term of the labor movement is, of course, a characteristic of European labor. The non-Communist left includes labor but extends also beyond it. Labor is the core. Much as the relations between political party and unions have changed over time, it is still impossible to understand what happened in the area of industrial relations without reference to the political parties of labor; nor can developments in the political evolution of the non-Communist left be analyzed without discussing events in the industrial relations field—hence, the sometimes difficult attempt to deal with both Socialist politics and trade union activities. Nor has it been possible to draw a clear demarcation line on the left. While Communist activities have been dealt with only when they impinged upon the life or structure of the non-Communist left, I felt it necessary to refer in somewhat more detail to the so-called Euro-Communist tendencies of the last few years.

The title may mislead the reader into a further strengthening of the already well-rooted misconception of a somewhat uniform Europe or even a somewhat uniform Western Europe. The fact is that the cultural, economic, and political variety of the area called Western Europe is tremendous. Between Sweden, Finland, and Norway in the north and Italy, Spain, and Portugal in the south are such gigantic differences in so many respects that almost no propositions can be formulated that would be valid for all of them. Not even the European Economic Community is a unified entity. In terms of economic power, for instance, West Germany ranks high above a bottom layer formed by the United Kingdom and Italy, or more recently, Greece and, in due course, perhaps Spain and Portugal while France is close to the top.

Of necessity the narrative parts of this study are brief to keep this book within manageable limits. But my aim in any case has not been completeness—which is impossible to achieve—but to provide material for what was for me the main purpose of this study, namely the discussion of the most important problems confronting Western European labor in a rapidly changing world.

The new Europe that emerged from World War II was very different from that of 1938 or the one that followed the end of World War I, almost three decades earlier. Some of the changes were temporary and gradually disappeared as reconstruction progressed; others proved permanent, lasting in more or less the same form throughout the period we are considering, which is roughly to the end of the 1970s.

Many of the changes are all too obvious. Europe was split into a Russian-dominated eastern part, which stretched into sections of central Europe, and a western part under strong but diminishing American influence. Both parts were extremely weak during the early postwar years, economically, politically, and militarily, and they were, to a large extent, if not totally, dependent for their protection upon one or the other of the two superpowers that had emerged from the war. Considerable social transformations occurred in Eastern Europe, mainly imposed by the Soviet armies, and in Western Europe, as a result of a complicated power play by native pressures and the influence of the United States or simply the desire to please American wishes. Other changes resulted from demographic facts: the reduced strength of the age groups lost in the war, the substantial influx of refugees from the East into the West, the almost complete disappearance of the Jewish elite in business, arts and sciences, and politics. Later millions of foreign workers, mainly from Southern Europe, responded to the severe labor shortage in Central, Western, and Northern Europe. In the 1970s a recession produced far-reaching changes in the political and economic make-up of Western Europe.

Gradually Europe began to be organized in response to these changes. The Atlantic Pact entrusted the defense of Europe to a decisive extent to the United States; the Marshall Plan, devised to assist in reconstructing the Old World, led to the formation of the O.E.E.C. (Organization of European Economic Cooperation) and, responding to American influence, restrained social experiments that appeared too wide-ranging. The unification of Europe in some vaguely defined sense, born out of ideas formed in the Resistance, gradually emerged on the political scene, powerfully stimulated by the strong personality of Jean Monnet who became its symbol, but falling far short of his ambitious plans.

Phase two of the Western European postwar history set in with the almost complete economic reconstruction and the stabilization of the political-economic system as a mixed economy, predominantly capitalistic, but with significant Socialist or state-controlled elements. Economic progress proceeded at an amazing rate. During the decade of the 1950s, according to the European Economic Commission (E.E.C.), gross domestic product per capita grew at an annual rate of 5.4 percent in Italy, 6.3 percent in West Germany, and 3.6 percent in France, considerably faster than the 2.0 percent in the United Kingdom and the 2.2 percent in the United States. In contrast with long period growth rates of 1.2 percent, 1.5 percent, and 1.5 percent for the first three countries mentioned, this was an amazing performance, continuing, as we shall see, into the 1960s and the early 1970s. For the United States and the United Kingdom, postwar and long-term domestic product growth rates were almost identical (the latter being 1.2 percent for the United Kingdom, 2 percent for the United States). The contrast between the rapid growth of the continental economies and the slow growth of the United Kingdom and the United States was to lead to a significant shift in the political and economic power relationships within Western Europe and ultimately between Western Europe and the United States. In general, this phase found the non-Communist left in most, though not all, countries of the West in the opposition, away from the levers of political power, but, given the strain in the labor markets, with growing union influence.

The third phase of Western postwar history is more difficult to discern. The most obvious expression of the change was the advance of the non-Communist left in politics. The great men of phase two had been Conservative leaders, though few, if any, in Britain measured up to the stature of historic figures such as Charles de Gaulle and Konrad Adenauer. In phase three Harold Wilson, Willy Brandt, Helmut Schmidt, and, as the French Socialists re-formed their ranks, François Mitterrand together with Bruno Kreisky in Austria and Tage Erlander in Sweden became the symbols of the renaissance of the moderate left. But these men no longer represented the ideas that had inspired the labor and Social Democratic leaders during the earlier period following the end of the war. Just as there was a new Europe, there had arisen a new labor leadership, primarily in the political arena and more slowly on the trade union side. There, the change was gradual, sometimes reluctant, uneven from country to country, to the point that in some countries the trade union movement tended to become one of the most tradition-bound of the organized social forces. Yet change did occur, mainly in response to the revival of a substantially reformed capitalism.

It is possible, perhaps even probable, that the economic slowdown that set in around 1974–75 has been the beginning of a fourth phase in the postwar evolution of Western Europe. On one hand, there were the triumphal victories of democratic forces in Spain and Portugal and signs of an alienation between some of the Communist parties in the West and Moscow. Indications of economic stagnation, on the other hand, a succession of balance of payments crises, the decline of that symbol of Western power, the U.S. dollar, and the break-up of the international monetary system were all symptoms of a substantial change in the economic growth of the West that had been the basis of so many of the economic, social, and educational reforms characteristic of the earlier periods. It is too soon, at the time of this writing, to do more than suggest possibilities as to the permanency of the change in the trend.

The stages in the evolution of the Western European society outlined here had their counterpart, and sometimes their origin, in corresponding changes in the character and behavior of the non-Communist left and the labor organizations with which it cooperated. It is not a mechanical application of vulgar Marxism to point out that in most cases the initiative of the transformation came from the economic and social foundations of the society at large rather than from labor and its political allies. But it would be equally misleading to neglect the role that the non-Communist left played in some of the most important changes, including the new orientation of West German foreign policy or the recent initiatives in social policy.

The first postwar phase was one of great expectations. Fascism and Nazism had been regarded by the left as the last bulwark of capitalism. The defeat of the Fascist powers was thus logically expected to mark the end of the capitalist system or at the least the beginning of a fundamental social change in the direction of democratic Socialism. The victory of the Attlee Labour government in Great Britain, the nationalization measures enacted in France by the government of de Gaulle with Socialist and Communist participation, the establishment of labor governments in Scandinavia, and the emergence of strong Socialist movements in Italy and Austria appeared to foreshadow a new Europe based on democratic Socialist principles. Kurt Schumacher's policy as leader of the German Social Democrats was based on the idea that a Socialist triumph would soon bring about the reunification of divided Germany. Only slowly did many of the Socialists on the continent acknowledge the duplicity of their Communist allies and cut the cords connecting the two parties. This separation was the easier, the closer the acquaintance a country had with the Red Army. It was total and undisputed for most of the time in Germany, followed by Austria. France and Italy found the break more difficult. For British Labour it represented no problem, given the extreme weakness of the Communist party in the United Kingdom.

The neocapitalist revival created difficult situations for labor. The new forms of business management, imported to a large extent from the United States, produced a far less authoritarian atmosphere in the factories than continental European workers were used to, even though employers continued to resist the entrance of unions into the plants. Instead, various types of cooperative institutions, bringing the workers themselves (rather than the unions) together with management, were set up in the plants and, at least at first, caused some appearance of harmony. More important, almost permanent full employment radically changed labor-management relations in favor of the workers. Skilled workers, in particular, became rare and precious. Unions acquired new power while a rapidly rising standard of living weakened the political fervor of working-class parties. In societies of expanding mass consumption the traditional appeals of the Socialist parties appeared hopelessly out of touch with reality, regardless of whether labor's share in the national product grew or not. The absolute increase of the workers' real income was undeniable and made the conventional references to the sad lot of the "exploited" and "oppressed" unbelievable and curious relics of an almost forgotten past. Mass consumption brought with it greater equality of living styles and of educational opportunities, though it took some time for some working-class groups to grow into their new status in society, and some—especially the "guest workers"—barely shared in this move toward greater equality.

The third phase of labor's adjustment to the new Europe was most clearly expressed in the abandonment of the Marxian tradition by the two parties that had earlier been its most loyal legatees, in words if not always in action: the German and the Austrian Social Democrats. The change was made in cautious terms: Marxism, instead of being the intellectual and moral basis of the left, now became but one of several potential motivations of the Socialist creed. Religious, ethical, and technocratic ideologies were put on the same level as Marxism. Quite conceivably, Marxism, perhaps in new expressions, might regain some of its former influence in the future if the economic performance of the mixed system should substantially deteriorate for long periods. Younger elements in the movement, desperately seeking for a meaning in a pragmatic world, may revive Marxism in a form that its creator would hardly recognize as his own; but for the foreseeable future Marxism plays no significant part in the practice and only a modest role in the greatly reduced theoretical work of the movement. New programs were adopted. Their main purpose was to drop the characterization of the party as a proletarian class organization, to turn it instead into a "people's party" open to everyone, to make peace with the church, and to make clear the break with the Communists—except for Italy and France. Beyond that, the programs had little impact on the orientation of a more and more pragmatically inclined movement.

This trend, mainly, though not exclusively, based upon the rising living standards and the social integration of the great majority of the population, was reinforced by growing disappointment with the traditional objectives of the movement. Now that nationalization of industry had been achieved on a substantial scale, it proved of far less significance in the life of the worker and of the nation than had been expected for so long. Even the new concept of codetermination, important as it was as an instrument of social harmony, held only modest appeal for the worker in the plant, though far more for the union leaders.

New problems had arisen: union-party relations were of necessity affected by the transformation of a class party into a people's party. Collective bargaining under full employment raised fundamental issues for price stability and the international monetary system. Later stagflation reared its ugly head. Further developments in programs like social security and fringe benefits for workers offered new opportunities for constructive action that did not affect the system too radically as long as prosperity prevailed. In foreign affairs the recognition that the United States was not prepared to risk World War III in order to intervene in any of the revolts in the East when subject nations made desperate attempts to free themselves from Soviet rule forced a revision of early hopes of rolling back the frontiers of Soviet power? Instead the issues involved in European unification and the reduction of tensions between East and West came to the fore. Not that the old hopes were ever forgotten, but they meant less and less to the rising generations in the West. Radical changes in power relationships would have to come about to revive the old ideas, and even then it was highly uncertain whether even the West as a whole would show much enthusiasm in supporting, for instance, the reunification of a powerful Germany.

There remained uncertainty about Soviet intentions. The fear of aggression from the East diminished, but it never completely died down. Could Europe really count on American help in a nuclear conflict? Was the United States willing to face such terrible risks—the same United States that appeared incapable in 1979 of accepting even minor sacrifices to acquire independence in energy to escape from the blackmail of the Organization of Petroleum Exporting Countries (O.P.E.C)?[1]

Further elaboration of these ideas can be found below.

Seen against a wider background, the post–World War II evolution of Western European labor appears, to large extent, as part of a trend of rising living standards, of higher levels of education, and of increased economic and political influence of the working men and women and their organizations that started long ago.

Real wages in most of the countries of Western Europe had increased three or four times since the beginning of the century. The upward trend appeared to accelerate substantially after World War II up to about the middle of the 1970s. The major break that occurred at that time may have indicated perhaps a temporary reversal but more likely revealed a slowing down of the upward move. Part of the increased productivity was transformed into shorter working hours—not necessarily always in reduced weekly hours of work but also in longer paid vacations and a sizable number of holidays dispersed throughout the year—a far cry from the monotonous, stultifying sixty-hour weeks of the nineteenth century.

One aspect of this almost revolutionary change in workers' lives is the far higher level of education of most workers in the West. While it sounds almost unbelievable that universal secular grammar school education in an industrialized country such as Belgium became a reality as late as after World War I, the period since World War II has witnessed a rapid and substantial expansion of high school and college education that has tested the ingenuity of educators and the adaptability of educational institutions.

Hand in hand with this evolution went a radical and rapid change in the industrial structure of the population. Technological changes have significantly reduced the proportion of the labor force in agriculture. A few figures may illustrate the rapidity of this change during a relatively short period since World War II. In Belgium between 1961 and 1977 the proportion of the labor force in agriculture dropped from 7.2 to 3 percent; in Austria, from 22.8 to 11.7 percent; in France between 1962 and 1975, from 19.8 to 9.6 percent; in West Germany between 1961 and 1977, from 13.4 to 6.4 percent; even in Italy with its lagging Mezzogiorno the drop between 1961 and 1977 reduced the agricultural labor force from 28.2 to 14.6 percent.[2] This meant huge population transfers from village to urban areas, and, if living conditions in the latter were often difficult and the cities incapable of providing reasonable comfort to the large numbers of new arrivals, hopes and sometimes opportunities for better work and living conditions were more readily available— even if with some delay—than in the isolated and narrow confines of the villages.

Most of the former peasants and farm workers ended up being employed in industry or in the rapidly growing ranks of the services. As a result of this and other factors, the reservoir upon which the unions and labor parties could draw expanded both absolutely and as a proportion of the total population. Even when the organizations could not take full advantage of these opportunities, especially of the growth of white-collar occupations, they did expand to some extent. Though mere numbers need not express themselves in power, some improvement in the status of labor in the post–World War II era resulted from the change in the social structure. Acceptance of unions as social partners became the rule rather than the exception and the formation of labor or Socialist governments was no longer a rare occurrence, as it had been during the interwar period.

Perhaps the most important phenomenom characteristic of the post– World War II period was—until recently—the absence of prolonged mass unemployment. Due to social insurance and assistance schemes, the fate of the unemployed is no longer necessarily one of devastating misery as it was during the Great Depression of the 1930s or in earlier crises. But the working population was no longer willing to endure prolonged mass joblessness, even if unbearable misery was no longer its necessary accompaniment. This became a fundamental fact of political and social life in Western Europe. At least equally important was the impact of full employment on labor-management relations, the internal structure and power distribution of the unions, the status of the unions in the community, and, last but not least, the influence that full employment had upon the entire economic system and the international economy.

The institution most directly influenced was collective bargaining. The system of regional or nationwide agreements widely used in Western Europe merely sets a floor under the basic wage rate upon which the rate structure of time wages is established. Traditionally supplementary plant agreements and sometimes understandings of a personal nature were superimposed on the large-scale contract, especially in more profitable firms. Shop stewards or works councils, though in many cases not legally empowered to do so, were most frequently the contracting party with plant or firm management as the counterpart. Under full employment and even more under conditions of the labor shortage, the gap between union-contracted and effective wage rates sometimes became so wide—in Swedish parlance, the "wages drift" became so large—that the union contract became meaningless for many, sometimes practically all, union members in a given industry. The attempt to regain control over effective wages caused some unions to attempt to conclude plant- or enterprisewide agreements. Such was the case at various times in France, West Germany, and elsewhere. Employers resisted such attempts, since, unlike contracts with unions, concessions made to individuals or works' councils are not legally enforceable and can be cancelled at will. Even some unions opposed these attempts as dangers to the solidarity of the working class that effectively undermined any central control over wages and wage policies; these issues still remain unsettled, though some German regional agreements lately contain clauses providing for adaptation of the agreement to plant conditions.

The transformation of the unions had its counterpart in fundamental changes in the membership and the style and ideology of the political parties to which the unions were related. This relationship itself was substantially altered. While workers, especially organized manual workers, remained a mainstay of the Socialist parties, the changes in the industry and the occupational structure of the labor force compelled the parties to make substantial, though not always successful, adjustments to the newly emerging employee groups. The discussion of the implications of this as well as the increasingly sharp separation from the Communist parties forms a large part of this volume.

With the exception of a short chapter on the relationship of British Labour to the European Economic Community, foreign policy has been neglected in this volume. This is not because of the author's failure to recognize the importance of the subject. Quite the contrary: foreign policy is too vital and complex a topic to be treated as part of this book without making it far heavier than appeared desirable.

It remains for me to express the customary thanks that in this case are intended to be more than merely conventional and polite. They go, first, to the German Volkswagen-Stiftung, the Friedrich-Ebert Foundation, the German Marshall Fund in the United States, and to my friends Richard Lowenthal, Jean-Daniel Reynaud, and John Windmuller. Assistance and advice have been given by W. Brugel, Ann Bergman, and others too numerous to name.

Secretarial assistance far beyond the call of duty was provided by Anice Birge and Christina L. Martinez and her collaborators at the Institute of Labor and Industrial Relations of the University of Illinois. Sincere thanks also go to the highly efficient librarian of the Institute, Margaret Chaplan.

NOTES

1. On this point various interviews of the author and articles, for instance in the summer 1979 issue of *Foreign Affairs* (vol. 57, no. 5), bear witness to the difficulties and "certain political tensions" that have arisen between Western Europe and the United States. They have been sharpened since the Ronald Reagan administration took office.

2. All figures are from the *I.L.O. Yearbooks of Labour Statistics*.

PART I
International Background

1

International Developments

EUROPEAN LABOR emerged from World War II in a state of organic unity, the extent of which it had not known for many years. Socialists, Communists, and many supporters of Christian unions had set aside for a short while their differences and had worked together against the Nazis and their Fascist allies in Europe. Cooperation reached its highest degree in the rank and file of the underground movements in Nazi- or Fascist-held countries, though rivalries continued among the leaders of many groups of the Resistance in the countries opposing Adolf Hitler and Benito Mussolini. This state of affairs was created only by the deadly danger of the combined onslaught of the Third Reich and Fascist Italy and the consequent wartime alliance of the capitalistic and democratic West with the Soviet Union. It required an extraordinary threat, such as the German attack on the Soviet Union in 1941, to bring together millions of people who up to then had fought against each other with the kind of bitterness that only profound ideological, almost religious, divergencies could produce.

A similar—temporary—cooperation had existed prior to the outbreak of World War II or, more precisely, prior to that fateful day of August 23, 1939, when Hitler's Germany and Joseph Stalin's Soviet Union surprised the world with the thunderbolt of a treaty of nonaggression—just a few days after an Allied negotiating mission had arrived in Moscow. This "diplomatic revolution,"[1] as it has been described, not only unleashed World War II but also destroyed the beginnings of working-class solidarity between Socialists and Communists that had set in during the middle and late 1930s. The key to this development had been the growing recognition by the Communists in general and Moscow in particular that the National-Socialist regime in Germany was there to stay and that it, rather than the Democratic Socialists, was the main enemy of the Soviet Union.

With the suddenness of policy changes characteristic of an authoritarian movement such as the Communists, this trend toward cooperation was reversed in August 1939 when Germany and the Soviet Union reached an agreement, and once again in June 1941. The Nazi attack upon the Soviet Union forced the Communists to return to an understanding not only with the Socialists but also with anyone who could more or less reasonably be expected to be willing to oppose Hitler and Mussolini.

The main result of this strategy in the labor field was the establishment of a unified trade union international, the World Federation of Trade Unions (W.F.T.U.). The Soviet trade unions participated in it, as did the U.S. industrial unions led by Philip Murray and Walter Reuther. This represented a major breakthrough for the Soviet organizations: for the first time in history they were part of a trade union international together with at least a significant group of U.S. trade unions. What mattered perhaps equally for them was that the American Federation of Labor (A.F.L.) was forced into international isolation, since it refused to cooperate with the Soviet organizations whose character as genuine trade unions the A.F.L. denied. In its view organizations whose leadership was not freely elected were only fictional representatives of the workers of the Soviet Union who had no way under the Russian dictatorship to express their free choices. From the outset, therefore, the A.F.L.—in due course with the support of the U.S. government—urged a relentless war against the W.F.T.U. as well as all other forms of united action or combination with Communists. Even more sharply, of course, it opposed the merger with Communist organizations that became the order of the day in Eastern Europe.

There was nothing startling about the victory of the Communist parties in Eastern Europe after the end of World War II. The Western powers had conceded control over Eastern Europe and parts of Central Europe to the Soviet Union. Indeed, U.S. troops withdrew from territories they had occupied in the course of military operations in order to make room for the Soviet armies, in accordance with the agreements concluded in Yalta. In exchange the West obtained a share of the control of Berlin and Vienna. With the support of the Soviet troops the Communists rapidly established their domination in the East. The limits of Communist power coincided quite closely with the boundaries of Soviet occupation. The Socialist parties were in most cases compelled to merge with the Communists, sometimes by splitting their party and expelling the recalcitrants; in some situations the Socialists were simply suppressed and jailed or executed. In all cases it was the use of force by the Soviet troops or the threat of such force that led to the result that the Communists desired.

Success in the West was more difficult to attain for the Communists and—as events were soon to prove—in many cases highly temporary. But for a while the threat of Communist takeovers in France and perhaps Italy, Greece, and even Austria was more than negligible, and leaders of the West took that danger quite seriously and acted accordingly.

The W.F.T.U.

The first and for a period principal offensive of the Communists outside the military field of action was waged on the trade union front. Its beginning followed soon after the German attack on the Soviet Union. The prewar International Federation of Trade Unions (I.F.T.U.), from which the Communist-controlled unions were excluded, had taken refuge in London. The German, Austrian, French, and other trade unions having been destroyed by the Nazi advance, the main pillars of the I.F.T.U. were the British Trades Union Congress (T.U.C.) and the A.F.L., which had joined the I.F.T.U. in 1937. To a considerable extent its motivation was to keep the rival U.S. union confederation, the Congress of Industrial Organizations (C.I.O.), out of the trade union international. This strategy was based upon the international statutes that provided that at any given time only one trade union confederation from a country could be affiliated with the I.F.T.U. By gaining admission to the international organization the A.F.L. stole a march on the C.I.O., which was thus isolated from the mainstream of the international trade union movement. True, Swiss and Swedish affiliates of the I.F.T.U. also continued to function, but they were of limited influence during the war.

Between the Nazi-Soviet pact in the summer of 1939 and the Nazi attack on the Soviet Union in 1941, the Soviet trade unions, like the Communist parties, engaged in a violent struggle against the I.F.T.U. and its affiliates. They and the Social Democrats came under the ominous heading of "Social-Fascists." They were described as the main enemy of the working class that had to be destroyed first if labor were to defeat the Nazis. Indeed, various informal methods of Nazi-Communist cooperation developed during the period 1939–41 while the full fury of the Communist attack was directed against the Socialists.

This stunning reversal of the Communist strategy following the Popular Front era, inaugurated in 1935–36, proved to be short-lived. Not that the Communists out of their free will set an end to it and reverted to their earlier search for collaboration with the Socialists and all other potential foes of the Nazis. The era of Social-Fascism was terminated by the Nazi surprise attack on the Soviet Union in June 1941. Overnight the Communists reverted to an even more pressing version of their Popular Front strategy.

The first objective of the Communists was the establishment of closer relations with the British trade unions. The latter were in a difficult position; the pressure for a closer understanding with the new Soviet ally was great, the ties to the rump I.F.T.U. mattered less than they had in the past, since the C.I.O. rather than the A.F.L. was powerfully represented in the war-essential industries of the U.S., and the White House maintained close and friendly relations with the C.I.O. Nevertheless, the great majority of the British T.U.C.

leaders were moving slowly and cautiously, restrained by the memory of the recent Communist attacks upon the Labour party, but pushed forward by the enthusiasm of the British workers for the heroes of Stalingrad. The A.F.L., of course, strongly urged the T.U.C. to refrain from organic cooperation with the Soviet trade unions.

The compromise at which the T.U.C. first arrived was to set up in October 1941 an Anglo-Soviet trade union center, which was to be enlarged to include all major U.S. trade unions. However, the A.F.L. put in a double veto: it objected to be included in any international organization of which the C.I.O. was to be a member and to any form of cooperation with the Soviet trade unions that, in the absence of free elections for union leadership, it did not regard as bona fide unions. While the first objection met with little understanding on the part of the British T.U.C., the anti-Soviet arguments did strike a responsive chord in the heart of most British union leaders. Their own experience with the first Anglo-Russian trade union committee (1925–27) had left them with little love for Moscow. Indeed, when in the days of the French Popular Front, French trade union leaders, who were also members of the I.F.T.U., sponsored a move for Soviet affiliation with the free trade union international, the British succeeded in blocking the move. Walter Citrine, the leader of the T.U.C., never concealed his strong feelings on the subject.

The result was an intricate game of international labor diplomacy. The British met with the Russians, on one hand, and the A.F.L., on the other hand, but never did all three sit down together. Moreover, the T.U.C. developed some unofficial ties with the C.I.O. without formally notifying the A.F.L. At the same time the C.I.O. with its then powerful pro-Russian bureaucracy moved closer to the Russians. This, the Russians hoped, would provide them with the handle they needed to destroy the I.F.T.U. They pressed for the calling of a world trade union conference to replace the I.F.T.U. with an organization that would include them and the C.I.O. For quite a while the I.F.T.U. and the A.F.L. resisted successfully. However, what Sir Walter Citrine could not do as president of the I.F.T.U., he was free to do as general secretary of the T.U.C. And the T.U.C. finally called a world trade union conference. It met in London in February 1945.

The Socialist International

The reconstruction of the Socialist International proved more complicated in some ways, simpler in others, than that of the trade union international. The last meeting of the prewar Labor and Socialist International (L.S.I.) took place in April 1940, a few days before the great German offensive destroyed or drove into exile the Socialist parties of Norway and Denmark and about a month before the same fate befell the affiliates of the L.S.I. in Belgium, Holland, and France. The surviving remnants of the organization were even fewer than those of the trade union international, and no affiliate of any significance existed in the United States. This paralyzed the international Socialist movement, but it also removed some of the diplomatic difficulties confronting the international trade union movement. No official act of dissolution of the L.S.I. occurred, except after the war's end. The L.S.I. simply ceased to exist. Its last general secretary, the Austrian Friedrich Adler, resigned, left Europe after the fall of France, and withdrew almost completely from the political scene. Some informal gatherings of continental European Socialists took place in London, but they were unofficial.

It was only toward the end of World War II, in March 1945, that on the initiative of the British Labour party an international Socialist conference met in London. Its chairman was Hugh Dalton, one of the leaders of the party. Thirteen Socialist parties were represented. Germany, Austria, and Hungary, the enemy nations, were excluded. The spirit of the conference was reflected in this fact, but even more in a formal declaration about Germany, which was the main issue before the conference. While recognizing the heroic acts of those Germans who opposed the Nazis, the conference nevertheless spoke of a "collective guilt" of the German people, exceeding any other in history. Military occupation and expropriation of heavy industry in the Ruhr and on the Rhine together with some necessary changes of frontiers but not the division of Germany—these were the price that Germany was to pay.

In addition, the conference appointed a committee to take the steps necessary for the reconstruction of the Socialist International; a plan of these measures was to be submitted to another conference to be held "in the near future." The Communist problem was tackled in the same spirit in which the new trade union international was to be born—the "recognition of the urgent need of the unity of the working class." Indeed, in a memorandum presented to a subsequent international Socialist conference Harold J. Laski, then at the height of his influence in the British Labour party, declared that cooperation of Russia with the Socialist international would turn Europe Socialist in two decades.[2] The alternative he saw was a Europe dominated by monopoly capitalism and carrying with it the danger of a third world war. For several years following the end of the war international developments dominated the labor scene in Europe. It is to these that chapter 4 herein is devoted. First, however, a framework for rapid historic evaluation is provided.

NOTES

1. Norman Luxenburg, *Europe since World War II: The Big Change* (Carbondale: Southern Illinois University Press, 1973), 41.

2. Julius Braunthal, *Geschichte der Internationale* (Hanover: Dietz Nachf., 1971), 3:169.

2

Three Stages in the Evolution of the Left

WORLD WAR II ended in widespread expectation of far-reaching social changes. Since Nazism and Fascism had been widely viewed as the last major defense of monopoly-capitalism against the left, and in view of the apparently endless crisis of the 1930s, a new social system seemed the inevitable consequence of the Nazi-Fascist defeat. A new era in Europe was about to start.

The first few postwar years seemed to confirm these expectations. A substantial majority in the House of Commons supported the British Labour government. Socialist governments existed in Scandinavia. Charles de Gaulle's government was firmly based on Socialist and Communist support and introduced a large number of Socialist-sponsored measures. The leftist vote in France in 1945 reached a staggering 60 percent. But there were also some conspicuous exceptions—primarily in Germany, Italy, and to some extent in Austria.

In West Germany, where Kurt Schumacher's policy was conceived in the expectation of an almost all-European Socialist-Democratic victory, the Social-Democratic party (S.P.D.) at the first federal elections in August 1949 obtained only 29.2 percent of the vote. In Italy in June 1946 the Christian Democrats (C.D.) won almost as many votes as the Communists and the Socialists combined. Alcide De Gasperi, the C.D. leader, emerged and remained the dominant political figure in the country for many years to come. Even in Austria the Social-Democrats, though running well, fell behind the Christian People's party, and the Communists suffered a devastating defeat.

This first semirevolutionary postwar period lasted no longer than five or six years, in some countries such as France even less, and was barely manifest in Central Europe. The fall of the British Labour government and the rapid decline of the French left eliminated the main pillars of left-wing power in Western Europe. Capitalist forces returned in new strength, though less stubbornly conservative and far more committed to democratic ideas and institutions than before 1939. The leftist parties established themselves as opposition. Within the left in France and in Italy the Communists soon outdistanced the Socialists. Thus at the French elections of June 1946 the Communists gained another thirty seats while the Socialists lost twenty-four. If, nevertheless, the Socialists held both the presidency and the prime ministership (in the persons of Vincent Auriol and Paul Ramadier), it was due less to their own strength than to support from the center and the right of the political spectrum. Ramadier paid the price for this support by maneuvering the Communist party out of the government in 1947. In Italy in 1953 when Socialists, right-wing Social-Democrats, and Communists ran separate lists of candidates—in 1948 the Communists and the Socialists had combined their lists—the Communist party with 143 seats vastly surpassed both the left-wing Socialists (seventy-five seats) and the Social-Democrats (nineteen seats).

From about 1952–53 on, the non-Communist left, if not the left in general, performed badly in the political field but developed growing power in the unions. The recuperative forces of a reformed capitalism proved remarkable. Full employment, indeed, labor shortages took the place of the prewar long-term mass unemployment that had contributed so much to the downfall of the democratic system in Europe and the demoralization of the antitotalitarian forces. Rapid economic growth, fostered in part by the replacement of the destroyed installations by modern equipment and in part by the U.S. Marshall Plan, led to an almost equally rapid improvement of living standards. Average gross investment ratios as a percentage of gross national product were in the range of 20 to 30 except for most of the Southern European countries and the United Kingdom.

The advance of the Communist regimes toward the West and the establishment of Communist-dominated governments in a number of Eastern and Central European countries had contradictory effects on the fate of the non-Communist left in Europe. Where the mass of the people came into direct contact with the Soviet armies, the experience was horrifying and its effect strongly anti-Communist. The behavior of the troops and the systematic looting of Soviet-occupied territories was—erroneously, no doubt—ascribed to the Socialism that these troops were allegedly representing. A large part of the population refused for some time to make a distinction between the "Socialism" of these Soviet troops and that of, for example, the S.P.D. in West Germany. The destruction of faith in the liberating and humanitarian force of Socialism greatly contributed to the weakness of the democratic Socialists in Central Europe right after the war; indeed, it may have been the main factor in their decline at that stage. A more permanent factor was, of course, the surprising power of recovery that capitalism exhibited.

In some of the countries that had no direct contact with the Soviet troops—like France and Italy—the prestige of the Soviet armies, the victors of Stalingrad, strengthened the extreme left. The local Communists basked in the reflected glory of the warriors who had so powerfully contributed to the victory of the anti-Nazi front, without suffering from the consequences of personal acquaintance with the Red Army.

Obviously, this can only have been one factor among many in the explanation of what happened in the West. For in other countries, e.g., Norway, Denmark, Belgium, Holland, and of course, Britain, some of which had been as protected from acquaintance with the Red Army as had France and Italy, the glory of the Soviet troops was not sufficient to strengthen the weak or almost nonexisting Communist parties; at the most it did so for short periods only. More profound economic and social factors such as industrial underdevelopment may have facilitated the Communist progress in France and Italy, and the reverse process may have taken place in the other countries mentioned above.[1]

A significant development occurred in the relationship of labor and church, as the old enmity or at least estrangement began to change on both sides. Not only did the Socialist parties accept or even emphasize religious Socialism and made Marxism only one of several motivations for the support of Socialist ideas but also the church and its related organizations abandoned a good deal of their traditional opposition to the Socialist parties and unions. The unification of the trade union movement in Germany, including the Christian unions, left behind only an insignificant religious (Christian) trade union group. In France the great majority of the Christian unions dropped their spiritual and organizational relationship to the Catholic church. The first steps in this direction were made in the immediate postwar years when the advisory (or supervisory) church committee of the C.F.T.C. (Christian Trade Union Confederation) was abolished, since many members of the upper church hierarchy had been closely associated with the occupation authorities. The completion of this separation took almost a decade, but by then the overwhelming majority of the C.F.T.C. changed not only the name but also the ideological direction of the organization and came ever closer to the Socialist movement. In Italy a rapprochement of the three trade union centers took place, mainly under the pressure of the powerful metal trade unions. While falling short of a repeatedly forecasted merger, the degree of cooperation among the long-time foes was at times astonishingly high.

The starting point of French postwar developments is to be found in the Resistance movement or rather movements (since there was a multitude of resistance groups throughout the country). Until Hitler's attack on the Soviet Union in September 1941, the French Communists, though disoriented and often acting half-heartedly, opposed the French struggle against the Nazi armies and managed to make Great Britain the villain in the drama. But when the Soviet Union became the victim of the Germans, the Communists threw themselves without hesitation into the underground struggle against the invaders. They soon managed to play a leading role in the various movements of the Resistance and were its most dynamic and most disciplined elements.[2] This helped to establish the Communists as the leading party of the left and the dominant faction of the trade union movement after the war.

The first phase of French postwar development was thus placed under the sign of powerful Communist influence that only de Gaulle's prestige and strong personality could offset. The Socialists played a secondary role to the Communist party. But the outbreak of the cold war made this first phase rather brief, and by 1947 it was over, but not without leaving behind a large legacy of reforms to be discussed in chapter 7 herein.

Most of the following years, indeed, more than the next two decades, with few and brief interruptions, were characterized by the sterility and the weakness of the French left. The Communists, who controlled the largest trade union confederation, were politically ostracized, and without Communist party support the Socialists were unable to claim governmental power, except as a partner in various coalitions with middle-class groups. Gradually, in this process, the Socialist party weakened until it almost disappeared.

It was only in the 1960s in England and Germany and at the beginning of the 1970s in France that a third phase may be said to have begun. The French Socialist party reemerged from almost total oblivion and the non-Communist trade union current was reenforced by the adoption of Socialist ideas by the bulk of the formerly Christian trade unions. Yet the relations between Socialists and Communists remained the key to the further evolution of the role of the non-Communist left in France. This fact continued to have considerable, if not decisive, impact on the ideological posture and the internal struggles of the Socialists and their allies as well as on the development of the trade unions. The Communist-dominated unions continued to be the strongest single union confederation, but the C.F.D.T. (Democratic Trade Union Confederation), formerly religious in its program, turned more and more toward the Socialist party, and its dynamism gave it influence beyond its numerical strength.

The British Labour party was defeated in 1951, even though it gained votes. There followed a period of dissension; the issue of nationalization divided the party and Aneurin Bevan's leadership aspirations brought personal animosities as well as ideological differences into the internal debates. In the elections of 1955 Labour lost more than 1.5 million votes. A change in the party leadership from Clement Attlee to Hugh Gaitskell—who made Bevan his prospective foreign secretary—was expected to create peace within the party. However, it did not suffice to reverse Labour's political decline. Gaitskell's attempt to set limits to the party's commitment to further nationalizations, except for iron and steel, did not succeed, even though in its election propaganda the party did speak only about "renationalizing iron and steel," but speakers seldom discussed it. Gaitskell and some of his colleagues did elaborate [on] the place of a public sector in a mixed economy, but many

Labour candidates shied away from the issue or even gave assurances that particular industries, such as a local branch of Imperial Chemicals, would not be touched. On the whole, nationalization was something of a handicap to Labour in this prosperity election."[3]

The 1959 election was a surprise and a disappointment for Labour. It lost close to 200,000 votes (2.5 percent of its 1955 vote) and twenty-three seats. Not only was this the third defeat in a row, but Labour also showed a steady decline in votes since 1951. While the party organization stayed with the traditional Socialist formulae, modifying them only in small steps, if at all, the Parliamentary party, which in England elected the party leader until 1981, maintained its loyalty to Gaitskell and his reform ideas, especially his doubts about the merits of the traditional demands for the nationalization of all or most industries. This in itself carried the germ of a sharp conflict because the Parliamentary Labour party, under the constitution of the party, is expected to "give effect as far as may be practicable to the principles from time to time approved by the Party conference." In the past this had rarely given rise to serious conflicts, but now the majority of the group in Parliament insisted on their right to act independently. Members of Parliament in Great Britain are not regarded as delegates of the party organization that nominated them but as representatives of their constituency, which includes nonparty members. When in 1960 the party conference decided by a small majority— not the two-thirds majority required by the constitution—to endorse unilateral British nuclear disarmament, the Parliamentary party came out in favor of multilateral nuclear disarmament. This particular conflict fizzled out when the party conference in the following year reversed its decision. Other conflicts remained. Nevertheless, all attempts at making the Parliamentary party the vehicle of decisions of the party conference, which usually is further to the left, failed, in spite of the fact that the left wing now enjoyed much stronger positions in the party. The party conference of 1978 declined to accept a proposal for a constitutional change that would have provided for the election of the leader by the usually more leftist party conference rather than the Parliamentary party, but subsequent conferences went far toward accommodating the left wing.

Recognizing these cleavages and their causes, the Gaitskell group organized a Campaign for Democratic Socialism that mobilized the reform element and led gradually to changes of the party attitude to bring it more in line with that of the Parliamentary group. Four issues dominated these debates: nationalization, wage restraint, unilateral disarmament, and, finally, British entry into the Common Market. These will be explored in later chapters. At this point it is sufficient to point out that Herbert Morrison requested the circulation among the members of the national executive committee of the party of a memorandum by Richard Crossman, one of the outstanding thinkers of the movement. In this document Crossman ascribed the decline of the party to the fact that it was divided "between those who favored consolidation and wooing the middle class on one side, and those who wanted more nationalization and the mobilization of the working class vote, on the other."[4]

A unifying factor in these debates was the growing emphasis of party propaganda on equality of opportunity rather than on massive nationalization measures. This, which was similar to developments in the West German S.P.D., became increasingly the hallmark of the party and helped to lead it into a third postwar phase, the recovery of the non-Communist left. In Britain, owing to Gaitskell's sudden death in January 1963, the fruits of this evolution were reaped by the party under the leadership of Harold Wilson.

This third phase in British Labour's standing began in the 1960s. The Trades Union Congress (T.U.C.) under its new general secretary, George Woodcock, the successor to Vincent Tewson, developed a distinct policy of moderation. While continuing to reject the Conservative government's attempts to involve the unions in various institutions devoted to wage restraint, the T.U.C. refused to be drawn into mass actions against restraint and, whatever the outward appearances, embarked as it traditionally did on a policy of bargaining with the government. At the same time, the T.U.C. made it clear that it would be less hostile to an incomes policy under a Labour government—which helped prepare the ground for a return of a Labour government in 1964. The party very effectively used its alliance with the trade unions as a device to attract middle-class voters by claiming that the unions would more willingly cooperate with a Labour than with a Conservative government. But beyond that Labour "appealed directly to middle class voters, to the professionals, the scientists, the managers and even set about to achieve an understanding with those 'progressive' elements in the City of London and among industrialists who were looking for a dynamic capitalism."[5] In this way the party adjusted to the advancing recovery of the country and its changing social structure and escaped from the "ghetto" of being merely a trade union or workers' party. To a considerable degree this accomplished the change of the party that Gaitskell had so long attempted to carry out.

The transformation of the German S.P.D. was in some respects far more difficult to achieve. It was the party of the Marxian tradition *par excellence,* though it was difficult to discern this during most of the interwar period, when its language and action more and more departed from its tradition. Its policy after its reconstruction at the end of World War II was based on the belief in the inevitability of a Socialist victory in Western and Central Europe, and its leaders who embodied and defended this policy were men of great moral stature: Kurt Schumacher, crippled hero of the anti-Hitler movement who had spent many years in a Nazi concentration camp; Erich Ollenhauer, the leading survivor of the pre-Hitler party who had returned from exile; Fritz Erler, one of the pillars of the Socialist underground organization "New Beginning"; and others of a similar caliber. Yet, while only these men had the moral authority to engineer the full adjustment of the movement to the changing times, party leaders had to change as well to make the new orientation of the party clearly visible to everyone.

The surprisingly poor performance of the party outside of Berlin immediately after the war, its decline in electoral support at the subsequent election of 1953, and its modest recovery (from just above 29 percent of the popular vote to 31.8 percent) in 1957 led to a revision of basic party tenets. In its traditional appearance the party seemed doomed to be an eternal minority and opposition. Konrad Adenauer, head of the increasingly conservative Christian-Democratic Union (C.D.U.), and Franz Josef Strauss, head of C.D.U.'s Bavarian ally, the Christian-Social Union (C.S.U.), were the permanent leaders of the government, especially after the elections of 1957 gave them a narrow majority of the votes. While in the various *Länder* (provincial) governments and cities the S.P.D. did not fare too badly and produced in Ernst Reuter, Wilhelm Kaisen, Max Brauer, and others leaders of high popular standing, at the federal level the party was less fortunate. After Schumacher's death in 1952, Ollenhauer represented honesty and realism rather than inspiration until Willy Brandt, the mayor of West Berlin, took over the party leadership in 1964. To be fair to Ollenhauer, one must point out that the recovery of the S.D.P. had started at the elections of 1961, when its share of the popular vote had risen to 36 percent. By then the party program had been profoundly changed. Still it was only in 1966 that the S.P.D. entered the government as junior partner of the C.D.U. and Brandt became foreign minister and deputy chancellor under Kurt-Georg Kiesinger of the C.D.U. The third phase of the postwar history of German labor had begun.

It is less easy to discern the three phases in the postwar history of Italian labor parties, for there appears an almost uninterrupted upward trend for the Christian Democrats, followed by the Communists, while the non-Communist left, weakened by a split between the Socialists of Pietro Nenni and a right wing led by Giuseppe Saragat, moved steadily downward. The issue over which the split occurred was the relationship to the Communists. Nenni, who even before the end of the Fascist regime, while in exile, belonged to the left wing of the Socialist International led by the Austrian Otto Bauer, favored cooperation between Socialists and Communists, the unity of the working class being his ultimate goal. However, he postponed a decision on this in order to avoid a split in the Socialist party. In the end he neither succeeded in obtaining the merger with the Communists nor in avoiding the split.[6] Saragat, the spokesman of a small moderate group, wanted to develop a "third force" that could effectively oppose both Christian Democrats and Communists. It was only after the repression of the Hungarian revolt of 1956 that Nenni looked for cooperation with Saragat and that Palmiro Togliatti, the Communist leader, began to speak of Communist "polycentrism," a forerunner of Euro-Communist ideas. This apparently strengthened the Communist

appeal. In the elections of May 1968 the Communists obtained almost 27 percent of the popular votes (from 25.3 percent) and added eleven seats to their previous 166; Nenni's party fell far behind, with 14.5 percent (previously 19.9 percent) of the popular vote and ninety-one (formerly 120) seats in Parliament.

On the trade union side, the threefold split of the left was reflected in the existence of three rival trade union centers, each consisting of national unions competing with each other in the plants. However, while politically Communist strategy aimed at a "historic compromise" with the ruling Christian Democrats and disregarded the declining parties of the non-Communist left, the three trade union centers cooperated increasingly after the late 1960s and even spoke of a merger—without ever acting on the issue. The driving force behind this move was the powerful metal workers' unions of the three centers. The Confederazione Generale Italiana del Lavoro (C.G.I.L.), the Communist-dominated confederation, even went so far as to loosen and ultimately break its ties with the Communist-dominated World Federation of Trade Unions (W.F.T.U.) in order to gain admission to the European Trade Union Confederation in which the unions affiliated with the International Confederation of Free Trade Unions play a dominant role.

It may not be too far-fetched to speak of a fourth phase in the postwar evolution of the non-Communist left, beginning perhaps with the sharp recession around 1975. The rate of economic expansion in Europe slowed down quite distinctly and with it the possibilities of further significant improvements in living standards and social reforms. But it is not quite so easy to discern the political counterpart to this change of the economic climate. The rise of an extremely conservative government in Great Britain, the fall of the Social-Democratic regime in Sweden and later in Norway, and the decline in the popularity of the Socialist-liberal coalition government in Germany point in the same direction as the election of Ronald Reagan in the United States. A countertrend can be discerned in the victory of the French and the Greek Socialists and perhaps to some extent in the democratic evolution of Spain and Portugal. But the predominant trait of the period since the mid-1970s appears to be to move the political center of gravity in the West toward the right. If that is so, then it may well be that the adjustment of the non-Communist left that assisted them in advancing with phase three may prove a highly unhappy development for the harsh conditions of phase four.

NOTES

1. George Lichtheim in his *Marxism in France* (New York: Columbia University Press, 1966) relates the Communist appeal in France and Italy to the persistence of the anarcho-syndicalist tradition in the two countries. By a curious mixture of confusion and pretense, the Communists succeeded in presenting themselves as the

successors to Louis Blanqui, the hero of early anarcho-syndicalism. In fact, while there were common themes in the thinking of Blanqui and later Georges Sorel, on one hand, and V. I. Lenin, on the other hand, there were also profound differences: the belief in a revolutionary elite was common. However, the objective of an individualistic society with a maximum of personal freedom, the very essence of anarcho-syndicalism, found the Communists at the opposite end of the philosophic spectrum. While Lichtheim's tracing of these intellectual traditions is of great interest, he really explains little about the movements of the mass of the workers. The underlying economic, social, and cultural factors that made one set of ideas more appealing to the workers are crucial. Michel Collinet's writings (e.g., his *La tragédie du marxisme* [Paris: Editions Ouvrières, 1948] and *L'ouvrier français; Essai sur la condition ouvrière* [Paris: Editions Ouvrières, 1951]) attempt to show these connections.

2. Hubert Beuve-Mery, editor of the definitely non-Communist *Le Monde,* in his *Reflexions politiques* (Paris: Editions du Seuil, 1951), 152, refers to the Communists as the *Aile Marchante,* the marching or advancing wing of the Resistance.

3. Carl F. Brand, *The British Labour Party: A Short History* (Stanford, Calif.: Stanford University Press, 1964), 287.

4. Quoted in Leo Panitch, *Social Democracy and Industrial Militancy: The Labour Party, the Trade Unions and Incomes Policy, 1945–1974* (Cambridge: Cambridge University Press, 1976), 45–46.

5. *Ibid.,* 53. Panitch also refers to Gaitskell's founding of the X.Y.Z. Society in which Labour leaders and economists met with sympathetic city men. This contact with the city grew as the election approached. *Socialist Commentary,* Apr. 1964, 13–14.

6. Nenni was then regarded as so close to the Communists that when a small number of British Labour members of Parliament sent a telegram to him wishing him success, Attlee had them expelled from the Labour group in the House of Commons.

3

The Outbreak of the Cold War

WITHOUT ENTERING into the debate on the relative responsibility for the break-up of the wartime alliance between the Western powers and the Soviet Union, it is perhaps useful to point out that the first signs of a change in the relationship became manifest as early as the last months of the European war, when Hitler's defeat appeared ensured. Yet, even in those few Western nations where Communists were represented in the governments, the possibility of a takeover by the Communists was, for all practical purposes, eliminated by 1947–48, when the Communist parties in France and Italy had left their government positions and the two countries still remained orderly and governable. It was quite otherwise in Eastern Europe.

While all those nations that were not invaded by Soviet troops during or at the end of World War II preserved or reestablished their democratic form of government (with the exception of most of Southern Europe), Communist dictatorships were rapidly set up where the Soviet armies penetrated. The crucial case was Poland. The attitude of the Polish population toward the Russian invaders, who were in alliance with Nazi Germany, and the terrorist regime that they had established was well known in the West. The technical-legal issue that brought Poland to the forefront of East-West discussions was the existence of two Polish governments—one was established in London by General Władyslaw Sikorski, the other was sponsored by the Russians, first as a Polish committee and then as the "legitimate representative" of the Polish people. For a while, especially while hostilities in Europe continued, both sides cooperated but with mounting mutual distrust. In Moscow on October 9, 1944, Winston Churchill attempted—in a somewhat desultory fashion—to divide Eastern Europe into spheres of influence between Britain and the Soviet Union; Franklin D. Roosevelt was not present because of the impending presidential election in the United States. Norman Luxenburg describes this meeting as follows: Churchill "wrote on a piece of paper which he handed to Stalin that Russian interests would be 90 percent in Rumania and 75 percent in Bulgaria. In Yugoslavia and Hungary British and Russian interests were to be 50-50 and the British were to have a 90 percent interest in

Greece. Churchill notes in his memoirs that Stalin looked at the paper and agreed by making a 'stick upon it.' Thus was to be decided the fate of millions of people."[1]

Poland is conspicuously missing in this list. Britain had arranged a meeting between the two Polish governments without any positive result. At the conference among Roosevelt, Churchill, and Joseph Stalin in Yalta agreement was reached about the new frontiers of Poland (at the expense of Germany), but no understanding was possible as to its government. The London government in exile, set up after the conquest of Poland by Germany and Russia, had been recognized by the Western Allies and the Soviet Union. The latter, however, withdrew its recognition of the London government in 1943, using the so-called Katyn incident as reason—or pretext—for this act. German troops had discovered a mass grave of several thousand Polish officers in the forests near Katyn and claimed that these had been executed by the Russians who in turn accused the Nazis of the crime. The Polish government in London asked for an investigation to establish the truth. The implied distrust of the Soviet claims enabled Moscow to break relations with the government. Only one member of the Polish government in exile in London, the leader of the peasant party, Stanislaw Mikolajcik, was declared acceptable after he had publicly agreed with the considerable territorial changes that the Soviet Union imposed upon Poland. Moreover, he had stated "that he regarded a close and permanent friendship with Russia as basis of future Polish policy." As a result, he had resigned from the London government in exile, which perhaps made him even more acceptable to the Soviet leaders. He became vice-premier of the "Provisional Government of National Union." Stalin regarded this as a loyal application of the Allied agreement. As he stated to Roosevelt's representative, Harry Hopkins, nothing was further from his mind than to "sovietize" Poland. Even the Communist leaders in Poland agreed with this, he said, since "the Soviet system is not capable of being exported." Poland, he declared, "would live under a parliamentary system just as it exists in Czechoslovakia, Belgium and Holland."[2]

Given the military circumstances and Stalin's promises, Roosevelt and Churchill recognized the Soviet-sponsored Polish government, with the understanding that the Moscow-sponsored authority should be broadened by the inclusion of democratic elements from abroad and from Poland itself and that this provisional government should then proceed to organize free and democratic elections. All democratic and anti-Nazi parties should participate in these elections. Answering a question by Roosevelt, Stalin responded that the elections could be held within a month.[3] The Western powers also impressed upon the Communist president of the Polish government, Boleslaw Bierut, the importance of genuinely free elections. Bierut responded that "Poland wished to develop along the lines of Western democracy."

However, Mikolajcik's return to Poland set off an anti-Communist movement of gigantic proportions, motivated largely, though not exclusively, by powerful anti-Russian feelings. The Communists, always a small minority party in Poland, had greatly suffered from the hands of the Russians: shortly before World War II, the Polish Communist party had been dissolved by Moscow, allegedly because its leadership had been penetrated by Fascist agents, an accusation that the Russians later officially withdrew. The entire party leadership had been executed. During the war—to mention only one outstanding incident—the Russian armies had deliberately stopped their advance on Warsaw until the German army had destroyed the Polish underground movement that had revolted, confident of relief by the advancing Russian armies. Moscow even prevented the Western powers from coming to the aid of the Poles. Democratic elections were likely to produce a government of anti- or at least non-Communist elements. Thus Mikolajcik's party had to be persecuted, its paper suppressed, its candidates jailed, and its election lists prohibited wherever possible.

Against the old Socialist party (P.P.S.), which had led the Warsaw rebellion, a somewhat different strategy was employed. As early as 1943 one faction had left the P.P.S., formed its own party, and entered into a pact of unity of action with the Communists. In due course, this group claimed to be the true P.P.S. Soon afterward, the general secretary of the P.P.S., Kazimierz Puzak, one of the top leaders of the anti-Nazi underground, was arrested and jailed by the Soviet authorities. An attempt to conquer the Communist-sponsored P.P.S. by requesting the members of the old party to join its rival, giving them the hope to be able to oust the Moscow-leaning leadership, failed. Under heavy pressure from Moscow, the P.P.S. and the Communist party merged in December 1948 into the United Polish Workers party (P.Z.P.R.).

In an atmosphere of terror and police-imposed restrictions on non-Communist activities, the elections were held and produced the expected result, perhaps going even further in its pro-Communism than would have made the elections appear possibly fair and democratic to an outside observer. The Communist-organized bloc received 80 percent of the votes and 394 of the 443 seats in the Polish parliament, the Sejm. Even before the elections, the Communist party and the new Communist–party-dominated P.P.S. had agreed on the distribution of the spoils. Each of the two parties received 119 seats, and together held a majority of seats in the Sejm. The United States protested against the way the elections were held, in violation of the agreements of Yalta and Potsdam. Nevertheless, the proud history of the genuine P.P.S. had come to an end.

The Polish events set the tone for the remainder of the Soviet-occupied territories in Eastern Europe. The Hungarian Communist party, strengthened by the presence of Russian occupation troops, polled almost as many votes as the Social Democrats in 1945, but this was still not more than 17 percent of the total vote in this peasant country. The main force of the Communist attack was therefore directed against the Peasant party which, with the assistance of the Communist-dominated state police, was gradually dismantled. The Communist leader Mathias Rakosi called that process the "salami tactic." While the majority of the Social Democrats favored cooperation with the Communists, they opposed submission or absorption. However, with the aid of the general secretary of the Social Democrats and terror and swindle, the Communist party succeeded in forcing the merger of the two parties in June 1948.[4]

As one more example of the Soviet intervention in the internal affairs of the occupied countries, it is worth briefly to refer to Romania.[5] The Communists started with the advantage of a split within the Social-Democratic party into a pro-Communist wing under Lotar Radaceanu and an anti-Communist wing led by Titel Petrescu and Serban Voinea. A further factor in favor of the Communists was the dictatorial system under the Iron Guard that had governed the country since 1940. The decisive element, however, was the occupation of the country by Soviet troops. When King Carol refused to appoint a Communist prime minister, Russian troops occupied the government buildings and disarmed the Romanian soldiers. Finally, the Soviet deputy foreign minister, Andrei Wyshinski, arrived in Bucharest and, while Soviet troops manned strategic positions in the city, threatened the king with the absorption of Romania into the Soviet Union, unless a Communist regime was set up. Subsequent elections—Romanian-style—simple confirmed the accomplished fact. The split within the Social-Democratic party facilitated the merger of the party with the Communists—with the latter taking the decisive positions in both party and government.

Communist control of Bulgaria, also occupied by Soviet troops, followed the pattern set in the other Soviet-dominated countries. More crucial were the events leading to the Soviet domination of Czechoslovakia and the struggle over control of Germany and especially Berlin, capital and symbol of German unity. Czechoslovakia, a heavily industrialized state formed out of parts of the Austro-Hungarian Empire after World War I, had been under strong left-wing influence during most of the interwar period. In the first elections following the end of World War II, the Communists, a powerful party from its beginning, emerged as the most successful vote-getter: 38 percent of the votes as compared with 13 percent for the Social Democrats. Together with the Czech National-Socialist party—a reform-minded democratic party not to be confused in any sense with the German Nazi party— these three parties clearly dominated the parliament. While in Poland, Romania, and elsewhere the Soviet troops were regarded as hostile intruders, the Czechoslovakian population welcomed them as liberators and their prestige redounded to the benefit of the Communists. A provisional assembly designated Eduard Beneš, a non-Communist but well-known as a friend of the Soviet Union, as president; Zdenek Fierlinger, a Social Democrat quite ready to accept Moscow's instructions, acted as prime minister. Klement Gottwald, leader of the Communist party, was vice-premier. Basic agricultural reforms and the nationalization of most large and many medium-sized industrial enterprises were carried out within a few months after the defeat of the Nazi occupation troops and the expulsion of most of the German- or Hungarian-speaking population from the territory. After the elections made the Communists the strongest single party, Gottwald became prime minister, but still within the framework of a parliamentary democracy. He claimed that Stalin had approved a "special Czechoslovak road to socialism."[6] The Russian army had left Czechoslovakian soil by the end of 1945.

The last step toward a definitive split of East and West followed Moscow's decision at the end of June 1947 to reject participation in the U.S.–sponsored Marshall Plan for the reconstruction of the war-torn European economy. The Czechoslovakian government, nevertheless, a few days later decided to accept the plan. Stalin compelled Gottwald to revoke this decision, which necessitated Czechoslovakian acceptance of Soviet economic aid and thus the dependency of the country on Moscow. Not long afterward the Soviet Communist party reestablished the Communist international, officially dissolved during World War II to please Russia's Western allies. Now the organization reappeared under the name of Cominform. The next step was the proclamation of a pact between the Social Democrats and Communists, ensuring an identity of policy in all important questions. This was, however, rejected by a large majority of the delegates to a Social Democratic congress, which wished to preserve the independence of the party. The pro-Communist party president, Fierlinger, was ousted and replaced by Bohumil Lausman, a left-wing Socialist who was by no means opposed to cooperation with the Communists but who wished to preserve the independence of his party. The Communists responded with a propaganda campaign against "American imperialism and its Czechoslovak agents," which grew more intense as polls indicated a decline of Communist popularity.

The immediate pretext for the destruction of what was left of parliamentary democracy was the promotion of a number of Communists to influential positions in the police. Three parties left the government coalition when Gottwald failed to respond to the question about whether these appointments had been revoked. Mass demonstrations in February 1948, organized by the Communist party, led to a reorganized government in which both Fierlinger and Lausman participated. This, in effect, symbolized the capitulation of the Social Democrats, even though Lausman still harbored some illusions about the preservation of his party. Fierlinger, using highly doubtful methods, took over the secretariat of the Social Democrats, and he agreed in April 1948 to the absorption of the party by the Communists. In fact, however, only individual members of the Social Democratic party joined the Communists. A large number refused to do so. Still, the Communist party was now all-powerful, and its internal purge, crowned by the execution of Rudolf Slansky, the general secretary of the Communist party, and his associates in 1952, ensured its total "Stalinization."

The West in fact, if not in words, capitulated. When President Harry Truman raised the issue of the Communist-controlled governments of Romania, Hungary, and Bulgaria, he did not even get the support of the British, whose only territorial interest was Greece—strategically vital for the West. Just as Stalin regarded a pro-Communist government in Poland essential to Russia's security, regardless of the wishes of the Polish population, Churchill proceeded to turn Greece toward the West, using British troops in the civil war that tore Greece apart.[7] Together with the developments in Poland, the end of democracy in Czechoslovakia destroyed the last glimmering hopes for the unification of the international labor movement in either the political or the trade union fields.

As Julius Braunthal puts it, "The Soviet Union itself . . . had become an imperialist power, having conquered the countries of Eastern Europe or submitted them to its imperialist domination. It had become a giant, second to America in its power. It did not appear, as in the pre-war period, to be threatened by capitalist-imperialist governments, but rather once the coup of Prague was accomplished, as a threat to the independence of the nations of Western Europe. This, in any case, was the image that Russia presented to the world in the post-war era. It explains the change in the attitude of the European Social Democrats toward the Soviet Union, as it manifested itself in their agreement with the Atlantic pact."[8]

NOTES

1. *Europe since World War II: The Big Change* (Carbondale: Southern Illinois University Press, 1973), 101.

2. Quoted in Julius Braunthal, *Geschichte der Internationale* (Hanover: Dietz Nachf., 1971), 3:130.

3. Winston Churchill, *Triumph and Tragedy* (Cambridge, Mass.: Harvard University Press, 1953), 387.

4. For details see Laszlo Reves, *Die Liquidierung der ungarischen Sozial-demokratie, Die Zukunft,* June 1968. This is published in Vienna.

5. Here, too, I follow the discussion in Braunthal's book, *Geschichte der Internationale.*

6. *Ibid.,* 209.

7. It is interesting to note that the British intervention was sharply criticized in the *London Times* and the *Manchester Guardian* but ignored by *Pravda* and *Izvestia.*

8. Braunthal, *Geschichte der Internationale,* 234.

4

The Internationals and the Cold War

JUST AS THE wartime alliance of the West and the Soviet Union was reflected in the founding of the more or less unified World Federation of Trade Unions (W.F.T.U.), combining Socialist- and Communist-led unions with the Congress of Industrial Organizations (C.I.O.) in the United States, the outbreak of the cold war led to the break-up of that organization. During its brief life the balance of power within the W.F.T.U. had clearly shifted to the Communists, not only because of the heavy weight of the huge Soviet trade union membership but also because Louis Saillant, elected general secretary as a non-Communist, had moved to the Communist side. The great prestige of Sir Walter Citrine, general secretary of the British Trades Union Congress (T.U.C.) and president of the W.F.T.U., was inadequate to offset the influence of Saillant. When the Chinese member of the executive committee took sides with the Communists, the latter obtained full control of the organization, and the break-up became inevitable.[1]

The Western non-Communist organizations proceeded to set up their own trade union international to be named the International Confederation of Free Trade Unions (I.C.F.T.U.). It was founded in late 1949 at a conference in London. It is not unfair to say that in view of the recent split and the events in the labor movements of the East, anti-Communism was the dominant theme of the conference. Nor is it surprising that the U.S. delegation dominated the meeting, for the American Federation of Labor (A.F.L.) and the C.I.O. represented the most powerful and richest unions of the West, and Walter Reuther was the author of the Manifesto to the Workers of the World that the congress issued.

Unlike the prewar International Federation of Trade Unions (I.F.T.U.), the new organization admitted more than one organization from any given country, which eliminated the dilemma of having to choose between A.F.L. and C.I.O. that had plagued the I.F.T.U. prior to the outbreak of the war. That organization was bound under its statutes to admit only one trade union center from any one country. Now both A.F.L. and C.I.O. could be members of the trade union international. Brussels was designated as the headquarters of the new I.C.F.T.U., removing the administrative center from the immediate influence of any of the big trade union confederations. The I.C.F.T.U. also covered a much wider territory, geographically and politically, than the prewar trade union internationals. From the beginning, the I.C.F.T.U. set up regional organizations, first in Europe and the Western Hemisphere and later in other areas. The first took over the functions of the former trade union advisory committee of the Marshall Plan. The Western Hemisphere organization, usually called Orit (from its Spanish abbreviation), has its headquarters in Mexico City.

The main emphasis of the new trade union international was on resistance to Communism. For the A.F.L. union leaders, especially George Meany, president of the A.F.L., David Dubinsky, the leader of the Ladies' Garment Workers' Union (which had almost been conquered by Communists and their sympathizers), and Jay Lovestone, former leader of the Communist party of the United States, who had turned into an uncompromising anti-Communist, fighting Moscow and its satellites was, if not the only, surely by far the dominant task of the new organization. Most of the European union leaders agreed, although with a not insignificant shading of opinion. The Socialist tradition was not forgotten and resistance to capitalist domination in the reconstruction of war-torn Europe was considered by them an equally important task. But the divergencies were covered up by such formulae as: "Where vested economic interests block the road to human progress, private planning for profit must yield to public planning for people." Yet the unifying theme of the congress was anti-Communism, and it was doubtful from the beginning whether this negative factor would be sufficient to keep the organization alive once the Communist threat receded or at least appeared to recede in the eyes of the European unionists. But this event was still in the future.

This was the period of the idea of the "Third Force" as an intermediary between hostile East and West, and Europe under Socialist-Democratic leadership was destined to play that role. "The choice is not between Stalin and Standard Oil" was the slogan, and the I.C.F.T.U. was to be the pillar of this new structure of international relations.[2] For most European trade unionists, this was a highly attractive slogan. In the early postwar years few of them had illusions about the power of Western and Central Europe to play an independent part. Yet, that Reuther, the leader of the United Auto Workers in the United States and of the C.I.O., defended this view of international relations with all the passion of which he was possessed and with his magnificent oratorical gifts made the idea of a Third Force plausible, if not for the immediate future, then for a few years hence. In the meantime the urgent tasks of reconstruction, of feeding the hungry millions of Europe, and of the defense against Communist aggression held this disparate alliance together. While William Green, president of the A.F.L. and soon to be succeeded by Meany, spoke of the need for a thirty-hour week and the Europeans of the necessity of higher production, the immediate tasks forged a union between the divergent wings of the movement. But this apparent harmony barely concealed the sharp internal disagreements and the abnormal power differences—political and financial—between the partners on the two sides of the Atlantic. As long as the fear of the threat from the East and the world-wide Socialist-Communist rivalry persisted, all other issues became secondary, and the newly forged unity had to be preserved in order to guarantee survival. But just as the "American century"—the unquestionable and unquestioned predominance of the United States—was bound to come to an end long before the end of the century, the recovery of the union movements on the eastern shores of the Atlantic gradually weakened the U.S. power position within the I.C.F.T.U. When, in addition, the internal tensions of the American trade union movement became obvious, the fundament on which the I.C.F.T.U. rested fell apart and with it the unity of the non-Communist movement.

In the meantime, however, non-Communist unions were set up in a number of crucial countries (mainly with U.S. assistance and through intermediaries): West Germany—then still divided into three Western Occupation zones—France, and Italy. In West Germany, where there was no significant Communist influence, what was required was mainly an effort to convince the Occupation authorities that a West German trade union confederation would be an instrument of neither Pan-German expansion nor of pro-Communist agitation. Once this effort of persuasion and political pressure was successful, due largely to the actions of U.S. unions, the D.G.B., the West German trade union confederation, could be set up. More difficult was the situation in France and Italy. In both of these countries the Communists had succeeded, partly by the effectiveness of their members in the anti-Nazi underground after 1941, partly by other less reputable means, in obtaining control of the trade union movement or at least of its strongest branch: in France the C.G.T. (Confédération Générale du Travail), in Italy the C.G.I.L. (Confederazione Generale Italiana del Lavoro). Since labor had played a decisive role in the Resistance movements of the two countries, the predominance of the Communists in the leadership of the unions gave the Communist party a tremendous political advantage. "Most of the nation's elites stood discredited: the military, the higher levels of the civil administration, the press, financial and industrial leaders. They were held responsible for failing to prepare the nation's defense, for preferring Hitler to the Popular Front [the Socialist-Communist-Radical coalition that had governed France under Léon Blum a few years before the outbreak of the war], for supporting Vichy and profiting from the occupation. . . . . Labor on the other hand, was then hardly blamed for the national catastrophe, for it had been virtually excluded from national decisions after 1938."[3]

Most of the Resistance groups in France, and almost all of labor, at the time were Socialist- or Communist-inspired. The programs of the Resistance drew heavily upon ideas elaborated by the C.G.T. and the C.F.T.C. (the Christian Trade Union Confederation) during the interwar period. Even Charles de Gaulle, in praising the role of labor in the Resistance, spoke in vaguely Socialist terms. Indeed, in large parts of France beyond the effective control of the provisional government a semirevolutionary situation developed.

The organizations of the C.G.T. expanded rapidly and claimed almost 5.5 million members in September 1945. The Catholic C.F.T.C. also profited from its role in the liberation and its rejection of those members of the Catholic hierarchy who had been especially close to the Occupation authorities. C.F.T.C. membership rose to about three-quarters of a million.[4] Attempts of the C.G.T. to induce the C.F.T.C. to merge with the bigger organization failed. "Unity of action"—whatever that might mean—was all the Christian unionists were willing to accept.

Being a government party, the Communists behaved as such. In behalf of reconstruction they resisted workers' demands for higher wages and urged their members not to slacken or to strike. And, in fact, for almost two years after the liberation there were no strikes of any importance. Nevertheless, the Communist party managed to obtain and maintain control of the C.G.T., using every means at its disposal including assassination.[5] By late 1945 Communist control was achieved. Their representative, Benoît Frachon, was elected co-secretary general, on a par with the long-time non-Communist leader Léon Jouhaux. Since Jouhaux assumed most representative functions along with extensive international activities, Frachon was free to devote himself to the internal organization and the policies of the C.G.T.[6] Early in 1946 the Communist party had a four-fifths majority at the union conference, the first held since before the war. Various authors offer a multitude of reasons to explain the stranglehold which the Communist party had acquired.[7] A major one was surely the discipline of the party, in sharp contrast to the endless theoretical discussions and squabbles of their rivals. Food shortages, black markets, severe wage controls, and lax price controls—all worked to the benefit of the Communist party.

But the Communists, anxious to be worthy of their ministerial positions, saw all kinds of ultra-left and other opposition groups arise, including some with considerable labor support. Within the C.G.T., however, the main opposition was the moderate group called Force Ouvrière (F.O.).[8] Its leading spokesman was Jouhaux.

In April 1947 the pressure from the left became too severe for the C.G.T. leadership. A strike at the nationalized Renault plant, which the C.G.T. opposed, spread further and came under Trotskyite leadership. Threatened from the left, the Communist party reversed its stand, voted against the government of which it was a part, and was promptly forced to resign from its ministerial posts by the Socialist Prime Minister Paul Ramadier. This break coincided with Russia's opposition to the developing Marshall Plan in aid of European reconstruction, which it regarded as a way of buttressing capitalism. In September 1947 the Cominform was instituted as a new model of Communist internationalism to replace the old Communist international that had been officially abandoned during the war in order to cement the new friendship with the Western Allies. Cominform was a clear signal of the widening split between East and West.

The small F.O. group, encouraged by the support offered by the A.F.L., defended the Marshall Plan in the midst of strikes against intolerable living conditions. Together with the C.F.T.C. and some "autonomous" unions, the F.O. group tried to resist the strike wave that swept the country. In December 1947 Jouhaux and his four supporters in the C.G.T. executive board resigned in the midst of fairly widespread demoralization of the workers following the failure of a strike. In April 1948 a new trade union confederation was set up by Jouhaux and his associates, the C.G.T.-F.O. It retained the age-old initials C.G.T., which have a profound symbolic value among French workers, but was commonly referred to as F.O.

A basically similar but perhaps more complicated process occurred in Italy, where the unified trade union confederation broke up into three parts. Together with the establishment of F.O. in France, the Italian evolution made possible the founding of the non-Communist I.C.F.T.U. (reported earlier), with representation in two such important countries as France and Italy.

As will be described later, the reestablishment of the Italian trade union movement started with the pact of Rome signed in June 1944, shortly before the liberation of the city by Allied troops, but, unfortunately for the non-Communists, after the execution of Bruno Buozzi, the outstanding non-Communist trade union leader, by German troops. The pact provided for the establishment of the C.G.I.L., comprising Socialists, Christians, and Communists, but independent of all political parties. Each of these three groups was to have equal representation on the executive board and three co-equal secretaries were to direct the organization.[9] But soon the Communist Giuseppe Di Vittorio emerged as the leading figure in the movement, because of his personality and his disciplined following.

In the political field, however, the Christian Democrats under Alcide de Gasperi took the lead. In December 1945 he assumed the post of prime minister, which he held for seven years. Communists and Socialists were expelled from the government less than two years later. In the first national elections held in June 1946 the Christian Democrats obtained 35 percent of the popular vote, the Socialists almost 21 percent, and the Communists 19 percent. This result contrasted sharply with the evolution in the C.G.I.L., where the Communists as the best organized and most aggressive group rapidly obtained full control.

Their position was strengthened by a split in the Socialist party. Early in 1947 the moderate wing led by Giuseppe Saragat broke away from the main body of the party under Pietro Nenni and formed the Partito Socialista del Lavoratori Italiani (P.S.L.I.) This, however, was only a small group compared with the Nenni following. In particular, Saragat had only a modest support among the trade unionists. Di Vittorio and the Socialist Fernando Santi, who later joined the Communist party, controlled the C.G.I.L.

The union divisions in France and those to come in Italy opened the way for a similar split in the international trade union movement. The only question left for the I.C.F.T.U. was the role of the Christian trade unions. While in France the C.F.T.C. from the beginning had opposed trade union unity, the Italian Christian unionists were part of the C.G.I.L. It was only in December 1947 after a politically motivated strike, which the Christian Democrats refused to join, that the issue of unity between the Christians and the Socialist-Communist majority in the C.G.I.L. came to the fore.

In June 1948 a democratic alliance was formed among Christian Democrats and Republican and Saragat-Socialist trade unionists. However, even within this group unity could not be preserved. In breaking away from C.G.I.L., each of the three groups had its own time table. Finally, two new trade union centers emerged, one a coalition of Christian Democrats with a small Socialist faction called the Libera Confederazione Generale Italiana del Lavoro (L.C.G.I.L.); another group under Republican and Saragat-Socialist leaders set up the Unione Italiana del Lavoro (U.I.L.). What separated the two anti-Communist confederations was the anticlerical tradition of many industrial workers, especially in the industrial north of the country.[10] No less important at the time were personal rivalries and financial issues.

For the I.C.F.T.U. the problem was now not too difficult. Since the old statutory clause admitting only one national confederation from each country had been dropped to permit both A.F.L. and C.I.O. to join the international organization, both L.C.G.I.L. (later called C.I.S.L.) and U.I.L. could be admitted, even though the two were engaged in bitter competition. Indeed, the I.C.F.T.U. addressed an appeal to all Christian unions to join it, the only condition being that they did not maintain any other international affiliation. This clause referred to the Christian Trade Union International, which in due course changed its name to World Confederation of Labor (W.C.L). It never attained any numerical significance, except possibly in some areas of Latin America and in Belgium.[11]

The reconstitution of the Socialist International offered some considerable difficulties. The prewar Labor and Socialist International (L.S.I.) had ceased to exist after the fall of France; indeed, its operations had been purely mechanical after the capitulation of the West in Munich in 1938. An attempt to reform an international grouping during the war had only partial success, especially since no one from Germany, Austria, or Hungary had been invited. However, the most consequential problems emerged only after the war.

There was, first of all, an attempt to establish an all-inclusive political international, which would include the Soviet Communist party. This proposal was patterned after the World Federation of Trade Unions in the trade union field and supported by such impressive leaders as Harold Laski of Great Britain, chairman of the Labour party that had just obtained a majority in the House of Commons, and the veteran Belgian Socialist Louis de Brouckère, who had represented his party for many years in the prewar L.S.I. and Belgium in the League of Nations. Pietro Nenni, whose Italian Socialist party had concluded a pact of unity of action with the Italian Communists, also advocated the reestablishment of international Socialist-Communist unity. The Eastern European Socialists, partly because they were under Soviet pressure, partly because of their own experience of Fascist oppression, favored a variety of "democracy" that would prevent the return to power of the feudal landowners and Fascist regimes.[12] This met with the approval of the Russians, but ran into absolute rejection by the British Labour party, the French Socialists, and others for whom no departure from a pure democratic system was tolerable. Indeed, it was difficult to see how an intermediate form of government between democracy and dictatorship could, over the long run, be distinguishable from a dictatorship.

Earlier small committees of Socialists of different nationalities met in Britain, sponsored by the Labour party. The main issue for them was less the Communist effort to establish a unified movement and more the relationship to the Socialists in the enemy countries and the fate of these countries themselves. While recognizing the resistance to Adolf Hitler by sizable numbers of Germans, an international conference held in March 1945 in London—without participants from the enemy countries—stated that the entire German nation must bear the consequences of its government's acts.[13] In May 1946 another international conference, however, faced up to the problem of Socialist-Communist relations. By that time the governments of Russian-occupied countries in Eastern Europe were oriented toward Moscow, while the Socialist parties of the West, represented in most governments of that part of Europe, accepted the leadership of Washington and even more of London where the Labour party governed with a secure majority. A unified international Socialist movement of the kind that existed prior to 1914 was possible only on the basis of an understanding between the Socialist and Communist parties in these two power blocs. But the inevitable rivalries of the two groups of countries as well as fundamentally different economic and social conditions in the East and West prevented the development of a unified strategy and organization. Some of the Socialist parties of the West, but even more the

Socialists in the Soviet-occupied countries of the East—Poland, Czechoslovakia, Bulgaria, Romania, and Hungary—opposed even the foundation of a purely Socialist International; the Westerners disliked the idea because they did not wish foreign intervention in their affairs, even on the part of other Socialists; the Eastern Socialists did not dare to join an organization from which the Soviet Union would inevitably be excluded. Moreover, substantial numbers—probably the majority—of Western Socialists also opposed the inclusion of the German Social Democrats in the Socialist International, and no decision could be taken for some time.

The German question was the focus of a conference held in Zurich in June 1947 at which twenty-four parties were represented. The German delegation invited to the conference included Kurt Schumacher, the uncontested leader of the party, and Erich Ollenhauer, who had been a member of the party executive in exile. Schumacher, crippled in World War I, had spent some ten years in a Nazi concentration camp and was a symbol of German Socialist resistance. A committee chaired by the veteran and highly respected Belgian Socialist de Brouckère recommended the affiliation of the German party to the nascent Socialist International. This recommendation was accepted by a vote of twelve to four (Palestine, Poland, Czechoslovakia, and Hungary) with two abstentions (Switzerland and Italy). A full-fledged international of the prewar style could nevertheless not yet be created since the Socialists in the eastern countries refused to join. Instead a temporary committee known as Comisco (Committee of International Socialist Conferences) was set up in which Morgan Phillips, general secretary of the British Labour party, played the dominant role. An executive committee consisting of representatives of the Socialist parties of France, Belgium, Holland, Austria, and Scandinavia was to assist him.

The Soviet-imposed absorption of the Socialist parties of Eastern Europe destroyed whatever illusions about a unified Socialist-Communist international existed in the West. The consequent renewal of the struggle between Social Democrats and the Communists made urgent the formal reconstitution of the Socialist International, which was finally accomplished at a congress at the end of June 1951 in Frankfurt, Germany. There were still some doubts as to the wisdom of forming a full-fledged international with any degree of discipline. With the proviso that the autonomy of the party not be restricted, the British Labour party finally agreed to a Belgian proposal to change the existing loose association to a hardly more disciplined Socialist International.

The choice of Frankfurt in West Germany as seat of the founding congress marked the renewed confidence of the Socialists in the democratic reliability of the German Social Democrats. The leading party of the international was the British Labour party. Consequently, its general secretary, Morgan Phillips, was elected president; Erich Ollenhauer (Germany) and

Louis Lévy (France) were vice-presidents, and Julius Braunthal, a former Austrian Socialist journalist, was secretary-general.

The crucial sentences of a declaration about the purpose and fundamental ideas of the parties unified in the International ran as follows: "There is no socialism without freedom. Socialism can only be achieved by democracy; democracy can only be completed by socialism." Hand in hand with this statement went a total rejection of Communism, which was described as incompatible with the critical spirit of Marxism. The declaration also emphasized that democratic Socialism does not require uniformity of views. Socialists may derive their conviction from Marxian or other methods of social analysis or from religious or humanitarian principles. In the debate both the Dutch and the British speakers even rejected Marxism altogether. The British Labour movement, Phillips said, had never accepted the Marxian concept of the class struggle. Other parties, however, claimed that Marxism was fundamental to their view of the Socialist movement or was at least a most useful method for the analysis of the capitalist society. The representative of the Austrian party even claimed that the newly constituted Austrian Socialist party regarded itself in all modesty as the successor of famed prewar Austro-Marxism.

Chapter 18 shows how unrealistic these last declarations of Marxian faith were or in due course became.

NOTES

1. Adolf Sturmthal, "Crisis in the International Labor Movement," *American Perspective*, 3 (May 1949), 87–99.

2. See Adolf Sturmthal, "The International Confederation of Free Trade Unions," *Industrial and Labor Relations Review*, 3 (Apr. 1950), 374ff.

3. Val R. Lorwin, *The French Labor Movement* (Cambridge, Mass.: Harvard University Press, 1954), 100.

4. *Ibid.*, 101.

5. See the examples quoted in A. Rossi, *Physiologie du Parti Communiste Français* (Paris: Editions Self, 1948), especially 443–45.

6. Lorwin, *French Labor Movement*, 108–9.

7. See, for instance, Alexander Werth, *France, 1940–1955* (London: Robert Hale Ltd., 1956).

8. Since at the time the Communists, anxious to stay in the government, were restraining their followers, the term moderate could also be applied to them. Perhaps it would be better to describe the Jouhaux-led current simply as non-Communist.

9. Daniel L. Horowitz, *The Italian Labor Movement* (Cambridge, Mass.: Harvard University Press, 1963), 186–87.

10. The Communists accused Luigi Antonini and David Dubinsky of the U.S. International Garment Workers Union and the U.S. Department of State of having ordered the split. Dubinsky and A. H. Raskin in *David Dubinsky: A Life with*

Labor (New York: Simon and Schuster, 1977) present their side of the events. The leading figure of the Christian movement was Luigi Pastore, of the U.I.L.–Italo Viglianesi.

11. It must be noted, however, that C.I.S.L. combined with A.F.L. leaders to delay the admission of U.I.L. until the end of 1957; see Horowitz, *Italian Labor Movement,* 236. Indeed, for a long time the relations between the two Italian organizations remained less than cooperative, in spite of I.C.F.T.U. efforts to achieve collaboration.

12. See the moving statement of the Hungarian veteran Social Democrat Emanuel Buchinger in 1947, as quoted in Julius Braunthal, *Geschichte der Internationale* (Hanover: Dietz Nachf., 1971), 3:170.

13. It is perhaps noteworthy that the Soviet position on the partition of Germany changed from one favoring the unity of Germany to one insisting on the existence of a separate sovereign East German state. In 1942 Stalin had stated, "Historical experience shows that the Hitlers come and go but the German people, the German state remains." Quoted in *ibid., 159n106.*

Part II
Developments in Western Labor

5

The United Kingdom

THE END OF World War II found the British Labour party, formerly the junior partner in the wartime coalition cabinet led by Winston Churchill, in full command of the House of Commons. Until 1950, under Clement Attlee, the Labour party dominated the political scene without any effective challenge; in 1950–51, it had a reduced majority.

The wartime coalition was never intended to last beyond the end of hostilities, and, in fact, it began to break up when the end of the war in Europe seemed to be in sight, even before hostilities in the Pacific were terminated. A Labour party conference in May 1945 clearly indicated its wish to end the coalition regime, and the prime minister promptly resigned. Elections were held on July 5. The Labour party entered the brief campaign with a manifesto entitled "Let Us Face the Future." Full employment, the nationalization of a number of key industries, mainly for the sake of efficiency, construction of public housing, and the establishment of a national health service were among the main items of its program. While Churchill painted a dark picture of a Socialist dictatorship, Attlee and his associates emphasized their social reform proposals. The elections gave Labour 393 seats in the House of Commons, 146 more than all other parties combined. In spite of Churchill's personal prestige and widespread doubts about Attlee's leadership qualities, the Socialists carried the day. The vote initiated a "revolution— British style."[1] Even though this was the third British Labour government, it was the first to have a parliamentary majority. With Attlee as prime minister served Ernest Bevin, the former leader of the Transport Workers' Union, as foreign secretary; Herbert Morrison, the spokesman of the London party organization, as lord president and leader of the House of Commons; Arthur Greenwood as lord privy seal; and Hugh Dalton as chancellor of the exchequer (comparable to a secretary of the treasury). The assignments given to Morrison and Bevin were mainly designed to keep these two old foes apart by giving them tasks that did not interfere very much with each other. In Sir Stafford Cripps, president of the board of trade, Emanuel Shinwell as minister of fuel, and Aneurin Bevan as minister of health, three men of growing stature were added to the cabinet. When late in 1947 Dalton was dropped from the cabinet because of a minor infraction of British tradition—he revealed one budget item to a journalist on the way to presenting the budget to the House—he was replaced by Cripps.

The economic situation facing the new government was deplorable. The abrupt ending of the U.S. lend-lease program in September 1945 "was a shock and a body blow to the government,"[2] faced as it was with the loss of many of its export markets and of one-quarter of Britain's overseas investments, the accumulation of a huge foreign debt, considerable physical destruction, and heavy wear and tear on most of its productive facilities. Lord Keynes managed to get a loan from the U.S. government and another from Canada, but only under U.S. conditions that were, given the war-created circumstances, utopian: the pound sterling was to be made convertible within a year! In fact, a few weeks after the conversion had been introduced in 1947, it had to be abandoned to stem the outflow of currency. Strict wartime controls and rationing had to be maintained, including wage restraints that the unions generally accepted, especially since the government's fiscal policy, under both Dalton and Cripps, tended to reduce income differentials. Indeed, a trade union conference on March 6, 1946, addressed by the prime minister, the foreign minister, and the minister of labour (G. A. Isaacs) adopted a resolution noting, among other points: "The conference declares its determination to do all in its power . . . to accomplish the speedy conversion of industry to peacetime needs; to increase production and to utilize the nation's manpower, financial and productive resources, in order to ensure full employment, and a steadily increasing supply of goods and services to meet the needs of the people and the demands of the export trade."[3] At the same time the unions pledged themselves to a simplification of their chaotic organizational scheme, primarily to avoid "demarcation" disputes, i.e., interunion conflicts of a jurisdictional nature. The historically disorganized structure of British trade unions tended to create such conflicts in large numbers, and the Trades Union Congress (T.U.C.), the national confederation of the unions, often lacked the willpower or the authority to settle disputes of this kind or at least to do so within a reasonable period.

For the unions, the most immediate advantage in the new political situation was the repeal of the Trade Union Act of 1927, the punishment that the then victorious Conservative government had inflicted upon the unions after the lost General Strike. Prior to 1927, British labor relations knew the system of "contracting out" (which helped greatly to support the Labour party). a worker who did not wish to pay the political part of the union dues, a portion of which went to support the Labour party, had to state his refusal in writing (and was then exposed to the social pressures of his fellow workers). The 1927 law changed this to the exact opposite: "contracting in" required that the union member state expressly his desire to pay the political levy. All this applied, of course, only to those unions—the great majority of those affiliated with the T.U.C.—that had decided, according to the rules laid down in their constitution, to become collective members of the Labour party. Affiliation was possible on both the local and the national levels. The intention of the 1927 act was to reduce the number of union members paying the political levy and thereby to weaken the Labour party. This the act accomplished quite well. While in 1927 some 3.2 million union members were affiliated with the Labour party, this number dropped to 2 million the following year. The opposite occurred in 1945 when the old method of "contracting out" was restored. By 1950 out of a total of 5.7 million union members almost 5 million paid the political levy.

Until 1918 the Labour party was simply a kind of holding company of unions, Socialist societies such as the Independent Labour party (I.L.P.) and the Fabian Society, and cooperatives; the revised statutes of 1918 permitted individual memberships. After a considerable decrease in their number during World War II, individual memberships increased fairly rapidly.

These and other developments are reflected in the change of the composition of the party executive that occurred in 1937. The number of trade union representatives was held to twelve while that of other groups or individuals was increased from eleven to thirteen. Several of these are elected by the party conference as a whole, while the union representatives alone determine their delegates to the party executive as did the local parties. Union strength in the party is further enhanced by the so-called bloc vote: the entire voting strength of a union is being counted the way the particular union majority decides, without regard for minority opinion. Thus to the extent to which the big unions agree, they can, with the support of one nonunion member, dominate the party, though not necessarily the parliamentary group that feels responsible to a wider electorate. There are many union members in the parliamentary group, but they do not usually act as representatives of the union to which they belong or which has financed their election campaign. In fact, the unions disagree among themselves on many questions.[4]

Major reforms enacted by the Labour government included a series of nationalization measures. Apart from the Bank of England, the industries selected for nationalization were mainly key industries in trouble: coal, the railways, aviation, telecommunications, gas, electricity, and iron and steel. Most of these had been running considerable deficits as private enterprises. Labor not only hoped to improve efficiency, but it also considered government control an indispensable tool for national economic planning.[5] Compensation was given to the former owners by way of guaranteed 3 percent bearing securities. In view of inflation this amounted to partial expropriation.

The only industry whose nationalization aroused serious opposition was iron and steel. First, the party in its prewar pronouncements had not included iron and steel among the industries to be nationalized. Moreover, it was difficult to determine which firms were to be included, since many steel enterprises engaged also in other, though mainly related, activities. Within the government opinion was divided on the wisdom of the measure: Dalton, Bevin, Bevan, and Cripps advocated nationalization; Morrison and Attlee were doubtful. It was only in 1951 that nationalization of the steel industry was finally enacted: the openly stated reason was that this was a necessary step toward Socialism. No wonder the Conservatives committed themselves to revoke the measure once they regained power.

Radical changes opened the educational system to less affluent students. At Oxford and Cambridge the great majority of the students obtained financial assistance from public funds. The driving force behind this radical change was Ellen Wilkinson, minister of education. Bevan was making a major contribution to the solution of the housing shortage, though he failed to meet all the objectives of his program. His name remains connected, however, with the National Health Service Bill of 1946. After considerable conflict the plan found the support of almost the entire population, in spite of difficulties in meeting the medical needs of the people. Even the Conservative party promised to maintain the service if it were to take over the government after the next election. The health service combined with a large-scale system of social security came close to realizing Lord Beveridge's "cradle to grave" plan.[6]

The most dramatic changes occurred in the international era. The transformation of most of the former colonies into self-governing members of the British Commonwealth gave in practice full freedom to India, Pakistan, Ceylon, and other countries. (That one of the by-products of this transfer of sovereignty was bloodshed between Moslems and Hindus was probably an unavoidable consequence of the suddenness of the process.) More dubious was the case for the rapid dissolution of the empire in Africa, where many of the British possessions were unable to organize effective and reasonably humanitarian governments. After unsuccessful efforts to solve the many intricate problems of the Middle East, the Labourites left the pursuit of solutions to the future. This applied in particular to the issue of Israel, which caused considerable disagreements even within the Labour party. The withdrawal of British troops in May 1948 was merely an act of despair after all attempts at a compromise had been defeated by terrorism and total Arab-Jewish disagreements.

Increasingly British foreign policy, contrary to the hopes of the Labourites, was determined by tension among the United States, the United Kingdom, and the Soviet Union. This adjustment went so radically against the expectations of a large part of the movement that internal debates became increasingly bitter, the more so as Britain played quite obviously the role of a junior partner in the Anglo-American alliance. The Marshall Plan was a clear indication of this fact, as was the assumption of responsibility for Greek and

Turkish independence by the United States under the Truman doctrine of 1947.

The elections of 1950, even though Labour stayed in office, marked the end of the first postwar phase. The prelude to the elections was a prolonged and sharp conflict within the party. The main issues in these debates concerned Bevin's policy as foreign secretary in the Labour cabinet, in particular his desire for a close association with the United States and his opposition to the Soviet Union's aggressive policies, especially the latter's efforts to penetrate toward the Mediterranean. As regards Germany, Bevin opposed the transfer of parts of East Germany to Poland, partly because the Western zones of Germany depended for their food supplies on these Eastern areas.[7] The Communist takeover of Czechoslovakia, which prior to 1938, in spite of shortcomings in its policies toward the German minority, had been a show place of democracy in Central Europe, compelled the government to introduce conscription and to conclude a defense treaty with France and a number of smaller continental nations; it led finally to the establishment of the North Atlantic Treaty Organization (N.A.T.O.), which brought the United States, Canada, and a number of European nations into a common security system. All the attacks of the left in the party ended in their defeat and the expulsion of some of the most outspoken pro-Soviet critics of Bevin.

In the election campaign of 1950 domestic issues predominated. The Labour party lost some 2.5 percent of the total vote compared with 1945 and had only a narrow majority in the House of Commons. Labour was clearly heading for a period of reflection in the opposition. It had carried out the commitments it had made in its 1945 election platform "Let Us Face the Future" and had changed the social structure of the country substantially. The next phase belonged to consolidation, the dying-down of some of the worst personal jealousies among party leaders, and the rejuvenation of the leadership.[8] All that meant a long period of Conservative rule. British Labour was to lose all three general elections in the 1950s after its bare survival as a government in the 1950 elections. It is true, however, that in the 1951 elections Labour, with almost 14 million votes, outscored the Conservatives, with 13.7 million, but it still elected only 295 members of the House as opposed to 321 Conservatives. This peculiar outcome resulted from the British electoral system, which does not reward the heavy concentration of one party's vote in some constituencies. It was only after thirteen years of Conservative rule that in the general elections of 1964 Labour succeeded in obtaining a narrow majority (317 seats as opposed to 304 for the Conservatives) augmented, however, by the support of nine liberals in the House—a short-run support as Liberal leader Jo Grimond put it.

Attlee retired after the elections of 1955 had decisively strengthened the Conservatives' hold on the government; Bevin and Cripps, two of the foremost leaders of the government, were lost by death and illness, respectively; Bevan—a most impressive popular speaker but no team player—and Harold Wilson had resigned from the Labour government in one of Bevan's many conflicts with his colleagues, and Bevan barely escaped expulsion from the parliamentary Labour group in March 1955 over the issue of the H-bomb. Only Attlee's pleading prevented the final break. However, as the elections to the party executive demonstrated, Bevan and his followers enjoyed the support of the active party membership but faced the opposition of a majority of the unions. Hugh Gaitskell was elected to the leadership after Attlee had retired, with an impressive majority over both Bevan and Herbert Morrison. Morrison was in due course sent to the House of Lords as a life peer—"an unusual position for one born the son of a London policeman."[9]

Gaitskell, an economist by profession—he spent one year in his youth at the University of Vienna, where he associated with Socialist students—had been one of Dalton's favorite disciples and turned toward Labour politics soon after his return to England. In 1945 Dalton made him part of his team when he became chancellor of the exchequer; Gaitskell had already been Dalton's private secretary during the latter's service at the ministry of economic warfare during World War II. By 1950, when Cripps resigned as chancellor of the exchequer because of ill health, Gaitskell at the age of forty-five became his successor, and five years later he became party leader. He succeeded in reestablishing harmony in the party by offering Bevan the post of foreign secretary in the "shadow" cabinet (the opposition front bench from which ordinarily the cabinet members are selected when the opposition party takes over the government). His main task, in his view, was to change the party's orientation in the light of the evolution of capitalism and the international scene. However, while the party shared Gaitskell's skepticism toward the past forms of nationalization, he failed to convince the party of the necessity of amending clause IV of the 1918 party constitution. That clause stated that one party objective was "to secure for the producers by hand or by brain the full fruits of their industry, and the most equitable distribution thereof that may be possible, upon the basis of the common ownership of the means of production." Gaitskell did not wish to see the party's aims to be totally and exclusively identified with common ownership. For him, this was but one of several methods to achieve the purposes that common ownership—i.e., nationalization—was to serve.

The party rejected Gaitskell's proposals at its annual conference in November 1959, and a majority was inclined to regard abandoning further nationalizations in their traditional form as a "surrender of principle."[10] Still, in due course the party executive, though not the conference, adopted a supplementary declaration that stated that community control of the commanding heights of the economy would be sufficient and that common ownership would include, in addition to outright state ownership, a variety of other institutions. The ideas of this declaration were best expressed in C. A. R. Crosland's words: "The ideal (or at least my ideal) is a society in which ownership is thoroughly mixed up—a society with a diverse, diffused, pluralist, and heterogeneous pattern of ownership, with the State, the nationalized industries, the Co-operatives, the Unions, Government financial institutions, pension funds, foundations, and millions of private families all participating. Since this is still a long way off, we need heavy taxation to limit profits and dividends. And it may be an unpopular solution amongst the traditionalists of the Left who still want (or will be made to want by *ad captandum* speeches) the steady creation of State monopolies."[11]

This conflict and another, more serious in some ways, over nuclear weapons and unilateral disarmament, could be settled without too much danger to party unity. When even Bevan came around to oppose unilateral British disarmament, its advocates lost most of their support. Still, the existence of British nuclear weapons continued to be a disputed issue, and a resolution in favor of unilateral disarmament passed at a party conference by a narrow majority. Gaitskell then proceeded to organize party and union opinion around his ideas and obtained a reversal of the antidefense resolution at the party conference in 1961. The internal struggle over Britain's joining the European Economic Community will be discussed in chapter 14.

The specific characteristic of the Labour party after all these decisions were taken was and remains the struggle for social equality. This Gaitskell made his main appeal to the party and the public. Just when he had won the internal battles and brought about a high degree of agreement, Gaitskell, in many ways the most brilliant of the younger leaders British Labour produced, died suddenly in January 1963.

His heir as leader of the party was Harold Wilson. James Callaghan and George Brown, the deputy leader, combined had a larger vote, but Callaghan withdrew and Wilson was the victor; Brown was his deputy as he had been under Gaitskell. With Wilson, another of Dalton's disciples took the lead of the party. Perhaps at first a bit farther to the left than Gaitskell—Wilson had been a Bevan follower—Wilson was primarily an opportunist, but a man of great talents. He inherited the results of the work of Gaitskell in adjusting the party to phase two of the postwar evolution of European labor, added his own not inconsiderable gifts, and led the party to a narrow election victory in 1964. So difficult was the parliamentary situation that a new general election was called in March 1966, which increased the Labour majority to ninety-seven.

Apart from the renationalization of the steel industry, which reversed a decision of the Conservative government, the main issue confronting the Labour government under Wilson was incomes policy (see chapter 13). The issue was connected with a serious balance of payments problem: a memorandum prepared by the treasury for the incoming government in 1964 forecast a payments deficit of 800 million pounds sterling for 1964.[12] Wilson wanted to solve the problem by cost reductions rather than devaluation, but a prolonged seamen's strike struck a hard blow against this policy. In the end, in spite of rising union resistance to Wilson's policy—the leader of the giant Transport Workers' Union, Frank Cousins, minister of technology, resigned from the government in July—the majority of the T.U.C. accepted a temporary wage freeze. The wage freeze and the following stage of "severe restraint" alienated a substantial number of union leaders and members from the Labour government without solving the payments problem. The government proceeded to a devaluation of the pound sterling by more than 14 percent under the new Chancellor of the Exchequer Roy Jenkins. The consequences—a combination of price increases and wage restraint, and thus a reduction of real wages—were accepted by the T.U.C.'s general council with the understanding that the T.U.C. itself would vet (check on) union wage demands. Direction of the incomes policy passed to the ministry of labour, relabeled department of employment and productivity. Barbara Castle, a former follower of Bevan, was its head. The main problem of this policy was that it required giving the T.U.C. far more authority over the policies, especially the bargaining activities, of its affiliated unions that it had ever possessed or asked for.

While the political direction of the country shifted back and forth between Conservatives and Labour, industrial relations remained a constant and central problem. As to its nature, the Donovan Commission report offers a convenient vantage point for an overview. The report of the Donovan Commission (Royal Commission on Trade Unions and Employers' Associations), which Wilson had created in 1965, and its preparatory studies illuminate the industrial relations problems of the late 1950s and 1960s that were thought to be central to the general troubles then confronting Great Britain. The chairman was a former Labour member of Parliament, now Lord Donovan. The main thesis of the commission was that there are two systems of industrial relations in Great Britain: a formal system based on the official institutions and an informal system resulting from the actual behavior of unions and employers' associations, of the managers of enterprises and plants, and of the shop stewards and the workers. The formal system, the commission found, is expressed in industrywide collective agreements setting minimum wages and working conditions; the informal system is the effective one. Resulting from formal and even more from informal agreements at lower levels, it describes what is really happening at the workplace. The fundamental causes of this dichotomy are partly institutional and partly economic. The first results from the weakness, especially the lack of power to enforce discipline, of both employers' associations and trade unions. This factor is more conspicuous in the United Kingdom than in most other countries in which the system of nationwide agreements exists because of the historically well-established lack of orderly structure, especially among the unions. Moreover, organizational discipline has also been weakened by economic circumstances: the high employment level maintained almost without interruption for close to three decades following the end of World War II induced employers to compete for scarce labor. As a result, the two systems—the formal and the informal—are frequently at odds with each other.

The key role in the real system is played by the shop stewards. Although differing from most works' councils on the continent in that they are a part of the union machinery, they act frequently on their own to adjust a contract to the particular conditions of a given enterprise or plant or to new situations arising out of changing technologies or other circumstances not foreseen when the nationwide contract was concluded. This trend toward plant and company bargaining

> was encouraged by the structure of the British trade union movement. Unions are for the most part not organized on an industrial basis, but according to occupational categories. Some of the largest and most powerful unions in Britain are "general" in their pattern of membership; that is, they organize irrespective of industrial boundaries or occupational grades. This pattern of trade union organization has led to a multiplicity of unions in most enterprises. . . . Each union is represented by its own shop stewards . . . but where, as is normally the case, a joint shop steward's committee exists, this committee is not subject to the authority or rules of any particular union. In these circumstances a joint shop stewards' committee has considerable freedom of initiative and independence. It is in fact responsible only to itself, and its constituents.[13]

This basic thesis has not remained without contradiction. It has been pointed out that there are many exceptions to this generalized view, such as the nationalized industries, and in private industry a fair number of firms do not belong to national associations.[14] In addition, there are the workers covered by wages councils or boards in poorly organized industries.

The Donovan report expressed the views of what in England is referred to as the Oxford School, whose spiritual leader was Allan Flanders and whose disciples are still among the leading industrial relations experts in the country. They exerted a good deal of influence upon developments in the late 1960s. Gradual adaptation to changing conditions rather than radical changes and persuasion rather than force were their guiding ideas.

That there has been a growing tendency toward plant bargaining seems to be well established, even though many if not most of these understandings are informal, unwritten, and often simply traditional. Related to this is the importance that the shop stewards acquired, especially since the end of the war. Instead of simply watching over the application of national agreements at the workplace—their traditional role—the shop stewards have increasingly endeavored to obtain better conditions for their constituents. Some management officials welcomed this development since it permitted a better adjustment to the particular situation of the individual workplace. The relatively tight labor market during much of the postwar era enhanced the power of the shop stewards.

A related development has been the growth of so-called productivity bargains. They appeared at first a welcome way of integrating the employees into the general functioning of the enterprise,[15] but with the introduction of an incomes policy in the second half of the 1960s they tended to turn into devices to circumvent the government restrictions on wage increases.

The growing stature of the shop stewards and the conclusion of group agreements has led to easier comparisons of group advantages that, in turn, have been held responsible for the high level of strikes, in particular of wildcat strikes. The Donovan Commission favored a voluntary arbitration system with some modifications. Apart from recommending wider use of factory or company agreements, one of the main proposals of the commission was to the effect that an Industrial Relations Act be passed with the stated objective of strengthening the voluntary system. One part of this act would require the registration of new agreements with the government; another part aimed at the establishment of a Commission on Industrial Relations (C.I.R.), which would examine and suggest further reform proposals. In spite of some opposition to this recommendation, the C.I.R. was duly set up, with George Woodcock, then secretary of the T.U.C., as its first chairman. While it did some useful work, events soon bypassed it. A seamen's strike in 1966 and a dockworkers' strike the following year contributed to balance of payments difficulties that led to the devaluation of the pound sterling. With Barbara Castle moving into the department of employment and productivity in 1968, the Labour government embarked on a new course of action, driven by the growing realization of the public that a Labour government was not much more successful than the Conservatives in handling strikes, particularly the large number of those called by shop stewards in breach of union rules and contracts.

The new approach of the Labour government was outlined in a White Paper entitled "In Place of Strife" in early 1969. Briefly, it affirmed that the right to strike was essential in a democracy but described strikes as a last resort "when all other alternatives have failed." While retaining C.I.R., the paper contained recommendations "on the other side" to strengthen the employer's position: government-enforced settlements in interunion jurisdictional disputes, cooling-off periods in wildcat strikes, and government-supervised strike ballots in official strikes. Union response was highly unfavorable, with the shop stewards in the automobile industry and in engineering leading the protests. Indeed, even the national executive committee of the party came out against the policy laid down in the White Paper. Finally, the government withdrew into a less exposed position that retained only the bare essentials of

"In Place of Strife." But even this did not meet with the unions' approval. While there was no danger of the unions disaffiliating or cutting off financial aid from the party, the new T.U.C. General Secretary Victor Feather was more effective than his predecessor in defending the unions' stand and presenting new T.U.C. proposals. Their main element was that the T.U.C. general council would help in securing settlements. For the government this was insufficient. Indeed, 1969–70 produced a wage explosion under the pressure of shop stewards and rank and file, with the union leaders rushing after them in new militancy.[16] The party election manifesto in 1970 could hardly conceal the split between the unions and the party and thus deprived Labour of its main political asset: that it could deal with industrial strife more effectively than the Conservatives. To many voters, the Conservatives thus appeared marginally as the lesser of two evils.[17]

The advent of a Conservative government in 1970 (which lasted until 1974) brought on a showdown between the unions and the government. While the Labour government's legislative plans could be interpreted as a temporary government intervention in what both unions and management wished to preserve as their private sphere, the Conservative proposals, coming from a government hostile to the unions, were regarded as attempts to introduce the government permanently into the system of industrial relations, a new departure for Great Britain, which had prided itself on keeping the law out of industrial relations. The Industrial Relations Act of 1971, an effort to regulate industrial relations by law remained a dead letter, for the T.U.C. embarked upon a policy of noncooperation.[18]

There is little point in discussing the details of this act beyond the following summary. In an effort to discipline unions, which since 1906 and 1965 were immune from legal actions on civil grounds in connection with an industrial relations dispute, the law introduced registration of unions as a device to tackle the widespread use of unofficial strikes. The act introduced principles of U.S. labor law, including the concept of exclusive bargaining rights and a bargaining unit. It also attempted to use the cooling off period of the Taft-Hartley Act in so-called emergency disputes. These clauses were rejected by the T.U.C. as surveillance of the unions by the state. Legislation in 1974 and 1976 reestablished the 1906 principle of union immunity .

This entire experiment failed. Not only did the Labour party attack it fiercely—in spite of some embarrassing similarities of the law with Castle's own earlier proposals—more important was that the unions simply refused to cooperate. Many refused to register as the act provided and equally refused to engage in legal actions required to obtain the advantages offered by the law. Since at the same time the government rejected statutory wage-price controls, the Conservatives obtained neither the possible advantages of union cooperation nor those of sharp antiunion measures. The result was that between 1970 and 1972 the government had to proclaim four national emergencies due to strikes over wages. Prolonged work stoppages occurred in such essential services as electricity, coal, the postal service, the services of local authorities, engineering, building, and the docks.[19] The law appeared to create and intensify industrial conflicts rather than reduce them. The imprisonment of striking dockworkers in July 1972 and the unsuccessful effort to reduce the miners' wage demands indicated the extent of the government's failure as did the results of a number of by-elections.

With new general elections approaching, the government attempted to establish better relations with the unions. The latter entered discussions with the Conservatives by presenting a list of demands topped by the repeal of the 1971 act. The failure of these discussions followed by a hardening of the government's attitude and its defeat in the elections of February 1974 demonstrated that a solution—imperfect as it might be—could only be found in consultation and cooperation with the unions.

The Labour government returning to office in 1974 drew lessons from its hapless predecessors' experience; it sought a social contract with the unions—as it had proclaimed during the election campaign. The contract, it developed, was not a written document embodying a trade-off of some kind, but, according to the prime minister, "a living and developing relationship covering the whole range of social and economic policies—a voluntary relationship, a constructive consensus between the Government and the unions."[20]

The Labour government's part included repeal of the 1971 Industrial Relations Act and a number of other measures, among them some progress toward industrial democracy.[21] In exchange, the T.U.C. announced that negotiated wage increases in 1974–75 should be limited to the maintenance of real wages; however, T.U.C. control over its affiliated unions—which carry on the bargaining—proved less than perfect and serious social conflicts arose.

The Labour party had returned to office but hardly to power. Its parliamentary support was short of a majority. Its main objective was to establish a "new social contract" to "rescue the nation from the most serious political and economic crisis since 1945," as the election manifesto put it. In 1972 the party had formed a liaison committee with the T.U.C. through which a joint policy to combat inflation was to be worked out. However, while the committee agreed on various objectives including that of reducing costs per unit of output, it failed to come to grips with the problems of an incomes policy. As a result, the first measures of the Labour government were negative: repeal of the 1971 Industrial Relations Act and abolishing the institutions connected with it such as the C.I.R. Later the government created a Conciliation and Arbitration Service and made preparations for legislation on industrial democracy. The T.U.C. in turn urged its affiliated unions—not always successfully—to limit wage demands for 1974–75 to the maintenance of real wages. T.U.C. support lasted two years. By late 1977 the limit for money wage increases was set at 10 percent.

Harold Wilson resigned and was succeeded by James Callaghan. The social contract, violated as often as it was observed, was changed. Real wage increases of up to 5 percent were permitted, but no radically new policy appeared on the horizon. Indeed, the government faced a growing union rebellion in 1978. Finally, the T.U.C. at its congress in 1978 formally rejected the 5 percent pay policy and called for a return to "responsible collective bargaining." This was followed by a similar resolution voted by the party congress. Prime Minister Callaghan's government threatened to use sanctions against employers who conceded more than the recommended limited pay increase. One of the first candidates on this list was the Ford Motor Company. At the same time strikes for wage increases above the recommended limit resumed. Finally, a wave of strikes in vital industries swept Labour out of office and led the Conservatives back to Number 10 Downing Street.

One of the most often repeated complaints about the state of industrial relations in Britain is the frequency and unpredictability of strikes, which appear to occur often in industries vital for the balance of payments. Sharp debates have occurred over the question of whether British unions are particularly strike-prone.[22] The problem is complicated by frequent unofficial strikes. However, the period of 1969 to 1972 saw also a sharp increase in official strikes. A study of the British Social Science Research Council in 1968 indicates that strike statistics are unreliable guides to an understanding of the frequency and intensity of industrial conflicts.[23] Quite possibly, the high occurrence of strikes heavily concentrated in relatively few industries could be related to the poor performance of the British economy in the postwar period, which did not allow for substantial improvements in living standards. It may reasonably be asked, however, to what extent the causal sequence can be reversed. Where the social responsibility for the frequency of strikes is to be placed is not as obvious as many observers seem to believe. An interesting phenomenon pointed out in the same study indicates, for instance, that the more decentralized managerial authority is in the industrial area, the lower is the strike frequency—by a significant margin.

In a new start the Conservative government enacted in August 1980 an Employment Act, which limits lawful picketing to a picket's own place of work and restricts other forms of secondary industrial action such as blacking[24] or sympathetic strikes; requires 80 percent ballot majorities for new closed shops[25] and widens the conscience escape clause for workers who object to trade union membership; abolishes statutory procedures for trade union recognition and arbitration on claims for parity of pay and conditions; provides public money for secret union ballots for the election of their officials, the starting and ending of strikes, basic rule changes, and mergers with other unions; and modifies existing unfair dismissal and maternity leave provisions in favor of employers—especially small employers. It is too early to judge the effectiveness of the new legislation.

In the political arena the advance of the Conservatives had far-reaching effects. At the Labour party conference in 1979 the left carried the day. It obtained organizational changes designed to put the leadership of the party in the hands of the party activists in the constituencies (election districts). Most of those who participate in the poorly attended local meetings tend to lean toward the radical left. Crucial, however, was the behavior of the big trade unions with their so-called bloc vote. In the 1979 conference vote, that of the Amalgamated Union of Engineering Workers, Britain's second largest union, shifted to the left. The delegates to the party convention in that particular union are elected in much the same way as in the party constituencies, namely in poorly attended branch meetings. Finally, all but one of the five women members of the executive, who are elected by the conference as a whole, now belong to the left, compared with the reverse situation fifteen years ago. A critical observer may also note that a sharp shift to the left may be expected to follow immediately upon an election defeat, but may not last for very long.[26]

Still, in this case lasting effects may derive from the conference decisions. The shifts in the party's leadership to the left while the majority of the Labour group in Parliament followed a moderate course led to increased tension within the party. Demands for Britain's withdrawal from the European Economic Community, for unilateral disarmament, for opposition to nuclear weapons, and for further nationalization measures and proposals for organizational changes that transferred the right to elect the party leader from the parliamentary group to a specially constituted electoral body and other changes brought the internal cleavages to the point of an open split. The last item, in particular, aroused passions. It was designed to bring to the leadership Tony Wedgwood Benn, the most articulate spokesman of the left wing in the party. As a result, four leaders of the moderates, including Roy Jenkins, formerly the chancellor of exchequer in the Callaghan cabinet, and Shirley Williams, another extremely popular former cabinet member, broke away from the Labour party.

In a loose alliance with the Liberal party they set up a new party, the Social Democrats. Although equipped with little organization and a program better known for what it opposed than what it advocated, the new party grew suprisingly fast and received the affiliation of several Labour party members of Parliament. With its organization and perhaps its policies patterned after the model of the German Social Democratic party, the new party refuses to accept the collective affiliation of trade unions. It clearly indicates thereby its desire to be a people's party rather than merely the political representation of the trade unions. Some astonishing electoral successes appeared to indicate that the new party may soon play a leading role in British labor and society, but later events greatly weakened the party.

NOTES

1. Carl F. Brand, *The British Labour Party: A Short History* (Stanford, Calif.: Stanford University Press, 1964), 236.

2. *Ibid.*, 239.

3. N. Barou, *British Trade Unions* (London: Gollancz, 1947), 221.

4. See Adolf Sturmthal, *Unity and Diversity in European Labor: An Introduction to Contemporary Labor Movements* (Glencoe, Ill.: The Free Press, 1953), 39–45. Note, too, that somewhat similar, though not identical, systems of collective union affiliation to a political party—typically a Social Democrat or Labour party—exist in Australia and Sweden.

5. For a detailed discussion of the forms of nationalization, see ch. 9 herein.

6. Brand, *British Labour Party*, 249.

7. *Ibid.*, 259.

8. A rather frank, though not completely unbiased, description of the internal quarrels is in Hugh Dalton's *High Tide and After. Memoirs, 1945–1960* (London: Frederick Muller Limited, 1962), esp. ch. 37. Bevan played a large part in these quarrels.

9. Brand, *British Labour Party*, 282.

10. *Ibid.*, 290.

11. C. A. R. Crosland, *The Future of Socialism* (London: Jonathan Cape, 1956), 496.

12. Harold Wilson, *The Labour Government, 1964–1970. A Personal Record* (London: Weidenfeld and Nicolson and Michael Joseph, 1971), 5.

13. B. C. Roberts and Sheila Rothwell, "Recent Trends in Collective Bargaining in the United Kingdom," in *Collective Bargaining in Industrialized Market Economies* (Geneva: I.L.O., 1974), 356. See also Allan Flanders, *Trade Unions* (London: Hutchinson University Library, 1968); B. C. Roberts, *Trade Union Government and Administration in Great Britain* (Cambridge, Mass.: Harvard University Press, 1956).

14. Nancy Sears in B. C. Roberts, ed., *Industrial Relations: Contemporary Problems and Perspectives* (London: Methuen, 1962); H. A. Turner, "The Donovan Report," *Economic Journal*, 79 (1969).

15. Allan Flanders, *The Fawley Productivity Agreements* (London: Faber and Faber, 1964).

16. Leo Panitch, *Social Democracy and Industrial Militancy: The Labour Party, the Trade Unions and Incomes Policy, 1945–1974* (Cambridge: Cambridge University Press, 1976), 218.

17. D. Butler and M. Pinto Duschinsky, *The British General Election of 1970* (London: Macmillan, 1971), 346.

18. Michael Moran, *The Politics of Industrial Relations. The Origins, Life and Death of the 1971 Industrial Relations Act* (London: Macmillan, 1977).

19. John F. B. Goodman, "Great Britain: Toward the Social Contract," in Solomon Barkin, ed., *Worker Militancy and Its Consequences, 1965–75. New Directions in Western Industrial Relations* (New York: Praeger, 1975), 68.

20. Quoted in *ibid.*, 71.

21. See ch. 11 herein.

22. E.g., H. A. Turner, *Is Britain Really Strike-Prone?* Occasional Papers, no. 20 (Cambridge: University of Cambridge, Department of Applied Economics, 1969).

23. Official statistics include only strikes lasting more than one day and involving more than ten workers. A great variety of other forms of industrial conflict—slowdowns, absenteeism, refusal of working overtime, rapid turnover—is not recorded.

24. "Blacking" is the British expression for boycotting.

25. Union shops in U.S. parlance. Further labor law changes of a far-reaching nature were planned in early 1982.

26. The data are derived from *The Economist,* Nov. 10, 1979, 36–37.

6

Germany

THE END OF World War II saw the Communists in full advance on the union and the political fronts. In Eastern Europe this coincided, after a brief transitional period, with the forward march of the Soviet armies. In Central and Western Europe, however, developments followed a more indigeneous and diversified course, though foreign influences were not absent, particularly in the first postwar years.

The most difficult, but also most important, problem in Europe was presented to the Communists by the German question. There was the shocking experience of looting, murdering, and raping by Russian soldiers and their allies in the course of their advance on Berlin. If not encouraged, this was at least not discouraged by the dispute among Soviet spokesmen as to whether all Germans or only the Nazis should rightly be treated as criminals. No less problematical was the political and social policy to be pursued; the wish not to provoke the Western Allies induced the newly re-formed German Communist party in its first appeal to the population (June 11, 1945) to state: "We are of the opinion that the method to impose the Soviet System upon Germany would be erroneous, because this method does not correspond to the present conditions of the evolution in Germany."

A further complicating factor was the urgent desire of the Communist party to merge with the Social Democrats (S.P.D.). This was dictated not only by the fact that the S.P.D. was probably much stronger among the working classes and far more acceptable to other groups of the population than the Communists but also by the almost irresistible wish of most workers to overcome the ideological splits in the labor movement.

Initiatives in this direction were started literally in the Nazi concentration camps, especially Buchenwald. Hermann L. Brill, sentenced in 1939 to twelve years imprisonment, was transferred to Buchenwald in 1943, where he met Benedikt Kautsky, the son of the famed German Marxist theoretician Karl Kautsky. Benedikt Kautsky had been in the camp for almost seven years. Together they drafted a manifesto in April 1945 when Hitler's defeat was assured. It was signed by thirty-three inhabitants of the concentration camp, all Social Democrats. In order to transform Germany into a Socialist people's democracy, the unity of the Socialist movement was described as indispensable. This, in the terminology of the time, meant a Socialist-Communist merger.[1]

The same theme was taken up by Kurt Schumacher after the end of hostilities. He had been a member of the S.P.D. in the Reichstag prior to 1933 and then spent ten years in jails and concentration camps. On May 6, 1945, a local organization of the party was set up in Hanover under his leadership; the city had just been occupied by U.S. troops. Since the Allies at the time prohibited all parties, this gathering had to keep its purpose secret. Schumacher, however, anxious to establish and preserve the independence of his party from all foreign powers—a policy the cold war soon rendered futile—rejected the idea of a united party since the Communists were tied to one of the victorious nations. This attitude was in full harmony with that of the great majority of both Social-Democratic and Communist sympathizers at the time. A contrary opinion was represented by Walter Ulbricht, the special representative of the Soviet Union in Germany, who had just arrived from Moscow in a Soviet airplane. The Soviet leaders were aiming at the establishment of broad anti-Fascist mass movements under concealed Communist domination. This policy was changed one month later by the arrival of Wilhelm Pieck from Moscow; he headed a small group of German Communists under the command of the Soviet army group of Marshall Shukov. The idea of the broad mass movement was retained, but the founding of a separate Communist party, which was to cooperate in elections with the S.P.D., was also urged. For this purpose, the Communist party was to oppose any attempts at introducing the Soviet system in Germany and, for the time being, to favor setting up a democratic-parliamentary regime. This policy could prepare the ground for a merger of the Communist party and the S.P.D. Schumacher was prepared to accept a community of action with the Communists but not a merger. This, however, was not the line that the Berlin S.P.D. under the leadership of Otto Grotewohl pursued. There the unification of the two parties was an "immutable goal," which the Communist leaders at first resisted. The reasons for the sudden change that Pieck engineered have never been made public. We can only guess that Moscow finally realized how the behavior of the Soviet troops and the expropriation of German production such as it was had ruined all prospects of a freely elected powerful K.P.D. (Communist party). A "blood-transfer" from the S.P.D. as Schumacher labeled it was urgently required.[2]

Thus, the new instructions given to Ulbricht to obtain control of all mass organizations but in an invisible fashion were probably decisive. To get total obedience, Moscow wanted to count not only upon its soldiers on German soil but also upon the group of leading Communists now reconstructing the party, namely those who had lived in exile in the Soviet Union. Among them were Pieck, Ulbricht, and Anton Ackermann, all three destined to control the party, although Ackermann soon stumbled over a feeble attempt to assert a small amount of independence. They were also to assume the leadership of a united S.P.D.–K.P.D. if and when the unification were to occur.

In spite of the four-power division of Berlin, the Allies intended to establish a joint administration of the city, treating it as a unit. Germany, too, was to be regarded as a unit, even though it was divided into four separate military zones, each occupied by the troops of a different power. Yet no all-German political parties extending over the entire country were allowed. Consequently, the S.P.D. at a conference near Hanover in October 1945 decided to entrust the leadership of the party in the three Western zones to Schumacher while the Berlin party committee was made responsible for the party in the Eastern zone. Grotewohl, Max Fechner, and Gustav Dahrendorf—the father of the present director of the London School of Economics—belonged to the latter. The conference agreed on the necessity of the unification of the labor movement in both politics and unions but felt that the decision had to be made on a nationwide scale; indeed, it stated that a "lasting unity capable of unified action" needed to be based upon an international agreement.

The more urgent the merger became for the Communists, the less hurried were the Social Democrats. They were greatly encouraged by the Communist defeat in Austria, where they obtained only four seats out of 165 in the National Assembly. Moreover, the difficulties that the occupation forces, especially the Soviet troops, created for the S.P.D. and its propaganda and organization efforts aroused a good deal of resentment. Thus the S.P.D. rejected unification prior to elections that would determine the relationship of forces between the two parties. Indeed, more and more the S.P.D. representatives referred to the need for a membership referendum on the issue of unification.

Berlin was the main battleground. A struggle developed within the Berlin S.P.D., where a sizeable group under the leadership of the veteran Social Democrat Franz Neumann—not to be mistaken for the Columbia University political scientist and former lawyer of various German unions of the same name—resisted to the bitter end. This was not only a struggle for independence but also an attempt to oppose the surprisingly moderate course the Communists were pursuing. For many of the Socialists, the downfall of the Nazi regime meant the end of capitalism or at least the first stage of the transition to Socialism. This the Communists in their accommodating mood were not willing to concede. Thus, the Socialists found themselves to the left of the Communist leadership, if not their followers.

When finally in March 1946 a referendum was held in Berlin, the Soviet authorities prohibited its being held in the sector of the city that they occupied. In the Western-occupied zones some 82 percent of the S.P.D. members who voted rejected the merger. Votes in various other parts of Germany indicated that, while a substantial minority favored the merger, a majority undoubtedly would have rejected it. Many S.P.D. members felt that the party had only the choice between lining up with the Western powers, which meant the reintroduction of capitalism, or with the Soviet Union, which could hold out only the promise of a dictatorial "Socialist" Germany. Moreover, in the Soviet zone the existence of a really independent S.P.D. would hardly be tolerated. Thus, in the Soviet zone and the Soviet-occupied sector of Berlin, the decision to merge became inevitable.

In the merged party in the East—in which the former S.P.D. members held a small majority—Grotewohl (S.P.D.) and Pieck (K.P.D.) were elected co-chairmen. However, the presence of Soviet soldiers gave the Communists control over the unified party in fact, just as in the parts of Berlin occupied by the Western powers support for the anti-Communist parties grew, especially once the fantastic ideas of the Morgenthau plan were abandoned.[3]

In the Soviet sector of Berlin, an independent S.P.D. continued to exist and at the elections of October 20, 1946 (held in all four sectors of the city), the S.P.D. obtained 48.7 percent of the votes; the S.E.D. (the merged part of the S.P.D. and K.P.D.), only 19.8 percent. Even in the Soviet sector the S.P.D.—that part that had remained independent—polled 43 percent of the votes; the S.E.D., only 29 percent. This event proved decisive.

In May 1946 the S.P.D. finally received permission to constitute itself as a party in the three Western zones of Germany and in the three Western sectors of Berlin. The founding congress took place in Hanover, Kurt Schumacher's city. Unanimously, the congress agreed with Schumacher's rejection of the merger. Even Dahrendorf, who not long before in Berlin had favored the merger, now agreed that it had been brought about by compulsion.[4] Schumacher was elected chairman; Erich Ollenhauer, formerly a member of the party executive in exile, became deputy chairman—a symbol of the unity between those who had remained in Germany under Adolf Hitler and the party in the emigration.[5] The Communist plan to take over the heartland of Europe by way of the merger of the two main working-class parties had failed, or at best only partly succeeded.

The Trade Union Movement

No less difficult and complicated was the reconstruction of the German trade union movement. True, many former trade union functionaries had survived in Germany, in spite of the Nazi persecutions. Others had remained active in exile, especially in Great Britain where a trade union center for German workers in Great Britain had been established. Among its leaders were men who later were to play leading roles in the trade union movement:

Hans Gottfurcht, one of the future leaders of the International Confederation of Free Trade Unions, and Ludwig Rosenberg, later president of the German trade union confederation (D.G.B.). However, the hindrances created by the military occupation of Germany, the removal of industrial equipment and other materials by the Soviet forces, the reparations exacted from the war-devastated country, the suspicion with which the military authorities viewed the emergence of German trade unions, the restrictions that, at least initially, the Morgenthau plan imposed upon the reconstruction of the country—all these elements combined to delay the rebuilding of the trade union movement in the four zones of occupation.

The best situation existed in the British zone, which included the heavily industrialized area of the Ruhr. Not that the great majority of the occupation officers that the British Labour government of Clement Attlee appointed were labor-oriented. Many of them were former administrators of British colonies and tended to transfer to Germany some of the practices they had employed in the colonial territories of Africa and Asia. There were, however, a few exceptions, such as Allan Flanders who came from the British trade union movement and who had sympathy for the newly emerging German labor organizations. And there was, at least occasionally, access to the London government itself, which could be of help, especially to Mr. Hynd and Lord Pakenham, who were responsible for German affairs. The main German figure emerging in the British zone was Hans Böckler, a former president of the Rhineland-Westphalia district of the D.G.B. and a former S.P.D. member of Parliament. As such he had been one of the first members of the Reichstag to be taken into "protective custody" by the Nazis.[6]

From time to time, the British Trades Union Congress (T.U.C.) representatives under the leadership of Vincent Tewson came to the assistance of Böckler and his collaborators. Tewson had taken the place of Walter Citrine as general secretary of the T.U.C. when Citrine had joined the board of the recently nationalized electricity industry. The T.U.C. and Gottfurcht succeeded in persuading Böckler to abandon his plan of an all-embracing single trade union in favor of sixteen industrial unions. These were to include the supporters of the former free—i.e., Socialist—unions as well as those of the Christian unions, leading in effect to a single unified movement instead of the former multiplicity of ideologically divided trade union organizations. The major remaining contentious issue was that of the white-collar workers. Böckler wanted to limit the white-collar union to the employees of commerce, banks, and insurance. Wilhelm Dörr, the leader of the white-collar workers, rejected this limitation; his D.A.G. (Deutsche Angestellten Gewerkschaft) was to include the white-collar workers of all industries. After Dörr refused to accept the decisions of the union congress of June 1948, which supported Böckler, he broke away from the trade union federation and set up the independent D.A.G., as it had existed in the Weimar Republic. White-collar unions that sprang up in the French and U.S. zones followed his example. The D.A.G. has maintained its independent existence ever since.

While the unions of the British zone took the lead, those of the U.S. and French zones were not far behind in forming their zonewide federations after the pattern established by Böckler. No understanding was possible with the organizations set up by the Occupation authorities in the Soviet zone, however, in spite of repeated attempts at finding some common basis for cooperation. There a separate Freier Deutscher Gewerkschaftsbund (Free Confederation of German Trade Unions) had been set up. Thus the founding trade union congress of the D.G.B. held in Munich in October 1949 did not include the unions of the Soviet zone, only those of the other three occupation zones (the D.A.G., of course, excepted). A long list of foreign union delegates to the congress indicated that the German unions had been welcomed to the international fraternity of labor. The support of the U.S. unions contributed a good deal to the reconstruction of the organization and its early survival.

The ideological orientation of the nascent D.G.B. was at first strongly influenced by men like Viktor Agartz, who expected radical social changes in the wake of the war. This period ended around 1952–53 mainly as a result of the S.P.D. defeat in the elections of 1953. Although earlier, at a conference in Hattenheim in January 1950 and again in March 1950, representatives of both unions and employers discussed forms of codetermination not only in the enterprise but also at the national level, the mood changed rapidly on both sides. In September 1950 Agartz proclaimed that "not only equality of capital and labor" was at stake but also "the future way of life of the German people, the construction of a political, social and economic democracy"; the conservative government of Konrad Adenauer remained unmoved. Two or three years later the unions shifted their attention away from general social reform plans and more and more to the narrower area of collective bargaining.[7]

The new D.G.B. was quite different in structure and ideology from the Weimar pattern. Then there had been over 200 unions, now there were sixteen. The ideological and religious splits of the Weimar era had been overcome. A tiny Christian union, mainly centered on the Saar Province, remained, but it was of little significance. The Communists, small in numbers, did not even consider setting up unions of their own. The D.A.G. was the only separate organization, and its relations with the D.G.B., though not friendly, were only rarely hostile. The civil servants' organization (Deutscher Beamtenbund) had never been a part of the union movement and continued to regard itself as a professional organization rather than a union.

A fairly strong executive board, consisting of nine full-time officials, heads the D.G.B. One of the two vice-presidents is traditionally a representative of the Christian current; all other officers as well as the presidents of the sixteen affiliated unions are Social Democrats. Thus, while in neighboring France, the Communist party assumed control of the largest of the divided trade union confederations, in West Germany Social Democrats are in charge, and the Communists have no significant influence.

The basis of the sixteen affiliated unions[8] is the local union, a geographic entity; the next higher stage is the district federation, and above it is the national union federation. The D.G.B. has full-time officers who represent the unions to the government, the European Economic Community, and the public. The leading spokesman in the early period was Böckler; later Christian Fette, Walter Freitag, Willi Richter, Ludwig Rosenberg, and Heinz O. Vetter took the presidency in succession. Collective bargaining is in the hands of the affiliated unions. Most agreements are regional in nature. Supplementary agreements, which do not have the same legal standing as the regional agreements concluded by the union, are arranged by works' councils[9] and individual workers. Some unions have made valiant attempts to set up their own shop stewards in the plants. The result is somewhat similar to the dual system that the Donovan Commission highlighted in Great Britain: the rates determined in the contracts are minimum rates; effective rates are normally above the contract rates and in periods of tight labor markets appreciably higher.[10] Another peculiar feature of German collective bargaining is the right of the government to extend the contract to firms and workers who are not members of their respective associations, provided the employers' association that concluded the contract represents employers with a majority of the employees in the respective industry. As a result, unions are directly interested in the growth of the employers' association. Moreover, this system reduces the incentive to join the union, and attempts by some unions to restrict advantages obtained in collective agreements to their members have failed. The courts have so far declared such differentiation to be inadmissible.

In general court decisions have created considerable difficulties for the unions: political strikes are illegal; strikes must be conducted only by the legitimate bargaining agents, which means that works' councils are acting against the law if they call strikes.[11] Lockouts are treated as the legal counterpart to the strike and are used not infrequently by employers. No lawful strike can be called during the lifetime of a contract. Moreover, the strike, even if called legally, must be "socially appropriate," i.e., correspond to the "moral social order . . . as it developed historically" and "to the principles of collective labor laws." Thus, a conflict in one plant rarely justifies a large-scale strike.

While strikes are infrequent, particularly since the 1950s, I.G. Metall, the largest trade union in the free world, carried on an aggressive wage policy until the 1960s. It was only after the S.P.D. entered the government and "Concerted Action" was organized[12] that the unions including I.G. Metall accepted a high degree of cooperation. This reflected a change in the political climate in the Federal Republic of Germany—a third stage of labor's postwar evolution.

In short, in the second phase of the evolution of West German politics (the first two decades following the liberation of the country), the political influence of the S.P.D. remained highly limited. Under Schumacher's leadership the party set its hopes on radical social change in Western Europe and the possibility of reunifying West and East Germany in the foreseeable future. The majority of the population longed for peace and order rather than revolutionary upheavals that might prolong the misery that most of the Germans had suffered.

Schumacher's policy, which has frequently been misunderstood, was determined partly by his personal experiences and partly by the fate of the Weimar Republic. Of strict Protestant background, he combined a total dedication to his political ideals with a sharp antiwar feeling strengthened by an injury he had received in World War I and his suffering in a Nazi concentration camp during the entire rule of Hitler. His insistence on a party policy dedicated to the reunification of Germany was motivated by his democratic devotion to the idea of the self-determination of all nations including Germany. Moreover, the experience of the Weimar Republic led him to avoid anything that could be used to brand the Social Democrats as traitors to the German national interest as had been the case after 1918.

While German prosperity and its growing acceptance into the community of Western nations weakened Schumacher's and later Ollenhauer's position to the benefit of the clearly pro-Western Adenauer, the failure of the United States to respond to the East German uprising in June 1953 created the first but still inconsequential doubts in the wisdom of betting exclusively on Western support. For the time being, this was more than offset by the revelation of the unpopularity of the East German Communist regime. The rising tide of East German refugees fleeing into West Germany via Berlin—estimated at 2 million "who voted with their feet"—added to the horror that the Eastern regimes aroused among the Westerners. While the Berlin wall, erected in August 1961, stopped the flow or reduced it to almost zero—crossing into West Berlin became a highly risky if not suicidal venture—it also indicated that Adenauer's pro-Western policy had failed in improving the fate of the East Germans and that the division of Germany had become irrevocable for a long time to come. In a way the wall marked the beginning of the end of the Adenauer era in West Germany and opened the door to a substantial change in its political configuration. However, before this could become a reality, the German labor movement in the Western part of the country had to undergo a radical change in ideology and leadership. The symbols of the new era were Willy Brandt, former mayor of West Berlin, and in the background, but of great importance,

Herbert Wehner. The latter, a former Communist, became the main strategist of the party.

The Conservative government, once it had stabilized the currency in 1948 and removed the nightmare of inflation, presided over a rapidly recovering economy. The availability of a large, highly skilled labor force, the self-restraint of the trade unions that permitted high profits and a high rate of investment, a favorable market situation for the kind of capital goods that the German industry was especially well equipped to produce, Marshall Plan aid, and many other factors combined to produce a high rate of economic growth in the 1950s and 1960s. Total real gross national product rose from 1950 to 1972 by 290 percent—an average annual rate of increase of more than 6 percent.[13] The labor shortage, only partly mitigated by the influx of some 2.5 million foreign workers, led to wage increases that paralleled increased worker productivity, i.e., a tripling of real wages in little more than the two decades beginning in 1950. This made social harmony easy to achieve and maintain for long periods. To a large extent, it also explains the failure of the Social Democrats to obtain a leading position at the federal level, even though their influence in the cities and several of the states into which the Federal Republic was divided was considerable.

Three elements combined to produce a change in what seemed for a long time a static situation: a change in S.P.D. philosophy followed by a renewal of the leading personnel of the party and a recession in 1966–67.

For quite some time the disparity between the official philosophy and traditional language of the party, on one hand, and its moderate and pragmatic action, on the other, had been obvious to any unbiased observer. The adjustment of philosophy and language to the policy of the S.P.D. was made official by the party congress of 1959, discussed later. Erich Ollenhauer, who had succeeded Schumacher as party leader after the latter's death, proclaimed the new moderate philosophy of the party. Moreover, most of the party's emphasis had been on issues of foreign policy and on opposition to the rearmament of West Germany with little attention to domestic issues. Along the same line the S.P.D. developed its "Plan for Germany," which advocated the release of West and East Germany from their respective alliances, NATO and the Warsaw Pact, as preparatory steps for the reunification of Germany. Needless to say, the plan remained a dead letter and the report of Soviet intransigence that two eminent party leaders, Fritz Erler and Carlo Schmid, brought back from a visit to Moscow set an end to the hopes the plan embodied.

The main change was the public and official statement of a different party philosophy to be voted on by a party congress. Some steps in this direction had already been taken. In 1954 the S.P.D. acknowledged that Socialism need not be based on Marxian theories and added that from being a "workers' party" it had become a party of the people. A party committee was appointed to prepare a new program.

Any change of a fundamental nature could be made credible only by a corresponding change in the personnel of the leadership. Ollenhauer, whose loyal service to the party was surpassed by no one else, lacked the power to inspire the broad masses of the electorate that Schumacher and—later—Brandt possessed. In some party circles this fact was held responsible for the poor showing of the party in 1957; even though the S.P.D. gained 3 percent of the votes, the Christian-Democratic Union (C.D.U.) retained the absolute majority.[14] In May 1958 Ollenhauer was reelected, but two deputy chairmen were elected to assist him: Waldemar von Knoeringen and Herbert Wehner. Wehner was regarded as representing the left wing of the party; Knoeringen, a moderate, was especially popular in Bavaria.

The committee named in 1954 to prepare a new party program had worked rather slowly and without arousing much interest among the party members. Ollenhauer, however, urged the committee to work with greater speed, and gradually the party membership demonstrated increasing and, finally, intense interest in the work. The text was submitted to an extraordinary party congress in Bad Godesberg in November 1959. This proved a decisive turning point in the history of German labor, inaugurating the third phase in its postwar evolution.

One of the outstanding characteristics of the program was its rejection of any particular ideological or philosophic foundation for the objectives that it set out. Although Marxism was not rejected, the program accepted on an equal footing any other philosophic or religious basis for party membership. One of the purposes of this opening up was to facilitate party access to religious groups, especially the Catholics, who so far had shown no sympathy for what they regarded as the "atheistic S.P.D." As the *Yearbook of S.P.D.* in 1960–61 put it, "Democratic Socialism . . . in Europe is anchored in Christian ethics, in humanism and in classic philosophy." And further on, "Socialism is only realized by democracy, democracy is completed by Socialism."[15]

The term socialization is missing in the program, but a somewhat vague term "communal property" appears and is described as a legitimate form of public control, opportune and necessary "where other means cannot ensure a healthy order of the economic power relationships." Codetermination[16] is held to be the beginning of a new order of the economy.

> Private property of the means of production has a claim for protection and advancement insofar as it does not hinder the construction of a just social order. Efficient medium and small enterprises deserve to be strengthened so that they can stand economic competition with large enterprises.
> Competition by public enterprises is a decisive means to prevent private market control. Such enterprises shall make prevail the interests of the community. Such enterprises become a necessity where for natural

or technical reasons services that are indispensable for the community can be produced in an economically rational way only by excluding competition.[17]

Perhaps the clearest expression of the turn of the party's new stand on basic issues is the following statement in the new program: "Competition as far as possible, planning as far as necessary."[18]

The new program took a positive attitude toward national defense while rejecting the production and the use of atomic weapons within the territory of the Federal Republic. Rejection of Communism and affirmation of the party's faith in democracy in its parliamentary form were stressed. These and other elements of the program were designed to make the S.P.D. a people's rather than a class party.

At the time of its reconstruction in 1945, the party had abandoned all attempts to build the giant network of associations and clubs that had existed in the days of the Weimar Republic. They had served to offer the workers social and sportive opportunities that the society at large did not offer or meeting places for workers who would not have felt at ease in the company of members of other social classes. The S.P.D. now signified that this "Socialist sub-culture" was no longer required or desirable in the genuinely democratic society the party expected to arise after Hitler's defeat.[19]

Equally important as these changes was a sensational speech that Herbert Wehner gave in June 1960 in the Bundestag (Parliament). Reversing the S.P.D. policy in foreign affairs, he declared that the party was now ready to cooperate with the government in foreign affairs. Recognizing that the reunification of Germany was at best a long-term objective and that the Federal Republic was an essential part of the West, the party executive unanimously endorsed Wehner's speech. With the nomination of Brandt, lord mayor of Berlin, as candidate for the position as chancellor, while Ollenhauer remained president of the party and of its parliamentary group, the new course of the party found its clear and impressive symbol.[20]

At the elections of 1961 the party increased its share of the vote from 31.8 percent (in 1957) to 36.2 percent; in 1965 the percentage went up to 39.3 percent and in 1969 to almost 43 percent. Under its new leader the S.P.D. started its comeback. In 1966 it joined the C.D.U. as its junior partner in the government after C.D.U. Chancellor Ludwig Erhard lost the support of his own party. In more than one sense this was a fundamental change. For the first time in the history of the Federal Republic the S.P.D. was a government party at the federal level, and Brandt as vice-chancellor proved to be impressive and increasingly popular. Professor Karl Schiller, also a member of the S.P.D., was an extremely competent, though rarely popular, minister of economic affairs. He introduced Keynesian economics into a system that was committed to unrestricted laissez faire, and he set up "Concerted Action."[21]

The year 1959, when the Bad Godesberg program was adopted, may be described as the beginning of the third phase in the evolution of German labor. It had abandoned policies based upon the expectation of a Socialist revolution or at least the victorious advance of Socialism in Western Europe. For the foreseeable future Western Europe would have a mixed economy just as the Godesberg program had advocated: "Planning as far as necessary."

A similar evolution occurred in the thinking of the German unions organized in the D.G.B., the confederation of sixteen industrial unions. The program adopted at its founding congress in Munich in 1949 was clearly anticapitalist: in addition to full employment, codetermination, and a full program of social security, it demanded the nationalization of key industries, transportation systems, and credit institutions. The foundation of the realization of all these demands was to be a central economic planning system.[22]

The spiritual leader of this radical program was Viktor Agartz, head of the D.G.B. economic research office. The congress of 1954 still welcomed him with great applause when he sharply criticized the economic and social policies of the C.D.U. government headed by Adenauer and Erhard. However, the mood of the workers hardly corresponded any more to the radicalism of the program. The year 1945 had not brought on a revolution which neither the military occupation authorities in the West nor the Germans themselves wanted. The changes that occurred—and some of them were dramatic—were the result of military defeat rather than of a working-class rebellion. Whatever dissatisfaction was expressed in the years following 1945 resulted from hunger, inflation, the removal of entire factories by the military authorities, and unemployment. After the S.P.D. defeat, especially in 1953, and in view of the growing prosperity—the German "economic miracle"—the unions rapidly returned to more pragmatic views. That the pre-Hitler divisions of the movement were practically eliminated by the merger of the Christian and the majority S.P.D.–oriented trade union currents contributed to this mood of the union membership as did the lack of self-confidence after the crushing defeat by Hitler. An action program adopted in 1955 indicated a good deal of this change, limiting itself to a list of immediate demands.

In 1956 D.G.B. Chairman Walter Freitag was replaced by Willi Richter, Agartz had disappeared from the scene, and the main emphasis of the congress was on questions of social insurance, health care, and unemployment insurance, the traditional union concerns. The new program of the D.G.B. worked out in 1963 under the spiritual guidance of Ludwig Rosenberg, who had followed Richter as chairman of the D.G.B. in 1962, confirmed this trend and brought the D.G.B. into line with the spirit of the Godesberg program of the S.P.D. The D.G.B. now officially accepted as the basis of its action the existing social system and asked for reforms rather than far-reaching nationalization measures. The embodiment of this thinking was the demand for equal codetermination on all levels of economic decision-making from the plant up to the highest levels as the instrument for the achievement of the substantive objectives stated in the program.

It may well be said that John Maynard Keynes rather than Karl Marx gave the main inspiration to the program. Especially the first part of the program could have been written by Professor Karl Schiller, the man responsible for the Keynesian twist in the S.P.D. policy. The main emphases were on full employment, economic expansion, a fair distribution of incomes and wealth, prevention of the abuse of economic power, and a stable currency. Whether and to what extent these various objectives were compatible with each other was not examined. In any case, Keynes would have had no difficulty in supporting this program, although he might have been more skeptical about the possibilities of economic planning that the program listed as one of the main tools for achievement of the objectives.

Major improvements were obtained in the system of collective bargaining. As mentioned earlier, the dichotomy between wide-ranging contracts and plant agreements that the Donovan Commission pointed out for the United Kingdom also existed in West Germany. In very much the same way industry agreements concluded for regions or the entire country were supplemented and improved upon by works councils' deals with plant management. Indeed, even though not all unions were happy about this apparent violation of working-class solidarity, some union-sponsored contracts contained clauses—so-called opening clauses—providing for supplementary agreements, and some unions aimed deliberately at the conclusion of union-sponsored plant agreements.

The acceptance of the limits of union demands set by Concerted Action contributed to a good deal of dissatisfaction among the rank and file. The great events that shook France in 1968 spilled over into the Federal Republic; part of the motivation for the workers' unrest was the growing discrepancy between the rates of growth of wages and profits. Wildcat strikes broke out in September 1969, "an event quite unprecedented for the German trade union movement. [They] strongly affected the unions' wage policy."[23] However, in actual practice the main change was a greater emphasis on *betriebsnahe* contract policy, i.e., a wages policy closer to the possibilities of the individual enterprise. To be fully implemented this demand would require a fundamental revision of the entire collective bargaining system.

A whole series of legislative measures had their political origin in the recession of 1966–67 and the subsequent strike wave. Among them were various training measures, an Employment Promotion Act, and, most important, union access to the plants.[24] Acceptance of these reforms by the employers was an indication of their willingness to resume cooperation with the unions after the storm of 1969.[25] The revision of the codetermination law resulting in harsh resistance by the employers was one factor that set a temporary end to this attempt at collaboration between the social partners.

With the economic decline in the mid-1970s a new objective took on primary importance: a shortening of the weekly working hours, a measure primarily designed to reduce unemployment, which for the first time in decades had become a major problem in the Federal Republic. The changed economic situation also found its expression in the new "fundamental program" of the trade unions of 1980. Full employment was given top priority; growth was to be primarily of a qualitative nature and shortening of working hours was to serve as an instrument of employment policy.

No change was made in the basic principles as expressed in the program of 1963, the second of the programmatic statements of the unions. This implied acceptance of a mixed economy, including profitability as a measure of success unless it contradicts the humanitarian principles of the unions. Hand in hand with the enhanced emphasis on full employment went the concept of economic growth modified by ecological objectives. An interesting modification also concerned the objective of price stability. According to the program, measures to that end should not be carried out at the expense of full employment. The top priority given to full employment was again expressed in the demand that mergers be permitted only with strict obligations to maintain the employment level. Similar conditions were to accompany public work contracts and subsidies. While competition was accepted as a basic principle, government intervention was to be required where the competitive system may lead to undesirable consequences.

Some of these formulations sound a bit more radical than the S.P.D. program of 1959, but these are at most differences of degree and even more adjustments to a greatly changed economic environment. Friction with the party is possible and occasionally unavoidable; an open break, however, appears unlikely.

In the period since the formulation of the second D.G.B. program, a profound change in the political situation had occurred. The entry of the S.P.D. into the government in coalition with the Christian Democrats produced contradictory effects. On one hand, it demonstrated that the S.P.D., having broken the government monopoly of the C.D.U., was capable of governing. This demonstration was the more impressive as the C.D.U. Chancellor Kurt-Georg Kiesinger, who had replaced the unlucky Erhard, proved to be a not more fortunate choice than his predecessor. However, the vote of the S.P.D. for the so-called emergency laws in 1968 created some dissatisfaction, as it appeared that the laws would restrict democratic rights. Of more lasting impact was Brandt's new start in the relations of the Federal Republic to its eastern neighbors. The new so called East Policy implied a commitment that West Germany would not attempt to change its eastern frontiers by force.

The great advantages that government participation brought to the S.P.D. were partly offset by internal cleavages, especially with the Socialist student organization and the party youth. With growing dissatisfaction these two groups watched attempts on the part of some of their elders to emphasize the changes in the party line that some critics described as designed to demonstrate that the S.P.D. was a better C.D.U.[26] In the long run, however, these discussions, troublesome as they were, may have helped to prevent intellectual stagnation in the party.

A new fact, favorable to the aspirations of the S.P.D., appeared in March 1969 when, with the assistance of the Free Democrats, Gustav Heinemann of the S.P.D. was elected president of the Federal Republic. This event was followed a few months later by general elections that gave the S.P.D. close to 43 percent of the votes. The Free Democrats (F.D.P.) who obtained 5.8 percent of the popular votes agreed to join the Social Democrats in their efforts to form a government, even though the C.D.U. and its Bavarian associate, the Christian-Social Union (C.S.U.), remained the largest single party in the Parliament.

The main achievement of this first Social Democrat–led government in the Federal Republic was in the area of foreign policy, where Brandt systematically continued his eastern policy, i.e., his attempts to normalize relations with Poland, the Soviet Union, and even the German Democratic Republic (D.D.R.). This policy ran into the opposition not only of C.D.U./C.S.U., but also of a small number of S.P.D. and F.D.P. deputies. This opposition and the resignation of Karl Schiller, who had become an outstanding member of the government combining the ministries of finance and economics, made new elections inevitable. The elections took place late in 1974. With close to 46 percent of the popular vote, the S.P.D. became for the first time the strongest party in West Germany. The C.D.U./C.S.U. followed closely with about 1 percent less.

The leadership of the party after Erler's premature death was in the hands of a triumvirate: Willy Brandt, Herbert Wehner, who dominated the party organization, and Helmut Schmidt, chairman of the parliamentary group as the successor to Erler in 1967. In due course Schmidt moved from the ministry of finance to the chancellorship when Brandt, partly out of fatigue and illness and partly as a consequence of an espionage case in his own office, resigned. He continued as party chairman and later was elected president of the Socialist International as well.

The main achievements of the government now dominated by Schmidt were in the area of combating inflation, the advancement of the European Economic Community, and a major step forward along the lines of expanded codetermination. If in the last area the government under the pressure of its coalition-partner, the F.D.P., failed to meet the far-reaching demands of the trade unions, some progress was being made. This will be discussed in greater detail in chapter 11. The achievement of one of the lowest inflation rates in the Western world (discussed in chapter 13) combined with a large surplus in the balance of payments enhanced the prestige of the government at home and abroad. A sharp decline in the popularity of the government occurred, however, as consequence of both the rapidly deteriorating economic situation in 1980–81 and the severe internal disagreements about the establishment of more nuclear weapons on the territory of the Federal Republic. These two developments may threaten the survival of the government and the leadership of the S.P.D. by Schmidt. A sharp contrast appeared on the nuclear issue between the political direction of the two neighbors, West Germany and France.

NOTES

1. Julius Braunthal, *Geschichte der Internationale* (Hanover: Dietz Nachf., 1971), 3:97.

2. That the Allies—still acting in concert—had ordered communal elections to be held in all of Germany in 1946 may have had a part in the decision in favor of a merger. No less important may have been the devastating defeat of the Austrian Communists at the elections of Nov. 25, 1945.

3. Secretary Henry Morgenthau advocated Germany be returned to the state of agriculture to deprive it of its war-making capacity. This plan was abandoned as East-West relations among the wartime Allies deteriorated and German support became increasingly important for both sides.

4. Braunthal, *Geschichte der Internationale,* 3:118.

5. The German S.P.D. was outstandingly eager to welcome its comrades home from exile.

6. E. C. M. Cullingford, *Trade Unions in West Germany* (London: Wilton House Publications, 1976), 6. The earlier history is well presented in Gerard Braunthal's *Socialist Labor and Politics in Weimar Germany: The General Federation of German Trade Unions* (New York: Archon Books, 1978).

7. Bernd Otto, *Gewerkschaftsbewegung in Deutschland* (Cologne: Bund Verlag, 1975); Erich Potthoff, *Der Kampf um die Montanmitbestimmung* (Cologne: Bund Verlag, 1957).

8. A seventeenth, a policemen's union, was added in 1978.

9. See chs. 10 and 11 herein for a discussion of the councils and of the systems of codetermination.

10. Employers preferred to make concessions in these supplementary agreements rather than in the regular contracts concluded with the unions, since the advantages conceded in the plant—or enterprise—agreements are revocable unilaterally. Recently unions have made efforts to conclude enterprise agreements with larger organizations.

11. This works both ways; it helps unions in asserting their authority over the works' councils but forces strikes to be more generalized than the unions may have wanted.

12. See ch. 13 herein.

13. Joachim Bergmann and Walther Muller-Jentsch, "The Federal Republic of Germany: Cooperative Unionism and Dual Bargaining System Challenged," in S. Barkin, ed., *Worker Militancy and Its Consequences, 1965–75: New Directions in Western Industrial Relations* (New York: Praeger Publishers, 1975), 237–38.

14. Susanne Miller, *Die S.P.D. vor und nach Godesberg* (Bonn–Bad Godesberg: Neue Gesellschaft, 1957), 36.

15. *Yearbook of the S.P.D.*, 404.

16. See ch. 11 herein.

17. *Yearbook of the S.P.D.*, 409, and *Protokoll der Verhandlungen des Ausserordentlichen Parteitags der S.P.D.* (Bonn–Bad Godesberg: Verlag Neue-Gesellschaft, 1959), 19.

18. *Protokoll*, 18.

19. Miller, *Die S.P.D. vor und nach Godesberg*, 39.

20. Ollenhauer died in December 1963, and Brandt became party chairman.

21. Concerted Action was a system of free exchange of views on economic policies among employers, unionists, government representatives, and experts. It will be discussed in ch. 13. The idea originated with the Council of Economic Experts in 1965 but was implemented by Schiller. The council—a group of experts appointed by the government but independent of it—had presented its first annual report on the economic situation and probable developments in 1963.

22. Otto, *Gewerkschaftsbewegung in Deutschland*, 108.

23. Bergmann and Jentsch, "Federal Republic of Germany: Cooperative Unionism," in Barkin, ed., *Worker Militancy*, 259. A large part of the conclusions to this article is utopian in character.

24. Under the revised Works Constitution Act of 1972.

25. Hans Günter and Gerhard Leminsky, "The Federal Republic of Germany," in John T. Dunlop and Walter Galenson, eds., *Labor in the Twentieth Century* (New York: Academic Press, 1978), 181.

26. Miller, *Die S.P.D. vor und nach Godesberg*, 48.

7

France

THE SOCIALIST-COMMUNIST relationship developed under quite different conditions in France than it did in its eastern neighbors. The Communist movement neither benefited nor suffered from the presence of Russian soldiers on French soil. Communism had been most of the time a minority current in the French labor movement prior to the outbreak of the war, but it was by no means ever a negligible factor. Just before 1939, the Communists may even have obtained a majority in the union movement. During the Popular Front regime (1936–38), the Communists had been part of the parliamentary majority supporting the government presided over by the Socialist Prime Minister Léon Blum. The unions, divided since 1921, united to support the government but split again in 1939 under the impact of the Russo-German pact. Indeed, the entire left had been given a devastating blow by that pact that preceded the outbreak of World War II, the more so as for years prior to August 1939 the Communists had been the most outspoken and most vigorous advocates of resistance to Nazi Germany. That the Nazi foreign minister Joachim von Ribbentrop and the Soviet commissar for foreign affairs V. Molotov could be associated in a friendly understanding involving the joint dismemberment of Poland would have appeared unbelievable to everyone in Europe, a few weeks, nay even a day or two before the announcement of the pact.

Later, Nazis and Communists joined in attacking Great Britain during the Nazi occupation of France, and there are some grounds for suspecting that some of the anti-Nazi refugees in France who did not fully agree with Joseph Stalin's newfound friendship with Adolf Hitler had been handed over by Communists to the German occupation authorities.[1] All this came to a sudden end and was followed by another total reversal of Communist policy when German troops invaded the Soviet Union in 1941. Once again, the Western democracies became the friends of the Communists and the Nazis the deadly enemies. Once again, also, the unions merged in the underground in 1943. This unity, too, was destined to be only temporary, but for a period it prevailed against the common enemy. The French Communists entered the anti-Nazi underground and soon became the most ardent foes of the very same men with whom they had so recently been associated in denouncing Britain. Many Communists distinguished themselves by their bravery and initiative in this phase of the underground movement, and some of them became heroes of the Resistance.[2]

Nevertheless, it is surprising that French public opinion soon forgot the Communist turnabout in 1939, the Berlin-Moscow pact, the joint Nazi-Russian attack on Poland, and the almost two years of Nazi-Communist tolerance. What may help explain this rapid forgiving and forgetting on the part of the French public is that, as a French Socialist leader explained to me shortly after the end of war, so many French people shared a feeling of guilt over their own collaboration—in different degrees and forms—with the Nazis. Even the Socialists themselves had a sizeable faction with no clean record. One wing of the party, including the majority of its deputies, had more or less openly collaborated, while another with Léon Blum at its head maintained its anti-Nazi posture. Paul Faure, general secretary of the party, Charles Spinasse, a member of Blum's former cabinet, and René Belin, a trade union leader, joined the government of surrender under Marshall Henri P. Pétain and Pierre Laval. Others, however, supported the underground movement. Among them was Jean Lebas, mayor of Roubaix in the industrial area of the north. A central resistance organization (C.A.S., Comité d'Action Socialiste) was soon formed under the leadership of H. Rubière and later Daniel Mayer, an associate of Blum's. The organization soon spread throughout the country and in November 1944, shortly after Paris had been liberated, held there its first public conference.[3] Mayer was elected general secretary of what was now officially the Socialist party, cleaned of most of the known collaborationists.

No similar purge occurred in the Communist party that earlier had acted severely against those party members who disapproved of the Hitler-Stalin pact. Still, the Resistance in the period after 1941 had produced a renewal of a kind of Popular Front with some major innovations: a tremendous increase of the Communist prestige and the replacement of the former amorphous middle-class party, the Radicals, by a Christian left-wing party, the M.R.P. (Mouvement Républicain Populaire). Its attachment to the Catholic church was loosened because of the support that many if not most top church leaders had given to Pétain. A by-product of this fact, which was later to call forth important social consequences, was the failure of the Christian trade unions (C.F.T.C., Confederation Française des Travailleurs Chrétiens) to reconstitute the "consultative theological committee" traditionally appointed by the cardinal of Paris. This committee had in the past controlled the ideological evolution of the C.F.T.C. Now, with the latter having played a part in the Resistance and the majority of the upper church hierarchy having sided with Pétain, it would have been morally impossible to reestablish the old relationship. For the C.F.T.C. this was the beginning of an evolution that twenty years later was to lead it further to the left.[4] This reconciliation between the left and the Catholic workers who after 1941 had worked side by side in the Resistance proved to have a lasting impact on the political and social evolution of France after 1944–45.[5]

Most important, in the long run, was the Communist effort to penetrate the hallowed trade union confederation, the C.G.T. (Confédération Générale du Travail), whose very initials were a venerated symbol among French workers. In May 1943 in Le Perreux they succeeded, in a meeting of two union leaders each from both sides, to undo their expulsion from the C.G.T. in 1939 and to reestablish "the physiognomy the movement had in September 1939" before the expulsions following the Hitler-Stalin pact. A central body of three Communists and five non-Communists was set up, giving the Communists greater proportional representation than they had before the war, a recognition of the important role the Communists played in the Resistance. By a multitude of methods, some fair, some foul, including the physical removal of some highly popular non-Communist labor leaders, the Communists succeeded in increasing their union influence rather rapidly. They were assisted by two major factors: first, a number of non-Communist labor leaders—Robert Lacoste, Christian Pineau, and Albert Gazier—accepted political assignments and, following the Syndicalist tradition, had to leave the union movement. Second, Léon Jouhaux, the outstanding non-Communist union leader, had been held in a Nazi camp in Austria and was late in being liberated and returning to France. In the meantime the pro-Communist faction increased its representation in the executive board of the C.G.T. (called the Bureau) and finally in 1946 at the first congress held since 1938 with 21,000 against less than 5,000 votes installed Benoit Frâchon as co-equal general secretary with Jouhaux. From this moment, the pro-Communist faction, with the assistance of some non-Communists or former non-Communists, controlled the C.G.T. and profited from the tremendous prestige of its name. The trade union movement became the main pillar of Communist power in France.[6]

In the political arena the dominant figure was, of course, Charles de Gaulle, who entered Paris as the great victor and by then undisputed leader of the liberation movement. The Socialist party, in spite of Blum's efforts to induce it to rethink its ideology in the light of the dramatic events since 1939, maintained unchanged its traditional antichurch and Marxian stance, the latter mainly in words rather than in action. The Communists had fewer scruples about throwing overboard most of their ideological ballast. Their propaganda anxiously avoided the words "class struggle"; instead, patriotic appeals to the "renaissance of France," French "grandeur," and the importance of France were not infrequent.[7] De Gaulle accepted them in his government but carefully avoided entrusting the control of armed forces to them. The Communists were limited to holding cabinet posts in the area of economics, which was, under the circumstances, the most unrewarding assignment. Still, this was the first time in French history that Communists were represented in the cabinet.

Just as in the trade unions, the question of a Socialist-Communist party merger came up toward the end of the war. At first there was only talk of a committee of cooperation, but soon the Communists proposed a full merger in a French Workers' party (Parti Ouvrier Français). The Socialists were divided on the issue. Blum, who also returned late from the German camp where he had been kept, and Mayer, who had replaced the collaborationist Paul Faure as general secretary of the party, were dubious, to put it mildly. Blum rejected any merger with a party whose loyalty to democratic principles and practices was doubtful, even though in the Resistance the Communist party had supported the reestablishment of democratic institutions after the liberation of France. Second, Blum asserted that the primary loyalty of the Communists was to the Soviet Union. As long as French and Soviet interests coincided, this did not matter. But when these interests were different or in conflict, the record would indicate that the Communist party would put the interests of the Soviet Union ahead of those of France (or of world Socialism).[8]

Blum's point of view won a tremendous majority (close to 10,000 versus less than 300 votes) at a Socialist party congress in August 1945. While the merger was rejected, continued cooperation between the two parties was endorsed. Maurice Thorez, who had returned to France after having been pardoned for his desertion from the French army, gave statesmanlike speeches emphasizing the governmental role and responsibility of the Communist party. Indeed, in view of the terrible destruction that the war, German looting, and the sabotage by the Resistance had wrought in the country, the Communists became the main protagonists of hard work, higher productivity, and restraint of consumption. Still the electorate appeared to approve the new Communist line by making it the strongest single party in the elections for the Constituent Assembly held on October 21, 1945. With 5 million votes (26 percent of the total), the Communist pary was ahead of the Socialists' 4.5 million. Together the two parties held 311 of the 586 assembly seats, a clear majority. The left-wing Catholic M.R.P. equalled the Socialists in votes and seats.

Socialists and Communists agreed about rejecting an armed revolution and favored changing France's institutions by legal methods. They also agreed on forming a government, by including the M.R.P., under the leadership of de Gaulle. The adoption of a new constitution for France and the transition to a Socialist system—these were the two tasks which the new government set out to perform.

The social reforms rapidly introduced and passed centered mainly on a whole series of nationalization measures (discussed in chapter 9). Other re-forms concerned industrial relations, including the creation of plant councils (*comités d'entreprise*) and in due course the resumption of collective bargaining, which had barely started on a large scale in 1936 only to be interrupted by World War II.

The adoption of a constitution for the country proved a major problem. De Gaulle, a powerful personality and charismatic leader, wanted a constitutional role commensurate with his authority and popular standing. The Socialist-Communist majority in the Constituent Assembly opposed any form of an authoritarian constitution. The first draft was rejected in a referendum in May 1946; the second draft was approved later the same year. In the November 1946 elections the Communists continued to be the strongest single party while the Socialists lost substantial support. Yet for a short period Blum became prime minister.

The government and party system that had emerged after World War II— the Fourth Republic as the French frequently call it—was in many ways simply a continuation of the prewar picture: multiplicity of parties, lack of party discipline—except among the Communists—and extreme government instability. As Jacques Fauvet said, "No country had made more revolutions than France, and . . . none was more conservative."[9] As far as the Socialists and Communists were concerned, their main strength was—just as before World War II—in the north, northeast, and especially the southwest. This localization of leftist preponderance even partly outlasted de Gaulle's advent to power: in the 1965 presidential elections, François Mitterrand, candidate of the left, obtained a majority of votes in twenty-four departments. All but one—his home department—were located in what used to be the unoccupied zone of France during part of World War II—in the south of the country.

The leadership of the Socialist party was at first in the hands of Daniel Mayer, who had rebuilt a party demoralized both by the large vote for Marshall Pétain and surrender and by the terror of the Nazi occupation. He presented in many ways the tradition of Blum. Yet the party, which at the time of liberation appeared stronger and more enthusiastic than ever before,[10] rapidly lost a part of its electoral support, primarily in favor of the Communists. The Socialists responded at their congress in July 1946 by adopting a more radical political line and replaced Mayer by the author of the new majority resolution presented at the congress, Guy Mollet. Mollet spoke of the danger of revisionism, of the weakening of the Marxist thought in the party, and of a false humanism, a term he directed against Blum. Negotiations with the Communist party about cooperation or even merger of the two parties were undertaken but failed when the Communists insisted upon the acceptance of the spiritual leadership of Stalin by everyone.

A whole series of events combined to introduce the second stage of the postwar evolution. As the French economy recovered, there was a profound rift between the Socialist and Communist parties and a sharp turn of the Socialists toward the right—with new General Secretary Mollet cooperating in the shift. Second, there was the outbreak of the cold war after the proposed Marshall Plan and the refusal of Communists everywhere under Moscow's pressure to cooperate with it. Third, the parliamentary group of the Socialists led by the rightist, Paul Ramadier, never agreed with the leftist ideas expressed, mostly verbally, rather than in deeds, by Mollet. The break between the Communists and their opponents in the C.G.T. led by the veteran trade unionist Jouhaux was the the fourth factor. The old C.G.T. was severely weakened by the establishment of the Socialist-inspired C.G.T.-Force Ouvrière (F.O.) and the departure of the National Education Federation and others. The event strengthened the anti-Communist course of the Socialist party, even though the division within the C.G.T. was by no means clear-cut and some official non-Communists—Alain Le Léap, Pierre Le Brun, and others—remained in it. An unsuccessful miners' strike in 1947, led by the Communists and opposed by F.O., provided the occasion for removing the Communists from the government. From then on, the Communist party was locked into a political ghetto and became the eternal opposition.

When de Gaulle retired from the political scene in disgust with the party quarrels and the Gaullists in 1951 also entered into opposition against the government, the Socialists were forced more or less willingly into an almost permanent coalition with conservative and mildly progressive groups in order to provide a parliamentary majority for the government. Even though they were not always or even most of the time represented in the government, they were an indispensable part of the support of the various governments. While the economy of the country strengthened, almost from year to year, the Socialist vote steadily declined.

The war in Algeria became the great turning point in the history not only of the Socialist party but also of France. Early in January 1956 general elections provided a progressive majority and strengthened the position of the Socialists. Many voters may have hoped that Pierre Mendès-France, in some ways a disciple of Blum, would become prime minister. Instead, it was Mollet. He was supposed to set an end to the bloodshed in Algeria. Parliament, including the Communists, gave him extraordinary powers to end the emergency.

During a visit to Algeria Mollet suddenly reversed his stand. Now he and his Socialist colleagues in the government continued the hopeless effort to suppress the rebellion of Algeria. Mollet's government was forced to resign by its failure to win in Algeria and in 1958 de Gaulle returned to power with Mollet as minister of state. A splinter group broke away from the Socialist party to form the Parti Socialiste Autonome (P.S.A.), later transformed into the P.S.U. The decline of the Socialist party from 1946, when it was strongest (with 21 percent of the electoral vote), to 1962, when it was deprived of almost half of its support (down to less than 13 percent) reduced the Socialist group from 145 deputies to forty-three after the elections of 1968.

Nor was fate much friendlier to the Communists, for the period following Stalin's death brought on a series of troubles. Having been among the most loyal supporters of Stalin, the French party was badly shaken by the revelations about his regime and its atrocities at the 20th Soviet congress (1956). Maurice Thorez waited for five years before he publicly acknowledged the crimes of Stalin.[11] The powerful attraction that the party exerted for so long upon the intelligentsia was shaken also by the Russian suppression of the Hungarian revolution in 1956. Internal conflicts led to the expulsion of well-known party leaders. The replacement of the dying Thorez by the pedestrian Waldeck-Rochet in 1964 did not add to the prestige and the attractiveness of the party. De Gaulle, upon his return to power in 1958, attracted numbers of former Communist voters.

Recovery from this low point, which reduced the number of Communist members of the Chamber of Deputies to ten, was exceedingly slow. Increasingly, the party sought to reestablish its position by efforts to form an alliance with the Socialists, but for a long time this policy proved a total failure. The Socialists tried to keep alive the memory of the Stalin-Hitler alliance and accused their rivals of being "not so much on the Left as in the East."[12] Gaston Defferre, Socialist mayor of Marseilles, referred to the Communist opposition to European unification and their stress on national independence as evidence that they had become Gaullists.

Yet, with the elasticity for which he had become known, Mollet, recognizing the demoralization of the left, began a policy of rapprochement with the Communists in 1962. However, the parties of the left could only agree on opposition to the Gaullists, without being able to work out a positive program of any kind. Even the traditional formula, according to which the less-favored leftist candidate in the first round of the two-stage electoral system "desisted" in favor of the leftist candidate who obtained a higher vote, was not universally applied.

The decline of the Socialist party was accompanied by sharp internal cleavages. Defferre and Mollet became leaders of two hostile factions, the main issues being the traditional obligation of the party to oppose religious education in the state schools and the possibility and desirability of cooperation with the Communists. More and more, non-Communist left-wing opinion expressed itself through a multitude of clubs; some clubs were also of different political orientation—conservative or moderate. Many clubs consisted of small numbers of people, but they were not without considerable influence on the general public. The idea of forming a federation of the non-Communist leftist clubs and the Socialist party, though widely accepted in principle, became a cause of further disagreements between Defferre and Mollet. François Mitterrand, a member of the Resistance, set up a Federation of the Democratic and Socialist Left in 1965, but it broke up after its failure to defeat the Gaullists in the election of 1968. It will be discussed later in this chapter.

In the meantime, however, the trade union movement had made significant progress. Collective bargaining received a new start in 1950 when new legislation came into being. The typical agreement under the law covers an entire occupation or industry—neither term is defined—on a national or regional scale. Agreements with a smaller scope were excluded, except enterprise agreements where an industry contract already existed. Thus enterprise agreements were concluded fairly frequently in larger enterprises in the 1950s, beginning with the Renault agreement of 1955, as were multi-industry agreements concerning national insurance schemes for old age (1957) and for unemployment (1958) to supplement social security or public unemployment benefits.[13]

Extension of agreements by the minister of labor was provided for in the legislation of February 1950. To be able to be extended, i.e., to be made applicable to all firms falling within their trade and territory, these agreements had to be negotiated by all the so-called most representative trade unions in the industry and to contain a number of prescribed clauses. This last requirement was abolished in 1971 to facilitate extension. Another modification passed in 1978 overruled the earlier requirement that the contract be signed by all of the most representative organizations. The major union confederations—C.G.T., C.F.D.T. (Confédération Française Democratique du Travail, the majority of the former C.F.T.C. now turned toward Socialism), C.G.T.-F.O., the remnant of the C.F.T.C., and the C.G.C. (General Confederation of Cadres, comprised of executive and other white-collar personnel)—all favor collective contracts, but in fact C.G.T. under Communist leadership refused to sign most agreements.

The main employers' organization is the Conseil National du Patronat Français (C.N.P.F.). Several other organizations represent small and medium enterprises and another the agricultural sector. On the workers' side, a multiplicity of unions are represented at the bargaining table, with the C.G.T. the predominant organization, employers are represented in most industry-wide or regional bargains by a single organization affiliated with the C.N.P.F. (National Council of French Employers).

French employers who were frequently regarded as the most reactionary—or at least the most conservative—in Europe preserved their attitudes far into the post–World War II period. Henry Ehrmann,[14] whose work, though dated, is the outstanding study of French employers, described their position as purely negative: against the state, against the unions, against collective agreements. "Immobilisme" and paternalism were the predominant features of their policy. The great changes that occurred after World War II in the social structure of France were forced upon the employers. It was only in the late 1950s and 1960s that the large companies at least, partly due to pressure from the Common Market and the increasing shortage of labor, began to realize that a new era had begun that demanded their willingness not only to accept new ideas but even to bring forth some of their own. Modern business schools were established, and French students began to appear in U.S. schools of business. Gradually the C.N.P.F. accepted discussion of modern reform ideas and even proposed some, particularly in the area of social security.

To return briefly to the problems of collective bargaining,[15] the closed shop or union shop—U.S. style—is forbidden, although in the printing industry the law of 1956 that confirmed previous court decisions is not always observed.

Given the multiplicity of unions with identical or overlapping jurisdictions, mainly separated by ideological differences, the term "most representative union" was introduced in the legislation of 1936 to indicate the union admitted to bargaining. However, this was rapidly and mainly for political reasons transformed into a plural so that a series of unions is "most representative" and present at the bargaining table. Throughout the post–World War II period the Communist-dominated C.G.T. has remained the strongest single confederation, although the C.F.D.T.—formerly C.F.T.C.—having abandoned its religious character and shown remarkable signs of activity, has increasingly influenced trade union developments and moved closer to the Socialist party. F.O., whose main strength is among public employees, and the C.G.C., organizing white-collar workers especially of managerial status, complete the picture as far as the main groups are concerned. However, all unions together represent only a relatively small fraction of those who could be organized. It has been said that the French worker is far more ready to offer his life to his union than to pay his union dues. The lag in union membership is particularly conspicuous in the light of the rapid growth of the proportion of dependently employed: from 1954 to 1972 this rose from less than 65 percent to almost 80 percent of he labor force,[16] thus close to the situation in West Germany or Belgium, while union membership lagged far behind. Though union membership figures are highly unreliable, the above statement is generally accepted by experts in the field.[17] The shifting relative strength of the different union currents can best be ascertained by way of the elections to the works committees (*comités d'enterprise*).

The growth of the labor force has been accompanied by large-scale changes of its structure. Agricultural workers (not counting independent farmers) dropped between 1954 and 1968 to 3 percent, less than half their earlier share; manufacturing gained 12 percent and even more since 1968; extractive industries lost 30 percent; construction gained 36 percent; commerce rose 28 percent; and banks and insurance companies gained 64 percent. Employment in administration increased by 54 percent.[18] At the same time industrial concentration has progressed rapidly, partly under the impact of the large-scale nationalization measures undertaken after the war and later stimulated by competition and other considerations. Still, the majority of French workers are employed by small or medium enterprises.

Collective agreements are thus concluded by organizations that usually represent only a fraction of the employees of the industry or occupation, but the minister of labor has made use of his authority—which exists in different forms in other countries—to extend the agreements, making them applicable to enterprises not members of the employers' organization that signed it.

However, as is well known, collective bargaining plays a lesser role in France than in the United Kingdom or United States in determining wages or working conditions. Originating in the French Revolution and its Napoleonic aftermath is the belief in centralization and the reliance on bureaucracy to maintain order and stability and, at the same time, to be an instrument of economic progress. David Jenkins and Michel Crozier's analysis shows how this factor influences the labor relations climate:

> The key to the situation is the position of the government, which inter-venes at numerous points in the relations between the two, in establish-ing certain aspects of working conditions and social security measures, as well as in direct participation in negotiations and in its own consider-able role as an employer. This arrangement has certain advantages— notably, it skirts "the emotional difficulty which direct contact would constitute"—but its cumbersomeness also carries obvious disadvan-tages. Though both parties have the theoretical possibility of influencing the other through pressuring for state action of some sort, this is not very efficient. As a consequence, both sides get increasingly locked into their rigid positions. The unions remain weak because whatever influence they are able or willing to apply on management is all but invisible to the potential dues-paying member. Management remains aristocratically backward because the resentment of the state's interference in company affairs "reinforces a complex of reactionary attitudes and an anachro-nistic attachment to prerogatives which, in fact, are largely outmoded."[19]

New developments during the period under consideration have produced interesting and, from a foreign point of view, peculiar or original changes; the best example is the so-called *accords interprofessionels*. No counterpart exists in the United States or the United Kingdom, and only a faintly similar institution is found in West Germany. Translated into U.S. terms, it approxi-mates an agreement among the National Union of Manufacturers, the A.F.L.-C.I.O., the U.A.W., the Teamsters, and other major unions. In some cases these agreements have served to prepare legislation embodying the principles agreed upon by labor and employers; in others they remained contracts. In the main, however, social and especially industrial relations in France are regulated far more by law and administrative rules than by collective agree-ments, even though, as we pointed out, some changes in this area can be detected, particularly in the third phase. Moreover, the legal regulations con-cern more the substance than the procedure—the inverse of the U.S. situation. Even this difference loses some of its significance, as one comes closer to realities: procedure and substance are not always clearly distinct.[20] Thus, the minimum wage (S.M.I.G) is set by the government with the advice of a multigroup committee. The extension of the agreement is a governmental act, but it is almost always automatic if the legal conditions are met. Perhaps, as Hugh Clegg has suggested,[21] a distinction ought to be made between bargaining and political action rather than between bargaining and law. In France advances of labor in the industrial relations area coincide most frequently with the progress of leftist parties.[22]

In addition to collective bargaining and interprofessional minimum wage determination, the first postwar years saw the introduction of a whole series of further social reforms. Among them was the creation of works committees, joint consultative bodies consisting of elected employee representatives and chaired by the employer. Personnel delegates, called at first workers' delegates, had been set up in 1936. Both of these are discussed in Chapter 10. Later still, union sections in the plant were recognized. This was already part of the third phase in labor's evolution.

The watershed between the decline of the left and the third phase is marked in France by the aftereffects of the riots and the general strike of May and June 1968. While this outbreak of popular revolt came as a surprise to the government and de Gaulle himself, the changes in the rapidly expanding and modernizing French society were bound to clash with the inflexibility of the existing institutions. As observers have pointed out, the most important initiatives in the rebellious movement came from "a new generation of highly skilled workers, technicians, and high-level white collar workers. . . . It was no accident that the first shut-down occurred at an advanced technology company, Sud-Aviation. Moreover, some of the most significant strike actions were conducted in electronics, atomic power, and other such sophisticated industries."[23]

France after 1968 was no longer the same conservative country it had appeared to be prior to the rebellion, even though the political direction of the country changed little. Some, at first sight inconspicuous, reforms indicate that the events of May and June had left their mark. A main step forward was the admission of union locals in enterprises with more than fifty employees. By 1975 almost half of these enterprises had union locals. The *comités d'entreprise* had a revival. In 1966–67 only 30 percent of the enterprises had such committees, six years later the percentage had increased to almost 60. Since most large enterprises had such committees in the earlier period, the increase must have occurred primarily in medium-sized undertakings.

Another major reform was the acceptance in April 1970 of the principle of the transfer of hourly paid workers to salaried status (mensualisation). By an interindustry agreement that set down the principle, the application was left to industry contracts. The works' councils were given a larger scope of activities, especially with regard to mass dismissals. Other reforms in 1973 gave the councils greater powers in the area of working conditions. The following year the Sudreau Commission was appointed to study how enterprises could be restructured to give the employees greater influence on management; it produced a very modest report. Proposals for some form of workers' participation in management—beyond a small measure of profit-sharing introduced by de Gaulle[24]—have found little support outside the leadership of the C.F.D.T. Perhaps the most significant change in the social climate was the multi-industry bargaining already mentioned and provided for in the Grenelle *constat* at the end of the 1968 strike movement. It led to two nationwide agreements, one on job security (February 1969) and another on vocational training (July 1970).

Another result of the May events was a tremendous increase in the number of collective bargaining agreements providing for shorter working hours. Quite a few of those were plant or company agreements.[25]

Yet most unions persist, at least in their public statements, in regarding collective agreements with some distrust; they protest that "negotiation is not integration" in the existing society. But this may very well be only a verbal separation from the established order.

In politics the recovery of the French Socialist party from almost total disintegration in the late 1960s to a position of governmental control was unique in Europe. Almost all other parties of the non-Communist left achieved their progress in the third phase by accentuating their rejection of revolutionary and antidemocratic ideas. In France recovery occurred by a shift to the left, at least, if that is implied by cooperation with the powerful Communist party. It is true that even before this turnabout occurred, the Socialists often used traditional revolutionary phraseology, but their practice was in contrast with their language. The divergence reached its highest point during the war in Algeria and was well perceived, though contradictorily interpreted, by different parts of the French public and accelerated the decline of the Socialists. A clear expression of the rejection of the party was the pitiful score of the Socialist candidate in the 1969 presidential elections, when he obtained little more than 5 percent of the popular vote. Intellectuals and young voters in particular turned away from the party.

In 1969 an effort was made to recreate the Socialist party by uniting what remained of the old party with some of the clubs and the P.S.U. The most important decision of a conference held in July 1969 was probably the election of a new general secretary, Alain Savary, who had been a member of the Socialist party until 1958, when he joined the new P.S.A. (later P.S.U.). He rejoined the Socialist party in 1969—after a brief stay in one of the clubs—and was soon a party leader. Two years later, the newly reorganized Socialist party that had in 1969 abandoned its description as French Section of the Socialist International (S.F.I.O.), part of its name since 1905, was again shaken up by its merger with the groups led by Mitterrand who, after a bitter battle, replaced Savary as general secretary of the party three days after joining it.[26] In the end this proved to be the definitive relegation of Guy Mollet to a back seat in the party, perhaps the only way to overcome the paralyzing stalemate between Defferre and Mollet.

The prospects of the new Socialist party seemed at the time less than promising. It could not hope for any substantial advance in popular support without attracting voters from the equally disorganized center and could have no serious governmental aspirations without an understanding with the Communists, two contradictory conditions.

The variety of political clubs and splinter parties on both the extreme right and the extreme left—with a few in-between—defies description. More than 100 existed at one time or another. Many were of only passing interest, and their lifespan often was limited to a year or two. To add the label unified to the name of a party almost inevitably meant that it was the result of a split from another party and was likely to split again in due course. As one example, the Unified Socialist Party (P.S.U.) found no partner worthy of cooperation. At the party conference of 1967, one delegate said: "We want unity on the Left, but on condition that it is not unity with the Communist Party, the Socialists, the Radicals—perhaps not even with members of the Convention [another left wing group]. With whom, then, are we proposing to unite? . . . The P.S.U., in its pure and solitary ivory tower, cannot defeat Gaullism by itself."[27]

The truth is that a great many, if not most, of these groups were far more interested in discussion and theorizing than in political action and had far more in common with university seminars than with effective political parties. Yet the end of the 1960s marked the beginning of the third phase in the evolution of the left, particularly for the Socialist party. The starting point was highly discouraging. At that time the percentage of the combined left in the popular vote dropped to 40 percent. Put differently, the four parties lost over 2.5 million votes while the total electorate increased by more than 3.5 million.[28] No less significant was the fact that the Communists, though sharing in the leftist losses, managed to surpass in 1968 the combined vote of the non-Communist left. The parliamentary representation of the Communists does not reflect this fact, as a new electoral system that operated against the Communists and the Gaullists—the "anti-system" parties—had been adopted prior to the election of 1951.

When Mitterrand, coming from the clubs, took over the leadership of the Socialist party, it had reached a low point in public support and esteem. Although circumstances—economic and political—played a major role in the recovery of the Socialist party, the personality of Mitterrand contributed a good deal. A brilliant speaker, not burdened by too much responsibility for the inglorious recent past of the non-Communist left, though not entirely free of it, Mitterrand succeeded in forming a federation of several clubs, the Con-

vention des Institutions Republicains. This, in turn, formed an alliance with
the remnants of the Socialist party and the small Radical party under the name
Fédération de la Gauche Démocratique et Socialiste (F.G.D.S.). The central
point in the political strategy of the slowly emerging party—then still under
the leadership of Savary—was the rejection of the "third force" concept: the
idea that European Socialism could form a political force independent of both
Soviet Communism and American capitalism. This, Savary maintained, had
turned the French Socialists into a second-rate party of the center because it
did not dare to admit publicly that it was following a "middle of the road"
policy. One implication of the new line was the rejection by the newly named
Socialist party of any governmental responsibility unless the Communists
were supporting the government.

Negotiations with the Communists led to a statement of agreements and
disagreements (*constat de convergences et de divergences*). The Socialist
party machinery was reorganized, and in 1971 at the congress of Epinay the
party was reconstituted by the merger with the F.G.D.S. Under Mitterrand's
direction the fundamental ideological discussions with the Communists were
abandoned as hopeless in favor of the elaboration of a limited common program of immediate reforms. As usual in such alliances, the main question
was who would profit more, or, as an election poster in 1973 that showed
the Communist leader Georges Marchais grinning above a worried-looking
Mitterrand put it, "Who will eat whom?"[29] In the elections of 1973 Socialists
and Communists obtained about the same number of votes, 20 percent each,
and the allied left Radicals plus various small left-wing parties including
Michel Rocard's Parti Socialiste Unifié added another 8 percent. When the
following year, after Georges Pompidou's death, Mitterrand ran for the presidency, he obtained 49.3 percent of the popular vote. This included the great
majority of the working class and of the young. Obviously, Marchais had
more reason to worry than Mitterrand.

A common program was worked out in 1972 providing for a limited
number of nationalization measures, a mixed economy, and cooperation in
the European institutions in addition to NATO. This program needed updating for the elections of 1978, which had been provided for when it was
first established. There is little doubt that this process could have been successful if all of the groups involved in the alliance had been willing to come
to an agreement. But the rapid growth of the Socialist party, which left the
Communists far behind, caused Marchais to prevent such an agreement. The
pretext was his demand for a longer list of nationalizations than had been
previously established. Few observers doubted that the real reason was the
unexpectedly rapid recovery of the Socialists who outdistanced the Communist party. The result was inevitable: the alliance that earlier had appeared
certain to win the elections of 1978 lost out, even though the Socialists as
well as the Communists gained votes. Obviously Marchais and most probably

Moscow preferred the more neutralist government of the right and center to Mitterrand toward whom the Russians have repeatedly shown their hostility.

The immediate consequences of the leftist defeat and the hardly concealed resumption of bitter hostility between Socialists and Communists meant internal crises of both parties. Mitterrand, whose main achievement had been his ability to hold together the highly diverse elements of his party, now faced rivals in his struggle to keep the leadership, especially opposition from Rocard and, perhaps, also from Pierre Mauroy, president of the strongest Socialist provincial organization, Nord-Pas-de-Calais. However, Mitterrand emerged victorious in the battle for the leadership of the party. Marchais's difficulties, though following Communist tradition less open to the public eye, are perhaps more serious. His belated and half-hearted move toward Euro-Communism[30] has appeared to few observers as genuine. Even the party's official rejection of the "dictatorship of the proletariat" did not prevent the return of the Communists to the political ghetto in which they had been living since the late 1940s. Marchais's assertion that the party since its 22nd congress clearly endorsed democratic principles was intended to make the average observer overlook the fact that the Communist party took notice of Nikita Khrushchev's revelations of Stalin's crimes as late as 1976, over twenty years later. The works' councils elections of 1978 held after the general political elections and in the midst of growing unemployment showed a C.G.T. loss of approximately 8 percent over the preceding year. The beneficiaries were the F.O. and to a lesser extent the C.F.D.T., which has increased its ideological distance from the C.G.T.

Among the most conspicuous signs of the rebellion in the Communist party is the loss of its prestige among the intellectuals and the expression of this fact in non-Communist papers. One example is an article by the philosopher Louis Althusser and five associates in *Le Monde*—the Communist party paper *L'Humanité* refused to print it—asking for a nationwide discussion of the party line, the later opening of the party press to such a discussion, and—differently from past pressures—free elections of delegates to an extraordinary party congress.

The Soviet invasion of Afghanistan, endorsed by the Communist party leadership, but sharply criticized by Mitterrand, has further sharpened the conflict between the two major parties of the left.

Nevertheless, the Communists were forced by public opinion to support Mitterrand against Valéry Giscard d'Estaing in the presidential elections of 1981. Not only did Mitterrand emerge as the victor with a strategy of cooperation with the Communist party and other leftist groups that many Socialists had opposed, but in the subsequent parliamentary elections the Socialists far outdistanced their Communist allies and rivals. The result was a Socialist majority government—the first in the history of conservative France—with a small Communist representation in the cabinet. Once again France had asserted its intellectual and political independence by turning left of center just at a time when the Western world led by the United States took refuge from its difficult problems in a move toward conservative ideas and parties.

It is not easy to discern the reasons for the French turn toward the left, especially since it was accompanied by a severe loss of votes by the Communist party. It would appear that the traditional issues dividing right from left in France played a less important role at these elections than in the past. The first impression of an insightful observer is that a movement toward decentralization, toward a less authoritarian system, and toward direct negotiations of social groups without government intervention has upset the traditional political structure of the country.[31] It is even more difficult to forecast the prospects of the new government that took office at a time of rapidly worsening economic conditions and sharpened international friction. The main asset of the Mitterand presidency is that it is new: new personnel, new ideas, and a new style of government.

NOTES

1. Twenty-one of the seventy-two Communists deputies in the French Parliament resigned from the party.

2. A prime example of the Communist ability to change policies from day to day was the behavior of the party leader, Maurice Thorez. At the outbreak of the war, he joined his regiment with all kinds of patriotic demonstrations, deserted a few weeks later, and called from abroad for immediate cessation of the war against Hitler.

3. No fewer than ninety-six of the 151 surviving members of the Socialist group in Parliament were expelled for collaboration with the regime of Pétain-Laval. Julius Braunthal, *Geschichte der Internationale* (Hanover: Dietz Nachf., 1971), 38*n10*.

4. See my discussion in the *Proceedings of the Twenty-Fourth Annual Winter Meeting of the Industrial Relations Research Association,* Dec. 1971 (Madison: I.R.R.A., 1972), 201, and Henry W. Ehrmann, *French Labor from Popular Front to Liberation* (New York: Oxford University Press, 1977), 265ff.

5. When the Allied troops approached Paris, the unions called for a "general strike for liberation." For the first time in their history the Christian unions joined this appeal.

6. Jean-Daniel Reynaud, *Les Syndicats en France* (Paris: Editions du Seuil, 1975), 1:99–100.

7. Braunthal, *Geschichte der Internationale,* 46.

8. Blum put heavy stress on human rights as he had in his book, *A l'échelle humaine,* written during his captivity and published in 1945.

9. Quoted in Dorothy Pickles, *The Government and Politics of France* (London: Institutions and Parties, 1972), 1:151.

10. Pierre Guidoni, *Histoire du nouveau Parti Socialiste* (Paris: Tema, 1973), 44.

11. Pickles, *Government and Politics of France,* 1:176.

12. A phrase coined by Mollet, general secretary of the Socialist party at the time.

13. Yves Delamotte, "Recent Collective Bargaining Trends in France," in *Collective Bargaining in Industrialized Market Economies* (Geneva: I.L.O., 1974), 226. The earlier post–World War II evolution of collective bargaining is well described in Val R. Lorwin, *The French Labor Movement* (Cambridge, Mass.: Harvard University Press, 1954). See also Adolf Sturmthal, ed., *Contemporary Collective Bargaining in Seven Countries* (Ithaca, N.Y.: Cornell University Press, 1957).

14. *La politique du patronat français (1936–1955)* (Paris: A. Colin, 1959). The original English edition was published as *Organized Business in France* in 1957.

15. This will be discussed in ch. 12 herein.

16. Reynaud, *Les Syndicats en France,* 1:21.

17. Thus for 1970, G. Adam *et al.* in *L'Ouvrier Français en 1970* (Paris: A. Colin, 1970), 16, estimate the membership of the C.G.T. at 1.5 million; the C.F.D.T., 600,000; the C.G.T.–F.O., 500,000; the C.G.C., 200,000; and the remainder of the Christian C.F.T.C. at 100,000.

18. Reynaud, *Les Syndicats en France,* 1:22.

19. David Jenkins, *Job Power, Blue and White Collar Democracy* (London: Heinemann, 1973), 138.

20. See Delamotte, "Recent Collective Bargaining Trends in France," esp. 235ff.

21. *Trade Unionism under Collective Bargaining. A Theory Based on Comparisons of Six Countries* (Oxford: Basil Blackwell, 1976).

22. Union growth also depends largely on political factors. Main spurts occurred after 1917 (Russian Revolution), 1936 (Popular Front), and 1946 (Liberation). However, no similar consequences followed the events of 1968 or the Socialist election victory of 1981.

23. Jenkins, *Job Power,* 145. The difficulty of finding a common theme in the mass rebellion is illustrated in the booklet of the Club Jean Moulin, *Que faire de la revolution de Mai?* (Paris: Editions du Seuil, 1968).

24. Which perhaps could be better described as a modest form of incomes policy, since it is a form of compulsory saving.

25. Delamotte, "Recent Collective Bargaining Trends in France," 246.

26. Pickles, *Government and Politics of France,* 1:193.

27. *Ibid.,* 256.

28. Frank L. Wilson, *The French Democratic Left, 1963–1969: Toward a Modern Party System* (Stanford, Calif.: Stanford University Press, 1971), 26.

29. Quoted by Jean-Pierre Worms in "The Rise of the French Socialist Party," *Dissent,* Summer 1977, 274.

30. See ch. 15 herein.

31. Communication of Professor Jean-Daniel Reynaud of the Conservatoire National des Arts et Métiers, Paris.

8

Italy

THE RECONSTRUCTION of all branches of the Italian labor movement after the long break imposed by the Fascist dictatorship and World War II was complicated by events during the last year of the war. In northern Italy Benito Mussolini with the assistance of German troops had established the Republic of Salo, which collapsed in April 1945. Southern Italy was occupied by Italy's ex-enemies and new allies, the U.S. and British troops. In Rome Marshall Pietro Badoglio ruled under an appointment of the king. Theoretically, his government controlled all of liberated Italy, but in fact the Allied military forces held most of the power. In early October 1943 Badoglio was forced by military events to transfer his government to southern Italy. There the anti-Fascist parties began to reconstitute themselves. In the north Resistance groups of various ideological orientation were operating under the overall direction of joint committees of national liberation (C.N.L.). The main components were Communists, Socialists, the Action party, Christian Democrats, and Liberals.[1] When Rome was liberated in June 1944, the Allies discovered that Badoglio had little support in the C.N.L., and he was replaced by Ivanoe Bonomi, president of the Rome C.N.L.

The diversity of the fate of southern and northern Italy greatly reinforced the economic and social differences between the two parts of the country. They were reflected in the attitudes of population and leaders. Southern Italy was freed by foreign military forces and suffered relatively little from the hostilities. In the north the destruction was more severe, and the liberation movement had done a good deal to rid at least the big centers of Fascist control before the Allied troops arrived. Thus the northern areas witnessed a political revival based upon the self-confidence of the successful underground movement while the south felt far more strongly its dependence upon the Allied forces. But the political revival in the northern industrial heartland of the country brought with it also political factionalism and its inevitable consequences, competition and rivalry. In the trade union field, however, the movement for unification became irresistible. Communists, having dutifully reversed their course in 1941 (just like their French colleagues), Socialists, and even Christian Democrats "were . . . convinced of the desirability of trade union unity and political cooperation."[2] The outstanding figure was the Socialist Bruno Buozzi, who had been a refugee in France. There the Germans had arrested him and had turned him over to the Fascist authorities. Marshall Badoglio released him and made him commissioner of the formerly Fascist Confederation of Industrial Workers. With him served Vice-Commissioners Giovanni Roveda, a Communist, and Gioacchino Quarrello, a Christian Democrat. Similar appointments were made for the formerly Fascist Confederation of Agricultural workers and other trade union confederations, with Buozzi heading a coordination committee of the various confederations. These appointments were approved by the anti-Fascist parties "on the condition that democratization be permitted, the Syndicates reorganized into genuine trade unions, and free elections held."[3] Very little could be achieved since a few days later German troops reoccupied Rome, and the trade union leaders had to continue their work underground. The result was a decision to reconstitute the trade union movement afresh, without using the Fascist organizations as the starting point. This was the result of an agreement among Buozzi, Giuseppe di Vittorio for the Communists, and Achille Grandi for the Christian Democrats. However, before the pact could be signed, an event of tremendous significance had occurred: Buozzi fell into the hands of the Germans in April 1944 and was executed just before Rome was evacuated by the Nazi troops. This deprived the non-Communist unionists of the one leader who in nationwide reputation ranked ahead of di Vittorio, the Communist labor leader. While many factors contributed to the growing Communist influence among the working class, Buozzi's death was undoubtedly one of the most consequential.

Some of the internal differences caused by regional, personal, and political rivalries were at least substantially overcome when the Naples unions joined the confederation based upon the Rome pact and called themselves the C.G.I.L. (Confederazione Generale Italiana del Lavoro), after a prewar Catholic organization. In September 1944 a congress was held with significant international representation and chaired by the secretary of the still surviving prewar International Federation of Trade Unions, the Belgian Walter Schevenels. Yet the main union power was in the north, and as soon as this was liberated, regional union organizations sprang up, the Camere di Lavoro, city or regional union bodies, which corresponded to the organizational tradition of the country. Fitting these into the framework of the C.G.I.L. in Rome did not create any major problems, since room had been left in the directorate for representatives of the north. Di Vittorio emerged more and more as the dominant personality, particularly since the Socialists were split into several warring factions.

The tendency of the Italian Socialists to divide into factions and even into separate parties had manifested itself already right after World War I. In

1921 the Communists split off; the following year the right wing of the Socialist party under Filippo Turati was expelled. The bulk of the party, the Maximalists under Giacinto Serrati, was further divided into different currents. Indeed, it is doubtful whether any major Italian party understands the function of a party in a democratic system, namely that of uniting citizens on a limited number of objectives that can be translated into practical actions. Instead, each party was subdivided into competitive currents to the point that at party conventions each submitted its separate resolution. The votes for each of these enabled the congress to elect the party executive on the principle of proportionate representation. Emphasizing internal differences rather than looking for integration and means to carry on joint actions became the rule rather than the exception in Italian politics. As Pietro Nenni, one of the outstanding Socialist leaders and a critical observer of events, noted in a discussion of the Italian left movement: "They did not discuss actions, they classified currents. Just as the theologians, they discussed the wording of the holy text while their world crashed in ruins. . . . Thus the fate of the Socialists was decided."[4]

Even during the Fascist period the internal friction continued. True, the situation had become somewhat simpler when Serrati, defeated in his own party, joined the Communists. But it was only among the emigres that serious discussions about a reunification started. Among the Maximalists who had fled to France, it was Nenni who most passionately sought unity, aware that the working-class divisions had paved the way for the Fascists. Within Turati's party the venerated party leader himself and his principal disciple, Giuseppe Saragat—many years later president of the Italian Republic—fought for reunification with the Maximalists. After some failures Nenni finally induced in 1930 a majority of the Maximalist emigres in France to agree to a unification with the Turati group. The merged party called itself the Partito Socialista Italiano (P.S.I.).

After liberation the political leadership of the country shifted a bit to the left, when the north made its influence felt. In June 1945 Ferrucio Parri of the Action party took over as prime minister. His support consisted of the six anti-Fascist parties then in existence; unfortunately, they quarreled a good deal among themselves. The terrible economic situation of the country made compromises difficult and forced the government to impose almost unbearable sacrifices upon the population. The left was unable to give leadership to the country. The result was a change in the direction of the government, and its leadership passed to Alcide De Gasperi, the head of the Christian Democratic party; this was the beginning of a long era of that party's predominance.

De Gasperi started out with a coalition of Christian Democrats, Socialists, and Communists, but this held together only for a year and a half. Then the growing conflicts between the Christian Democrats, on one hand, and the Socialists and Communists, on the other, induced him to expel the two leftist parties from the government in May 1947. The main issues were the beginning of the cold war and a division among the government parties as to which side they were to support, the United States or the Soviet Union. Thus ended the first phase of the postwar era.

One of the inevitable victims of these conflicts was the unity of the trade union movement. Heavy unemployment and underemployment combined with an incredibly high rate of inflation contributed to a rapid growth of the trade union movement. Under the circumstances most union activities were directed against the government or at least were designed to put pressure on it. At the same time the leadership of the movement passed more and more into the hands of the Communists, with di Vittorio the dominant figure. By 1946 they had effective control.[5]

Strangely enough, it was not their radical attitude that gave the Communists control. Palmiro Togliatti, after eighteen years in exile in Moscow—where he operated under the name Ercoli—returned to Italy with directives for moderation. He rejected Socialist reforms, favored freedom for private initiative, and agreed to continue the arrangement with the Catholic church that Mussolini had concluded in 1929. Clearly Nenni now was to the left of the official Communist line, but he refused to break the ties that connected the two parties. The electorate responded by giving the Communists in the elections of June 1946 almost as many votes (19 percent) as the Socialists (21 percent)—under the circumstances an astonishing success for the Communists. Not only in the Resistance while the war still lasted but also in the trade unions and in the plants themselves after the war were the Communists the most active group. They more than anyone else had the initiative in the trade union movements, regardless of their numbers.

Di Vittorio was far superior in organizational ability to his Socialist colleague Oreste Lizzardi or to Achille Grandi, the Christian-Democratic representative, in the leadership of the C.G.I.L. The Communists also had a large well-trained, experienced, and dedicated cadre; some of its members had fought in the Spanish Civil War, and many others in the underground movement, especially in the industrial north. They combined their elastic tactic in political matters with a more aggressive strategy in economic issues, such as wage adjustments exceeding cost of living increases.[6] As one close observer put it:

> The period was a painful one in the accomplishment of the enormous tasks confronting the nation, and the Communists took full advantage of the situation in playing the role simultaneous with participation in government, of chief critics and rallying point of the discontent which manifested itself, especially among wage earners. . . . Unemployment and underemployment were high and took on the chronic pattern which characterized the economy in succeeding years. Inflation, which had as-

sumed major proportions through the war, took on a more and more serious aspect during the two years following the war. . . . Cost of living, using 1938 as 100, stood at 2823 in 1946 and 4575 in 1947 reaching its peak in September 1947 at 5331.[7]

By 1946 the Communists outdistanced the combined numbers of Socialists and Christian Democrats in the unions and were in control of the C.G.I.L. The union stand for the Republic against the monarchy in the referendum in 1946 aroused no conflicts, since all union factions agreed on that particular issue. Differences began to arise over automatic wage adjustments to cost-of-living changes, but these were minor compared with the threats to unity that developed as a consequence of the divisions that emerged among the Socialists. The Nenni group favored closest cooperation and at times even a merger with the Communists, but the moderate wing led by Saragat was totally opposed to this strategy. Seeing that the Nenni-wing controlled a majority of the party, Saragat and his followers left it in January 1947 and founded the P.S.L.I. (Partito Socialista dei Lavoratori Italiani), colloquially called the Piselli. This party was doomed to remain a small but not uninfluential group. At the 1947 C.G.I.L. congress the Piselli supporters had 2.2 percent of the votes.

The Socialist leadership within the C.G.I.L. passed into the hands of Fernando Santi without producing a major change of direction. The Socialists endorsed the election of di Vittorio as secretary general and accepted the post of secretary subordinate to him.

De Gasperi's new cabinet was based upon the Christian Democrats and three minor parties including the Saragat-wing of the Socialists. The new government could count upon strong economic and diplomatic assistance from the United States. In due course, after a period of hesitation, the other leftist parties and the unions responded by intensified opposition. Italy had become one of the focal centers of the Cold War.

The trade unions were one of its main battlefields. The Communist majority engaged in a strategy of "short stoppages, slow-downs, and general strikes affecting different areas and sectors of the economy in rotation, gradually encompassing the entire country."[8] The non-Communist minority refused to carry out the majority decisions, claiming that they were politically inspired. The outcome of the general elections in 1948 added fuel to the fire. Christian Democrats and Communists were the main victors, the first getting 48.5 percent of the votes and 306 out of 574 seats in Parliament, and the Communists 31 percent of the votes and 131 seats. The Socialists were far behind with fifty-three seats. This was shortly followed by the break-up of trade union unity. Christian Democrats, Republicans, and the Saragat Socialists prepared the way for the split by founding a committee, somewhat ironically called the "Alliance for the Unity and Independence of the Trade Unions." Its main task was to convince the Italian workers for whom trade union unity was a most precious good of the necessity of a split.

However, before these careful preparations could be completed, events precipitated an unplanned and disorganized breakup of C.G.I.L. An attempt on the life of the Communist leader Togliatti led to a confused situation that included spontaneous strikes and fear of an armed revolt. The trade union executive board was unable to agree on uniform action. The Christian Democrats in particular insisted upon an end of the strikes. It is doubtful whether at that moment the Communists had the power to bring it about, though they were trying desperately to get control of what was essentially a spontaneous movement. Nevertheless, the Christian Democrat leader Giulio Pastore asked his followers to resume work. The C.G.I.L. executive thereupon announced that the Christian Democrat supporters had put themselves outside the organization. Republicans and Saragat supporters in the P.S.L.I., not having been informed by the Christian Democrats of their plans, were resentful of this neglect and decided to stay in the C.G.I.L. They held separate conferences that criticized both Communists and Christian Democrats for the split. The latter proceeded in October 1948 to set up their own nationwide trade union, the Free Italian Confederation of Labor (L.C.G.I.L.). Pastore was elected general secretary.

This proved to be only the first stage in the disintegration of the trade union movement. Republicans and right-wing Socialists were a tiny minority in the C.G.I.L., so their influence upon its policy was negligible, and growing East-West tension soon made their situation within the C.G.I.L. untenable. Their anticlericalism, a long and powerful tradition of the bulk of the Italian labor movement, made it impossible for them to join an organization dominated by Christian Democrats. In the spring of 1949 a third confederation came thus into being: the Federazione Italiana del Lavoro (F.I.L.), representing the Republicans and the Saragat Social Democrats. The Communists declared that the new group was secretly directed by the United States, in particular by David Dubinsky and his associates of the International Ladies' Garment Workers.[9] Some elements of F.I.L. then joined the Christian Democrats; the resulting organization called itself Confederazione Italiana Sindacati Lavoratori (C.I.S.L.). The remaining F.I.L. group stayed in that organization, renaming it Unione Italiana del Lavoro (U.I.L.). With this threefold split the movement repeated the pattern of its pre-Fascist divisions. A Communist-led organization, the C.G.I.L. now represented the majority of the organized workers, including most of the left-wing Socialists. The C.I.S.L., dominated by Christian Democrats but with a substantial Socialist element, was second in size. The U.I.L., the weakest of the three, combined Saragat Socialists and Republicans. A few splinter groups of various ideological orientations completed the picture. C.G.I.L. became increasingly combative as the cold war intensified but showed also genuine concern with the everyday problems of the workers in the plant. C.I.S.L. and U.I.L. were either too ideological or too timid to attract many of the non-Communists who remained in the C.G.I.L.[10] Moreover, they appeared more interested in combatting each other rather than the Communists.[11] The latter gained a good deal by their emphasis on the two problems that most concerned the average worker: job security and unemployment. In exchange most workers were willing to accept C.G.I.L. leadership on political issues.

When the April 1948 elections provided the Christian Democrats with a firm majority in Parliament, Communists and Socialists were forced into a minority opposition role. No revolutionary possibility existed any more, and the country was firmly aligned with the West in the cold war.

Phase two of the postwar evolution of Italian labor coincided with a rapid expansion of the Italian economy. Just as in most industrializing countries, the structure of Italy's labor force changed radically during the postwar period. The exodus from agriculture—by 1975 its share of the total labor force had dropped to less than one-sixth—led to a vast expansion of the service sector that in many cases represented a form of concealed unemployment.[12] Yet both hourly earnings and productivity in manufacturing rose rapidly and steadily, and the rate of inflation as measured by the cost of living index declined. The result was either price stability in some years or small rates of increase by the end of the 1950s.[13] Perhaps more important, the unemployment rate dropped below 3 percent in 1963, due largely to the emigration of large numbers of Italian workers to other countries in Europe but also as a result of economic expansion in Italy itself. The employees' share in the net national product rose almost steadily during the same period.[14]

In politics the revelations of Joseph Stalin's crimes at the 20th Soviet party congress, the "Polish October," and the uprising in Hungary brought about a cooling-off between the Nenni Socialists and the Communists. Even the Communists, under the influence of the humanistic tradition of their early leader Antonio Gramsci, tended to have a liberal current in their midst; they now gained a certain distance from Moscow. Nenni and Saragat met for discussions on a possible rapprochement. Combined with the rapid economic expansion, particularly in northern Italy, these events tended to bring some movement into what appeared until then an unshakeable stability, the "immobilismo" in the Italian political system.[15] At the elections of 1958 both Saragat's and Nenni's parties gained, the Communists had a slight loss, and the Christian Democrats had a notable success. Perhaps more important was that the left wing of that party—which was even more than most Italian parties a fairly loose confederation of various currents—advanced. It had to battle the conservative and authoritarian influence of Pope Pius XII who was hostile to the tendency of the Christian Democrats to look for allies on the left. In April 1959 "the Holy Office, just when the idea of the opening to the Left was gathering force, issued a decree condemning political collaboration with the Socialists as with the Communists."[16]

It took the election of Pope John XXIII, who favored the opening to the left, before the Nenni party was admitted, not yet to the government, but to the support of the administration of A. Fanfani, who belonged to the left wing of the Christian Democrats. Fanfani proposed a program of social reforms, including the nationalization of electric power. He also undertook to introduce economic planning into the almost chaotic economic system of Italy, an attempt that had few chances to succeed given the inefficiency of the Italian civil service.

Influenced by the repression of the Hungarian rebellion, Nenni moved away from cooperation with the Communists. Nevertheless, it took some time before center-left coalitions began to emerge in various cities (Milan in January 1971, then Genoa and Florence). In a few months forty city coalitions had been set up.

In the general elections of April 1963, after a campaign in which the Communists bitterly attacked the Socialists for having betrayed the working class by supporting the Christian Democratic government, the Communist party gained more than a million votes. However, both the Social Democrats (Saragat's party) and the Nenni Socialists gained as well, while the Christian Democrats lost nearly three quarters of a million votes. The issue of the "opening to the Left" remained on the agenda, even though the form in which Fanfani had implemented it, namely support by the Socialists without admitting them to the cabinet, obviously failed to stem the Communist tide.

It was only under Fanfani's successor, Aldo Moro, that the Nenni Socialists entered the government. Nenni became deputy prime minister and represented Italy in NATO! A new party leader was elected in the person of Francesco de Martino, who took Nenni's place. Saragat, the leader of the moderate Social Democrats who had split off from the Nenni party over the issue of cooperation with the Communists, was elected president of Italy in 1964—a mainly representative post except when a new government was to be formed. Then a strong president might have some influence on the choice of the prime minister. New divisions developed among the Socialists as a consequence of their joining the government, and the electorate responded by further reducing the Socialist vote at the elections of 1968. From 19.9 percent their share of the popular vote dropped to 14.5 percent, while the Communists increased theirs from 25.3 to 26.9 percent, almost double the Socialist vote.

Not until 1976 did the Socialists finally leave the coalition with the Christian Democrats, but the Communists, not the Socialists, profited from the government crisis that followed. The Socialist vote dropped to less than 10 percent. As a result, the party forced de Martino to retire and replaced him by a man in his early forties, Bettino Craxi. This represented a change of generations as well as a modification of strategies.

Though almost unknown when he was elected, Craxi soon demonstrated leadership qualities that appear to have enabled the party to enter what may be labeled a third phase. He changed gradually the international policy of his party according to the slogan that Italy is "a friend of the Soviet Union and an ally of the United States."[17] When the Communist leader Enrico Berlinguer referred to Russia as "a Socialist society with a few illiberal traits," Craxi responded that it was "an illiberal society with a few Socialist traits."

As one consequence of this new policy of greater independence from both Christian Democrats and the Communist party, a merger of the Socialists with the small Social Democratic party (4 percent of the vote) had become a possibility. The Social Democratic party chief Giuseppe Romita, Saragat's successor, was now replaced by Pietro Longo, who was friendlier toward the Socialists. In the not too distant future a revived Socialist party hoped to replace the Communists as effective support of a non-Communist government and friendly words directed at the Christian Democrats were frequent at the party congress in early 1978. But this is not an undisputed strategy.

One of the consequences of the splintering of the parties on the left was a series of dramatic developments among the trade unions. To a considerable extent, they performed functions that belonged to political parties. In the early stages of postwar reconstruction the unions concentrated on agreements that set minimal rates and standards for wages and working conditions. These were typically nationwide agreements covering an industry or a branch of an industry. The rapid industrialization of Italy and the emigration of large numbers of jobless workers created early in the 1960s a state of affairs approaching full employment—a rare phenomenon indeed in modern Italian history. As wages started moving upward more rapidly, the unions became more aggressive, their objectives less political and more economic, and a more "articulated bargaining" system was one of their immediate aims.

While a more detailed discussion of developments in the collective bargaining field is reserved for chapter 12, reference must be made here to the strike movements of 1969—wildcat strikes and "rolling" strikes alternating from firm to firm or department of a firm to another department. New forms of workers' representation developed, as did opposition to the Internal Commissions. While representatives to the latter are elected by all workers, the so-called delegates represent the union members. A mood of rebellion, perhaps a sequel to the Paris events of the preceding year, went through the factories and workshops. By the "hot autumn" of 1969, plant assemblies had formulated demands that were quite often at variance with those proposed by the union leadership. At the same time a "Workers' Charter," similar to the Wagner Act in the United States and French labor legislation of 1968, was passed by Parliament. Its essence was that representative trade unions should be given recognition at the workplace. The exact functions and the organizations to be involved in plant bargaining remained to be settled, but developments in the direction of expanded plant bargaining were due to occur.

This became clear in the agreements concluded in various industries in 1970 and 1971, some of which—in rubber and glass—expressly recognized trade union bargaining rights at the plant level. Gino Giugni refers to an estimate of 4,400 plant agreements.[18] They vary considerably in content and cover wage increases, incentive wages, and shorter working hours. Some deal with the working environment and job enrichment. The election of workers' delegates has spread, which means that the rank and file who can oust delegates anytime has far more direct influence on bargaining than by way of the old Internal Commissions. No uniform regulations exist as to the election of the delegates and their relation to the unions. The key to the further developments lies probably with the progress—or absence of progress—of the unification of the unions. That C.G.I.L. has left the World Federation of Trade Unions and the growth of Euro-Communism may be indications of future developments, but a failure of unification is still possible. Indeed, so far there has been far more talk than action on this score.

A good deal depends on the move toward unity, since the main strength of the labor movement is still in the divided nationwide unions rather than in the political parties. Yet at the same time supplementary agreements and contract administration are becoming more and more decentralized. Since, however, consultations between government and unions at the national level have become a normal event, the system of bargaining reaches all the way from the highest to the lowest level.

The main issue Italy had to face since the late 1960s was a new kind of "opening to the Left," the entry of the Communist party rather than the weakened Socialists into a coalition government headed by the Christian Democrats. This the Communists presented as the "historical compromise." There are indications that this has been an objective of the Communist party since the end of World War II. When Togliatti returned to Italy from Russia, he was deeply convinced of the need for the party to come to terms with the Catholics. The first major occasion he had to demonstrate his strategy occurred when article 7 of the constitution of post-Fascist Italy became a matter of bitter dispute. This article incorporated the Lateran agreements of 1929 between Mussolini and the Vatican into the new Republican constitution. These agreements gave the Vatican the right to claim obedience from all Italians to its dogmas about marriage and education.[19] This would virtually turn Italy into a religious state. Togliatti supported the text, even though this did not guarantee in exchange any help for the Communist party on the part of Pope Pius XII.

The subject of an understanding between the Christian Democrats and the Communist party had been put again on the political agenda by the elections of May 1968. The Christian Democrats made slight gains, but the Communists and their allies, the party of Proletarian Unity—a splinter of the Nenni Socialists—made substantial advances, mainly at the expense of the allegedly united Socialists and Social Democrats. The coalition between them and the Christian Democrats now looked impossible to maintain. The Russian invasion of Czechoslovakia in August 1968 gave an occasion to the Communist and the unions to condemn the Soviet Union and to start upon their career as "Euro-Communists."[20] The rise of various leftist opposition groups combatting, often with terrorist methods, the official line of the Communist party helped to advertise the moderation of the latter.

The beginnings of Italian Euro-Communism were, however, rather feeble and uncertain. The protests against the invasion of Czechoslovakia became weaker as time went on, and the new Communist leader from Sardinia, Enrico Berlinguer, almost ruined his party's chances for government participation by asking in a speech in Parliament that Italy leave NATO and the alliance with the United States.

Still in 1970, when the C.G.I.L. and the French Communist–led Confédération Generale du Travail (C.G.T.) were included by their respective governments in their nominations of representatives to the Economic and Social Commission of the European Economic Community, the non-Communist unions decided to admit the C.G.I.L. representatives to the meetings of the trade union side of the committee, but under the influence of Force Ouvrière and the German Trade Union Confederation (D.G.B.), the French C.G.T. was kept out. The Italians had successfully made the first step toward cooperation with the non-Communist unions.[21]

After the "hot autumn" of 1969, when strikes in various forms shook the country to its foundations,[22] the Communist party advanced again in popular votes at the general elections of 1976, obtaining 34.4 percent of the total. The presidency of the lower house of Parliament and the chairmanship of a number of parliamentary commissions were handed over to the party. A long period of economic troubles and political terror followed, bringing the country close to chaos. A new government formula was invented: the Christian Democrats under Giulio Andreotti formed a *monocolore* (one-party) government that Socialists, Socialdemocrats, Republicans, and Communists were to support by abstaining from voting.

This formula did not last long. A major change in the situation occurred when the three trade union centers—C.G.I.L., C.I.S.L., and U.I.L.—held a joint conference in February 1978. They proposed that in exchange for their abandoning a wages policy of permanent conflict, they be given codetermination in a long-term economic policy program. This moderate course found unanimous support among the Communist trade unions, but some opposition arose among the members of C.I.S.L. and U.I.L., as well as the metal workers' unions of the three confederations. The metal unions in Italy always regarded themselves as the spearhead of the labor movement. The opponents pointed out that the new union strategy served the political ends of the Communists rather than union objectives.

In December 1978 the Communist group in Parliament voted against Andreotti's decision to have Italy join the nascent European Monetary System. Socialist abstentions prevented the fall of the government over this issue, but the government's days were numbered. While the Communists would have preferred to produce a government crisis over a domestic rather than an international issue, Berlinguer felt compelled to express his party's stand against the proposed monetary union, especially since it involved radical measures of economic restriction. To a not insignificant extent, the action indicated Communist fears of being outflanked on the left by a multitude of extremist groups, without being able to show to its followers the advantages of the cautious policy that the party pursued.

Thus, the Communist party regarded the time ripe to make the decisive step of entering the cabinet. Craxi supported Berlinguer's demand, partly because the internal stresses of the country seemed to him to demand open assumption of governmental responsibilities by the Communist party and partly because he hoped that this would reduce Communist propaganda advantages at the Socialists' expense.

In view of the possible consequences of a government formation that might give Communists access to NATO secrets, the foreign relations importance of the issue was obvious. A public statement by the U.S. Department of State spoke clearly to this point: "The U.S. and Italy have in common profound democratic values and interests, and we do not believe, that the Communists. . . . share them."[23] In the end, the Communist party was kept out of the government while the stranglehold of the Christian Democrats on the job of the prime minister was at last broken. At the same time Socialist leader Craxi was clearly in the ascendancy. For the second time in several decades, Italian politics was in flux, in part at least because of the victory of François Mitterrand in France. The events in Poland provided the Italian Communist party with a further occasion to criticize Moscow and to assert their independence from the Soviet Union.

NOTES

1. Muriel Grindrod, *The Rebuilding of Italy: Politics and Economics, 1945–1953* (London: Royal Institute of International Affairs, 1955), 8–9.

2. Daniel L. Horowitz, *The Italian Labor Movement* (Cambridge, Mass.: Harvard University Press, 1963), 185.

3. Ivanoe Bonomi, "Diario di un anno," 74–76, quoted in *ibid.*, 185.

4. Pietro Nenni, "Storia di quattro anni, 1946," quoted in Julius Braunthal, *Geschichte der Internationale* (Hanover: Dietz Nachf., 1971), 2:230.

5. Horowitz, *Italian Labor Movement*, 204.

6. *Ibid.*, 205.

7. *Ibid.*, 203.

8. *Ibid.*, 211.

9. American support for the anti-Communist labor organizations was undoubtedly of crucial importance at this stage.

10. *Ibid.*, 225.

11. Since Italian union membership figures are traditionally overstated, there is little to be gained from quoting their official numbers.

12. Ettore Massacesi and Maria Grazia Finze, "The Labour Market in Italy," *Review of the Economic Conditions in Italy*, XXXI (May 1977). The authors stress the lack of reliability of official labor force statistics, in view of "illegal employment" to escape legal and trade union restrictions and of the size of the labor force engaged in "moonlighting."

13. Charles P. Kindleberger, *Europe's Postwar Growth: The Role of Labor Supply* (Cambridge, Mass.: Harvard University Press, 1967), 38.

14. G. H. Hildebrand, *Growth and Structure in the Economy of Modern Italy* (Cambridge, Mass.: Harvard University Press, 1965), 222.

15. Elizabeth Wiskemann, *Italy since 1945* (London: Macmillan, 1971), 34ff.

16. *Ibid.*, 39.

17. *The Economist*, Aug. 5, 1978, 36.

18. Gino Giugni, "Recent Trends in Collective Bargaining in Italy," in *Collective Bargaining in Industrialized Market Economies* (Geneva: I.L.O., 1973).

19. Wiskemann, *Italy since 1945*, 7.

20. See ch. 15 herein.

21. B. C. Roberts and Bruno Liebhaberg, "The European Trade Union Confederation: Influence of Regionalism, Detente and Multinationals," *British Journal of Industrial Relations*, XIV (1976), 262.

22. According to the *I.L.O. Yearbook of Labour Statistics*, the number of working days lost rose from 9.2 million in 1968 to 37.8 million in 1969 and declined to 18.3 million in 1970.

23. It is worth noting that the developments in the Italian Communist party had considerable influence on the Greek Communist movement. There a split has existed since 1968 between what are frequently called the Communist party of the exterior and the domestic Communist party. The first is led by Charilaes Florakis, who enjoys Moscow's support, and the second, which is more Euro-Communist in its views, is led by Babis Drakopoulos. While Berlinguer has addressed friendly messages to Drakopoulos, he has been careful not to spoil his relations with Florakis. During a visit to Greece by an Italian Communist party delegation led by Gian-Carlo Pajetta in January 1978, however, Pajetta made a statement endorsing the European Economic Community and objecting to Greece leaving NATO, declarations that ran counter to the policies of Florakis and of Andreas Papandreou, leader of the left-wing Socialists. The reasoning behind this, as stated in Italian Communist party papers, was to bring about reunification of the Greek Communist movement.

PART III
Evolution of Industrial Relations

9

Nationalization

THE DEMAND FOR the nationalization of all or at least a substantial part of industry has long been a standard feature if not the core of Socialist party programs and propaganda. It has also been taken up by a large number of unions. In the view of the Marxists[1] private ownership of the means of production and of distribution has been the source of surplus value and hence of profits and exploitation. A Socialist society devoted to the abolition of production for private profit would, therefore, wipe out the sources of private profit and transfer them to public property by nationalization or socialization.

However, most of the post–World War II expropriations were only to some extent a means of appropriating the property income of the capitalist. "Given that we pay full compensation," wrote C. A. R. Crosland, "it [the degree of appropriations] relies on (a) the difference between the yields on gilt-edged and equities, (b) the fact that nationalization precludes rising dividends and share-values, and (c) occasionally, the lower level of salaries in the public sector."[2] And he quotes John Strachey: "We [nationalize] in order to extinguish the great *unearned incomes* which are today derived, not from anything that those who draw them do, but from what they own. . . . The real purpose of socialization is to secure the proper distribution of the net national product among those who create it."[3] As nationalization was first carried out by compensation, the transfer of income was initially almost insignificant. Moreover, studies of the distribution of the national income show that the confiscation of all profit would add only small amounts to the incomes of the nonprofit-deriving citizens. For England, Crosland quotes a figure of 3 percent of net personal income after taxes as a possible increment.[4]

The distribution of private profit among the citizens in one form or another has not been the only motive of nationalization. Such measures have been undertaken throughout modern history by ideologically diverse governments and for a variety of reasons: from nationalist and militaristic impulses to the need to bail out essential or politically influential enterprises threatened by bankruptcy. Socialist governments have often found it convenient to na-

tionalize enterprises in the name of efficiency, sometimes mixing two different motives for the sake of political appeal.

Still, the large-scale nationalization measures taken shortly after World
War II, especially in Great Britain and France, were to a considerable extent
the work of Socialists or forces allied with them. Industries that were regarded
as essential for the life and safety of the community (a criterion that was often
interpreted to include industries vital for economic planning), industries that
were highly concentrated (which could well mean monopolies), and industries
whose operations were excessively dispersed through an inefficiently large
number of enterprises (coal mining in Britain and the electricity industry in
France) were the prime candidates for nationalization. In such cases nationalization was to provide the advantages of large-scale production, efficient
coordination, and more complete integration.[5]

Crosland describes the order for nationalization as follows: first, public
utilities where the basic capital equipment is very large; second, monopolies
that "inevitably constitute a threat of exploitation (political and social even if
not economic)"; third, basic industries. While these arguments relate to the
strategic position of the industry in the economy, a fourth argument—that of
efficiency—referred to the economies of scale that nationalization could produce.[6] Lastly, economic planning required substantial nationalization measures, especially of heavy investment industries, since the profit motive and
the national interest were viewed as "always in conflict." This was shown
quite clearly in decisions on the location of new plants or the closing of old
ones. Behind all this was of course the traditional Socialist demand for nationalization as a device to establish public ownership of all industries, to
destroy the profit motive, and to abolish profit as a source of income.[7] Politically—this was stressed more in France than in Britain—nationalization was
to free democracy from the pressures of private monopolistic powers. In the
area of industrial relations, it was to lead to more humane conditions.

In post–World War II Germany a number of currents merged to put the
socialization of industry into the background. At the first postwar congress of
the Social Democrats (S.P.D) held in Kurt Schumacher's domain, the city of
Hanover, Viktor Agartz, then the leading theoretician of both party and unions,
explained the position of the movement mainly in negative terms. The party
rejected traditional liberalism, monopoly capitalism with its imperialistic
tendencies, a nondemocratic corporate state, a centralized state capitalism
with a nonmarket economy, and, finally, the developing neo-liberalism.[8]

In the light of the Marxist tradition of the movement the failure to
emphasize the demand for nationalization of industry represented a sharp
break with the past. It was only later that the party spoke again of basic
industries to be socialized, but by that time the domestic political situation
had changed against the S.P.D. In 1947 even the later so conservative Christian-Democratic Union (C.D.U.), Konrad Adenauer's party, had expressed

Socialist ideas in its so-called Ahlener program. But by the summer of 1948 the Occupation forces made clear their objections to Socialist policies that would give the government powers that could be used in an antidemocratic fashion. The belated S.P.D. demand for nationalization measures was by now determined by the party's conviction that it would prove impossible to reestablish capitalism after the Nazi defeat, especially since the S.P.D. expected the masses to be inspired by powerful anticapitalistic sentiments. Even Schumacher's firm demand for a reunified Germany was based upon his conviction that democratic Socialists would become the dominant force in Western Europe.

However, the British Labour party and the government of Charles de Gaulle showed little inclination to support Schumacher's domestic or foreign policies, for a multitude of reasons, including U.S. pressure and a generalized distrust of Germans, even of S.P.D. members. At least equally important in preventing the enactment of nationalization measures in West Germany was the surprising weakness of the S.P.D. at the first postwar elections held in the Federal Republic. Only in Berlin in 1946—before the division of the city into Communist and non-Communist sectors—did the S.P.D. score impressively: almost 49 percent of the vote as against 22 percent for the C.D.U. and not quite 20 percent for the Communist-led S.E.D. (Socialist Unity party). At the elections to the first federal parliament on August 14, 1949 (in the three Western zones), the S.P.D. obtained 29.2 percent of the votes; the C.D.U./C.S.U. (Christian-Social Union), 31 percent; the Free Democratic party (F.D.P.), 11.9 percent; the Communists, 5.6 percent. A non-Socialist government was ensured.

The S.P.D. now represented the opposition to the more and more conservative C.D.U. This also meant the definitive rejection of major socialization measures by the West German electorate eager to protest against anything that smacked of the policies pursued in the Soviet zone of Germany. Different ideas such as codetermination and workers' control came to the fore.

Codetermination, as a generalized formula, appears together with a demand for "equal participation of the unions in the self-government of the economy" as point 7 of the so-called 16 Durkheimer points adopted shortly after the S.P.D. election defeat in August 1949. This was the first major programmatic document of the party since 1945. Point 8 asks for the socialization of the basic and key industries (Grundstoff- und Schlüsselindustrien) which was primarily designed to deprive the big capitalists and managers of their power. The pre-Hitler idea of nationalization as a means of distributing property income was obviously no longer a primary objective, although the wording did not specifically exclude this idea.

By 1952, at the party conference in Dortmund, a formula was advanced that indicated the long distance the party had traveled since the end of the war. Now the demand was for genuine competition of efforts in all branches of the economy for which it was appropriate. Less than ten years later, the party adopted a slogan that symbolized its turn from the Marxian tradition: "Planning as far as necessary, competition as far as possible." American New Dealers would have found this slogan probably too conservative. Of course, it is possible to interpret this as competition among separately administered nationalized enterprises or between the latter and private enterprises in the same industry, and the party program of Bad Godesberg stated that "competition by public enterprises is a decisive means to prevent private market domination." Crosland of the British Labour party found the latter version rather attractive in his book, *The Future of Socialism,* published in 1956, and was roundly criticized for his "revisionist" views by some of his fellow party members.

As early as 1950, Fritz Erler, one of the party leaders who had played a significant role in the Socialist underground movement "New Beginning" in the Third Reich, pointed out: "We must know that in the present situation of our society, we are swimming against the current, not with it." At that time, this was far from being generally accepted by the movement, still expecting the "inevitable" collapse of the capitalist system.

At the time of the Bad Godesberg congress in 1959, the issues presented themselves quite differently. One of the questions that led to internal debates was whether or not to adopt a separate program of principles and another program for the election scheduled for 1961. This division was rejected at the urging of Schumacher's successor, Erich Ollenhauer. But the concern with the forthcoming election, indeed with electoral success in general, emerged clearly in Ollenhauer's introductory speech at the congress. "If we were to follow these ideas [to make the political program of Karl Marx and Friedrich Engels the content of a program of social democratic principles in the year 1959] one result would be assured: within a short foreseeable time we would become a sect without political influence in the political struggles of our time." Admitting that the economic part of the program had given rise to sharp debates, Ollenhauer continued: "It is undeniable that pure nationalization . . . no longer solves the problem of the maximum increase of production and the unconditional control in favor of the community." Nationalization was assigned the role of a last resort, "where a healthy order of economic power relationships cannot be assured by other means." And the program itself described public enterprises as a necessity where "for natural or technical reasons indispensable services for the community can be produced in an economically reasonable way only by excluding competition." The main other purposes of public enterprise were to regulate prices and to prevent the development of private economic power centers.

While "workers' control" can be conceived of independently of nationalization or even as opposed to it, the demand for workers' control has most frequently appeared in history in combination with nationalization. The main exception was an early version of French, Italian, and Spanish syndicalism, which opposed nationalization as an instrument of centralized power. However, after the collapse of French syndicalism in World War I, nationalization and workers' control were merged in French labor propaganda. At about the same time, guild Socialism with its decentralizing tendencies made a valiant effort to break into the efficiency-oriented intellectual structure that the Fabians had established in Great Britain.

The trade unions were also early and ardent advocates of nationalization. The French unions adopted a program providing for nationalization of industry as early as 1919, even though the Communists rejected any such measures prior to a proletarian revolution and refused to allow for any compensation for the former owners. Catholic unions more and more accepted the idea, following Pope Pius XI's Encyclical Quadragesimo Anno (1931), though in subsequent statements the pope limited greatly the scope of nationalization he approved of. The decisive push came with the Resistance in France, which adopted a program in 1944 providing for "the establishment of a real economic and social democracy which implies the ousting of the great economic and financial feudal lords from the direction of the economy" and "the return to the nation of the great means of monopolized production, fruit of common work, of the sources of energy, the wealth underground, the insurance companies, and the great banks."[9] The Socialists and the Communists took up the demand, while the Catholic M.R.P. (Mouvement Républican Populaire) accepted the nationalization of key industries as far as efficiency required.

In Britain and in France substantial nationalization measures were enacted rapidly after the end of World War II. The Bank of England, coal mining, electricity and gas, civil aviation, telecommunications, inland transportation, and later iron and steel were nationalized. French nationalization measures went even further by adding a large number of banks and insurance companies to the list. Moreover, nationalization was used in a small number of cases as a means of punishment for real or alleged collaboration with the enemy during the Nazi occupation. One well-known case was that of the Renault automobile factory.

The main issue at the time was how to administer the nationalized enterprises. Quite different solutions were implemented on the two sides of the English Channel. In the United Kingdom one powerful current of opinion was guild Socialism, whose intellectual ancestor was William Morris and its later and most articulate spokesman was G. D. H. Cole.[10] French syndicalism, American industrial unionism, and a small admixture of Marxism merged to produce a program that was rarely clearly defined. The main points were "that, in the normal conduct of manufacture, the producer must be the dominant partner," but that "the community as a whole must always reserve an ultimate power to override the producer's will."[11] As formulated by the review *New Age,* guild Socialism was "a proposal for the co-management of industry by the State and the Trade Unions."[12] The bargaining union would change into the producing guild. Differing from the guild Socialists, the Fabians used their tremendous intellectual influence to present Socialism as a process of rationalizing society with the supreme objective of achieving maximal efficiency. The competent ministers would appoint the expert management of nationalized enterprises, with the managers responsible to the ministers and, through them, to Parliament. No room was left in this design for workers' control or even a share of management by unions.

By 1920 Beatrice and Sidney Webb—the main guides of the Fabian Society at the time—had come to accept some of the guild Socialist ideas. In a rather complicated fashion they now allowed for some representation in the management of nationalized enterprises of three or four main interest groups: workers, chief administrators, consumers, and the community at large. These were to form the management of the companies, under the supervision of a social parliament elected on a geographical basis by the citizenry but exclusively devoted to economic problems.[13]

However, when Herbert Morrison as minister of transport in the Labour government elected in 1929 introduced the London Passenger Transport Bill, he omitted any reference to union participation in the appointment of the proposed board that was to direct the large enterprises coming under its control. Instead the board members were to be chosen solely on grounds of merit. This was the beginning of a prolonged and sharp debate between Morrison and Ernest Bevin, then the leader of the Transportworkers Union. The issue was finally settled by what appeared at first a victory of the Bevin group but was soon revealed to be essentially a decision in favor of Morrison. While the boards could include trade unionists nominated by the unions in the industry concerned, they would resign their union offices upon appointment to the board and would be responsible only to the minister in charge of the particular industry. Thus the union viewpoint would be represented but not the union itself. It was, of course, not difficult to list union experience among the qualifications of a successful board member of an industrial enterprise. This remained T.U.C. (Trades Union Congress) policy in later statements for many years. The formula most frequently used was that the "viewpoint of the work people engaged in the industry" but not the union itself should be represented, in the interest of the efficiency of the industry. This was the policy carried out in the numerous nationalization measures following the end of World War II.

French nationalization proceeded differently. In line with proposals of the Austrian Socialist Otto Bauer, the French established governing boards on a tripartite basis; one-third of the members each representing the government, the union, and the consumers. In fact, however, the Communist ministers in charge during the first period following the liberation of the country often appointed fellow party members for all three groups. After the Communists left the government, radical changes—a "repolitization"—of the boards took place. To indicate the confusion which the politization and repolitization of the boards created, a decree of 1949 may be mentioned as symptomatic. It required that the board member be independent "with regard to the category of interest which he is not instructed to represent."[14]

Board membership is part-time and only small attendance fees are paid.[15] Meetings are infrequent and brief. As a result, a question soon arose: "Is a board autonomous which consists of persons who, almost all of them, have jobs outside of the house and who, therefore, with few exceptions do not have the time to devote themselves to the running of the enterprise and who are compelled to give to the president and the director general practically all power?"[16] Given the limited role of the boards, it is difficult for the workers or even the unions to feel involved in the management or the policy-making of the enterprise. This had important consequences for the performance of the nationalized enterprises.

Increasingly since the 1960s, the civil service and the nationalized enterprises have adopted systems of collective bargaining that approach those of the private sector. The French theory of public law makes it a basic principle to distinguish between "statute" and "contract"; in the nationalized enterprises the "statutes" were acts of sovereignty. In the civil service a peculiar contradiction has existed since the end of World War II. While civil servants were given the right to organize and later the right to strike, collective bargaining remained excluded.[17] This contradiction was eliminated in the 1970s, when the civil service unions were given the right to negotiate annual agreements about salaries, job classification, and some of the working conditions.

Bargaining in the nationalized enterprises was subject to a basic distinction between those cases where individual enterprises were nationalized— Renault and aeronautical enterprises, for example—and the nationalization of entire industries. The first were made part of the general collective bargaining system created in February 1950; the second group was subject to a statute (or law), similar to that of the civil servants. The first group was thus subject to the collective agreement of its industry, the second had almost civil service status.

The latter arrangement gave the employees distinct advantages as far as security of employment and professional training and advancement were concerned. In other areas including pensions, wages, and increases in wages due to seniority, the early advantages of the nationalized enterprises rapidly vanished. A major miners' strike in 1963 and frequent strikes on the railroads and in the electricity industry indicated the dissatisfaction of the employees. At the same time changes occurred in the bargaining system, at first in practice and then in the law.

The role of the union representatives on the boards was soon revealed as symbolic. They hardly ever influenced board decisions. Then the power of the managers themselves in wages and working conditions gradually diminished as the government took over authority in these areas. Finally, in August 1953 the government assumed ultimate control on decisions on wages. Negotiations were carried on through intermediaries. Through their immediate bargaining partner, the trade unionists spoke to a distant authority, rarely accessible, and tried to influence the all-powerful ministry from where, one day, a decision would come.[18]

Toward the end of 1963 an official report (Rapport Toutée) pointed out the shortcomings of the system. The following year the government introduced a three-stage negotiation process. First, an objective investigation was to be made of the changes in wages and salaries in each enterprise, year by year; then the government, after consulting the unions and the indicative plan,[19] would determine the percentage by which aggregate wages and salaries could increase during the following year; third, management and unions would agree on the distribution of this total. This procedure, while operating for a number of years, resulted in new difficulties, created in part by necessary adjustments to changes in the structure of the labor force, in part caused by changes of the cost of living. It required several years, the upheaval of 1968, and the government's concession of greater flexibility to the nationalized enterprises before the way was opened for new forms of collective bargaining in 1969. The pioneer contract was concluded at the Electricité de France between management and C.G.T.–F.O. (Confédération Generale du Travail–Force Ouvrière), C.F.D.T., and the union of higher employees (cadres). The resistance of the C.G.T. proved ineffective.

Following the recommendations of the so-called Rapport Nora, the new system makes wage increases dependent on the progress of productivity of the enterprise and the growth of gross national product. The unions commit themselves not to engage in conflicts during the lifetime of the contract, at least as regard the subjects settled in the agreement, but they have the right to renounce the agreement by giving notice three months in advance. In general the agreements following this pattern tend to compress the wage pyramid, but the "peace clause" remained limited to the Electricité de France. In most respects, however, other nationalized industries follow what may be properly described as a process of collective bargaining, with a particular emphasis on a reduction of wage differentials. What is lacking to make these agreements full-fledged contracts is the absence of a legal basis.

Certain variations in the text of the agreements that occurred in the 1970s are significant. The commitment to "social peace" originally introduced and to which the C.G.T. objected has disappeared. Instead a cost-of-living clause has been added, as demanded by the C.G.T., but the progressive inflation since 1971 has made the enforcement of this clause increasingly difficult. Strikes in public enterprises have become frequent since the end of 1973.

In the United Kingdom the problem of sovereignty that French legal tradition created did not play a significant role. The British never expected nationalization to cause any departure from the principle of negotiated determination of wages and working conditions. The main new principle—of a highly limited practical significance—was that collective bargaining became enshrined as a duty in the laws governing the nationalized enterprises. This produced little or no change, since collective bargaining was already the accepted practice in these enterprises. The new element was the higher degree of centralized decision-making on the management side which, in turn, required centralization on the part of the labor organizations. This may have been one of the factors involved in reenforcing the dualism of the industrial relations system—national agreements of limited significance and local understandings of high relevance—to which the Donovan Commission later referred.

It is up to the boards in Britain to designate the union that it regards as the appropriate bargaining agent. This has not only strengthened the power of the established unions and made it difficult for new unions to enter the industries but also involved the boards occasionally in jurisdictional disputes among different labor organizations. Moreover, centralized bargaining has led to uniform wage rates—London excepted—but these have been counteracted by local agreements supplementary to the national ones.[20] Finally, since the boards were in most cases more susceptible to government directions than lower management or private enterprises, industrial relations policies in nationalized industries are likely to be regarded as signposts of governmental policies. In a somewhat contradictory fashion centralization has at the same time enhanced the power of the unions in the nationalized industries and put additional pressure of public opinion on them. This has been particularly true in periods when the Labour party provided the government of the country and the trade unions were eager to assist the government of their choice. Still, only rarely have the unions abandoned policies vital to them for long periods, if only because of threatened revolts from their membership.

This danger was the more serious as the employees expected rapid and substantial changes in management and industrial relations practices following the nationalization of the enterprises. "They had expected a more rapid improvement of conditions—probably a more rapid improvement than was practicable." Not appreciating the difficulties, they were apt to assume that the delay was due to management's intransigence and to blame their representatives for not insuring more rapid change.[21] A good deal of the workers' disappointment was directed at the small number of changes that occurred in managerial personnel. Worse still, the few that did occur took place in jobs far removed from the daily life of the workers. At the workshop and the colliery level the former managers continued in their functions and very much in their old ways. The union position was further weakened by the transfer of

outstanding union leaders to the boards of the nationalized enterprises at
various levels—national, regional, or area. The second—or sometimes third—
line leadership that took over was lacking in authority and in some instances
in ability as well.

As in France, consultative committees that were set up with great hopes
in the United Kingdom proved of little value in introducing workers' participation on general managerial problems. Since the committees had little or no
authority in general management, a sense of futility and frustration became
unavoidable. The matters that were handled with considerable authority by
the committees were problems of welfare and safety—vacation homes belonging to the enterprise, common in France, were rare in Great Britain.[22]
This was partly a carry-over into consultation of attitudes appropriate to
collective bargaining, partly of inadequate preparation of labor representatives
to discuss questions of finance and technology, and to a large extent the result
of a feeling of frustration, given the committees' lack of decision-making
power.

The greatest disappointment of nationalization was the lack of a radical
change in the workers' morale. That change was one of the pillars upon which
the case for increased efficiency after nationalization rested. The thwarting of
that belief caused many labor circles to question nationalization itself.[23]

Productivity did increase in the nationalized enterprises but at about the
same pace as in private industry and appeared most probably to depend upon
the rate of investment rather than upon worker enthusiasm.[24] Indeed, unlike
France, coal mining in Britain suffered for long periods from labor shortages;
nationalization alone was not a sufficient attraction for the necessary expansion of the labor force. Up until 1950 it was regarded as necessary to maintain
the so-called ring-fence, which restricted the freedom of miners to leave their
occupation. It was then removed, partly for reasons of principle, partly because it was believed that the "ring-fence" kept youngsters from entering the
industry. Manpower thereupon dropped by nearly 21,000.[25] On the other
hand, strikes were far less frequent than after World War I, but this was true
for private industries, too.

In industrial relations, then, nationalization produced no miracle, neither
in Britain nor in France. For Britain, the comment of a study of the Acton
Society Trust may be worth quoting:

> The general public hardly realises to what a large extent nationali-
> zation of industry appeared to the workers in it as the promise of a new
> era of opportunity. It was widely felt that before nationalization all the
> best jobs were reserved for those who had the benefit of special educa-
> tional opportunities, particularly in the Public Schools. One of the strongest
> expectations of the new nationalized boards was that they would rapidly

institute a system whereby every employee would have the chance of rising to senior positions—that is to say, a system which would draw primarily from within the industry, even for the most senior positions, and one which would be completely free from all favoritism or class bias.[26]

Little of the kind has in fact occurred so far, except perhaps on the boards. In France the key to the economic consequences of nationalization[27] was the attitude of the dominant trade union confederation, the Communist-led C.G.T. The revolutionary mood created by the liberation of France combined with the enthusiasm that the Communists—then in government—succeeded in inspiring in their followers and the restraints that the union leaders imposed upon the organizations that they controlled explain a good deal of the growth of production in postliberation France. Communist opposition after 1947, when the party was expelled from the government, may similarly have been a main factor in the subsequent difficulties.

It is, therefore, highly unlikely that nationalization by itself had any noticeable impact on workers' morale, except possibly—an important reservation—in so far as it may have helped avoid serious social troubles. "On the basis of the past record, one is entitled to assume that in the absence of nationalization large-scale strike movements, revolutionary attempts, perhaps bloodshed, would have been likely in France and that in Britain reconstruction would have been at least seriously endangered. In both countries, but particularly in France, the record of private management in some industries in its dealings with the unions was such as to make fruitful cooperation unlikely, if not impossible."[28]

Still it is difficult to reject the thesis that changes in property rights alone do not involve a fundamental alteration of the workers' situation in the factory or mine. Enthusiasm for nationalization measures clearly declined in most European countries.

A major attempt at revising the basic concepts underlying nationalization was put forward by C. A. R. Crosland in 1956.[29] Long before that—in 1948—the *Tribune,* the Labour party's principal left-wing organ, had admitted: "Socialism does not necessarily mean an endless flow of nationalization measures. . . . By themselves they do not constitute Socialism or anything like it." The right wing had no answer to give and the party, divided and without direction, lost the elections of 1951.

The nationalization issue was now reduced in Britain for practical purposes to the steel industry. Labour had proceeded to nationalize it; the Conservative government returned it to private enterprise.[30] It became partly a matter of prestige, partly one of economics and ideology for Labour to undo what the Tories had done. Beyond that no groundswell for further nationalization existed. Crosland questioned the importance of changes in ownership and placed management in the foreground of his program, following the research of A. A. Berle and G. Means, as well as that of James Burnham. He also pointed out that beyond a certain size economies of scale are likely to be offset by the disadvantages of centralized administration and the attendant delays in decision-making. While these disadvantages were not too conspicuous in the case of industries with a fairly uniform output directed at the home market—as was the situation of most of the early nationalization measures—they appeared quite large for most of the manufacturing industries that would have been next in line for transfer to public ownership and management.

Experience thus pointed toward the quality of management as the crucial factor for the success of nationalization, and in this respect the public enterprises suffered from a severe handicap. It was easy—often all too easy—for them to recruit trade union leaders, especially those close to retirement, for the boards of the nationalized industries, given the low salaries traditionally paid in Britain to union officers. However, the situation was the reverse as far as the other board members were concerned. While labor people were protesting against the excessive salaries paid to the board members, the fact was that public enterprise was not competitive with private industry in the salaries that it provided. Apart from a number of public-spirited citizens, few of the former managers of the newly nationalized enterprises—the people with the knowledge and experience of the industry—were attracted by the salaries being offered.

This disadvantage was not always offset (or increased?) by enhanced willingness on the part of the board members to accept the directions of the government and to facilitate whatever planning measures the government wished to enact. Some board chairmen in particular—Walter Citrine, former T.U.C. general secretary and later chairman of the electricity board, is usually mentioned in this connection—proved to have highly independent minds. Whatever modest attempts at planning the Labour government attempted to make had to adapt to the strong will of men like Citrine.

Serious problems, Crosland pointed out, were created by the price policy that the nationalization laws imposed upon the public enterprises. Over the long run, these businesses were neither to make profits nor to suffer losses. This meant, as the laws were interpreted, that they could not accumulate any reserves for expansion or modernization. Research was neglected. Moreover, savings were "more heavily concentrated than they need have been in private hands. A quite different pricing policy would have been required to achieve the objective of greatly increasing public relative to private capital."[31]

One basic issue was and remains how to make compatible the conflicting objectives set for the nationalized enterprises. They were at the same time to be businesslike and to fulfill a social mission. Most of them ran up heavy losses that general tax funds had to cover. Conservative and Labour ministers appeared equally uncertain as to the advisability of price increases. Not only electoral considerations but also the threatened impact of, for example, higher coal prices entered the ministerial decision-making process.[32]

Contrary to the intentions of the law, an uneasy and informal relationship between the ministers and the chairmen of the boards developed that considerably influenced the pricing policy of nationalized enterprises.

> Because the relationship between minister and board chairman is loosely defined, it is informal in character. Because it is informal, it is often secret. Because it is secret, it is often unaccountable. . . . It is in the sphere of prices that this backstairs pressure has most frequently been used; the best-known example is the "gentlemen's agreement" whereby the Coal Board consults the Minister of Power before raising its prices. Conservative Ministers have on several occasions intervened to prevent price increases which were economically justified, but which might have been electorally unpopular. For this is the crux of the matter. Interference based on some genuine conception of the public interest would be tolerable, even if one disagreed with the conception involved. But, in fact, interference has been largely motivated by short-term political considerations.[33]

Finally, while the basic industries lent themselves more readily to the kind of centralized and routinized management that nationalization created, manufacturing industries required different leadership. Creativity, individuality, constant search for better production methods and technology, new markets, new sales methods, and new products are more likely to develop in pluralistic forms of organizations, even though in research and development a case for substantial economies of scale can easily be made. The high degree of British dependency on foreign markets for its output added to the importance of the marketing process and the need for continuous, rapid adaptation to the vagaries of a buyer's market, as Crosland has pointed out.

Yet the first substantial change in the administration of nationalized industries in Britain came only after the renationalization of the steel industry in 1967. It was felt that in the resulting giant organization—one quarter of a million employees—a spirit of genuine employee involvement had to be created.[34] One of the means used—at first viewed as an experiment—was the appointment of three worker-directors to each of the four divisional (not the top) boards. They were to retain their jobs in the industry, receive £1,000 a year, and resign what union jobs they held. The appointments were made by Lord Melchett, then chairman of the board of the British Steel Corporation, after consultation with the T.U.C. A more detailed examination of this experience is found in chapter 11. What is relevant in this context is that this first step was part of an evolution toward increased and direct worker participation in management. Increasingly, this idea became separated from nationalization and was proposed by some Labour people as a universally applicable solution for all larger corporate enterprises whether private or public.

An important change in ideas had been made when Crosland proposed in 1956 that nationalization be separated from monopoly and that the Labour party take into account the "reaction against making state monopoly the central feature of Labour policy."[35] As one item of evidence he referred to the "regular rejection of sweeping nationalization proposals" at the annual congresses of the party and the vacillations of the party programs on the issues of whether there should be further nationalization and the changes in the list of industries to be nationalized. Even the left wing of the party was no longer certain that Socialism should be identified with public ownership. "Keeping Left," a statement by twelve left-wing members of Parliament, including Richard Crossman, Ian Mikardo, and Barbara Castle, devoted five of 114 lines of conclusions to the subject of nationalizations.

In this climate of opinion, Crosland states, nationalization must be justified in the name of economic improvement. Moreover, rather than taking over entire industries, he proposed that only individual firms be taken over or new government-owned plants be set up. This step is to be taken where the existing industry is clearly performing poorly; where competition either cannot or is not permitted to enforce an improvement; where physical or fiscal controls are incapable of curing the situation; and where public ownership will not bring attendant disadvantages of its own.[36]

The first three conditions, Crosland felt, clearly applied to the British steel industry, which has consistently underestimated the expansion required to accommodate the rising needs of the metal-using industries. Another example that Crosland cites is the machine-tool industry, where long delivery delays occur every time there is a spurt in investment. The most obvious example of the need for public enterprise is atomic energy, an industry in which the risks were too high for private enterprise.

In support of his thesis that individual industries and firms be treated according to their particular circumstances, Crosland pointed out that contrary to standard U.S. clichés, some nationalized industries demonstrated a high degree of efficiency while others—especially coal and the railways—are quite inefficient. But there are also official investigations of a whole series of privately owned industries, from food-marketing and machine tools to construction and construction materials, that pointed out various degrees of inefficiency. In other words, efficiency depends largely on the quality of management, and in modern large-scale corporations management depends little on ownership. To obtain high quality management for the public enterprises, Crosland advocated higher salaries.[37] He feared that nationalized concerns are under a hopeless handicap in competing with private enterprise.

Crosland thus proposed what he called the "competitive public enterprise": a state-owned company in competition with privately owned enterprises in the same industry. This may sound surprising, if not shocking to many Americans, but it is far from exceptional, and Crosland himself could refer to a whole series of examples in other countries. Perhaps the best known case is Renault, the state-owned automobile firm in France, which is highly successful in competition with a large number of privately owned enterprises. There are other examples: SNECMA, the largest French aircraft firm, and various banks and insurance companies; in no case was the entire industry nationalized, just parts of it. Sweden owns and runs a bank, a chain of restaurants, iron and steel works, saw and pulp mills, bus services, and shale oil production companies, all in competition with private enterprises.

One method of such expansion of nationalization would be for the existing nationalized enterprises or other socially owned firms to extend their operations laterally. Transport enterprises, for instance, might add hotels to their operations as do the Canadian and many other railroads. The Swedish state forestry runs pulp and saw mills. In Britain this would require a change of pricing policy to enable the nationalized industries to acquire the funds necessary for expansion, either through the purchase of existing enterprises or establishment of new ones.

It remains to be added that the Labour government in 1974 nationalized ship-building and aircraft construction. The basic controversy as to further nationalizations had been settled at least officially within Labour by the adoption of "Industry and Society," a statement moved by Harold Wilson at the party conference of 1957. In fact, however, this statement was hardly ever mentioned. Yet the document contained a fundamental idea, namely that Labour would take into public ownership any industry which "failed the nation." Thus nationalization was to become a salvage measure to prevent the collapse of unsuccessful companies. These takeovers were to be financed by death duties, and the procedure proposed was the purchase of shares of such companies that were in private hands.

It is doubtful, however, whether at this stage the party has an agreed-upon program of nationalization. True, the party conference in 1977 adopted a long list of nationalization measures including a number of banks and insurance companies, but Prime Minister James Callaghan made it quite clear that he and the parliamentary party, i.e., the Labour members in Parliament, were not prepared to implement the party conference decision, which he regarded as "suicidal." The prospect of such a party conference vote led Callaghan to set up the Wilson committee to review functioning of financial institutions. The unanimous conclusion of this eighteen-member committee (containing four trade uionists) on the issue of nationalization was:

> We do not believe that the British banking and financial system is ideal. Had we been designing a completely new financial system some of us would have believed that there was a role for publicly-owned insurance companies and a greater role for publicly-owned banks. But there is considerable difference betweeen this and attempting to change an already functioning system. Any economic gains from nationalizing ex-

isting financial institutions have yet to be demonstrated and there would undoubtedly be costs, though it would be difficult to quantify these exactly. We recommend therefore against any extension of the public sector in banking and insurance by way of nationalization of existing institutions. This should not, however, be taken as an indication that all of us are satisfied with the relationship between the financial institutions and industry and trade, or with the flow of funds into industry.

It is noteworthy that bank and insurance employees had indicated quite strongly that they did not want nationalization. This, obviously, would not make it easy for a future Labour government to proceed with the nationalization of the financial institutions against the wishes of those most directly concerned.

The Morrison-type of management remained unquestioned for several years, even though its proponent originally had met with powerful opposition. The bulk of the unions clearly opposed worker participation in managerial bodies after the style of German codetermination. By the mid-1960s that attitude changed. In its evidence to the Donovan Commission, the T.U.C. argued that the conflict of interest between employees and management did not present an insuperable obstacle to worker representation on management boards or any other organ of management. In the T.U.C.'s view a distinction had to be made between the "negotiating function of the employer, and the overall task of management. Once this distinction is established, it can be seen that it does not detract from the independence of the trade unions for trade union representatives to participate in the affairs of management concerned with production, until the step is reached when any of the subjects become negotiable questions as between trade unions and employers."[38] A few years later the T.U.C. prepared a Green Paper on industrial democracy in which it stated that "to be seen to be relevant, schemes of industrial democracy must be seen to be effective by workers at their own place of work. Yet some of the most basic aspects of the work situation and the security of that employment stem from decisions taken at extremely remote levels. . . . It is for this reason that any policy for the extension of industrial democracy must operate at all levels, from shop floor to board room and indeed affect the process of national economic planning itself."[39]

In the meantime, in March 1968 a practical step in the direction of workers' participation had been made, in the newly (1967) renationalized steel industry. A Fabian Society publication criticized the old forms of nationalization because they lacked "bold experiments," a lack characterized by the industries' "preoccupation with sterile forms of joint consultation and collective bargaining."[40] And a Report of the Working Party on Industrial Democracy published by the Labour party in 1967 suggested in recommendation XVIII that experiments be undertaken in placing "representatives of workers directly concerned on the boards of publicly owned firms and industries. . . . This representation should not be confined to full-time officers of the unions."

At about the same time, the T.U.C. criticized its own 1944 stand against workers' participation as "unduly sharp." Instead it recommended that "union representatives—lay, rather than full time union officials—of work people employed in those industries participate in the formulation of policy and in the day-to-day operations of those industries." Such appointments were to be made at all managerial levels. The contrast with the Morrison-type of management of the immediate post–World War II nationalizations is striking. Beyond this, consultative committees were to be established and their members provided with all of the necessary information in sufficient time ahead of the meeting to enable the members to be adequately informed about all the elements that may enter the decision-making process.

The road to participation seemed wide open since many unions agreed that radical reforms in the structure and operations of the industry were required and that these could not be carried out without management having the cooperation of a fully informed workforce. Not all unions, however, supported the new departure. The electricians, in particular, remained loyal to the old idea that management should manage and the union form a loyal opposition, a position the union had maintained consistently all through the later debates on the so-called Bullock plan to be discussed in chapter 11. Several other unions agreed with them. If there were to be worker-directors— an idea that rapidly gained support—they should not be union representatives. The proposal that finally emerged from the discussions was to appoint three part-time worker directors to each of the four divisional boards, each controlling a different part of the steel industry, as described above.

In general, the experience can hardly be described as successful, except as a symptom of an evolution away from Morrison's concept of the public corporation. The divisional boards on which the worker-directors were represented were regarded by the board members themselves as having limited significance.[41] However, the division management committees consisting of full-time directors—thus without labor directors—that met monthly were regarded as important.

Names of worker-directors were proposed to the T.U.C. by the individual unions. The twelve finally selected—average age, fifty-three—met each other for the first time after their selection. White-collar workers were overrepresented, at the expense of manual workers; most of them, however, came from working-class families. They accepted the value system of their fellow directors without question, i.e., efficiency and profitability ranked first among their priorities. Occasionally this was qualified by references to the "national interest" or "social responsibility." In this way the interests of workers and management were presented as more or less identical. Moreover, being in most cases ill prepared for their new assignment and given a minimum of guidance, the worker-directors oriented themselves toward the behavior of their better prepared, better educated colleagues. Whatever training courses they were given fitted them to perform as directors rather than worker-directors. Indeed, there were no clear standards of what a worker-director should do as distinguished from the other directors. At the most they regarded themselves as middlemen, "who will try to link together management, especially senior management, the unions, and the workforce. In this way, they will attempt to create more harmony and understanding in the industry; this in turn will lead to greater efficiency."[42] As time passed, the worker-directors increasingly stressed the directorial aspects of their job rather than the worker aspects. That they were most reluctantly accepted by their fellow directors added to their eagerness to favorably impress their colleagues to whom they felt inferior—educationally, socially, and in many other ways. No wonder the "full-time directors were able to ensure that the worker directors conformed generally to the normative code of the board room, and did not become a source of 'trouble.' "[43] At the same time, the T.U.C. demonstrated little interest in the worker-directors until about a year and a half after they had assumed their offices. Their work colleagues felt at least a measure of jealousy toward their director-colleagues, especially with regard to the time off from the job that the worker-directors were to be given: how much, when, by whom? Reforms instituted at the end of 1969 established closer relations between worker-directors and unions and enhanced the position of the labor directors. Under the circumstances, it was not surprising that a majority of the members of the Donovan Commission felt unable to recommend the appointment of worker-directors to the boards of companies, although three commission members favored experimentation along these lines, and two—not union representatives—advocated mandatory arrangements of this kind.[44] The Labour government responded with a White Paper, "In Place of Strife," in which it expressed its willingness to experiment with the institution of worker-directors and intended to engage in consultation as to how this could best be done. Yet the basic position of the British unions—as of the Donovan Commission—remained that collective bargaining was the best method so far devised to advance industrial democracy.

The decisive break came in 1973 when Britain entered the Common Market. The German example of codetermination now became something worth considering, even though generally speaking British Labour does not like to follow foreign models but rather wishes to play the role of model itself. This will be developed further in chapter 11.

The conservative government under Margaret Thatcher instructed the so-called think-tank (the central policy review staff of the cabinet office) to investigate the control of nationalized industries and propose methods of improving it. It submitted its report in 1981, but it failed to deal with cost overruns that have become a major issue of the nationalized industries. (These overruns often result from a reluctance to accept the politically damaging responsibility of raising prices.) The committee did identify five problem areas (which had been noted before): lack of marketplace pressures or threat of bankruptcy; the extent of union power in the industries; the absence of any strategic framework for production, labor, and marketing; the impact of political decisions that unavoidably clash with straightforward business objectives; and failure of communication and understanding between industries and government.[45] However, the think-tank did not put forward any startlingly new proposals. The basic problem still open is the choice of the criteria for success or failure of a nationalized enterprise, a decision particularly difficult for monopolistic enterprises.

In France the idea of nationalization was revived in the election campaign of 1978. The coalition of the left, consisting of Socialists, Communists, and a small Radical party, agreed on a program of nationalization. The closer the election date came, the more the Socialists under François Mitterrand outdistanced the Communists in the public opinion polls. The Communists responded by asking for a considerably enlarged program of nationalization measures, which the Socialists rejected. This developed into a sharp disagreement between the two parties. Many observers referred to this conflict as the main cause of the failure of the left to obtain an election victory. Internal conflicts developed over that issue also within the Communist party. The opposition to Georges Marchais, the Communist leader, was so strong that the party did not dare take the customary disciplinary measures against the dissidents. In any case, the election outcome ensured that no further extensive nationalization measures would be taken in France in the near future. The fundamental change had to wait for the year 1981 and new presidential elections.

Once again Mitterrand, defeating his rivals within the Socialist party, forged an alliance with the Communist party. The Communists, torn by internal quarrels and weakened by a mass defection of intellectuals and artists who had given the party a large part of its prestige, were compelled to support the Socialist candidate. Mitterrand succeeded in defeating Valery Giscard d'Estaing by a narrow—but under the circumstances surprisingly substantial—margin. The first Socialist president of France since the end of World War II to be equipped with the great powers that de Gaulle's constitution provided took office in 1981. Confronted with a hostile majority in Parliament, he dissolved it and called for new parliamentary elections. The outcome added tremendously to his victory, for not only did the leftist parties obtain a clear and massive majority in Parliament, but also the Communist party was driven back into the role of a small minority that had to accept a minor role in the cabinet. All of the key positions of the cabinet were occupied by Socialists, and the government, in spite of the presence of four Communist ministers, was committed to a pro-Western and anti-Soviet policy.

Nationalization measures were now again on the agenda. The remaining privately owned banks and insurance companies were transferred without compensation into public ownership, as were a number of monopolistic or otherwise market-dominating industrial enterprises. This increased the size of the publicly owned sector of the economy from about 12 to 16 percent. What role, if any, these measures were to play in the struggle against the massive unemployment, flight of capital, and other problems confronting the new government remained to be seen when I wrote these lines in the fall of 1981. Equally open was the question of possible changes in the administration and industrial relations of public enterprises. The government's intention, obviously supported by the majority of the electorate, to decentralize the administrative system might lead one to expect new institutional arrangements to emerge in both these areas.

Issues concerning nationalized enterprises have come to the fore as a result of talks that Economics Minister Jacques Delors had early in October 1981 with union leaders about voluntary wage restraints to cut inflation from 14 percent to 10 percent in 1982. While the union leaders stood ready to support this policy, if the low-paid workers were exempted from such restrictions, lay-offs at the nationalized Renault plant caused sharp disagreements with the unions. They were especially important as Renault is a pattern-setter for the entire industrial relations system.[46]

NOTES

1. During the period before 1914, some French Marxists, led by Jules Guesde, opposed nationalization, which would add to l'Etat Gendarme the Etat patron. The impact of the war seems to have changed their opinion. If human beings are being mobilized to serve under conditions set by the state, industry should be subject to the same regime. Cf. George Lichtheim, *Marxism in Modern France* (New York: Columbia University Press, 1966), 42.

2. *The Future of Socialism* (London: Jonathan Cape, 1956), 483. "Gilt-edged" refers to government bonds with which the compensation was paid to the former owners and "equities" to the stock of the companies.

3. "The Objects of Further Nationalization," *Political Quarterly,* 24 (Jan.-Mar. 1953).

4. Crosland, *Future of Socialism, 484n1.*

5. See my article "Nationalization and Workers' Control in Britain and France," *Journal of Political Economy,* LXI (Feb. 1953).

6. Crosland, *Future of Socialism,* 462–63. However, as one commentator pointed out: "Whatever the intentions of the original nationalisers may have been, they certainly were *not* that the state enterprises should operate in a manner indistinguishable from that of private firms. If the companies are going to pursue only their commercial interests, then what is the advantage of having them owned by the state?" William S. Rukeyser, "Creeping Capitalism in Government Corporations," *Fortune,* Sept. 15, 1968, 127.

7. Michael Young in *What Is a Socialized Industry?*, a Fabian publication, no

date (apparently written in 1947 or 1948), adds the theme of industrial democracy to the discussion, interestingly by connecting it with the issue of efficiency.

8. Susanne Miller, *Die S.P.D. vor und nach Godesberg* (Bonn-Bad Godesberg: Neue Gesellschaft, 1973), 15.

9. Bureau International du Travail, *La Participation des organizations professionelles à la vie économique et sociale en France* (Geneva: B.I.T., 1948), 103.

10. *The World of Labour*, 4th ed. (London: Macmillan, 1919), was the most influential of Cole's numerous writings.

11. *Ibid.*, 367.

12. *Ibid.*, 363–64.

13. See the 1920 edition of the *Fabian Essays* (London: Fabian Publications).

14. Commission de vérification des comptes des enterprises publiques, "Rapport d'ensemble"; *Journal Officiel de la République Française* (Annexe Administrative), Aug. 21, 1949, 375. The Greek Socialists under the leadership of Andreas Papandreou are planning nationalization measures by way of government purchase of controlling shares in troubled industries. These are to be administered by boards composed of workers, consumers, and government representatives. This follows the French pattern. These plans are reported in the New York *Times,* May 6, 1982, by Nicholas Xenos.

15. In contrast to the fairly high salaries of the full-time board members, which made these appointments so attractive that union leadership was rapidly depleted.

16. Christian Pineau, minister of transportation, speaking in the National Assembly on May 31, 1949, *Journal Officiel de la République Française,* June 1, 1949.

17. François Sellier, "Les Problèmes du Travail en France: 1920–1974," paper submitted to the 4th World Congress of the International Industrial Relations Association, Sept. 1976, Geneva, Switzerland.

18. Jean-Daniel Reynaud, *Les Syndicats en France* (Paris: Editions du Seuil, 1975), 1:218.

19. The plan was a projection of probable economic developments worked out in joint committees of government officials, employers, union representatives, and experts, but it was not to be imposed on industry.

20. Hugh Clegg, *Labour in Nationalized Industry* (London: Fabian Publications, 1950), 26, states that "in gas and electricity instructions have been given by the Boards to local managers that they must settle all problems that they can within their establishments."

21. Action Society Trust, *The Future of the Unions,* in the series Nationalized Industry, vol. 8 (Claygate: A.S.T., 1951), 17.

22. Empirical investigations of the topics handled by district councils in the British electricity industry from approximately 1946 to March 1950 indicate that barely 1 percent of the topics came under the headings of "efficiency." All others concerned welfare, education and training, health, and safety. A. M. F. Palmer, *Joint Consultation in Nationalized Industry,* in the series the Nationalized Industry (Claygate: A.S.T., 1951).

23. Cf. the debates at the 48th Labour party conference in Blackpool in 1949. C. A. R. Crosland, "The Transition from Capitalism," in R. H. S. Crossman, ed., *New Fabian Essays* (London: Turnstile Press, 1952), esp. 63–64.

24. A study of the British National Coal Board for the period 1947–51 shows the

highest rate of productivity increase to have occurred in 1949, not 1947, the first year after nationalization and, furthermore, that the rate of increase tended to level off with the passage of time.

25. National Coal Board, *Report for 1951,* 11–16.

26. Action Society Trust, *Problems of Promotion Policy,* in the series Nationalized Industry, vol. 3 (Claygate: A.S.T., 1951), 1.

27. Disappointment in the results of nationalization in France, particularly in the human relations area, was expressed as early as 1953 by, for example, Jean Rivero in "L'Expérience des Nationalisations," *Preuves,* 34 (Dec. 1953).

28. Sturmthal, "Nationalization and Workers' Control in Britain and France," 77.

29. *Future of Socialism.*

30. It is noteworthy that the Conservatives while in power did not attempt to undo the other basic nationalization measures of Labour. The National Health Service in particular was left practically untouched.

31. Crosland, *Future of Socialism,* 468.

32. As to the issue of the losses of nationalized enterprises, see the discussion later in this chapter. Needless to say, if some form of profitability is not accepted as the yardstick for success or failure of the nationalized enterprises, some other criterion for the evaluation of their performance must be found.

33. Foreword by Roy Jenkins to "Lessons of Public Enterprise," in Michael Shanks, ed., *A Fabian Society Study* (London: Jonathan Cape, 1963), 8.

34. Quoted in Peter Brannon *et. al., The Worker Directors: A Sociology of Participation* (London: Hutchinson, 1976), 4.

35. Crosland, *Future of Socialism,* 475.

36. *Ibid.,* 477.

37. Crosland speaks of "stingy salaries in the public sector." *Ibid.,* 480–81.

38. T.U.C. evidence to the Donovan Commission, 1966, H.M. Stationery Office, London.

39. Interim report by the T.U.C. General Council entitled "Industrial Democracy," 1973, 27. See ch. 11. In so far as these ideas related to the nationalized industries alone, they are discussed here.

40. John Hughes, *Nationalized Industries in a Mixed Economy,* Fabian pamphlet no. 328 (London: The Fabian Society, 1960).

41. Seventy-five percent of the directors who responded to a questionnaire considered the board either not very important or not important at all. Brannon *et al., Worker Directors,* 108.

42. *Ibid.,* 132.

43. *Ibid.,* 191nl.

44. Andrew W. J. Thompson, "New Focus of Industrial Democracy in Britain," *Annals of the American Academy of Political and Social Science,* 431 (May 1977), 34.

45. *The Economist,* Aug. 8, 1981, 49.

46. *European Industrial Relations Review,* 94 (Nov. 1981).

10

Workers' Councils

WORKERS' PARTICIPATION, European style, runs along at least two and in some cases three channels: (1) at the enterprise managerial level—mainly through board representation of union or workers or both; this is known as codetermination; (2) at the national level—by formal or informal consultation among government, unions, employers, and sometimes experts (It is interesting to note that in general collective bargaining, in contrast to the overwhelming majority opinion in the United States, is rarely regarded as a form of industrial democracy or codetermination, except perhaps recently in Sweden for reasons discussed in Chapter 11); (3) at the plant floor level—by way of shop stewards or workers' councils sometimes called works' councils.

It is possible to trace the development of workers' participation in management fairly far back in history, if the concept is interpreted in its widest possible meaning. Thus, advisory works committees are included by some analysts even though their history is overwhelmingly one of disappointments and failures. Moreover, in most cases these committees at first were not compulsory institutions. It was only during World War I that the imperial governments of Germany and Austria-Hungary, in order to placate the increasingly weary workers in the war industries, instituted compulsory works committees and committees of the office staff; they were mainly to deal with industrial relations problems, but without power of decision.

A second root has its basis in the British system of union organization and collective bargaining. This consists of national agreements with highly limited content, leaving details, supplements, and grievance-handling to shop stewards elected according to the constitutions of the individual unions. In the mining industry the checkweighman and in the printing industry the father of the chapel may be regarded as forerunners of the modern shop steward. In France personnel delegates (*délégués du personnel*) and in Italy the commissione interne played a somewhat similar role.

There is, however, a fundamental difference between the British shop steward and the various plant and enterprise organizations on the continent in their relationship to the unions. British shop stewards, whether they disobey orders from union headquarters or act on their own, are part of the union structure. The corresponding continental organizations are not union organs and are not subject to union discipline. In most cases they are means of worker-management collaboration, frequently presided over by the employer, sworn to secrecy, and not entitled to call lawful strikes. When workers raise a problem that proves impossible to solve in peaceful negotiations and it is important enough to call for measures of industrial strife, the councils step aside to let the unions take over the matter. However, their power has greatly increased in the last ten or fifteen years.

Right after World War I there was a strong current within the working class that aimed at making the councils counterparts of the Russian Soviets, i.e., organizations that move aside the existing political parties and unions and lead the working class into a revolutionary movement. In Russia this was a device to bring the unorganized masses of workers and soldiers under the leadership of the numerically weak, but well-disciplined working-class and Socialist (Menshevik or Bolshevik) organizations. Since, contrary to the Russian situation, parties and unions of the working class in Central Europe were strong organizations, the tactic misfired. The councils of workers and soldiers in Central Europe, which were elected by all workers whether unionized or not, were far less combative and less well-disciplined that the existing political parties of labor and the unions. At about the same time the British guild Socialist movement sought to transform the shop stewards into elements of a future government of industry. In all countries the radical attempts failed.

Germany

In Central Europe a further stage was reached after the end of World War I when two reforms were introduced in Germany and Austria. One made consultation of the works committees obligatory in social and the most important economic questions; however, this was still only consultation not codecision-making. The second reform enabled the employees of larger enterprises to delegate two members to the supervisory board, which is the policy-making, nonmanagerial agency of the corporations. Neither of these measures changed the internal power structure of the enterprise to any substantial extent. Advice could be accepted or not, as management wished, and the two employee board members could easily be outvoted or by-passed in preliminary, unofficial meetings of the other board members representative of the stockholders.

Two channels of codetermination were outlined in these early reforms, however: participation of the employees in decision-making at the plant level and employee representation in the top policy-making boards of the larger companies. While the Nazi period put an end to any developments along either line with its Order of National Labor Act of 1933, some new departures began after World War II. In many cases councils were set up by the workers in Germany, quite spontaneously, as soon as Allied forces destroyed Nazi control of a given area. Council functions consisted at the time mainly of organizing the clearing of the rubble in the factories, of finding food for the workers, raw materials for production, and spare parts for the repair of the machinery, and of making feeble attempts at resuming production. In fact, the councils were managing what there was to manage, since the previous members of management had either fled for fear of being accused of collaboration with the Nazis or had lost all authority.

A legal foundation for the councils was created by the Occupation authorities through the Allied Control Council Act No. 22, which essentially reproduced the Works Council Act of 1920, a creation of the Weimar Republic. On that basis, the individual states of the newly created Federal Republic enacted their own council acts. Some of these limited council rights to social and personnel matters; others gave the councils co-decision or information rights, in matters relating to production as well. Once again two members of the councils were to be delegated to the board of directors.[1]

These reforms appeared too weak and too diverse to the growing trade union movement. As the Occupation authorities gradually permitted the formation of unions on a larger and larger territorial scale, union pressure for a uniform and a more far-reaching council law increased. In May 1952 the newly formed German Trade Union Confederation (D.G.B.) issued a manifesto to the workers of West Germany that contained the following statements:

> In 1945, the German economy was in ruins. While you were working at the reconstruction of the factories, offices and administrations, the men responsible for the breakdown of Germany disappeared from sight.
>
> You alone have accomplished what others have called the miracle of the economic reconstruction of Germany. Now attempts are made to prevent the achievement of a real codetermination of the employees in the plants and the administrations.
>
> This emerges from the draft of the works constitution law. It shows a clear design to prevent the realization of real codetermination of the wage-earners. It confirms the sacred privileges of the employers. It leaves the wage-earners in an economically subordinate position. Moreover, the bill deprives you of rights that were yours in 1933, which were guaranteed after 1945 in the constitution and laws of some of the *Länder* and which have demonstrated their worth in the difficult period of reconstruction.[2]

In this document the unions asked for the extension of the system already established in coal and steel[3] to all or most of industry. Soon, however, labor had to realize how rapidly public opinion in West Germany had turned against radical reforms. The clearest expression was the shift in the position of the dominant political party, the Christian-Democratic Union (C.D.U.) and its

Bavarian ally, the C.S.U. (Christian-Social Union). Earlier, in the so-called Ahlener program, the combined Christian parties had come out for codetermination. This program was confirmed in 1949, during the campaign for the first parliamentary (Bundestag) election in July and at the Catholic congress of Bochum in September. But the appointment of Ludwig Erhard as minister of economic affairs in September 1949 initiated a rapid doctrinal revision of the C.D.U. Erhard's neo-liberal program, the "social market economy," soon became the official doctrine of the C.D.U. and left little room for extended codetermination. The reconstruction of German capitalism, supported by the United States and by a growing proportion of the German population, was under way.

Thus the Works Constitution Law of 1952, which applied to industries outside coal and steel, provided only for a one-third representation of the employees on the supervisory boards and determined works' council functions as a mixture of negotiating and advice-giving. Being an organ of labor-management cooperation, the council cannot legally call a strike or organize other forms of social conflict. The main tasks of the councils were grievance-handling, concluding agreements supplementary to the union-sponsored collective agreements on wages and working conditions, but without legally binding character, hiring and firing of groups, and the administration of works' welfare institutions. Elections are held every three years.

This law gave neither side full satisfaction and was replaced in 1972 by a new Works' Constitution Law that, in line with the stronger position of the Social Democrats and of the unions, extended the functions of the workers' councils. A symbol of the increased power of the unions is perhaps the fact that now upon the demand of one-quarter of the council members a representative of the union may be invited to take part in a council meeting. The old cleavage between the council—representing all employees—and the union can now be eliminated or at least greatly reduced.

The impact of the council on the economic policies of the enterprise is greatly enhanced by a variety of clauses in the new law, such as one providing for the formation of general works' councils in enterprises with several plants or of a works' council of a group of companies. Arbitration is possible in the case of conflicts between council and employer, but the arbitrator's award is binding only in a limited range of matters. A deluge of legal actions was started by a new definition of senior management members who are exempted from representation in and by the councils. In part this conflict reflects the desire of the Liberal-Democratic party (F.D.P.)—coalition partners of the Social Democrats in the federal government—to separate a group of senior employees from the rest and to attract them to their party, leaving the rest to the influence of the S.P.D.

The functions of the council were greatly enlarged. It has codetermination rights in the regulation of the hours of work, including daily working hours and breaks and temporary short time or overtime work, the fixing of job and piece rates, the laying down of principles of remuneration and the introduction of new remuneration methods, the setting of principles for suggestion schemes, the time and place for payments of remuneration, the preparation of the schedule of leaves, the installation of technical devices for controlling employee performance, safety regulations, the administration of welfare services limited to the individual undertaking, and the assignment and notice of lodging provided for employees. Another codetermination right is granted in the event of any technological change affecting the workplace, the work flow, or the work environment.[4] In such cases the works' council may demand appropriate measures to consider approved findings of ergonomics. There is also the important right of codetermination in matters of issuing guidelines for personnel selection and in carrying out occupational training. In the event of major operational changes within the enterprise employer and works' council shall set up an agreement fixing the balance of interests and, in case of economic disadvantages for employees, introduce adequate social planning. The council subcommittee on economic affairs must be kept informed of all matters relevant for the economic and financial situation of the enterprise, including any plans of management that may affect the employees of the company. Arbitrators may settle disputes between the economic committee of the council and management.[5]

The essential point about the councils is that they are elected by all employees, whether union members or not, and therefore they are not subject to union discipline. In some industries like the metal industry the overwhelming majority of the council members are also trade unionists and likely to be inspired by union ideas.[6] However, that powerful unions like I.G. Metall are trying to establish their own steward network suggests that the union is not totally satisfied with the existing relationship, a result of the fact that the lowest level of union organization is regional and does not reach the individual plant.

The councils may sue the enterprise before a special labor court if they believe the enterprise violated law or agreement, but they cannot call a strike. Since German collective agreements most frequently are regional or national and cover a multitude of firms, they are typically brief. This brevity greatly enhances the importance of the supplementary understanding between the council and management, and often the council is of greater significance to the individual worker than the union. In conflicts, on the other hand, it is the union upon whom the workers must rely, although a well-developed but not always used internal grievance procedure adds to the stature of the council and makes the workers somewhat less dependent on the union. The dangers of "company-mindedness" are always present, due to the structure of the councils, but they do not materialize too frequently. The extent to which council activity gives the individual worker an opportunity to participate in decision-making depends on circumstances and personalities.[7]

The extent to which the German councils represent an effective instrument of industrial democracy is difficult to determine. By negotiating actual wages—contract rates being regarded as minima—piece rates, and working conditions, they undoubtedly strengthen the influence of the workers in the plant in these matters. On the other hand, only a small proportion of individual grievances is handled by the councils; most of these conflicts are passed on to labor courts. In any case, the link between the union and the plant is less close than in the United States. All in all, the councils are on balance a step forward toward industrial democracy, but at times they create tensions between the union and the workers in a given plant. For the rest, the new law has been in force too short a time to permit more than impressionistic judgments. Some of these are summarized in the next chapter.

France

French employers, whose firms are still, in spite of a trend toward concentration, to a large extent small or middle-sized, have traditionally been extremely hostile to trade unionism. Any form of workers' participation in business management, even in questions directly affecting personnel, was abhorrent to their paternalistic thinking. Indeed, it is probably no exaggeration to state that French employers were more hostile to unions and industrial democracy than those of any other Western European country except Spain and Portugal. The percentage of unionized nonagricultural workers is low relative to that of many other countries in Western Europe, but the figures of union membership issued by the unions themselves are so unreliable that any precise statement can only be made with extreme caution. Moreover, since the published figures are overstating the size of union membership, they are probably exaggerating the number of actual dues-paying union members. Interestingly, the wild membership fluctuations are more closely related to political events than to the business cycle, a curious phenomenon in view of the official antipolitical line of French union tradition.[8] Moreover, most of the great advances of French labor in the social field are the result of political and legislative actions rather than of collective bargaining and other usual forms of union pressure.

Thus, the establishment of plant committees (*comités d'enterprise*) owes its origins to a decree of 1945 and a law of 1946—high points of political working-class strength following the liberation of the country. At the plant level joint committees were introduced in all enterprises, whether public or private, with at least fifty employees. With the employer as chairman, they were to act as consultative committees. In the first enthusiasm following the defeat of the Nazis, they were regarded as instruments of "social liberation."[9] It soon developed that their best work was performed in the administration of welfare institutions (*oeuvres sociales*) attached to the enterprise—vacation colonies and kindergartens, for example, where the committees have powers of decision. In economic and technical matters "the . . . task of the committees must be regarded in the great majority of cases as practically dormant; the committees are not being consulted before decisions are taken, and it is already regarded as highly satisfactory when they are informed afterwards and can still establish a certain liaison between management and staff."[10]

In an effort to revive the stagnating committees a law of June 18, 1966, listed the issues about which committees must be consulted: professional training and general operations of the enterprise especially with regard to employment. In addition, the law indicated the kind of information to which the committees are entitled. However, the committees still offer only advice, and the employer is merely required to report how and why he has or has not followed the advice. The power of the committees is thus far less than the authority of the German works' council.

That the committees succeeded in functioning effectively, or even at all, in the only area in which they have power to make decisions, namely, in welfare activities, gives a fairly clear indication of the reasons of their failure elsewhere: their lack of power. Admittedly, most committees were ill prepared to discuss complicated financial or investment issues, but even members who might have useful contributions in a discussion of such issues found themselves unable to speak about them without reference to the interests of the employees rather than the enterprise as a whole. As Yves Delamotte put it, the activity of the committees outside the welfare area could only be a "participation conflictuelle"—participation with conflicts.[11]

It was only in the late 1960s that the functions of the committees were enhanced. Thus an agreement of 1969 gave them increased powers in matters relating to employment. A law in 1971 entrusts them with an examination of professional training arrangements in the enterprise. Similarly a law of December 1973 confers on them certain rights in checking on working conditions. In many instances discussions in the committee serve to prepare collective negotiations, especially since enterprise agreements have lately acquired a higher status.

While the committees are consultative and organs of cooperation, the personnel delegates, elected the same way as the plant committee members, serve as instruments of grievance-handling. In this activity they operate as if they were representatives of the union. They are to be given free time by the employers to carry out their duties and are protected against discharges.[12] However, the effectiveness of this process of grievance-handling is highly limited, unless the issue represents a clear violation of legal or contractual obligations. Otherwise only strikes or other methods of collective action are likely to be used, since the appeal to the labor courts is usually too expensive. Moreover, many of the conflicts arise out of the vagueness of the agreements or other arrangements that regulate the life of the enterprise.[13] Thus lay-offs and dismissals are often based upon "qualification and seniority" without indicating the relative weight to be given to each factor. In the end, therefore, top management makes the final decision.

Since 1968 a third form of personnel representation has a legal foundation: the union local (*section syndicale*). The demand for such a legal basis had been raised as early as 1945, but employer resistance had prevented the realization of this demand, even though the union local performed legally recognized functions in the enterprise, e.g., in the election of *comités d'entreprises* and personnel delegates. Only the major upheaval of 1968, followed by the Grenelle agreement, forced the legal recognition of the presence of the union in the enterprise. Even so, in 1975, seven years later, less than half the enterprises with fifty employees or more had union locals.[14] Most of them were concentrated in the larger enterprises with 1,000 or more employees, 96.4 percent of whom in 1975 had such union groups. The union designates its representatives who are protected against dismissal and are given paid time to fulfill their mission. What their mission is compared with those of the personnel delegates and that of other employee representative committees is unclear. They are to represent "the professional interests" of their members, a task that obviously overlaps with the duties of other representatives of the employees. There is what the French call *"un embarras de richesses."* Is the union in the enterprise a countervailing force, which is the view of the C.G.T. (Confédération Generale du Travail), or is it part of the administrative machinery of the enterprise, which comes closer to the ideas of the C.F.D.T.? In any case, the difference is rarely seen as clearly as stated here.[15] It is too early to determine whether the legal recognition of union sections in the plant will make a substantial contribution to the development of industrial democracy on the factory floor.

A decree, dear to the heart of Charles de Gaulle and less enthusiastically received by unions and employers, has introduced a measure of profit-sharing in French enterprises. It has some parallels with systems introduced in West Germany and Holland. This, too, is of so recent date that judgments cannot be made. In any case, the experiment concerns only the results, not the running of the enterprise.

Recent reports indicate that the Socialist government elected in 1981 proposes to extend workers' rights considerably.[16] Among other items are proposals to enhance the status of part-time workers and to ensure that disciplinary sanctions imposed on workers are not excessive and that work rules established by the employer are limited to matters of health, safety, and issues necessary to ensure the effective running of the firm. Further measures are intended to strengthen the protection of workplace representatives and candidates for such offices and to provide the members of the enterprise committees with the information they may need on company operations. In multiplant establishments a group council system is to be set up. Arrangements for union-employer committees chaired by labor inspectors and government representatives—appointed civil servants empowered to enforce labor legislation—will be made where no collective agreements exist.

Attempts to introduce codetermination, German style, into France have met with little sympathy. Only the C.F.D.T. among the major unions has shown any interest, but it is not clear whether any definite plan is in preparation.

Great Britain

The nature of the British shop stewards is quite different from that of their German or French counterparts. They are "trade union lay representatives at the place of work."[17] This differentiates them sharply from the typical continental council that, while often dominated by union members, is not a part of the union structure. The British shop steward is the result of union penetration into the plant. The continental enterprise or plant committees had their origins precisely in the failure of the union to enter into the plant. While these contrasts do affect the way the two sets of institutions function, the differences as regards their substantive tasks are less clearly delineated. Especially when we study the areas of their work rather than what the law or the rules say, we find many parallels.

Being active in the plants, the shop stewards are closer to the rank and file than the full-time union officials, particularly since the British unions are rather poor and have only a small number of such officers, far fewer than their American colleagues. Even if the British unions so desired, their full-time officers could not maintain close contacts with their members. By numbers, place, function, and daily contact with the rank and file, the shop stewards are far better situated to be organs of industrial democracy than are the union leaders.

The main emphasis is placed on the stewards' functions in negotiating the effective wages and benefits of the workers whom they represent. This is the basis for the well-known statement of the Donovan Commission that Britain has a double industrial relations system: one fictional, consisting of the national agreements concluded by the union leaders and the employers' associations, and a real system based upon the effective wages and benefits negotiated by the shop stewards and usually improving substantially upon the terms of the national agreements. In fact, the stewards "negotiate over a wide variety of issues, from the level of piece work earnings to non-financial questions such as discipline and conditions of work. On the whole they tend to be most prominent and influential where they can secure a measure of influence over the determination of earnings, and in this respect systems of payment by result may be said to assist their growth and development. On the other hand, even where earnings are not determined at shop floor level they can usually find plenty to do, unless special arrangements are made to curtail and restrict their activities."[18]

Bargaining is largely based upon comparison with what is regarded as a similar job. "Shop stewards in one factory, region, or industrial group learn what is happening in other factories, regions, and groups from their unofficial company-wide co-ordinating committees and from their quarterly A.E.U. [Amalgamated Engineering Union] district meetings. Increases in earnings in industrial groups growing fast lead to pressures for increases in groups which are growing more slowly; increases in earnings in one works of a company create pressures for increases on grounds of 'comparability' or to restore 'fair relativities' in the region where the works are, in works of the company elsewhere, and hence in other regions."[19]

While the negotiation of effective wages and fringe benefits is one of the most important tasks of the stewards, their key role in questions of discipline—in the United States this is commonly a large part of grievance-handling—is of almost equal significance. In plants with satisfactory labor relations, management relies to a large extent on stewards "to help solve problems of absenteeism, sloppy work, quitting early, loitering on the job and drunkenness. . . . With the aid of a shop steward a foreman may be able to persuade workers to change shifts or places of work as production orders vary. . . . Not only the foreman, but the rest of management, too, use stewards and other union representatives to help them apply the provisions of the collective agreement to new situations and to help solve problems."[20] This also gives the stewards their power: withdrawal of cooperation is a strong means of pressure. As a result, the shop steward plays a key role in the daily working life of the union member while the union leader becomes a figure of immediate relevance only sporadically and even then at a distance.

The relative independence of the shop steward from his union hierarchy to which he is officially subordinated is enhanced by the presence of several unions in the same plant. This follows from the existence of numerous separate skilled workers' unions within most enterprises and their component parts. In such cases joint or combined steward committees are set up; their decisions usually are binding on the stewards regardless of their union affiliation. This makes it impossible for the individual union to impose its discipline upon the shop steward, who acquires autonomy and a status of his own.

NOTES

1. See ch. 11 herein.
2. Quoted in Adolf Sturmthal, *Workers' Councils: A Study of Workplace Orga-*

nizations on Both Sides of the Iron Curtain (Cambridge, Mass.: Harvard University Press, 1964), 60–61.

3. See the discussion later in this chapter.

4. Friedrich Furstenberg, "West German Experience with Industrial Democracy," *Annals of the American Academy of Political and Social Science,* 431 (May 1977), 47.

5. *Ibid.*

6. Reports in *Gewerkschaftliche Monatshefte,* no. 11, 1981, show that the overwhelming majority of the works' councilors are union members. For I.G. Metall the percentage that year was 83.1; 14.3 percent belonged to no union.

7. A small empirical study reported on in *Gewerkschaftliche Monatshefte,* no. 3, 1979, by Lothar P. Schardt, seems to indicate that the council is regarded by almost half the employees of a large industrial plant as part of "management" or as "they" rather than "we." This does not seem to prevent a large majority of the employees from regarding the council members as highly competent. White-collar employees were far less inclined to vote for union candidates to the council, but, more important, participation in the elections was surprisingly low among both workers and white-collar employees. Even though the council is legally independent from the union, almost all employees, workers and white-collar people, believe the council is working closely with the union. The latter is thus, rightly or wrongly, held responsible for council action or inaction. Since the number of council members is much too small to enable them to maintain close contact with the mass of employees, Schardt concludes that only the organization of union shop stewards would make such contacts possible.

8. See François Sellier, "Les Problèmes du Travail en France, 1920–1974," a paper submitted to the International Industrial Relations Congress, Sept. 1976, Geneva, Switzerland.

9. Ordinance of Feb. 22, 1945, and legislation of May 15, 1946.

10. "L'éxperience des comités d'entreprises: Bilan d'une Enquête," *Droit Social,* 3 (Mar. 1952), 169.

11. Quoted in Jean-Daniel Reynaud, *Les Syndicats en France* (Paris: Editions du Seuil, 1975), 1:242.

12. In practice, however, this merely means that they are paid severance pay in case of dismissal.

13. *Ibid.,* 1:244–45.

14. Sellier, "Les Problèmes du Travail en France," 21.

15. Following Reynaud's discussion, *Les Syndicats en France,* 250.

16. *European Industrial Relations Review,* 94 (Nov. 1981).

17. W. E. J. McCarthy, *The Role of Shop Stewards in British Industrial Relations. A Survey of Existing Information and Research* (London: H.M. Stationery Office, 1967), 2. This is one of a series of research papers prepared for the Donovan Commission, officially termed the "Royal Commission on Trade Unions and Employers' Associations."

18. *Ibid.,* 16.

19. S. Lerner and David Marquand, *Regional Variations in Earnings, Demand for Labour and Shop Stewards' Combined Committees in the British Engineering Industry,* Manchester School of Economic and Social Studies, Sept. 1963, 290.

See also Milton Derber, *Labor-Management Relations at the Plant Level under Industry-Wide Bargaining. A Study of the Engineering Industry in Birmingham* (Urbana: University of Illinois Press, 1955), 56.

20. James W. Kuhn, *Bargaining in Grievance Settlement* (New York: Columbia University Press, 1961), 30–31.

11

Codetermination

THE INSTITUTIONS of codetermination at top management level have their main origin in West Germany. While minority representation of workers on the boards of directors—the policy-making level in the two-tier system of enterprise administration—existed after World War I in Central Europe, the institution had little impact on the life of the enterprise. A new departure of lasting and growing importance was the enactment in 1947 in West Germany of the codetermination principle in the iron and steel industry by the Occupation forces. The so-called articles of association provided for a supervisory board consisting of an equal number of representatives of stockholders and employees. The managing board was to include a "labor director" to administer social and personnel matters.

This system was inspired by the necessity of refusing control of heavy industry to people who had been among the main supporters of Hitler and his regime. It was regarded as highly unlikely that German workers would be willing to work under the direction of the men who had done their best to destroy German democracy and the labor unions of the Weimar Republic. The British Labour government in whose area of occupation most of the German iron and steel industry was located was understandably open to ideas of this kind (even though many of the British Occupation officials in Germany came out of the colonial service and were not inclined to look favorably at Socialist or semi-Socialist ideas).

In subsequent years the principle was extended under the pressure of the trade unions to the coal industry and received support through legislation. The law of May 1951 established a precedent that became increasingly important over time, both nationally and internationally. The typical model was for the upper level of the two-tier board to be composed as follows: five shareholders' representatives, five employees' representatives, and a neutral eleventh representative. On the lower managing board, which most frequently consists of three members, there was to be a labor director to be appointed with the approval of the employees' representatives of the supervisory board.

In practice, this meant that the labor director came from the ranks of the trade unions.[1]

This law corresponded very well to the ideological compromise upon which the newfound unity of the German trade union movement was established. It restricted property rights without completely abolishing them by equating them with rights acquired by work in the company. At the same time it recognized the rights of the employees who had invested their working lives or parts of them in the life—and in many cases in the reconstruction from the war damage—of the enterprise. While one part of this pleased the Socialists, the other corresponded in some ways to ideas that the Christian unions could accept and even defend. Codetermination thus became a tie between the formerly hostile or at least competitive branches of German trade unionism and helped to cement the unity of the movement. The new concept also permitted the movement to acknowledge openly its distance from the Marxist tradition. This had been accomplished for many decades in the daily practice of German labor, and the first attempts at formulating a corresponding theory had been made during the Weimar Republic as, for instance, in Fritz Naphtali's work, *Wirschaftsdemokratie, ihr Wesen und Ziel,* published in 1929. Now its underlying concept became the official program of the trade unions. Communist criticism of the system could easily be disregarded given the state of hatred and contempt in which the followers of Joseph Stalin were held after the terrible experiences that accompanied the Russian presence on German soil. Codetermination also fit well into the general trend of the Socialist and labor movements in many countries in Europe of deemphasizing the issue of property rights and their abolition or radical change in the light of the growing importance and independence of management. Supplementary legislation passed in 1956 extended the law to cover companies whose subsidiaries are engaged predominantly in coal and steel.

For corporate enterprises outside of coal and steel and for limited liability enterprises, labor representation on the supervisory board was limited to one-third of the board membership. This was the subject of increasingly sharp criticism on the part of the unions, whose aim it was to enlarge labor's share in board membership. The growing power of the Social Democratic party made a move in this direction politically feasible. A commission under the chairmanship of Professor Kurt Biedenkopf of the Christian-Democratic Union (C.D.U.) was appointed by the federal government to examine especially the experience under the "parity" codetermination system of coal and steel. After two years of empirical investigations, the report published in 1970 came to the conclusion that no fundamental changes had occurred in coal and steel as a consequence of the introduction of *parity* on the supervisory boards, that most decisions were made by unanimity, and that the management board was the main power center.

The Biedenkopf findings confirmed the widely held impression that the supervisory board merely endorsed policy decisions previously arrived at by management and accepted in informal consultation with works council members and union officials.[2] In many cases these discussions served as an effective method of conflict management. In spite of Biedenkopf's political affiliation with the conservative C.D.U., strong objections, especially as regards the process of restructuring the German coal industry, arose because of the support that the unions apparently could derive from the findings. The report, however, did not recommend the generalization of the parity system, but rather a five to seven relationship between employee and shareholder representatives, to ensure the dominance of the latter group. Against this, the unions desperately fought for parity representation.

As legislation was required, the issue became the object of prolonged negotiations between the parties represented in the federal government, the Social Democrats and the Free Democrats. Although the unions obtained some concessions, the Free Democrats won out on what was regarded—rightly or wrongly—as the crucial issue, namely the parity representation of labor on the supervisory boards. As a result, three rules exist as regards labor's representation on the supervisory boards of different enterprises: (1) the parity arrangement in coal and steel and the holding companies in these industries; (2) the one-third representation of labor according to the 1952 legislation, which applies to enterprises with more than 500 but less than 2,000 employees; (3) the new codetermination system enacted in 1976, which applies to firms with at least 2,000 employees. This new system provides for supervisory boards with an even number of members, half of whom represent the employees. This group includes at least two union representatives, one member selected by the office staff, and one representative of senior (managerial) employees. It is this last member who was the object of prolonged wrangling, since he is expected to vote in most cases with the shareholders' side. In spite of this compromise favorable to the employers' side, the Employers Association instigated an unsuccessful lawsuit against the act, claiming that it violated constitutionally protected property rights. Not all employers, however, agreed with this action, which they feared might poison the otherwise quite reasonable and cooperative relationship between what the Germans have come to describe as the "social partners."[3]

In the meantime, the implementation of the new law on labor representation on supervisory boards has made considerable progress. According to the 1976 act, all West German companies with a work force of 2,000 or more had to complete the process by June 30, 1978. The most interesting aspect of the new development has been the nomination by German unions of leading non-German members of their international professional associations as candidates for the boards of multinational companies. For example, Herman Rebhan, general secretary of the International Metalworkers' Federation with headquarters in Geneva, has joined the Ford board, and Charles Levinson, general secretary of the International Federation of Chemical Workers with headquarters in Geneva, is a member of a Dupont-subsidiary board.

A rather important issue due to arise when the boards are reconstituted is the selection of the labor director. While the new law prescribes that such a director be appointed, the worker members of the board do not have the right to veto the selection of a particular person. The unions are thus left only with the argument that the appointment of a person whom labor can support would have advantages for the enterprise as well as the unions.

While the German codetermination system is undergoing rapid changes, it has called forth attempts to introduce the system or variations of it in other European countries. The argument is usually that codetermination is responsible for the extraordinary degree of prosperity in West Germany. There is, however, no evidence connecting the two factors, nor can the possibility be excluded that the causal relationship is in the opposite direction, i.e., that it is German prosperity that ensured the success of codetermination. In any case codetermination has not prevented the extraordinary resurgence of the West German economy.

One of the countries especially concerned with the German model is the United Kingdom. We have seen in Chapter 9 that in the battle between Herbert Morrison and Ernest Bevin over union participation in the administration of nationalized enterprises an apparent compromise was arrived at which, in fact, represented a victory for Morrison's position of rejecting official union representation on the board. Strong theoretical underpinning was provided for this view by outstanding industrial relations scholars. Hugh Clegg, for instance, in a widely read book[4] defended the view that industrial democracy was best obtained by unions functioning as a countervailing power rather than as a partner in administration or management. His views were based on three elementary principles: unions must be independent of the state and of management; only unions can effectively defend the interests of the workers; ownership is irrelevant to good industrial relations.[5]

About the time when Clegg's book appeared, however, sentiment in the British labor movement began to change. The basic reasons were manifold. The rising power of the shop stewards brought them rather than the union functionaries close to the shop floor. The former unionists on the boards of nationalized industries were too far removed from the rank and file to be regarded as effective organs of industrial democracy, even though they might meet some of the requirements of what was described as one of the channels through which workers' participation might express itself.

A minor departure from the Morrison concept had already occurred in the steel industry. There, after its renationalization, part-time divisional labor directors had been appointed who retained their jobs in the shops. On the whole, this experiment was not regarded as a major step forward on the road to industrial democracy on the shop floor. Yet the problem itself remained on the agenda. Its importance was strongly underlined by the work of the Donovan Commission, which published its report in 1968.[6] Although a majority of the commission members rejected the idea of workers' directors (see chapter 9 herein), three members did favor experiments along these lines; two other members, not representing unions, even wished to make such arrangements compulsory.

In 1968 the European Economic Commission decided to prepare a statute for a European company in contrast to the great majority of multinational corporations that are, in fact, conglomerates of national companies operating under the various company laws of the different countries in which they do business. In connection with the statute attempts were being made to provide for some form of workers' representation in the direction of enterprises functioning under that future statute. C. Lyon-Caen and others proposed that the specific form of such representation be decided by collective bargaining, but the commission of the European Economic Community came out in favor of a uniform system. The model for this was to be the German codetermination scheme.

These various events combined to focus attention on the issue of worker directors in Great Britain. One result was the preparation of a paper by the research staff of the Trades Union Congress (T.U.C.) in 1973, which broke sharply with the tradition of British unionism. It made a major issue of labor representation on company boards, even though it reaffirmed the primary significance of collective bargaining. The new argument was that collective bargaining did not extend to the general economic policies of the different enterprises such as investment, location, or closures that are of vital interest to the workers. The T.U.C. adopted the paper at its congress in 1973 without much debate and made its contents part of the discussions with the Labour party in what came to be known as the "social contract." This was a bargain in which the unions accepted voluntary wage controls in exchange for various reforms to be enacted by the Labour government, including some form of industrial democracy.

The preparation in detail of proposals to this effect was entrusted to a Royal Commission under the chairmanship of the distinguished Oxford historian, Lord Bullock, author of a well-known book on Hitler and a leading student of German affairs.[7] Three of the eleven members of the commission were trade unionists, and the majority of the commission members were rather close to the T.U.C. or the Labour party. The instructions of the commission were very close to the ideas of the T.U.C.: "Accepting the need for a radical extension of industrial democracy in the control of companies by means of representation or the board of directors, and accepting the essential role of trade union organizations in this process, to consider how such an extension can best be achieved, taking into account in particular the proposals of the Trade Union Congress report on industrial democracy as well as experience in Britain, the EEC and other countries. . . ." The findings of the committee were to apply only to the private economy while another committee was to investigate the public sector.

The appointment of the commission was announced by the government in August 1975. As early as May 1966 the Labour party had set up a "Working Party on Industrial Democracy." Its chairman was Jack Jones, then a rising star in the leadership of the giant Transport and General Workers Union (T.G.W.U.) and a member of the Labour party's national executive committee. Its report published the following year went only marginally beyond the traditional commitment to collective bargaining.[8]

However, in the evidence given by the T.U.C. to the Donovan Commission the idea of union participation in management was touched upon, even if only tentatively. Companies were to be encouraged, said the T.U.C. document, "to recognize and take advantage of the mutual benefits to be obtained from more active participation by trade union representatives in company policy and day to day practice." This suggestion aroused only a modicum of interest.

The decisive step in the new direction came in 1973, as mentioned above. In July of that year the T.U.C. published a major policy document based on the paper prepared by its research staff. The T.U.C. document stated:

> The traditional British trade union attitude to schemes for "participation" in the management of private industry has been one of opposition. It has been considered that the basic conflict of interest between the workers and the owners of capital and their agents prevents any meaningful participation in management decisions. The reasoning behind this opposition has varied from the claim that the trade unions' job is simply and solely to negotiate terms and conditions, and not to usurp the function of management, to the proposition that trade unions should not be collaborationists in a system of industrial power and private wealth of which they disapprove.[9]

However, although the T.U.C. made a number of recommendations about improving industrial democracy based on the strengthening of union organization and the widening of the scope of collective bargaining, it now saw the need for something more: "it is clear that this leaves a wide range of fundamental managerial decisions affecting workpeople that are beyond the control—and very largely beyond the influence—of workpeople and their trade unions. Major decisions on investment, location, closures, takeovers and mergers, and product specialisation of the organisation are generally taken at levels where collective bargaining does not take place, and indeed are subject matters not readily covered by collective bargaining. New forms of control are needed."[10]

The T.U.C.'s basic proposal to achieve this objective in the private sector was that there should be a new Companies Act, to be introduced in stages, initially applying to the six to seven hundred enterprises employing more than 2,000 workers. In these companies there would be a two-tier board structure with supervisory boards that would be responsible for determining company objectives and for appointing the management boards. One half of the supervisory boards should be elected through trade union machinery, and the new provisions would only become operative in unionized firms. Representation of workers on boards could only be through bona fide unions choosing to exercise this right. Finally, the change in structure should be reflected by a statutory obligation of companies to have regard for the interests of working people as well as shareholders.

This pattern was in keeping with, and was undoubtedly influenced by, other European developments. But another element of continental practice, the works councils, was emphatically rejected by the T.U.C., which argued: "An attempt to introduce a general system of works councils in British industry would lead to one of two things. Either they would duplicate existing structures at plant levels, in which case works councils would clearly be superfluous; or they would displace and supersede existing trade union arrangement; this latter approach would be even more unacceptable to the trade union movement."[11]

The T.U.C. evidence later submitted to the Bullock committee departed from this text in one major point: the T.U.C. was willing to accept a one-tier board with half the votes going to the union representatives. These should be designated by the union according to rules to be determined by each individual union. At the same time the T.U.C. was prepared to accept a number of shareholder and management representatives on the board in excess of the number of union representatives provided that the voting power of all these representatives taken together would not exceed the number of union votes.[12] The voting parity between this group and the number of union representatives need not lead to a stalemate: a rotating chairman from the two groups with deciding vote or an independent outside chairman could be appointed. No need existed, however, to appoint a consumer representative as some continental nationalization measures provided, the more so as he would have no clearly defined constituency to whom to report. This ran counter to a submission by the National Consumer Council (N.C.C.).

The Bullock Commission submitted its report in early 1977. More than 200 pages long, including a minority dissent of employers' representatives on the commission, the report is a substantial document. Its underlying philosophy, quite close to the T.U.C. document, was stated in the following paragraph, which is part of the conclusion:

During our inquiry we found a widespread conviction, which we share, that the problem of Britain as an industrialized nation is not a lack of native capacity in its working population so much as a failure to draw out their energies and skill to anything like their full potential. It is our belief that the way to release those energies, to provide greater satisfaction in the workplace and to assist in raising the level of productivity and efficiency in British industry—and with it the living standards of the nation—is not by recrimination or exhortation but by putting the relationship between capital and labour on to a new basis which will involve not just management but the whole workforce in sharing responsibility for the success and profitability of the enterprise. Such a change in the industrial outlook and atmosphere will only come about, however, as a result of giving the representatives of the employees a real, and not a sham or token, share in making the strategic decisions about the future of an enterprise which in the past have been reserved to management and the representatives of the shareholders.

While referring frequently to the West German model and its success, the report recommends retention of the traditional unitary board rather than the division between a supervisory and a management board. There are fundamental decisions that only the board of directors can make, ranging from liquidation of the company to the appointment, removal, and pay of senior management officials. Employee representation is to occur at the level of the board of directors. These representatives are to report back to the employees whom they represent but keep confidential information "the disclosure of which might damage the company."

The most widely disputed proposal of the committee concerns the constitution of the board. The formula "2x + y" has been used as an abbreviation: "Minority but equal representation of shareholders and employees, entailing a third group of directors on the board." Minority employee representation without that third group was rejected on the basis of experience in Sweden and West Germany, where it was found that this system provides no effective transfer of power from shareholders and management to the workers. The third group is to be elected in an uneven number greater than one by agreement of a majority of each of the two other groups.

In principle, agreement should be reached about the organization of the board between the recognized trade unions and the existing board. If no agreement is reached within six months, the law would prescribe the necessary rules based on the "2x + y" formula. The chairman should be selected by the shareholder representatives unless the board unanimously decides otherwise. However, a preliminary basic decision is a vote of all employees by simple majority constituting at least one-third of the employees in favor of board representation. Employee representatives are to be elected by the union shop stewards' organization to prevent the development of an employee organization competitive with the recognized union.[13]

The delicate problem of the relationship between employee representation and collective bargaining is treated with somewhat surprising optimism: "Employee representatives are most unlikely to demand that senior management reveal their bargaining position and strategy and if they did make such a demand, they would almost certainly not be supported by the Shareholder representatives and the co-opted directors."[14] The main evidence cited to support this happy perspective is Swedish experience. However, the Swedish law prohibits employee representatives from taking part in board discussions on collective bargaining and related issues, although in practice this is reported to be only rarely observed. More important, the harmonious labor relations of Sweden can hardly be used as analogy for the much less friendly industrial relations of the United Kingdom.

There is, of course, a good deal more in the report, including proposals on an Industrial Democracy Commission and another on training facilities, but this text must refrain from going too far afield. Moreover, events since the report was published tend to indicate that it is unlikely to be translated into fact without considerable changes, if at all.

While the Bullock Commission adopted fairly completely the T.U.C. views, the T.U.C. did not represent the entire trade union movement on the issue of workers' participation. Opposition arose on the left as well as on the right of the labor movement. Indeed, the opposition had little in common with the traditional ideological divisions of the movement. Thus the Amalgamated Engineering Union with its 1.3 million members, usually regarded as leftist, opposed the report as did the Electricians Union with some 450,000 members whose leadership stands for right-wing strategies within the movement. Both unions view their role as a countervailing force to capital rather than as a partner in management.

As might be expected, opposition came from other sides as well. Indeed, very few influential voices outside the committee were raised in favor of the report. The three industry representatives on the committee strongly dissented from several of the main proposals. They advocated the adoption of the German two-tier system of administration. On the supervisory board the workers' representatives would be in a minority, since, when no agreement on the selection of the third outsider group of members could be obtained, the shareholders could elect them at their annual meeting. Moreover, this part of the scheme would not be in force until three years after employee councils on the shop floor had been in operation. The candidates for the supervisory board would have to be properly trained, have at least three years' experience on the employee council, and have been employed by the company for at least ten years. Different categories of employees—blue-collar, white-collar, managerial—would be entitled to separate representation on the boards. No board representation was to be in force unless either all unions represented in the company agreed or two-thirds of the employee council members so requested. No election of worker representatives could take place unless 60 percent of the employees participated.

On its own the Confederation of British Industry (C.B.I.) also waged war against the Bullock proposals and threatened that if they were to become law the C.B.I. would refuse to consult with the government. The main objections, as formulated by the *Economist,* were as follows.[15] (1) The report gave too much influence in the selection of the labor directors to the shop stewards, neglecting the union rank and file and the nonunion workers. (2) Parity of labor and shareholders representation on the board went farther toward a new social order than would correspond to Labour party electoral strength in the country. (3) The Bullock proposal of "$2 \times + y$"—which the *Economist* called infamous—went further than the West German system in twenty-five years of evolution. An inflexibly uniform formula does not fit the internal divisions of both of the T.U.C. and the C.B.I.

Yet the *Economist* favored some form of workers' participation. Indeed some minimal level of participation, the journal said, should be legally enforceable on employers if unions and workforce demand it. Thus while the report undoubtedly went further than circumstances permitted, the issue of industrial democracy remained on the agenda not only of Great Britain but also of many other industrially advanced nations. Whether Lord Bullock's committee has shown the way toward a solution of the problem remains an open question, which will most probably not be settled before the next general election in the United Kingdom, if then.

Worker directors have been instituted in a number of continental countries. However, small minority representation of the employees started after World War I in a number of countries, frequently in the wake of the creation of workers' councils at the plant level. This form of labor representation on the boards—introduced in Germany, Austria, and other countries after World War I and in Sweden in the 1970s—proved disappointing. It was too easy for the shareholder directors to hold separate meetings without workers' directors or to take major decisions in small committees that the full board then just had to ratify. Moreover, the fundamental problem of how to handle situations in which the objectives of the shareholder directors differed from those of the worker representatives was hardly envisaged, let alone examined. As a result, worker representatives rapidly became ordinary board members, eager to increase efficiency in the plant.[16] The workers themselves regarded collective bargaining and other traditional practices as more relevant to the defense of their interests that they did the worker directors. The introduction of worker directors appears to have interfered little with the authority of management. On the contrary, in a number of cases managerial power seems to have been strengthened and a kind of joint labor-management oligarchy has sometimes emerged inside the enterprise, leaving the union more or less free to represent members' interests against this coalition.

Symptomatic of this trend is the fact, revealed in public opinion surveys, that in Germany about three-quarters of the workers knew that codetermination had been introduced in their enterprises, but only half the workers knew with any degree of precision what that meant. As might be expected, knowledge of codetermination declined in line with the skill level of the workers concerned.[17] In Great Britain only 9.5 percent of a sample of employees in the steel industry realized that the worker directors were members of the (product) divisional boards.

While in Germany the works councils are in principle independent of the trade unions and in Britain the shop stewards, though part of the union structure, often act independently from the unions, in Sweden the labor movement found an interesting solution for the integration of the worker representatives in the union structure. While stressing the importance of effective workers' participation in determining conditions on the shop floor, the movement realized that employee influence on decisions at the board level had to be strengthened as well. However, the right to negotiate about the issues to be settled at board level is not enough. To make this right meaningful, employees must be provided "with full insight into the company's intentions and plans."[18] While main emphasis was laid upon company policies in the area of conditions arising in daily work, the importance of extending employee insight into, and influence upon, company management was stressed.[19] Most important, the labor movement demanded the abolition of paragraph 32 of the statutes of the Swedish Employers Confederation, which confirmed the employer's exclusive right "to direct and distribute the work" and to "hire and fire" at his discretion.[20] Following the publication of this report a law on codetermination was passed in 1976 that made decision-making on all company levels subject to collective bargaining; strikes on codetermination issues were legal even after an agreement on wages had been concluded. Employers were obligated to negotiate and conclude the negotiations before making decisions on important matters (reorganization, expansions, or shut-downs). Employers must provide the unions with all information they require to safeguard the interests of their members. In the case of local disputes, negotiations by the union at the national level were to settle the disagreement, thus maintaining the ultimate authority of the national union. Negotiations at the local and at the national level were in this way connected, and industrial democracy at the work place combined with collective bargaining, a problem that the British unions have found difficult to solve so far.

Austria has developed a special form of codetermination that in effect means union participation in all public bodies determining economic and social policies. In Parliament the unions are strongly represented, especially by the Socialist party with which most of the trade union leaders and members are affiliated. Politics permeates Austrian life to such an extent that even the unified trade unions determine the composition of their governing bodies by a system of proportional representation of the political leanings of the membership. This is ascertained by the votes of union members for the different candidate lists for the executive established by the political groupings of the union members.

Most of the large industrial establishments of Austria are nationalized and even a number of nonnationalized firms are government controlled, as the nationalized banks hold the controlling shares of these enterprises. Thus iron and steel, aluminum, metal-fabricating firms, oil, coal, most of the chemical industry, and the two largest banks are in the hands of the state. The governing boards of these enterprises are appointed by the government according to the relative strength of the political parties in Parliament. Until 1974 two representatives of the employees were also designated as members of the board. Since then this number has been increased to one-third of the total number of board members.

The control of the nationalized enterprises takes two forms; one is the proportional distribution of the board membership according to party votes at the latest parliamentary election, the other the distribution of control of different enterprises between the two leading parties, the Socialists, which acquired a majority in Parliament, and the People's party, which is the leading opposition party.[21] In general the Socialists are likely to be underrepresented since public employment has been dominated for many decades by a Catholic student fraternity whose former members have long acquired civil service status and cannot be removed.[22]

This discussion of an evaluation of codetermination, highly tentative as regards especially the results of the German 1976 legislation, will deal only with the West German experience, as empirical studies that have come to my attention concern only that country.

The primary fact that emerges from the literature and through personal observation is the importance of information. Works council members and labor members of the supervisory board both stress the need for information about the enterprise and point out that the success of their participation depends upon the willingness of management to provide the necessary information.[23] No less important is the training of the workers representatives in the knowledge necessary for the fulfillment of their tasks.

The degree of workers' interest in the various institutions of codetermination is documented by their participation in the elections. In workers council elections voting rates of more than 80 percent have been recorded.[24] This is undoubtedly high, though it compares unfavorably with participation rates in political elections in West Germany. Among those elected as representatives, older workers and white-collar personnel are overrepresented.

Relations between council members and the respective unions appear to be evaluated differently by different observers. In the nature of the facts only open conflicts of some significance would be recorded. Of those there are only very few that are known to occur. Some inferences can be drawn, albeit tentatively, from two observations: unions persist in efforts to establish their own network of representatives in the plants, and 76 percent of works' councilors reported[25] that union officers participated in council meetings. The first fact suggests union concern over their influence on the councils; the second suggests a fairly high degree of cooperation. No firm general conclusion seems possible.

It is especially difficult to establish a clear generalization about the workers' approval of codetermination. The highest degree of approval is found in coal and steel where parity codetermination exists.[26] Some further support for this positive view can be possibly found in the sharp resistance of the I.G. Metall to attempts to weaken this system by changes of corporate structure. As Friedrich Fürstenberg puts it, a rather favorable attitude exists among employees toward works' councils, in spite of criticism in detail.[27]

As to employee participation in supervisory boards, the influence of labor depends largely, if not decisively, upon its members' ability to come to an agreement among themselves prior to the official meeting. The main inspiration for the unanimity of most decisions in coal and steel lies in the parity of the two sides on the boards, a situation that compels compromising. Since the boards meet infrequently and for only a few hours, the role of the management board (Vorstand) and of prior consultation is predominant. The issue of the "managerial employees," who have separate representation on the supervisory boards and most often vote with the shareholders' representatives, remains a problem for the unions. Against this, union attempts to nominate managing labor directors after the pattern of coal and steel in the companies covered by the new codetermination law have aroused shareholders' resistance, as no such connection between labor directors and unions is provided for in the law.

With codetermination maturing in age, the system works quite effectively as an instrument of conflict management. Whether it gives employees a sense of participation in managerial decision-making remains to be seen. But that question is unanswered for most cases of collective bargaining as well. Admittedly, however, bargaining is not intended primarily to be an instrument of workers' participation in decision-making. In so far as it is, it is a desirable side effect for the point of view favoring industrial democracy.

NOTES

1. Dietrich Hoffmann, *The German Co-Determination Act of 1976* (Frankfurt/ Main: Alfred Metzner, 1976).

2. Friedrich Fürstenberg, "West German Experience with Industrial Democracy," *Annals of the American Academy of Political and Social Sciences,* 431 (May 1977), 51.

3. Since this was written, the Constitutional Court has rejected the employers' claim.

4. *European Industrial Relations Review,* 48 (Dec. 1977), 8–9.

5. See his *A New Approach to Industrial Democracy* (Oxford: Blackwell, 1960), 21; Adolf Sturmthal, "Unions and Industrial Democracy," *Annals of the American Academy of Political and Social Science,* 431 (May 1977), 12–21. Clegg's view corresponds to the one put forward by Sidney and Beatrice Webb at the turn of the century. They assigned to the consumers the function of deciding indirectly (by way of capitalist entrepreneurs or their salaried agents) what should be produced; to the managers how it should be done; and to "the expert negotiators of the Trade Unions . . . to state the terms under which each grade will sell its labour." This established the mixture of cooperative and adversary relationships of the unions that for so long has been the hallmark of British trade union thought. Selig Perlman then transferred this view to the American unions where it dominated industrial relations theory for several decades—in so far as any need for a theory was felt by the trade unionists and their academic students.

6. *Report of the Royal Commission on Trade Unions and Employes' Associations* (London: H.M. Stationery Office, 1968).

7. See my paper, "Bullock and the Aftermath," *Industrial Relations,* vol. 32, 299–309.

8. John Elliott, *Conflict or Cooperation. The Growth of Industrial Democracy* (London: Kagan Page, 1978), 206.

9. Trades Union Congress, *Industrial Democracy* (London: T.U.C., 1977), 14.

10. *Ibid.,* 34.

11. *Ibid.,* 38. Jack Jones described the councils as "tea party committees" (Elliott, *Conflict or Cooperation,* 213). This was prior to the substantially enhanced function of the councils in Germany and France in the 1970s.

12. This presentation follows closely Andrew W. J. Thompson's article, "New Focus on Industrial Democracy in Britain," *Annals of the American Academy of Political and Social Science,* 431 (May 1977), 32–43.

13. The British Employment Protection Act of 1975 provides procedures through which unions may claim recognition and establish that they are independent of employers.

14. *Report of the Royal Commission on Trade Unions and Employees' Associations,* 125, paragraph 56.

15. *The Economist,* May 21, 1977, 84–85.

16. See the results of various research efforts in Norway and the report of the German Biedenkopf Commission 1968–70.

17. Ralf Dahrendorf, *Das Mitbestimmungsproblem in der Deutschen Sozialforschung* (Munich, 1965), gives a succinct survey of the results of empirical stud-

ies—e.g., Pirker, Popitz, and Neuloh. See also Friedrich Fürstenberg, "Workers' Participation in Management in the Federal Republic of Germany," *International Institute for Labor Studies Bulletin*, 6 (June 1969), 94–148.

18. *Codetermination as the Foundations of Solidarity. A Report to the 1976 Congress of the Swedish Trade Union Congress* L.O. (Stockholm: n.p., n.d.), 11.

19. *Ibid.*, 10.

20. *Ibid.*, 11, and Bernt Schiller, "Industrial Democracy in Scandinavia," *Annals of the American Academy of Political and Social Science*, 431 (May 1977), 68.

21. The Alpine-Montan Company and the Bohler Company are commonly regarded as belonging to the People's party. The famous Austrian Steel Works and the nitrogen companies are the domain of the Socialists. For qualified job seekers who do not belong to either party the disadvantage is obvious. See Kurt Steiner, *Politics in Austria* (Boston: Little Brown, 1972), 391n29.

22. A history of plant-oriented codetermination is presented in Wilhelm Filla, *Zwischen Integration und Klassenkampf* (Vienna: Europa-Verlag, 1981).

23. Gundolf Kliemt, *Die Praxis des Betriebsverfassungsgesetzes im Dienstleistungsbereich* (Tübingen, 1971). Friedrich Fürstenberg, *Die Anwendung des Betriebverfassungsgesetzes im Hause Siemens* (Munich: G. C. B. Mohr, 1970). Cf. also Fürstenberg's paper at the IRRA Conference, Denver 1980, and the so-called Biedenkopf Report: officially the Report of the Mitbestimmungs-Kommission (Bonn, 1970).

24. Horst Udo Niedenhoff, *Praxis der Mitbestimmung* (Köln: Deutscher Institutsverlag, 1979), quoted in Fürstenberg's Denver paper.

25. Otto Blume, *Normen and Wirklichkeit einer Betriebsverfassung* (Tübingen: G. C. B. Mohr, 1964).

26. Rigga Graf Blücher, *Integration und Mitbestimmung* (Sennestatt, 1966).

27. Fürstenberg's Denver paper. The Mannesmann case was only the most publicized among some thirty incidents of the same kind.

12

Collective Bargaining

A WIDELY QUOTED statement of Sidney and Beatrice Webb points out that collective bargaining originated as a defensive device designed to prevent competition based on deteriorating wages and working conditions. Labor then in excess supply in the industrializing countries of Western Europe, the unions' main effort was directed at establishing a floor below which wages could not be depressed and a level at which minimal working conditions had to be maintained. The collective contract took the place that the courts or justices of the peace had held earlier when they fixed minimum wages. This method had gradually fallen into disuse and "towards the end of the eighteenth century . . . free bargaining between the capitalist and his workmen became practically the sole method of fixing wages."[1] It was then that the struggle for the right to combine, to form unions, and to engage in collective bargaining began, even though some forms of union activity can be traced back even further.[2]

Another defensive device, primarily European, but also in use in other parts of the world, is the so-called extension of agreements. Under certain conditions (which vary from country to country), the validity of an agreement can be extended by the government and enforced by it from the firms and the workers represented at the bargaining table to all others in the same industry. This gives the agreement something of the character of a law and prevents competition based on below-contract wages. The impact that extension may have on union recruiting is discussed later in this chapter.

Even before World War I collective bargaining was not unusual in some of the advanced industrial nations, such as Great Britain and West Germany. Hitlerism, World War II, and the period of reconstruction set limits to the scope of the institution, although the British wartime coalition government was careful not to introduce direct wage controls. A few years after the end of hostilities, collective bargaining was resumed, though changes in the institutions and the economic basis of the bargaining process made significant alterations unavoidable.

The interim period—roughly until 1950—saw a variety of devices designed to cope with the extreme scarcities in the wake of the war. Britain continued for about two and a half years the wartime policies of compulsory arbitration, food subsidies, and a reliance on the good sense of the unions and their willingness to assist the Labour government elected in 1945. A wage standstill followed but had to be abandoned in early 1950 when a conference of trade union executives "approved it by so small a majority that it clearly could not be put into effect."[3] The return of a Conservative government in 1951 ended all expectations of union restraint.

France, where collective bargaining on any significant scale came into being only during the Popular Front government in 1936 and was soon terminated, permitted collective bargaining once again at the end of 1946—but only on working conditions. Wage determination remained the province of the minister of labor.[4] Moreover, even the agreements on working conditions required the approval of the minister upon the advice of the Commission des Conventions Collectives, an advisory body to the minister. This somewhat elaborate machinery was used only once, however, as only one collective agreement, that of the bank clerks, was concluded under the rules of 1946.

As price controls and rationing were rapidly dismantled, the pressure for unrestricted collective bargaining rose and in February 1950 a law on collective bargaining on all industrial relations issues including wages was passed. It will be discussed later.

West Germany—the three zones of occupation apart from the eastern Soviet-occupied zone—slowly returned to a system of collective bargaining after the war; the main hindrance was that the unions whose reconstitution had been permitted on a local and state level "found no partners with which to deal. They were accustomed to bargaining with organized employers, so that transfer to a company-by-company basis appeared utterly impossible. . . . The unions were not organized into plant locals . . . and thus had no local unit capable of signing a contract, nor were there enough trained negotiators to go from plant to plant negotiating agreements on behalf of the area-wide union organization."[5] The result—surprising, at least for U.S. unionists—was that the unions asked the Occupation authorities to permit the reestablishment of employers' associations. When those came into being, they soon reestablished also the iron discipline among their members for which they had been known in the past.

Great Britain

The institutional set-up varied, and continues to do so, from country to country. Great Britain, the prime example of voluntarism among the major Western nations, shows a "complex pattern of overlapping and interlocking bodies which exist on both sides."[6] Unions range from very large to very small in the number of members, from the giant Transport and General Workers Union and the almost equally large engineering union to a craft union limited to one locality, such as the London Typographical Society. Craft and industrial unions coexist with so-called general unions, which organize workers whom other unions have neglected. Expansion has followed to a considerable degree changes in the industrial structure: white-collar and professional employees and public workers have joined union ranks in increasing numbers. Workers in nationalized industries have been among the best unionized groups and—as was described earlier—engage in unrestricted collective bargaining. In industries with a low degree of unionization, minimum wages and some other conditions of employment are set by wages councils, pending the time when collective bargaining becomes possible. Unionization is relatively high so that collective bargaining is by far the most important method of setting wages and working conditions.

Most agreements have been industry-wide since the end of World War I, which is common in most other European countries. (We shall return in due course to the problems raised by this system.) The Trades Union Congress (T.U.C.) with which most unions are affiliated has no control over their collective bargaining activities, except by way of persuasion or moral authority. The T.U.C. general council may offer help to a union involved in a conflict, and it expects to be informed of a major dispute. The T.U.C. has no authority to make commitments in behalf of its affiliates unless specifically empowered to do so. Nor is there any legal authority that could enforce agreements. British unions and employers have consistently refused to make collective agreements legally enforceable. Indeed, large numbers of agreements, especially below the level of the industry, are not even put into writing. Agreements on working conditions ae often traditional and informal.

The impact of full employment on this and other European collective bargaining systems will be explored later in this chapter and in Chapter 13. However, other issues that arose since the end of World War II need some brief mention at this time.

An outstanding event was the investigation of the entire British industrial relations system by a Royal Commission on Trade Unions and Employees' Associations (the Donovan Commission), appointed by the Labour government in 1965. The appointment was the result of the inflationary tendencies that the British ascribed at least in part to the existing system, its failure to achieve central pay and price control, and "a growing tendency for agreements not to be kept and a steady rise in industrial conflict."[7] A report published in 1963 pointed out that Britain had in fact two industrial relations systems: one based on the industry-wide agreements, the other related to the informal supplementary understandings achieved primarily by the shop stewards at plant or shop-floor level. The latter system, which often mattered far more than the former to the individual worker, was not based on any particular procedure, and the behavior of shop stewards and workers escaped almost completely the control of the unions. This results in part from the failure of the unions to have a sufficient number of representatives available to maintain effective contacts with shop stewards in the plant, an inevitable consequence of the poverty of British unions. It also derives from the existence of a multitude of unions in the same plant, each having its own shop stewards. The latter form joint shop stewards' committees with the stewards of the other unions represented in the plant, and the result is a committee not responsible to any particular union. "In these circumstances a joint shop steward committee has considerable freedom of initiative and independence. It is in fact responsible only to itself, and its constituents."[8] Violations of agreements concluded by the shop steward carry no legal penalty and the unions—against whom shop steward actions were about as frequently directed as against the employers—were unable or unwilling to enforce their discipline. Thus a second system of industrial relations developed, creating a good deal of unrest, outside of legal or union control, even in the rare case of the Amalgamated Union of Engineering Workers that since 1971 has striven to replace national agreements by local arrangements made by its shop stewards.

An attempt by the Conservative government in 1971 to regulate industrial relations by legislation was defeated when many of the unions refused to cooperate.[9] Nor has the report of the Donovan Commission, which did not remain undisputed, led to any substantial and permanent changes. There has been a trend toward more plant and company bargaining, but the corresponding development of formal grievance procedures has been sluggish. Some legal regulations have attempted to fill part of the gap. A redundancy payments act of 1965 provides for some compensation in the case of a permanent loss of jobs. Another law (1970) provides for equal pay for equal work.

The industrial relations problem that has created the most intense public resentment is the frequency and unpredictability of strikes and other forms of industrial unrest. A good many of them result from the actions of shop stewards.[10] The harm done by industrial strife to the British economy in general and the balance of payments in particular looms large in public opinion. There is little reason to doubt that the frequency and duration of strikes during the winter 1978–79 contributed substantially to the defeat of the Labour government at the elections of 1979. Yet, given the strength and the resolve of the British unions, it is not easy to think of basic reforms without their cooperation.[11]

The use of arbitration, usually as a final stage, is more frequent in the case of disputes about the terms of a new contract and quite exceptional in grievances under an existing contract. Even so, while most nationalized industries and the public sector have arbitration clauses in their contracts, they have rarely been used.

France

While collective bargaining dominates the British industrial relations scene, it has never played a comparably large role in France. In part, this has been the result of French tradition and the constitution, which instinctively look to the government rather than private initiative to solve difficult social problems. To another extent, the weakness and poverty of French unions and the "master in the house" philosophy of many French employers combined to make collective bargaining essentially a post–World War II phenomenon; the brief episodes of 1919–20 and even that of the Popular Front in 1936 did not make a lasting impact on the country. Thus the history of collective bargaining as a significant phenomenon begins in 1950.

The legislation then enacted allows for national agreements for any industry—a term not defined in the text—and for plant agreements provided they fit into the framework of an industry contract. While on the employers' side usually only one organization is represented, the workers' representatives may belong to a multitude of organizations. There are, ideologically divided, the Confédération Generale du Travail (C.G.T.) under Communist leadership, the French Democratic Confederation of Labour (C.F.D.T.), which originated in the Confédération Française des Travailleurs Chrétrens (C.F.T.C.), but is now close to the Socialists, the remnants of the C.F.T.C., and the C.G.T.– F.O. (Force Ouvrière), moderately Socialist. In addition, there is a special organization for higher white-collar workers, the General Confederation of Cadres (C.G.C.). C.G.T. is the strongest of the organizations, although in the absence of closed shops and checkoffs as well as the widespread reluctance of workers to pay union dues, even though they regard themselves as union members, no reliable membership figures are available. Unlike under U.S. rules, several unions representing the same category of workers may sit side by side at the bargaining table and compete with each other. The scope of an agreement depends less on the importance of the union or unions that signed it, as long as at least one did so, but on the number of firms affiliated with the employers' organization. However, the minister of labor may extend the validity of the contract to all firms of the industry. In any case, a valid agreement whether extended or not, applies to all workers employed by the firms affiliated to the signatory employers' association. The scope of application of an agreement that has not been extended thus depends more on the size or density of the employers' association than on union membership.

While agreements are usually concluded for one year, it is customary to keep them in force until a new agreement has been worked out. If no new agreement is reached, the old one continues in force.[12] Bargaining is thus an "erratic phenomenon." Moreover, strikes can be called any time; a union that has signed an agreement may not call a strike, but it could "break out spontaneously."[13] Nor does a strike represent a contract violation, at least since

1950, unless the employee commits a "severe fault," the contract is merely suspended. Though some categories of public employees do not have the right to strike—the *fonctionnaires d'autorité*—the "French law in this area is very tolerant, far more than that of the U.S. or of England."[14] When the collective bargaining law was passed in 1950, it was of limited significance for large parts of the labor force, compared with the "guaranteed interprofessional minimum wage" (S.M.I.G.), since wage levels were very low at the time. When the S.M.I.G. was raised substantially, not only the lowest rungs on the wage ladder but also the entire wage structure were affected by the changes. Contracts gradually introduced a number of benefits such as paid vacation, pay for public holidays, and severance pay. Later, mainly in the late 1960s, pay for sick days was included in some contracts. At about the same time a significant change occurred in the character and forms of collective bargaining, and in the subject matter covered. This development bridged the traditional French gap between contract and law in the area of industrial relations.

One of the most important changes of this kind concerned employment questions. In the early 1960s collective agreements limited themselves to severance pay, and this benefit often applied only to salaried staff. The Lorraine iron and steel agreement of July 1967 set a new model. According to this contract, natural attrition is to be the primary device for reducing employment, which will be supplemented by early retirement and internal transfers, among other methods. The works council (*comité d'entreprise*) is to be informed in advance if more than 100 workers are to be dismissed. Other firms may cooperate in the process of placing workers. While the government did not officially participate in the negotiations, it was kept informed and involved itself insofar as financial contributions were concerned.

On other subjects, the government encouraged direct negotiations, and after the strike explosion of 1968 and due to government initiative new forms of collective bargaining were introduced. Thus agreements on employment policy following the pattern of the Lorraine agreement and on vocational training were concluded between the national employers' confederation and the five main trade union confederations. "Salaried status" (mensualisation) was introduced gradually, also on government initiative, in a number of industries in an effort to reduce the class distinctions in French society. In this case, a nationwide principle was first agreed upon, whose translation into detail was left to negotiations in the different industries. These methods of "three-cornered" negotiation are a kind of "concerted action," similar in some respects to the German model discussed in Chapter 13.

While there is a pronounced trend toward negotitions at the highest possible level, an opposite trend has also been significant. The events of 1968 made clear the importance of the workplace as the locale of many decisions of vital impact on the daily life of the worker. Legal status was given in December 1968 to trade union branches in the plant, and plant agreements have been legally recognized. In fact, they existed since the Renault agreement of 1955. In practice they have been limited to larger enterprises. However, in somewhat chaotic fashion and frequently without legal status, contracts of some kind have become more frequent in what Jean-Daniel Reynaud calls "mini-branches," small numbers of enterprises of a similar kind, subgroups of an industry.[15]

Germany

Three main features characterize collective bargaining in the post–World War II era as contrasted with the corresponding institutions of the Weimar Republic: less close association between the unified trade union movement and any political party; compulsory arbitration was not reintroduced after 1945; and unions have become an accepted institution of West German social and economic life. In many other respects industrial relations are quite similar to those of the Weimar Republic prior to 1933. The typical agreement concerns working conditions and is regional (one or several provinces [Länder]) or industry-wide and is consequently limited to general principles. Another agreement may set a basic wage rate, called the "corner wage." This contract is usually limited to one year, while the agreements on working conditions are valid for longer periods. The remaining clauses, including the rates of pay, are filled in at lower levels, especially in the plant, by nonunion organizations such as the works council or even by bargaining by an individual. However, these agreements do not have the same legal force as those concluded by the union.

The contracting partners are thus principally superplant unions, frequently covering large regions, and employers' associations. With rare exceptions individual employers do not bargain with unions; the latter are traditionally not organized in the plant, but on a local or regional multiplant or multienterprise level. As a result, when collective bargaining was resumed after the war, the unions needed the reestablishment of employers' associations.[16] This fact underlines the original defensive purpose of collective bargaining, namely to set minimal wages and prevent competition based on below-tariff wages.

Collective agreements are thus a combination of various documents and understandings. At the top stands the so-called *Manteltarif,* a union-bargained document at the state, regional, or nationwide level, usually and of necessity brief, since it concerns a multitude of highly diverse establishments. Customarily it defines the industrial and geographical area and the time period of its validity, overtime and night shift rules, and other matters that can be uniformly regulated for a number of enterprises. There are several thousand such master agreements in the Federal Republic. Separate wage agreements setting forth some basic wage rates for different occupational groups are usually concluded for shorter periods and allow for more frequent adjustments than apply to the master agreement. For white-collar employees a separate salary agreement is almost always negotiated.[17] The crucial wage rate to which all others are related is that of a skilled worker in a metropolitan area.

Works council understandings and plant rules agreements (*Betriebsordnung*) go into the specific details that the large-scope agreements could not settle. The union is not involved in these agreements, and this is sometimes the source of disagreements and tensions between the councils and the union.

Grievance-handling under the contract is rarely carried on by the union, but mostly by the works council[18] and, if the case appears important, by the labor court. There the union may provide assistance, usually by way of its district office.

One "social partner," as the German terminology now goes,[19] is the unions. Sixteen—all industrial unions—were originally admitted in 1949 to the D.G.B., the main trade union confederation, and a seventeenth has recently been added. Sizeable numbers of white-collar workers are organized in a separate association (D.A.G.). Quite a few white-collar workers, however, belong to an industrial union. There is no clear-cut definition of industries, and U.S. students would frequently be tempted to speak of multi-industry unions. Civil servants have their own union, the Beamten-Bund (B.B.).

The D.G.B. started out with tremendous authority over its affiliates, mainly due to the powerful personality of its first president, Hans Böckler, a veteran trade unionist and participant in resistance movements under the Nazis. This relationship, reflected also in the financial strength of the D.G.B., has changed over time in favor of the affiliates, who now retain a larger proportion of their dues.

The pattern in collective bargaining has usually been set by the giant metalworkers' union (I.G. Metall) or, to a considerably lesser extent, the building trades. Most negotiations have been settled peacefully, sometimes by way of conciliation or by voluntary arbitration. Strikes have been infrequent, for reasons stated elsewhere in this volume, to which should be added that they are very costly for the unions since German workers expect strike subsidies from their union. While it was true as stated in an earlier report[20] that in the past settlements arrived at by the union officials were seldom, if ever, rejected by the rank and file, this has been less true since the late 1960s. Even the powerful I.G. Metall had difficulties in obtaining rank-and-file approval for the agreements reached in 1977–78 and even more so in 1978–79. A hardening of the attitude has also occurred on the employers' side: lock-outs—which are legal—have become a not infrequent method of social combat since 1976. In the metal industry three lock-outs have occurred in short succession.[21] Conflicts over lock-outs have contributed to the cessation of the "concerted action" discussed in Chapter 13.

Extension of contracts, on the request of one of the parties to a contract, can be ordered by officials of the ministry of labor, if the contract applies to employers with more than half the employees in the industry and the area concerned and extension is viewed as in the public interest. It thus depends more on the strength of the employers' association than that of the union. The response to the question at what level are wages set—which, often by way of extension or example, influences the wages of all employees in the industry concerned—is most frequently some vague reference to an "average." The follow-up question then is: Do you mean that half the firms in the industry find that wage level higher than they could afford?" The typical answer: "No, we mean the most frequently paid 'corner wage.' " In practice this means a wage level tolerable also for most of the least efficient firms in the industry. The national or regional contract thus performs somewhat the functions of a minimum wage, and it is understood that effective earnings, not negotiated by the union itself, will in many, if not most, cases be higher that the contract rates would provide. This gap, modest in the first years after collective bargaining resumed, became considerable as the rapid expansion of the West German economy absorbed the unemployed, the refugees, and finally more than 2.5 million foreign "guest-workers." Attracting and holding competent workers—at times workers of even modest abilities—during long periods of labor shortage required making not inconsiderable concessions in wages and working conditions beyond the contract terms. Job evaluation schemes play a large part in determining contract rates. Working conditions have been consistently improved over the years. Improvements include special arrangements for job security for older workers, for assistance in the event of unemployment (apart from the state-controlled social insurance system), reduction of working hours, and an annual paid leave of at least four weeks for most workers (88 percent in 1977). The terms of collective agreements appear to be accepted also often outside the reach of the agreement.

The system of regional or national agreements and the extension of such agreements by the government greatly reduce the importance of union membership for the average worker. Unless ideas of solidarity or pressure on the part of unionized colleagues exert their influence, union membership offers few tangible advantages that would not also belong to the nonmember. Attempts to introduce differential advantages for union members have failed, mainly on legal grounds. The federal labor court in 1967 held such distinctions to be in violation of the constitution.

Unions made considerable efforts to gain some measure of control over what happened in the plants. Collective agreements with a single employer who is not a member of his association—such as the one aimed at in 1965 by the I.G. Metall with the German subsidiary of the Ford Company following a strike—are lawful. However, by joining the employers' association, Ford avoided this solution and subscribed to the national agreement. Still, "about one third of current collective agreements have been concluded on a company basis (*Firmentarifverträge*). These include collective agreements in the public sector concluded with individual employers such as the German Post Office . . . and the German Railways."[22]

Plant-level agreements concluded with the works council concern "normal hours of starting and finishing work, breaks, the time and place of payment of wages . . . the establishment of the holiday schedule (which now frequently involves a collective shut-down of the whole works or of individual units), vocational training in the light of new statutory requirements, the administration of welfare facilities at plant or enterprise level, and internal regulations including workers' conduct. The last of these items covers such delicate subjects as clocking in, checks to prevent filching, no smoking rules, and fines for offenders."[23] Time and piece rates as well as job evaluation of new or radically changed jobs are also frequently treated in these agreements. A "peace obligation" makes it illegal to force changes in the union-sponsored agreement during its lifetime. Conflicts about the interpretation of agreements are usually settled by a conciliation board.

Union stewards have no official standing in enterprise negotiations, and union efforts to obtain recognition and functions in the enterprise have become increasingly intense since the wildcat strikes of the late 1960s. The situation is usually easier for the union when the shop steward is also a member of the works council. However, for the person performing this double role a basic conflict of conscience is almost unavoidable; as works council member he is legally committed to maintain "social peace"; as union representative his obligation may require his taking the opposite attitude.

The unions have been long aware, especially during the long period of labor shortages, that their vitality and relevance for their members have been affected by this double-track system. Events in the plants are most often of far greater importance to the individual than the high-level negotiations about the contract. The I.G. Metall has been successful in some of its contracts to obtain recognition and protection for the union representatives in the plant. But this is only a first step, and other unions are far behind.

Thus, it remains true that the union is a rather distant body for the average worker. The works council member who handles grievances and negotiated wage supplements and additional fringe benefits is often a more important figure for the individual worker than the union representative—a result of the fact that union structure stops above the plant level, in a union local with a geographic scope. The lowest level of the union structure may thus serve a multiplicity of plants without, until recently, operating within the plant. Employers favored this system because concessions made to the works council are not legally enforceable while collective agreements concluded with the union are.[24] It is true that some unions, for example, I.G. Metall, have endeavored to build up a network of union shop stewards next to the works council and that recent legislation has enabled union representatives to obtain access to the workplace itself. But these are only beginnings.

During periods of excess demand for labor as prevailed for many years in West Germany, France, Switzerland, Austria, Sweden, and other countries effective wage rates tended to be set above the rates agreed upon in the collective contract; in many cases rates and other benefits—such as a definite number of overtime hours to which the employer committed himself—resulted in earnings substantially above those based on contract rates. This phenomenon, which reduced the importance of the collective agreement and of the union for many workers, came to be known as "wage drift."[25] The counterpart on the employers' side was the often widespread disregard of individual firms for the contract that the association to which they belong had concluded with the union or unions. As a result, German union membership as a percentage of the labor force, while still higher than in the United States, has become stagnant or even declined. This trend has been reinforced by the decline of class-consciousness as constitutional, legal, or social discrimination against the workers disappeared or at least weakened.

The right to strike or lock-out is not established explicitly in legislation but is derived from the federal constitution and applies in principle also to public institutions of all kinds. In fact, however, strikes in essential activities such as hospitals have never occurred; strike frequency in general is exceedingly low, though in the late 1970s conflicts have become more frequent: this was probably due to the deteriorating economic situation. It is customary for German unions to pay their members strike subsidies that sometimes come quite close to net earnings. In turn, employers' associations in a number of industries provide financial support for their members involved in a conflict. Conflicts are thus costly to both sides, and they are interested in keeping down the frequency and duration of strikes and lock-outs. More important, however, is the basic acceptance of things as they are—due to high real income—by the social partners and the bulk of their membership, even though there is criticism, particularly among the younger generation, of the lack of ultimate objectives.

In the discussion of incomes policies in Chapter 13, more detailed reference is made to the role of the government in collective bargaining. In principle, the autonomy of the bargaining partners is recognized. "Concerted action," which provides for discussion by government representatives, experts, and the social partners, has been established under legislation enacted in June 1967. The purpose is to provide "orientation data" for actions of all concerned to foster economic growth, full employment, and stable prices. The degree of success and duration of this institution that served as a model for many countries is discussed later.

Italy

The three main trade union confederations in Italy are the Confederazione Italiana Sindacati Lavoratori (C.I.S.L.), whose leanings are predominantly Communist with Socialist support, the Confederazione Italiana del Lavoro (C.G.I.L.), which is Catholic/Socialist, and the Unione Italiana del Lavoro (U.I.L.) which can be described as Socialdemocratic/Republican. After their reconstitution collective bargaining set in on a national level, both for industry in general and for particular branches of it. As elsewhere in Europe, these agreements were either supplemented or superseded by plant agreements concluded by the works councils, which were outside the union structure.

One of the consequences of this procedure—again as elsewhere—was the existence of substantial differences in actual wages and working conditions between different plants in the same industry, especially between larger and smaller plants. In the 1960s the unions themselves increasingly took over plant- or enterprise-wide bargaining, which was given official recognition by state-owned concerns. This shift of the center of gravity of union action toward the plant was resisted by the confederations, which had aimed at establishing model agreements for all industries combined. This, however, proved to be of limited value. One new departure under this procedure concerned the works councils, which were now deprived of the right to conclude plant agreements, and they gradually withered away. Another—later embodied in a piece of legislation—concerning dismissals was essentially a renewal of a 1947 agreement, though with some improvements.

The return to some form of plant agreements to be concluded by the provincial union federations rather than works councils marked a move to more decentralized negotiations; in Italian parlance this was called "articulated bargaining." Thus two tendencies observed in other Western countries manifested themselves in Italy as well: highly centralized bargaining on general principles and increased emphasis on plant agreements. In Italy and France the first tendency went so far as to provide for all-industry agreements.

There are thus agreements concluded on a series of levels. At the top are interconfederal agreements involving confederations on both sides of the bargaining table. Such agreements concern issues of a general nature and usually cover entire sectors of the economy, such as industry, agriculture, or commerce. These agreements concern sliding wage scales and procedures to be followed in the case of substantial lay-offs. Sometimes such agreements, as is also the case in France, become the basis for legislation. On the next lower level are national agreements, often covering the same category of workers in several industries, e.g., "the national agreement for workers in mechanical industries which covers all iron and steel metal working, automobiles, household appliances, machine tools, and engineering works in general."[26] There are also a few regional agreements covering mostly small firms. Enterprise agreements are the lowest level. They often cover more than one establishment and implement or modify national agreements. They deal especially with issues deriving from technological change or with the work environment and the activities of unions in the plant. These are fairly new issues that were added to those more traditionally handled in enterprise contracts (such as wage supplements, piece-work rates, job evaluation, and bonuses).

There are also joint discussions of union and employers' confederations and the government on issues not directly related to industrial relations. Though not a normal form of collective bargaining, union proposals raised in these discussions (comparable to the West German "Concerted Action" discussed later) are sometimes backed-up by strikes and other forms of pressure.

In the 1970s group agreements developed dealing with huge industrial concerns such as Fiat or the state-owned Institute for Industrial Reconstruction. Their subject matter extended into new problem areas such as investment and employment policy. Thus issues formerly regarded as coming under managerial prerogative have become the subject of collective bargaining—a form of codetermination similar to one that developed in Sweden.[27]

On the employers' side of the bargaining table, Confindustria is the most important, followed by a confederation of small enterprises (CONFAPI) and a grouping of artisans. Since a sizeable part of the Italian economy is nationalized, there are also associations of publicly owned enterprises (INTERSIND and ADAP).

The amazingly rapid economic expansion of Italy conflicting sharply with an outdated, cumbersome public administrative apparatus led to tensions and conflicts that at times seemed to endanger the fabric of organized social and political life. Most directly affected in some ways was, of course, the industrial relations system as a whole, and collective bargaining in particular. One main factor was the rapid influx of unskilled workers, mostly from the south of Italy, into the industrial centers of the north. Another major element in the situation was the progressive rapprochement of the three main trade union confederations that culminated in talk of a complete merger—without so far decisive action in this direction. However, joint actions became possible during the wave of unrest in the fall of 1969, especially among the metal industry unions. This was accompanied by a reassertion of the unions of their traditional role: away from a limitation of their concerns to their own members and toward a representation of the working class as a whole.[28] One symptom of this trend and of the growing power of the unions was their role in negotiations with the government and employers' associations on issues of general interest, beyond the employment conditions of workers and white-collar employees.

The relatively peaceful evolution of collective bargaining was sharply interrupted by the unrest of 1969, following the semirevolutionary events in France in 1968. Wildcat strikes in various forms occurred, as well as the election of "workers' delegates" in the plants, who now took the place of the former works councils. Directly elected in the various departments of a plant, sometimes in cooperation with the unions, sometimes independently, by no means all union members, they acted often without any reference to national agreements, even though the unions frequently joined in the bargaining process. This role of the unions was reenforced by the legal enactment of the Workers' Charter, which began to operate in May 1970 and gave the unions status in the plant. Employers' resistance to union tendencies to reopen negotiations in the plant on issues already settled in the national agreement prevented full agreement, however. Moreover, the unions reserved to themselves the right to reopen negotiations during the lifetime of a contract while the employers were expected to observe its validity. A shift in emphasis to negotiations on working conditions ("humanizing work"), the implied union intervention in work organization and work rules, and the delegates' efforts to check on the observation of agreements added to the growing tensions between unions and employers.

Collective Bargaining under Full Employment

If, as we have seen, collective bargaining came into being essentially as a defensive device on the part of the workers, its function changed fundamentally when long-term full employment developed. Admittedly, the term full employment lends itself to a multitude of interpretations, ranging from the highly exacting one that Lord Beveridge proposed in his famous report to the increasingly elastic interpretations used by U.S. authorities. For the purposes of this study—and since it deals with Western Europe only—no intricate analysis is required. The leading industrial nations of Western Europe exhibited throughout a large part of the post–World War II period until the mid-1970s an excess of the demand for labor over its supply at prevailing wages and working conditions. This excess was only inadequately met by the millions of refugees streaming into the West and the millions of guest workers imported primarily from the countries bordering on the Mediterranean.

This state of affairs presented problems that the established institutions in the area of industrial relations found difficult, if not impossible, to solve. While the shift in employment to the service sector tended to weaken the unions—people in the service industries being notoriously difficult to organize—the supply-demand relationship on the labor market tremendously enhanced union power in general. Skilled workers in particular became a rare and valuable item, and employers were eager to attract and to keep them by wages and benefits at levels far exceeding those laid down in union contracts.

The gap between contract and effective earnings, always present in the European system of predominantly large-scale agreements, now became frequently so wide that unions lost track of the effective earnings of their members. Accompanying this development was a rapid growth in the participation of females in the labor force, with the result that many families had multiple incomes. The era of the mass consumption society had begun.

The most immediate problem created by long-term full employment was the incompatibility of that state of affairs with price and exchange rate stability—the latter because rates of inflation in different countries with full employment were unlikely to be identical and, in fact, diverged widely. This problem will be explored in chapter 13. Here it may be sufficient to point out that the traditional view of collective bargaining as a private matter between private organizations could be maintained under the new circumstances only with great difficulty and sometimes a high degree of pretense. Economic policy-making became the result of arrangements among corporate powers, primarily management, unions, farmers, consumers' groups, and the government. If not all of them sat at any given bargaining table, they were implicitly represented if not by any of the private groups, then by the government conscious of the various interest groups' impact on the outcome of the next elections. Governing was more and more openly the art of arranging compromises among various interest groups; they were increasingly difficult to achieve as the cohesion of many of the large interest groups weakened. Class consciousness lost its appeal with the decline of political and social discrimination against the workers and their increasing occupational differentiation. Skilled groups insisted upon maintaining or reestablishing their differential positions in the wage structure, and wage drift often helped them to succeed in this effort, in spite of ideologically inspired equalization policies pursued by some of the trade union confederations, as for example, the Swedish L.O., which represent manual workers. The maintenance of differentials in wages and working conditions was facilitated, as we have seen earlier, by the existence of works councils, more or less independent of the union, capable of concluding supplementary agreements that employers favored because these agreements could not be legally enforced and concessions made in them could be withdrawn at will.[29] Collective bargaining in the widest sense of the word thus became an instrument of defending group rather than class interests.

The greater part of the unionized workers and by way of the extension referred to earlier in this chapter their nonunionized associates became members of a new lower middle class, distinguished from the upper middle class by their life-styles rather than by real income differences. The higher education standards of large parts of the working class and the shift within the labor force toward higher skill workers, technicians, and semiprofessionals added to this blurring of class distinctions. Professional identification has largely taken place among the upper middle class of engineers, administrators, and other highly educated groups. The real proletariat in Western Europe consists largely of foreign guest workers. The lowest-paid jobs and the least attractive working conditions are their lot.

Rising living standards and high employment levels have produced a shift in values and objectives, especially among the upper strata of workers and even more of technicians and professional employees. This trend, expressed in some of the more recent collective agreements, aims at longer paid vacations, more opportunities for part-time work, here and there in what has come to be known as "flexi-time" (arrangements of working hours within reasonable limits according to the wishes of the employee), and shorter hours of work, partly to redistribute job opportunities among more people during a period of economic slowdown but also to meet the rising desire for a different distribution of time between work and leisure. Job enrichment ideas are beginning to penetrate into the conventional area of industrial relations. Unlike the United States, these and other new developments are not, or are only rarely, used by management in Western Europe to combat unionism.

The most important trend, however, has been the growing recognition—most forcefully resisted in Great Britain—that collective bargaining can no longer be regarded as a purely private affair involving only management and labor. The public, most often represented by the government and sometimes with uneven success by the trade union confederation, has become a partner to the negotiations that affect so strongly the entire social life of the community. Both labor and management still have much to learn to adapt to the new times and the new problems that they bring along.

Another set of conclusions that can be drawn from the experience presented in these pages relates to the relative weight assigned to collective bargaining and alternative, principally legislative, administrative or political methods of labor action. There is little doubt that the growth of labor's political influence, especially during the first phase of the postwar evolution, was the primary factor in the social environment shaping the strategy and structure of the labor movements.[30] The major exception was West Germany, which in the first postwar phase had its political and social life under strict control by the occupation forces. The domestic influence of labor in the three Western zones and West Berlin was mainly directed at growing resistance to Communist domination.

The era of collective bargaining as the main weapon in labor's arsenal began with the second phase of the postwar evolution. There was a growing national income to distribute and the situation on the labor market became more and more favorable to union action. At the same time the revival of capitalist institutions, though modified by sizeable nationalization measures but supported by powerful forces, especially in the United States, weakened labor's political influence. This process was enhanced by the fact that the Communist parties, even where they had substantial popular following, were pushed or withdrew voluntarily into a political ghetto.

If, as various indicators seem to forecast, the era of high-pressure economic expansion in Western Europe has ended, a change to greater political activity on the part of labor is likely to occur. The economic weapons may prove less effective if the labor market were to shift toward higher levels of unemployment than in the past. But these are long-term trends, and consequently we should not expect rapid changes in labor's strategy.

Next to the change in the character of collective bargaining the most significant development in industrial relations is likely to be the employment protection legislation developed in the 1970s and unlikely to undergo fundamental changes in the near future. The May 1968 near-rebellion in France and Italy's hot autumn of 1969 gave impetus to this trend, and it has since been extended into most of Western Europe's industrial nations, with the result that labor has now often become almost a part of fixed overhead costs. The legislation and other institutions that brought this about vary from country to country. In Britain a group of employment protection measures was part of the social contract concluded between the Labour government and the unions in 1973. In Germany, Belgium, and Holland the government can postpone mass dismissals and force management to consult with the unions, to give advance notice, and to provide for substantial severance pay. In France the government-appointed labor inspectors have the authority to prevent or at least delay massive lay-offs. The costs of retaining the workers is usually divided between the employer and funds provided by industry in general. While undoubtedly beneficial to the workers and the communities concerned, the system has tended to reduce labor mobility and to slow down the hiring of new entrants into the labor market. A case can probably be made that incentives are thereby provided to bring jobs to the workers rather than to locate new enterprises where other conditions, such as location, are favorable and then bring the workers there.

It should perhaps be added that the seniority principle in lay-offs and new hiring so widely used in the United States is of far lesser importance in Western Europe. For temporary business slowdowns, generalized shorter worker hours are frequently used as a first remedy, and in cases of permanent dismissals social considerations—family responsibilities, illness, e.g.—often count for as much or more than job seniority.

NOTES

1. Sidney and Beatrice Webb, *The History of Trade Unionism* (London: Longway, Green and Co., 1950), 72.

2. Allan Flanders, "Great Britain," in Adolf Sturmthal, ed., *Contemporary*

Collective Bargaining in Seven Countries (Ithaca, N.Y.: Cornell University Press, 1957).

3. *Ibid.*, 49.

4. Adolf Sturmthal, "Collective Bargaining in France," in Sturmthal, ed., *Contemporary Collective Bargaining*, 135.

5. Clark Kerr, "Collective Bargaining in Postwar Germany," in Sturmthal, ed., *Contemporary Collective Bargaining*, 171. The problem of extension of agreements also entered the consideration of the unions in desiring the constitution of strong employers' associations.

6. Flanders, "Great Britain," 18–19.

7. B. C. Roberts and Sheila Rothwell, "Recent Trends in Collective Bargaining in the United Kingdom," in *Collective Bargaining in Industrialized Market Economies* (Geneva: I.L.O., 1973), 354.

8. *Ibid.*, 356.

9. Michael Moran, *The Politics of Industrial Relations. The Origins, Life and Death of the 1971 Industrial Relations Act* (London: Macmillan, 1977). The law was repealed in 1974. The repeal reestablished the legal status created by the Trade Disputes Act of 1906, which gave unions legal immunity under civil law in the case of disputes. Collective agreements were not legally enforceable. The Employment Protection Act of 1975 contains provisions on the disclosure of information for collective bargaining purposes. Other parts of the act deal with union recognition. The closed shop is permitted if both parties agree to it.

10. "Some 95 percent of these strikes [i.e., of fairly short duration not normally involving very many people] were unofficial; that is they were in breach of the union rules and of the national agreed procedure." Roberts and Rothwell, "Recent Trends in Collective Bargaining in the United Kingdom," 371.

11. *The Economist* (May 11, 1979) wrote: "The British trade unions are not badly behaved school boys requiring only a stern usher with a big stick. They are an immensely powerful estate of the realm with quite sufficient power to savage, if not obliterate, Mrs. Thatcher's strength of purpose. . . . The unions must be reformed; they must be made subject not just to natural justice (the courts have already done much here) but to the laws of contract. But Mrs. Thatcher, if she keeps to her present stance, will ensure that this reform will be the subject not of consensus but of confrontation."

12. Yves Delamotte, "Recent Collective Bargaining Trends in France," in *Collective Bargaining in Industrialized Market Economies*.

13. *Ibid.*, 229.

14. Jean-Daniel Reynaud, *Les Syndicats en France* (Paris: Editions du Seuil, 1975), 1:150.

15. *Ibid.*, 197.

16. Kerr, "Collective Bargaining in Postwar Germany."

17. *Ibid.*, 202.

18. See ch. 10 herein.

19. A long way from Marxian concepts.

20. Kerr, "Collective Bargaining in Postwar Germany," 192.

21. See the extensive discussions in *Gewerkschaftliche Monatshefte*, 30 (Mar. 1979).

22. O.E.C.D., *Collective Bargaining and Government Policies in Ten O.E.C.D Countries* (Paris: O.E.C., 1979), 61.

23. Hans Reichel, "Recent Trends in Collective Bargaining in the Federal Republic of Germany," in *Collective Bargaining in Industrialized Market Economies,* 262. See the further discussion on German collective bargaining in ch. 13 herein.

24. In fact, during the recession of 1966–67 some of the advantages granted beyond the contract were withdrawn so that there was a negative wage drift in terms of effective, not contract, rates.

25. This phenomenon existed in Germany even in pre-Hitler days. Some individual workers were always granted rates above the contract rates which were regarded as a minimum wage acceptable even to relatively inefficient firms. Skilled workers, in particular, were proud not to have to work at contract rates—or ashamed when they had to do so. However, the spread between effective and contract rates widened appreciably during the periods of acute labor shortage from about the mid-1950s to the mid-1970s. As Arthur M. Ross has pointed out ["Prosperity and Labor Relations in Europe: The Case of West Germany," *Quarterly Journal of Economics,* LXXVI (Aug. 1962)], reliable statistical data on the wage drift are hard to come by. I know only of a study of the I.G. Metall in West Germany and one by the corresponding employers' association that contained quantitative data. Henry C. Wallich's book, *Mainsprings of the German Revival* (New Haven: Yale University Press, 1955), refers to wage drift, but contains no figures. See also Reichel, "Recent Trends in Collective Bargaining in Germany," 263.

26. This section owes a good deal to the article on Italy in *Collective Bargaining and Government Policies in Ten O.E.C.D. Countries.*

27. See ch. 11 herein.

28. Gino Giugni, "Recent Trends in Collective Bargaining in Italy," in *Collective Bargaining in Industrialized Market Economies,* 275. In fact, Italian unions have always claimed to represent the working class as a whole.

29. Hence, as we have seen, the efforts of at least some of the unions to obtain control of the councils. See the references in Ross, "Prosperity and Labor Relations in Europe," especially the quotations from Heinz Hartmann, *Authority and Organization in German Management* (Princeton: Princeton University Press, 1960).

30. Cf. my observations in "Industrialization and the Labor Movement—A Set of Research Hypotheses," in *Proceedings of the Second International Conference on Industrial Relations* (Tokyo: Japan Institute of Labor, 1967), 61–62. Although these hypotheses were presented in the context of discussions on developing countries, I believe they stand up quite well also for industrialized nations.

13

Incomes Policies

IT IS A CORRECT though trite observation that organized societies at all times have and had an incomes policy. Taxation, subsidies, and
tariffs have always tended to influence the income distribution, and even the
absence of any of these elements could be described as a policy in the sense
that the income distribution as arranged by the market is accepted as proper
or desirable or inevitable. This, however, is not the problem that presented
itself to the Western world since approximately the end of World War II or
more precisely since the end of postwar austerity and the emergence of a
deliberate policy of full employment.

The term incomes policy has in itself no precise meaning. Following
definitions frequently cited in the literature I shall use it to mean the establishment by the government of "specific criteria or guides for incomes and prices,
and the attempt to gain adherence to them through various forms of public
pressures."[1] Swedish policy may then barely fit into the definition, but, in
view of the international attention paid to it, it has nevertheless been included
in this study. However, this definition does not include the main element of
incomes policies, namely their purpose. While earlier incomes policies were
concerned with influencing the distribution of the national income among
different groups, however constituted, the post–World War II version had a
new purpose: to maintain, as far as possible, a stable price level or at least
one that did not rise substantially faster than that of other countries. The
second of these alternative objectives changed its character when the gold
standard (or the dollar standard) was abolished, and thus the price discipline
imposed by it no longer existed.[2]

As long as the quantity theory dominated economic thinking, no need
for an incomes policy in this new meaning of the term seemed to exist. Price
stability required merely a proper monetary and credit policy just as in recent
discussions Milton Friedman has advocated. It was only after the Keynesian
revolution that a new theoretical basis for a policy designed to influence
changes in money incomes was laid. While at the time of John Maynard
Keynes's presentation the need was for an increase in incomes to combat the

long-term depression of the 1930s, the post–World War II era was confronted with inflationary trends and saw the need for limiting increases in money incomes. The most recent years presented a third type of problem—stagflation, inflation combined with large amounts of idle resources.

The issue that has plagued governments and labor movements almost the entire period since the end of World War II was that of the apparent incompatibility of high employment levels, rising money wages, and price stability, all equally or almost equally desirable. Upon closer examination and with growing experience, other factors have been added to the list of desirable objectives that do not appear to fit into any one set of economic policies. Among them were stable exchange rates and greater social justice, especially in income distribution. Free collective bargaining has also frequently appeared in this conundrum of aims for social and economic policies. How to combine these objectives in one set of consistent policies proved to be one of the fundamental problems of post–World War II economics. Later the even more intractable problem of stagflation was added to this list.

With varying intensity these problems have appeared in practically all countries of Western and Central Europe at one time or another and in some, almost constantly. Some of the difficulties were already foreseen in the pathbreaking study on full employment which Lord Beveridge published during World War II. He "solved" the problem by eliminating free collective bargaining from the "magic triangle" and replacing it by arbitration of wage claims. The explanation for the need for arbitration was simply that when the supply of labor barely matched or was inferior to the demand at prevailing wages, the latter would tend to move upward and increasing wage costs exceeding productivity gains would in turn lead to increased prices. Later the Phillips curve appeared; it operated with only two variables: the rate of unemployment and the rate of price inflation. This relationship, astounding in its simplicity, did not pretend to be a theory or to be based on a theory, but was simply presented as an empirically established fact compatible with almost any theory.[3] Hence this relationship was also compatible with any set of policies that would affect unemployment. This, however, turns the problem over to politicians. Which rate of unemployment combined with which rate of inflation is politically most acceptable? Obviously the answer will depend on a vast array of circumstantial factors varying not only from country to country but also from one period to another. Thus controls sharply enforced were more readily acceptable as an alternative to high unemployment in the period of extreme scarcity following the end of World War II. Yet even then they were in dispute.

An early demonstration of the variety of objectives that could be assigned to incomes policies emerged in the discussion following the British government's issuance of a White Paper on "Personal Incomes, Costs, and Prices" in February 1948. This presentation made the volume of money incomes dependent on the volume of production, with the single exception that a greater increase of wages could be justified in behalf of an industry suffering from lack of manpower. The Trade Union Congress (T.U.C.), while claiming to accept the principles of the White Paper, added further exceptions: recognition of free collective bargaining, increased wages where output (presumably per hour) increased, special treatment of workers whose wages were "below a reasonable standard of subsistence," and—finally—maintenance of "those wage differentials which are an essential element in the wages structure of many important industries and are required to sustain those standards of craftsmanship, training and experience that contribute directly to industrial efficiency and higher productivity."[4] Clearly, some of these conditions went far beyond the terms of the White Paper.

If considerations of the balance of payments are introduced, not only does the rate of inflation but also the price level and its stability become objectives of economic policy unless another possible objective, currency stability, is abandoned. Since most of the Western European countries are heavily dependent on foreign trade, balance of payments considerations are vital. Currency fluctuations under these circumstances are likely to affect prices and to be affected by price changes. Another set of incompatibilities thus arises: price stability and exchange equilibrium may not be achieved and maintained at the same time.

Given this variety of policies and objectives, we shall limit our discussion to a few particularly significant cases, leaving a more complete and detailed presentation to the available literature.

Great Britain

The United Kingdom is an impressive case of being in perpetual danger of an imbalance in external payments. The terms of trade have moved sharply against the country; it had lost its income from its overseas investments since it had been forced by the war exigencies to sell them. Thus while its exports did grow after the war, they did not provide an income sufficient to cover the cost of imports whenever the economy started an expansionist boom. That in turn induced the government to raise interest rates, restrict credits in various ways, raise taxes, and reduce government expenditures. The result was a check on investment and consumption, which resulted in a decrease of output and an increase in unemployment. The well-known "stop and go" cycle of the British economy had its origin in this sequence of events.[5]

The British example marks in many ways one extreme of a gamut of situations in Western Europe that create the need for incomes policies. In the United Kingdom the prime factor calling for restrictive measures was a series of balance of payments crises. As was pointed out earlier, of all Western countries the United Kingdom was the one with the lowest growth rate of gross national product (G.N.P.) during almost all of the post–World War II period. It was no preconceived notion, but "successive acts of expediency 'that led governments of different political persuasion to adopt various forms of incomes policy.' "[6] In 1948 the Labour government introduced a two-year freeze in wages, salaries, and dividends and declared that "it is not desirable for the government to interfere directly with the income of individuals otherwise than by taxation. To go further would mean that the Government would be forced itself to assess and regulate all personal incomes according to some scale which would have to be determined. This would be an incursion by the Government into what has hitherto been regarded as a field of free contract between individuals and organisations."[7]

Sir Stafford Cripps, then chancellor of the exchequer and close to the left wing of the party, helped to make this policy acceptable to the "radical" groups in Parliament, the unions, and the country. But even in the desperate situation of the United Kingdom—most conducive to a policy of restraint— union acceptance from the beginning was vaguely defined. By June 1950 union rebellion had grown to the point that the government was forced to abandon the policy of restraint.

With the fall of the Labour government of 1951, whatever modest degree of willingness remained on the part of the unions to cooperate with governmental restraint policies disappeared altogether. Neither the Conservative government in 1956 nor that of 1961 was successful in obtaining union cooperation.

When Labour returned to power in 1964 under Harold Wilson a new era of incomes policies started, primarily again under the impact of balance of payments crises. One underlying cause was apparently clearly seen by the government: the slow growth of productivity in British industry that made exports costly and difficult and imports cheap and attractive combined with the painful adjustments of the United Kingdom to the status of a middle-sized power. Wilson in his memoirs points out how the problem of lagging productivity growth was misunderstood by the civil servants: "In a Board of Trade document . . . I was actually told that production in one of the key sectors had risen by ten percent in ten years."[8] A reflection of this low rate of productivity growth was the equally low rate of growth of G.N.P. to which reference was made in an earlier chapter.

It appeared that only a Labour government could induce the unions to accept wage restraints—a fond illusion as events were to show. Still union refusal to cooperate with any body that the Conservative governments appointed to discuss settlements with the parties concerned became a main factor in the eventual downfall of the Conservatives while the possibility that a Labour government could obtain the cooperation of the T.U.C. where the Conservatives had failed helped to bring Labour back to power in 1964. Indeed, unions and employers promised "to cooperate with the Government in endeavoring . . . to give effective shape to the machinery that the Government intends to establish." At the end of 1964, in any case, a statement of Intent on Productivity, Prices, and Incomes was signed by the government, the unions, and the employers. A National Board of Prices and Incomes was created to which the government could refer proposed settlements for review; at the same time a "general guideline for wage increases of 3 to 3.5 percent, and for price increases was issued."[9]

The main differences from the system the Conservatives had attempted to put into service were that the new departure dealt with prices as well as with wages and that it was set up by a Labour government. Thus the early incomes policy that Wilson and his Chancellor of the Exchequer James Callaghan pursued was based on the idea of willing union support.[10] The T.U.C., eager to avoid government controls, undertook to review wage demands of its affiliates.[11]

The main campaign of the government was directed against some of the time-honored union rules that stand in the way of raising productivity. As Wilson put it in a speech to the Amalgamated Engineering Union in what he called "an impassioned appeal for modernization of trade practices": "The sooner your rule book is consigned to the industrial museum, the more quickly the union will be geared to the challenge facing industry and the nation."[12]

The pillar of the government's policy in the wage question—the cooperation of the T.U.C.—proved time and again too weak, demonstrating what was known to everyone concerned with British industrial relations, namely that the T.U.C. did not control the actions on wages and conditions of the affiliated unions just as the latter failed to control the shop stewards. The seamen's strike of 1966 was but one example of this situation. Still, a statutory freeze and later severe restraint on wages and prices (July 1966 to June 1967) did in fact lead to a slowdown in the rise of earnings and prices.[13] The next stage, one of moderation, produced much more rapid wage increases and ended in a currency devaluation.[14]

It would lead us too far astray to follow all of the gyrations of British incomes policies during the Wilson era up to 1970. Only one or two main points deserve to be made. The first is a reference in Wilson's memoirs[15] claiming that during his visit in Washington in the summer of 1966 President Lyndon B. Johnson stated, "What really amazed him was that we [the British] had secured parliamentary approval and union 'acquiescence' for an incomes policy that no democratic country had introduced even in wartime." The Dutch, who were far more enduring and successful in their policies, must have been amused by this example of combined Anglo-Saxon "insularity" and ignorance—unless this was simply an expression of diplomatic nicety.

The second point refers to the issue of union discipline. Attempts at maintaining an incomes policy were abandoned at the end of 1969, partly at least in view of the approaching general elections. Instead, the Labour government turned its attention to another disturbing phenomemon in the industrial relations area, the rising number of wildcat strikes that not infrequently permitted a small group of workers to paralyze important industries. The government was eager to leave control of such matters to the T.U.C. and to intervene only if the T.U.C. failed in its efforts to maintain union discipline. The T.U.C., while willing to show its readiness to cooperate with the Labour government, did not feel that it had the power to use "every penalty in the rule book to enforce compliance with a T.U.C. call for a return to work."[16]

Under extreme pressure by the government the T.U.C. finally accepted an obligation to intervene in conflicts between unions and in wildcat strikes. Whether this understanding was effective or not is difficult to decide. Even Wilson, who regarded this commitment as one of his greatest achievements, was frank to admit that "strikes did not diminish in number, scale or duration, following the agreement of June 1969, any more than in an increasingly militant situation abroad, where legal restraints operate."[17] It is, of course, impossible to establish what the situation would have been in the absence of the T.U.C. agreement. In any case, the Conservative government that came to power in June 1970 refused to rely on T.U.C. intervention.

In addition to securing T.U.C. cooperation, the Labour government reintroduced the milder provisions of the Prices and Incomes Act of 1966—prior notification to the government of intended price or wage increases. The right of the government to impose compulsory conciliation in unofficial strikes and to have members of a union threatening to go on strike vote in a secret ballot were reforms that the Labour government intended to introduce. However, these were defeated by the combined opposition of the unions and of a sizeable group within the Labour party.[18]

The Conservative government made an attempt to regulate the whole field by the 1971 Industrial Relations Act, the first major effort to transform the British voluntary system into a legally regulated one. To a large extent this was modeled after the U.S. example. The great majority of the unions responded by boycotting the act and the institutions set up under it. As a result, sharp conflicts developed between the government and the unions. In particular, the unions objected to the registration provisions of the act, which tended to limit and make conditional rights that the unions regarded as well established. These included especially what the British call the closed shop and exemption from legal liability for inducing breach of contract in the case of industrial action.[19] The failure of the act contributed a good deal to the downfall of the Conservative government and the return of Labour to office in 1974. The expectation that Labour could deal more easily and effectively with the unions contributed to its electoral success. Upon taking office the government immediately sought an agreement with the T.U.C. on pay policy and a method of cooperative enforcement by all three partners: government, T.U.C., and C.B.I. (Confederation of British Industry). The symbol of the new style was the repeal of the Industrial Relations Act, which the Conservatives had passed and which in the view of labor embodied the ideas presented by industry spokesmen before the Donovan Commission.[20]

However, the expectation that the minority Labour government under Callaghan could get along more easily with the trade unions was unfounded. A "social contract" for two years was concluded: the T.U.C. undertook to monitor wage demands so as to keep them to 5 percent annually in exchange for government policies favorable to the unions, e.g., employment protection and support for closed shops. However, the contract expired and no further agreement with the unions was possible for 1977–78. The government, in order to limit wage increases to about 10 percent for the entire economy, threatened sanctions against employers—a forerunner of Alfred Kahn's "voluntarism" in the United States. Thus no public works orders were to be issued to firms violating the rule. No subsidies that had been used under the title of Temporary Employment Subsidy for textiles, clothing, and shoe industries—against the protest of the European Economic Commission—were to be given to enterprises violating the rules.

The renewal of the contract in early 1979 was not taken seriously by anyone. Pay raises ran about 15 percent per annum, and conspicuous strikes (including a hospital strike) shook confidence in the government's ability to come to reasonable terms with the unions. Clearly, the new agreement served primarily to support the election propaganda of Labour—to no avail as the outcome of the general elections of May 1979 demonstrated. A whole series of variations in policy details and institutions took place to adjust to economic and political developments and to take into account the tendency of the effectiveness of all methods of wage and price restraints to wither away after an early and rather brief period of relative success. An important lesson apparently manifested itself: even given a fair degree of initial union cooperation, incomes policies in the United Kingdom lost rather rapidly whatever effectiveness they may have had at birth.

Other inferences have also been drawn by some authors from the British experience. A crucial fact is the British system of collective bargaining: industry-wide agreements with supplementary understandings at the enterprise or plant-level and the shop floor. Within limits, this system eliminates employers' fears of being undercut by competitors paying wages below the rates set in the nationwide agreement. However, it does not set an upper limit for wage demands outside the national framework. While incomes policies agreed to by union leaders may reduce their aggressiveness, shop stewards as a rule do not feel bound by commitments made at national levels, and effective rates negotiated in the shop may be set far above the limits determined by governmental policy or national agreements. This applies particularly to joint shop steward committees, when members belong to a variety of unions and thus do not feel responsible for collective actions to any particular union. Wage drift may be especially significant in periods of severe labor shortages when employers are frequently willing to cooperate with the shop stewards in circumventing existing rules and contracts or even take the initiative in doing so. But even in the absence of acute labor shortages employers often put up little resistance to wage demands exceeding the rate of increase of productivity. They were confident "that they will be able to cover that rise by raising prices without loss of business. That belief has been reinforced by the experience of twenty years. It is also strengthened by the expectation that governments pledged to full employment will not let capacity lie idle for lack of monetary demand sufficient to employ it at the current level of costs."[21] While resistance to a wage claim and the consequent conflict may be costly, giving in will be justified in due course by competitors doing the same.[22] This leads to the perhaps surprising conclusion that for an incomes policy to succeed for more than the short term, the authority of national union leaders has to be strengthened, especially with regard to the shop stewards, but often also with regard to the affiliated unions.[23]

While the British case may be regarded as going fairly far in the application of incomes policies, other countries have not been less inventive in their approaches.

Netherlands

Physical destruction—estimated in Holland at about half the prewar productive capacity—played a significant role in the Dutch government's decision at the end of the war not to leave real income distribution to the forces of the market. Moreover, the government expected that within a few years a worldwide depression would occur and that in a country as dependent on foreign trade as Holland a rapid rise of prices had to be avoided. Enemy occupation had developed a sense of national solidarity that enabled the government to count upon the willing cooperation of all elements of the population. To a large extent this fact explains the longevity of the success of Holland's incomes policy, in spite of the ideological and religious divisions of the population, which are reflected in the multiplicity of unions and employers' associations.

Two main institutions were set up at the end of the war: the Labor Foundation, a joint board of employers and trade unions to examine collective agreements, and a Board of Government Mediators, which was to determine whether these agreements were consistent with the national interest. Contrary to their designations, the mediators could approve or reject agreements even if they were approved by the foundation, and their decisions were enforceable in the courts. The objectives of these institutions were to resist inflationary pressures and to compress the wage structure. The first was to be achieved by restraining wage increases; the second was to be attained by dividing all workers into three skill classes. The unskilled were to be paid a "social minimum"; the semiskilled wage was 10 percent higher; the wages of skilled workers were increased by another 10 percent. A nationwide job evaluation scheme was to operate and to permit some deviations from the rigid scheme set out at first.[24]

The three main union confederations cooperated; these were the Netherlands Federation of Trade Unions (N.V.V.), which was Socialist and comprised about 36 percent of organized workers, the Protestant Federation of Labor (C.N.V.), which enrolled about 16 percent of organized workers, and the Catholic Workers' Movement (K.A.B.), which comprised about 30 percent of organized workers. The employers associations also participated.

In 1950 a third organ was added, a Social and Economic Council of forty-five members, one-third nominated by each of the three components (unions, employers, and government). The advice of the council was to be sought by the government in all important economic and social matters. Even if only advisory, the council had great authority that the government could not lightly disregard.

Under this highly centralized system by 1962 collective agreements covered some 70 percent of the privately employed workers, as compared to 15 percent in prewar days.[25] Part—but only a part—of the explanation for this expansion of the validity of collective agreements was the government's authority and eagerness to extend the terms of any agreement approved by the Board of Government Mediators[26] to all employers and employees of the particular industry.

With the creation of the Social and Economic Council (whose functions overlapped those of the foundation), the latter declined in importance but did not cease to exist. The lack of clearly demarcated functions of the three institutions had certain political advantages as far as open responsibility for unpopular decisions was concerned, advantages that, apparently, no one wanted to abandon.[27]

A rather influential role in the operation of this approach to incomes policy was played by the macroeconomic forecasting models, which served as a guide for examining the results of various possible policies. Annual forecasts were prepared by, among others, Jan Tinbergen, the world-renowned economist, a member of the Labour party. One of the difficulties in using these models as guides for wage policy was that wages appeared as both dependent and independent variables, i.e., wage changes determined the rest of the model while the model was supposed to determine what increases in the global wage mass were compatible with the remainder of the model, given the objective of price stability.

With many variations and adaptations, this system worked quite well until the late 1950s. One of the factors, but by no means the only one, that led to the downfall of the system was the attraction that neighboring West

Germany, with its far higher wage level, exerted upon workers in the border area. In order to retain workers, Dutch enterprises had to pay "black wages"—higher than those permitted—and this violation of the rules spread beyond the border areas by various devices that were difficult to control. Labor contractors "entered the scene and recruited workers for jobs in Germany and Belgium."[28] Although the discrepancy between "legal" and "black" wages was often rather insignificant, it did reach at times 10 percent.

Upon the advice of the Social and Economic Council, the failing control system was replaced in 1963 by one providing greater freedom and making the Foundation of Labor rather than the mediators the main controlling body. While the government retained reserve powers to disallow collective agreements and price increases that it regarded as incompatible with the public interest, the interest groups were given greater freedom than before. But the boom of the countries of the European Economic Community led to extremely tight labor markets in 1964 and to what has been called a "wage explosion," pioneered by a ship-building firm. The union leaders found themselves confronted by a threat of a membership rebellion. The pressure from below paralyzed the Foundation of Labor; this, together with a change of government that brought the Labour party back into the government coalition, opened the door for substantial increases of wages. No serious balance of payments problems threatened until 1966 when the Board of Government Mediators, in the presence of a refusal of the Foundation of Labor to accept the responsibility, was called upon again to enforce both the limits on wage increases set by the government and the prior notification of intended price increases. Wages kept rising faster than productivity, and while the institutional framework of wage and price controls remained in existence it had ceased to function. The slow down in the wage escalation in 1967–68 was the result of a mild recession rather than of a return to effective wage regulation.[29] This was demonstrated by the failure of a new attempt on the part of the government, with the consensus of the three trade union confederations, to set a ceiling on wage increases for 1970. This may have been the result not only of a new tightening of the labor market but also of a strategic mistake on the part of the government. It introduced a Wages Act that would have given it powers to intervene even in individual agreements. While this law was adopted, its enforcement against the resistance of the most powerful trade union confederations proved impossible. Social unrest followed and even some partial concessions of the government proved of limited value in reestablishing cooperation among the three partners on which the Dutch incomes policy had rested.

What this record tends to show is, first, that even an elastic incomes policy, based upon intimate cooperation among the main social groupings can hardly be maintained indefinitely; second, in the long run market forces will tend to assert themselves against laws and regulations; and third, in any especially small country the relevant demand and supply curves may have to take into consideration factors outside the country itself. By way of the "iron law of comparisons," wage advantages obtained in one sector tend to influence wage behavior in others. Finally—but perhaps this should be much higher in this list—trade unions cannot indefinitely transform themselves into engines of restraint without losing the support and confidence of their members.

What has remained of the bold Dutch experiment in incomes policies is an annual meeting of unions, employers, and government to discuss a central wage accord. Usually no agreement emerges. The negotiations are then carried on sector by sector and in some cases separately by large companies and their union counterparts. Wage freezes have been used, for example, at the end of 1975 when all negotiations failed and again in 1976. Wage indexation has been retained as a result of strikes in 1977, and fringe benefits have acquired a higher standing in the list of union demands. In this respect unions have not been too successful. In 1979 a proposal for work-sharing by a reduction of the work week to thirty-five hours, similar to a West German union demand in the metal industry, failed, partly because it aroused only modest enthusiasm among union members, partly because of friction among the union federations, and finally because of widespread fear that it would impair Dutch competitiveness on the world markets. Attempts to reestablish the annual three-party discussions on the state of the economy in order to determine how much allowance could be made for wage increases have failed over the issue of the duration of the wage contracts. Employers want longer wage contracts; the unions do not wish to go much beyond a year.[30]

West Germany

An entirely different approach from the Dutch system was chosen in West Germany. The rapid expansion of its economy made possible substantial increases in incomes of all kinds and in fringe benefits for employees and other groups of the population. For a long time the government, guided by its laissez-faire philosophy, refrained from intervening in the collective bargaining process beyond expressing its views on the economic situation. Similarly an annual report submitted to the government and the public since 1963 by a council of economic experts contains no explicit recommendations (as the law that set up the council stipulated).

Underlying this rather passive attitude of the government in a country that traditionally had relied on government action on a wide range of social and economic problems was one major startling fact: "labor's muted and unaggressive policy."[31] This was facilitated by a number of factors: labor's failure to stem the rising tide of Hitlerism had greatly weakened the self-confidence of the workers; recovery had been surprisingly fast and made possible wage increases that, after the years of deprivation during the Great Depression and then during and right after the war, satisfied the immediate demands of the workers. Concern for job security and fear of inflation exerted a powerful restraining influence on labor.

Significant inflationary pressures on the labor market did not manifest themselves until the influx of refugees and foreign workers had ceased or been reduced to a trickle, and unemployment had been virtually eliminated. This was roughly the case at the beginning of the 1960s. Tightness on the labor market coincided with a slowing down of the previously very high rate of productivity increases. This change may have been partly the result of the need to employ less skilled workers, such as foreign workers or women.[32]

The first attempt at some kind of an incomes policy designed to restrain wage increases occurred in January 1960, when at the request of Chancellor Konrad Adenauer the president of the central bank in a memorandum proposed that wage increases in 1961 be limited to 4 percent. This rather primitive effort failed miserably: earnings rose by 9 percent and the predicted growth of productivity upon which the 4 percent figure was based proved to be a gross underestimate.

Whether the organization of a Council of Economic Experts in 1963, to which reference was made earlier, should be included among the methods of restraining wages is unclear. The council was not supposed to make policy recommendations, but it was perhaps unavoidable that council reports made, either openly or implicitly, policy recommendations extending into the wage and price area. This became more systematic in 1966 when the new minister of economic affairs, Professor Karl Schiller, then a member of the Social Democratic party, organized what came to be known as Concerted Action. This was based upon a law enacted that year "requiring the government to formulate and interpret guidelines for maintaining or restoring economic stability through what was termed 'concerted action' by the regional authorities, the trade unions, and the employers association."[33] The purpose of these meetings, which were held irregularly, was described by the minister as "not to negotiate specific prices and wages; it is to promote understanding, and especially the realisation that there is a link between the reasonable interests of individual groups and economic necessities."[34] Concerted action worked quite well, even though it took several years before the two main participants—employers' and employee associations—agreed on a joint procedure to promote stability. Just prior to this the customary quiet in West German industrial relations had been badly shaken by a number of wildcat strikes and other expressions of unrest that in the wake of the Paris events of 1968 swept through large parts of the continent.

German workers were accustomed to expect a steadily rising income, and the deflationary developments of 1967–68 came as a shock to most workers. Moreover, the factors that explained the cautious behavior of the unions and their members mattered less and less as new age groups joined the labor force without a vivid recollection of the great defeats of labor in the 1930s and the misery of the war and the early postwar years.

Both employers and unions agreed that collaboration among all the partners in the concerted action was required to bring about stability. In June 1971 the central employers' associations and the union confederation agreed to set up a standing committee to examine price and cost trends to eliminate disputes about facts and numbers. But even though the authority of the German Trade Union Confederation (D.G.B.) had been very great at the time of its foundation, it had steadily and visibly declined as its affiliate obtained greater autonomy. Moreover, tight labor markets had greatly undermined employer discipline.

Nevertheless, the rate of inflation in West Germany remained one of the lowest among the industrial nations of the world.[35] Concerted action operated quite successfully until the central employers' association (B.D.I.) decided to contest the constitutional validity of the new codetermination law of 1976 before the Federal Constitutional Court, claiming that it violated the protection of property rights guaranteed in the constitution.[36] Although this attack ended in a defeat for the employers when the court ruled against them in early 1979, relations between what the Germans call the social partners remained strained, and Concerted Action has officially ceased to function. A further deterioration of the relationship occurred as a result of a decision of some of the employers in the metal industry to respond to a union-called partial strike by a lock-out. Yet, as long as a government led by the S.P.D. under Helmut Schmidt remains in office, the unions have little interest in spoiling the otherwise peaceful atmosphere of German industrial relations.

Austria

Both Switzerland and Austria went further than the Germans in maintaining price and wage discipline. The Austrian case is the more remarkable as soon after the end of the war unionization covered some two-thirds of the labor force, and 85 percent of the employees in private industry work for members of the Federation of Austrian Industry.[37] Beyond this, all of the important economic interest groups are organized in official representative bodies called chambers: Chamber of Labor, Chamber of Agriculture, Chamber of Industry. There are close connections among the respective chambers and the unions, employers' associations, and other interest groups. In 1947 the three chambers and the Trade Union Federation formed an "Economic Commission," which sponsored a series of price and wage agreements to which government and Parliament gave the power of law.

Compared with the domestic political tensions that existed in pre-Hitler Austria and that culminated in the civil war of February 1934, the era of cooperation that followed the end of World War II offers a sharp, indeed almost unbelievable, contrast. Some of the causes explaining this turnabout coincide with those mentioned in the case of West Germany: lack of self-confidence among the unionized workers and the recognition of the need for unity among the formerly competitive and ideologically divided trade unions. However, there were also factors special to Austria, among them the fact that the leaders of the bitterly hostile factions involved in the bloodshed of 1934 met each other as fellow-victims in the Nazi concentration camps after 1938, and again as members of the same government after 1945 and jointly opposed the threat from the East.[38]

The importance of the organized interest groups was enhanced by the large proportion of nationalized industries that the Economic Commission could directly influence and by the extreme centralization of the organized interest groups. Thus the unions control all forms of workers' representation from the works councils up and the Trade Union Confederation keeps a tight reign on its affiliates.[39] Given the high degree of unionization—some two-thirds of the dependently employed are now union members—this makes for strict discipline on labor's side. Still, nationwide collective agreements combined with full employment produce considerable wage drift, mainly by way of agreements between works councils and plant managements. Strikes are highly infrequent, unemployment and inflation very low, and living standards, when considering the extensive fringe benefits,[40] very high, especially when compared with the miserable economic situation during the interwar years. Selective price controls, mostly on staple foodstuffs, have helped somewhat in keeping inflation rates very low.

In 1957 the Economic Commission gave way to a "Joint Commission," a form of Concerted Action, whose decisions have to be unanimous. Its three components are labor, employers, and the government. Two subcommittees were set up—one to deal with prices, the other with wages. Applications for wage negotiations pass from the union concerned through the trade union confederation to the wages subcommittee; a good deal of preparatory checking is done by the union confederation before the matter reaches the subcommittee. The Joint Commission cannot prevent a wage agreement it does not believe to be in the public interest, but it can postpone it. Price increases, however, if not approved, can under the circumstances detailed in laws enacted in 1962 and 1971 be made subject to sanctions. On the wages side, wage drift could not be entirely avoided; its importance first gradually diminished but then increased again, though not in all industries.[41] Efforts of the trade unions to raise the lowest earnings more than the higher ones have had some success.

A third subcommittee of the Joint Commission was set up at the end of 1963, an "Economic and Social Advisory Board," which provided a form of workers' codetermination above the plant level. In practice the government most often carries out the board's recommendations, which are usually a compromise unanimously adopted by the board and thus are an agreed policy of the different interest groups represented on the Joint Commission.[42]

France

A very different approach was used in France. In the first postwar years all emphasis was on restraining wages. This policy met with the approval and support of the Communists then represented in Charles de Gaulle's government. Strict wage controls were part of a series of emergency measures designed to deal with the inevitable and extreme scarcity caused by war and enemy occupation. Incomes policies designed to deal with the problems caused by full employment or even labor shortages were a product of later policy-making and had to be fitted into the French framework of "indicative planning." This requires a few brief preparatory remarks.

Indicative planning, as distinguished from the conventional enforced "dirigisme" of the 1930s, was introduced into France gradually after World War II. It relies mainly on using the market mechanism to obtain the desired results rather than on direct controls or price fixing. It is, therefore, a rather liberal method of public intervention in the market. It offers incentives rather than coercion to achieve its ends and searches for consistency among both objectives and methods employed to attain them. In particular it aims at prior coordination among the policy measures used.

Incomes policies were introduced into the plan during the preparation of the Fifth Plan (1966–70). Prior to this, after 1950, when collective bargaining on wages was resumed, the government had relied primarily, but sporadically, on price controls as an indirect way of controlling wages.[43] Beginning with the Fifth Plan the government introduced a system combining price freedom with *contrats de programme*. This followed a period of price freezes that had started in October 1963.

Contrats de programme are contracts concluded between the government and enterprises, based upon a decree of May 1966. These arrangements provide guidelines by sectors for price increases and for the distribution of productivity gains among wages, dividends, and investment and research expenditures. Industries have freedom to determine prices if they agree to a review by governmental agencies, including the newly established "Study center of income and costs." Industries that did not accept such contracts remained subject to the controls established in 1963. Most industries accepted contracts, and even the wage explosion of 1968[44] did not lead to a change of the principle of the contract policy, though in the public sector price restraint became a significant factor. Nevertheless, a devaluation of the franc became necessary in 1969, followed by a short period of price freezes and then a return to the contracts.

A counterpart in those nationalized industries where the remaining private sector, if any, was insignificant was progress-contracts; these began with the electricity industry (E.D.F.) in December 1969. The latter set wages for two years in relation to productivity increases in the enterprise and to the growth of the national income; the Socialist-leaning C.F.D.T. (Confédération Democratique du Travail) signed the contract, the Confédération Generale du Travail (C.G.T.) refused to do so. The example of the E.D.F. was followed by other nationalized enterprises, in some cases, e.g., the coal mines, with important variations. While the more refined clauses of the E.D.F. did not last very long, the simple cost-of-living indexation of the coal mines remained—with the approval of the Communist-led C.G.T., which had opposed the other formulae. The victory of the C.G.T. was so complete that the E.D.F. contract when renewed in 1972 was signed by the C.G.T. while the C.F.D.T. refused to do so.

Since the law does not provide for legally enforceable contracts for this group of nationalized industries—those with no or an insignificant private sector—all these contracts have not only no legal validity but are also in direct violation of the law and thus not really collective agreements in the French meaning of the term.[45] They come under the heading of incomes policy primarily because they tended to increase low incomes by a larger percentage than high incomes and to limit aggregate wage increments.

Progressive inflation weakened the entire contract program both for prices and wages. Strikes on the railroads in 1973 and at E.D.F. early 1974 bore witness to these difficulties.[46]

Sweden

Once again we are confronted by an entirely different approach to incomes policy, and again it becomes comprehensible only in the light of the particular circumstances of the country: the existence of highly centralized organizations on both sides of the bargaining table and an exceptionally high degree of organization and of discipline within the organizations. Also on both sides there was a common desire—keeping the government out of industrial relations. Moreover, most of the unions, being closely connected with the Social Democratic party, were inclined to follow policies that would support the party, especially since it controlled the government most of the time.

The first stage was a voluntary freeze in 1949–50 to meet a balance of payments crisis. The L.O. (trade union confederation) accepted it, but soon discovered that, owing to the wage drift resulting from the frequency of piece rates, the freeze had only limited effects. A currency devaluation proved necessary.

The L.O., guided by two distinguished economists, Rudolf Meidner and

Gösta Rehn, worked out a labor market policy designed to avoid premature bottlenecks that might develop in certain types of labor long before full employment had been attained. In this way they hoped to avoid premature restrictions on demand.[47] This has since become one of the cornerstones of Swedish incomes policy, together with a centralized system of wage bargaining by the main employer and employee confederations. The latter system may be described as a "privately operated incomes policy,"[48] but we would prefer to label it an element of such a policy since manpower policy is also an indispensable part.[49] Moreover, while normally in Sweden the framework for wage movements in collective agreements and other forms of wage settlements is established by national negotiations between employer and employee organizations, the government has occasionally stated what it regarded as the proper average wage development.

The government's contribution to economic stability has in the main been limited to monetary and fiscal measures plus its role in the implementation of labor market policies designed to improve the mobility and adaptability of labor to economic change. In addition, the Swedish government has created a tax-free investment reserve system, which allows companies to set aside, free of taxes, some of their profits in boom periods. These reserves can then be used for capital investment during recessions.

The total wage increment available is set in top level national bargains; internal negotiations then follow about the distribution of this aggregate. These are sometimes quite difficult, as the top leadership of the L.O. wishes to compress the wage structure to favor the low-paid groups (the so-called solidaristic wage policy) while wage drift tends to widen the gap.

This policy has remained a bone of contention between L.O., an organization primarily of manual workers, and other union confederations, especially S.A.C.O., which represents academically trained managerial and other high-level employees, and, to some extent, T.C.O., the white-collar union confederation. Less in dispute has been L.O.'s pressure for equality of earnings between men and women.

A classic example of interunion rivalry, centering on the issue of equality, occurred in 1966 when civil servants were given full rights to bargain and to strike. In the spring of that year L.O. and S.A.F. (the employers' association) concluded an agreement for a three-year period providing a 12 percent increase in wages and fringe benefits. Shortly afterward white-collar workers and civil servants, excluding teachers, obtained a three-year contract with 18 to 20 percent increases. In the fall of the same year S.A.C.O. managed to get a 35 percent increase over three years, mainly because teachers' salaries had remained unchanged for several years. The timing of the agreements of the various groups became a major issue. It was then that the reasoning of the Norwegian Aukrust report[50] with appropriate adjustments for Sweden entered the consideration involved in collective bargaining.

Hidden behind these arguments were disputes over the possibilities, limits, and desirability of the solidaristic wages policy of L.O. and the then Social Democratic government. Opponents of this—mainly ideologically motivated—policy have claimed that it has an innate inflationary tendency.[51] And T. L. Johnson quoted an L.O. economist: "It is no exaggeration to state that the task of establishing just and reasonable relative wages between different groups is still in the main unresolved."[52]

Some of these stresses and strains and also rank-and-file dissatisfaction with the high degree of centralization of collective negotiations found their expression in the series of strikes that shattered industrial peace at the end of the 1960s and early 1970s. These ranged from miners in the state-owned mines in the north to the railroads, Saab, Volvo, Goodyear, Electrolux, SAS, schools, universities, and various services; they induced the government to take stern measures, quite at variance with the tradition of keeping the state out of industrial relations.

One of the puzzles confronting the confederations on both sides and governmental policy-makers was the coexistence of domestic inflation with a satisfactory international performance of the Swedish economy. The same phenomenon had been observed earlier in Norway and analyzed by Odd Aukrust. Basically, his analysis proceeded by dividing the economy into an international and competitive sector, and a sheltered domestic sector mainly consisting of construction and services.[53] Under the pressure of competition, productivity increases rapidly in the first; without the pressure, productivity increases slowly in the second. Wages rise rapidly in the competitive industries, and, by way of the solidaristic wages policy of the unions, these increases are transferred to the domestic sector. Since the productivity increase in the latter was inadequate to offset the wage increment, prices on the domestic market increase without substantially affecting the international competitiveness of the Swedish (or Norwegian) industry, although at times balance of payments problems arise. Some of these may, however, have resulted from a more rapid increase of Swedish investments abroad than of foreign investments in Sweden.

These problems, reinforced by industrial conflicts in the public sector and growing resistance to the high tax rates (probably the highest in the Western world) created a tendency for increased state intervention in industrial relations. Tax changes and wage adjustments were combined in 1973.

Reference has been made earlier to the solidaristic wages policy of the L.O. Combined with wage drift, this became an important element in creating inflationary pressures. In 1976 a codetermination law was enacted that in some way reenforced this trend by providing that collective agreements are legally binding and are automatically extended to cover new members of the signatory organizations.

The rate of inflation has been in line with the average rate of the member countries of the organization of Economic Cooperation and Development, while the unemployment rate has been considerably below their average.[54] This has been made easier by the relatively favorable economic growth rate of Sweden. The high degree of centralized bargaining combined with a high measure of discipline on the employers and also, though to a lesser degree, on the union side, plus the well-known Swedish labor market policies aiming at rapidly eliminating, if not anticipating, supply requirements of labor appear to be big factors in this achievement.

Conclusions

The issue of how to combine full employment with other desirable objectives, primarily free collective bargaining and price and exchange rate stability, has remained one of the great unsolved problems of the post–World War II era. It has its difficult political and economic aspects.

Politically, incomes policies aiming at achieving these ends are most easily introduced and enforced under either of two conditions: (1) when a high degree of social harmony is combined with high economic growth rates, so that in fact no incomes policy is needed; or (2) when a severe national emergency—war, immediate postwar crises, or natural catastrophes—occurs that makes income regulations acceptable to all or at least most elements of the population. A unified trade union movement greatly contributes to the success of the policy. The politically difficult cases lie outside these extremes and, unfortunately, cover the great majority of critical situations since the end of World War II reconstruction.

The methods used ranged from mild persuasion or exhortation ("jawboning"), sometimes reinforced by threats of various kinds, to strict controls, sometimes of prices, at other times of wages or both, with a large variety of measures in between.

A similar variety exists with regard to the objectives and even more with the priority given the objectives when their simultaneous achievement appears to be difficult, if not impossible. Thus many incomes policies started with the aim of defending the external value of the currency and then changed into devices aimed at combatting inflation of domestic prices.

The level of unemployment, its rate of change, and the intensity of the national commitment to full employment are obvious factors in governmental considerations and so is the degree of the dependence of a country on international trade. The strength, degree of centralization, and discipline of unions and employers' organizations, the distribution of income and national attitudes toward equality and inequality, the rate of growth of national income, and public tolerance of industrial unrest and warfare—all these and probably many more factors enter the decision-making process, stimulating or restraining the introduction and the degree of enforcement of incomes policies. Generalizations are thus difficult, if not impossible. A few tentative conclusions will nevertheless be attempted.

I begin with some negative conclusions. The attempts to turn the issue into a moral one will be helpful only in extreme national emergencies. Only then can a society built upon the search for profits in particular and maximizing income in general appeal successfully to moral sentiments to prevent people and institutions from pursuing their traditional objectives. Nor is the reference to oligopoly and market power of any validity unless there are changes in the degree of such power or unless those who hold it have in the past failed to make full use of it. Market power by itself may explain why a price or a wage is higher than it would be under perfect competition, but it cannot explain why prices or wages keep on rising over time unless market power also increases over time. It is possible to make out a case of retained market power. A monopolist or oligopolist may decide for public relations purposes or to avoid political dangers not to make full use of his power to raise the price or the wage. This retained market power may later, at a more propitious time, come into use. Once again this may explain a once-for-all raise of prices or wages, but it would require a gradual use of the retained power over a period to explain a prolonged upward trend of prices or wages. "Cost-push" theories of inflation would have to meet these conditions to be acceptable.[55]

Other negative generalizations derived from the experiences discussed in this chapter are summarized in the following paragraphs.

1. Incomes policies are no substitute for currency devaluations.

2. The attempt to make average productivity increases the measure of wage and price changes fails as a rule in maintaining stability. This policy suffers from a lack of symmetry. It requires that industries or firms with above-average increases in productivity lower their prices to offset the price increases of industries with less than average productivity increments. Public opinion, which is to be used as a means of pressure, is, however, more conscious of price increases than of missing price reductions. Pressure for the latter is, therefore, much weaker than opposition to price increases.

3. Many incomes policies are based upon the expectations that unions in the public interest will assist in holding down the rate of increase of money wages. While it may be true that the general interest would be served by such behavior of the unions, it is not necessarily true for the interest of any particular union and even less for that of an individual union member. Nor is it clear how unions can long survive if they appear to their members as devices that prevent them from obtaining money wage increases that, under conditions of full employment, their employers may be quite willing to grant. Few workers will continue to pay union dues to be denied wage increases that would otherwise be obtainable. For the long run, such a policy would thus

mean the self-destruction of unions and probably the diversion of workers' energies into political channels to obtain radical institutional changes.

4. Yet, in some countries to be discussed below, union cooperation in incomes policies has proven possible. It is easier the more centralized and powerful union leadership is. The inference from this consideration is that incomes policies, in order to be successful, require strengthening the power of top union leaders so as to insulate them to a high degree from rank-and-file pressures.[56] Even then wage drift under the collective bargaining systems of Western Europe is likely to defeat a good deal of what union leaders may wish to arrange, unless management, facing the same problems as union leaders, also cooperates.

5. Incomes policy appears to be a device of temporary effectiveness. More permanent and basic solutions can only be found in fiscal and monetary restraint, i.e., in reducing the level of economic activity, with a great likelihood of calling forth a recession. Public opinion does probably prefer a recession to continued inflation, partly because the burden of unemployment is likely to fall upon a relatively small minority—often groups of little political influence such as guest-workers in Europe or the racial minorities in the United States whose voting participation is abysmally low—and partly because social insurance measures, e.g., unemployment benefits, make temporary unemployment far less of a catastrophe than before World War II.[57]

6. The outstanding exceptions to these considerations appear to be West Germany, Austria, Switzerland, and possibly Sweden. These success stories deserve closer examination, precisely because they are so rare. Even though none of them has totally escaped the worldwide wave of inflation and to some extent an increase in the level of unemployment, the data are fairly conclusive in demonstrating the relative but probably temporary success of their policies.[58]

In West Germany, Austria, and Sweden the main though not the only instrument of the antiinflationary policy was some form of social contract, a high-level agreement of two partners, the trade unions and the employers' confederations, with the government either openly or behind the scenes acting as a third participant. Switzerland does not fit this pattern unless the old pre–World War II peace agreement in the metal industry is interpreted as an embryonic form of social contract. In any case, the ideological and religious divisions of the Swiss trade unions and their relative weakness assign to them a modest role in determining the price level or the distribution of the national income.

It would, however, be erroneous to classify all European countries that have undergone experiments in establishing one or the other form of the social contract in the group that has attained the typical objectives of incomes policies. The outstanding example of a failure is the United Kingdom, with its high rate of inflation, unstable currency, and sharp social conflicts. Obviously, the social contract alone is not the magic key to success. It is only in connection with other factors that the contract seems to hold out hope of success in attaining the objectives of stabilization policies. The contrast between the British case and the successful countries mentioned earlier opens the possibility of formulating some hypotheses about the conditions of success and the limitations of the applicability of the continental model—by which term we shall refer to the cases of West Germany, Austria, and Sweden. The suggested explanations should be taken as no more than highly tentative hypotheses, pending a more thorough study that I intend to undertake in the near future.[59]

There are obvious organizational requirements. Both the employers' associations and the union confederations must be unified. A divided labor movement is inevitably competitive and more concerned with the survival and the strength of each group than with national interests. Any ideological, religious, or other division of the trade union movement would destroy the most essential precondition for the success of the policy. The labor movement must not only be unified but also highly centralized. The organizations must have strong discipline and powerful leadership. This immediately excludes countries with ideological or religious divisions of trade unions and—less frequently—employers' associations and countries with highly decentralized industrial relations systems and collective bargaining methods. Austria is perhaps the outstanding case in meeting these requirements, followed—until the late 1970s—by West Germany and Sweden. Holland was an earlier example.

The more centralized the industrial relations system is, the more obvious are the connections between the conditions laid down in the agreements and macroeconomic considerations and restrictions. There is full insight into the economic possibilities of the system, with divergent views relating only to different estimates of the probable rate of change of the national product. The more information leaders on both sides have, the more they can pay attention to macroeconomic considerations and the more they are insulated from pressure from below. A precise representation of various group interests would appear to make impossible or at least exceedingly difficult the smooth functioning of the social partnership. The distance of the leaders from the rank and file gives them the necessary authority to accept moderate or even unpopular solutions. On the other hand, some successes must be obtained in order to prevent outbreaks like those in the late 1960s that affected even West Germany and Sweden (though not Austria). Repetitions of such rebellions would destroy the system. In the long run, economic growth is therefore an almost indispensable prerequisite of continued social partnership, although it may not always be a sufficient condition.

A further device that has been successfully used in West Germany is the payment of wage increases in the form of blocked accounts, available to the employees at a later date, e.g., upon retirement. While this may affect the savings rate to some extent, it does seem to have practically achieved the intended reduction in the pressure of current demand for goods and services.

The other set of conditions seems to be in the area of politics and ideology. Workers must not only have a high standard of living but also the confidence that they share fairly in the benefits of economic growth. Even more important is their trust in their leaders and to a considerable extent also in the reasonableness of the other side in the agreement. Thus the opposition of the West German employers to the extension of the codetermination system and later the lock-out in the metal industry threatened the survival of the system of social partnership that has, in fact, continued only in an informal but nevertheless quite effective way.

Perhaps the principal *political* condition is the existence of a government close to the unions. On the European continent, this means in practice a Social Democratic government or at least one strongly influenced by the Social Democrats.

It would appear that underlying the operation of partnership is the acceptance of the existing distribution of the national income. This is not necessarily the case, first, because in general, collective bargaining is hardly a device for radical changes in the social system, and second, because the transfer of the class struggle into the conference room may lead to gradual changes, such as the participation of the workers in the ownership of productive capital as proposed in Sweden by the Meidner plan.

Finally, public approval of the partnership leads to a strengthening of the trade union movement and most probably also of the non-Communist left parties supporting the system. The idea has been expressed in conversations in these three countries that union leaders may be induced to cooperate by the prospects of political rewards, such as a seat in Parliament or other forms of public recognition. While this may be true in a number of cases,[60] it is less applicable to West Germany. Only one of the seventeen trade union presidents in the D.G.B. holds a seat in the Bundestag—and he is not the leader of the strongest union, I.G. Metall. No doubt the latter could obtain a seat if he so wished, but it is likely that he can exert as much influence on policy and public affairs in his capacity as president of the largest trade union in any Western country.

While these considerations are plausible hypotheses, there is no clear explanation of why incomes policies do or do not work. In summarizing British experience, Joan Robinson said a decade ago: "Incomes policy is an expedient to cope with a pressing situation. There is no articulate philosophy behind it. The philosophy which it implies is both a rejection and acceptance of laissez-faire. It emphatically rejects laissez-faire, since it expresses an acknowledgement that the free play of the market does not establish an equilibrium price level but rather a progressive deterioration in the value of money. At the same time, it tacitly accepts the distribution of real incomes that the market throws up." While this may stand as a necrology of British (and possibly other) incomes policies, the experiences of other countries permit a slightly more positive evaluation, though they still require further analysis.

In the last few years the traditional full employment–inflation issue has been radically changed. Under stagflation an entirely new issue has come to the fore, and few, if any, labor leaders (or economists) were prepared for it. That inflation could coincide with massive unemployment of labor and considerable idleness of productive facilities contradicted the wisdom of the late 1930s. While labor, led by the Swedes, had come in most cases—belatedly— to adopt Keynesian policies, the left, as did the Conservatives, found itself without intellectual guidance in the face of the new and unexpected problem. No wonder, then, that the governments were helpless when confronted with the new challenge.

With the exception of the Scandinavian and Austrian labor movements, many other Western unions and Socialist parties accept the thesis that the top priority must be antiinflationary measures. Others remain uncertain what their main assignment is. This leaves the battlefield to the Conservative battalions who seek in an artificially induced depression and its consequent persistent mass unemployment the answer to the riddle of inflation in the midst of idle resources.

Even in the countries with relatively low unemployment, labor has bypassed rather than solved the problem. By giving low unemployment top priority and tolerating fairly high inflation rates, the labor movements of some Western countries have not solved the problems but rather rejected them. No doubt, however, that the problem of stagflation remains a top item on the agenda.

NOTES

1. David C. Smith, *Incomes Policies: Some Foreign Experiences and Their Relevance for Canada* (Ottawa: Economic Council of Canada, 1966), 166.

2. J. R. Hicks in his *Essays in World Economics* (Oxford: Oxford University Press, 1959) included an article "Economic Foundations of a Wage Policy," in which he referred earlier than most members of his profession to the newly arising problems. He says: "Since 1931, wages questions have been closely associated with monetary questions; it is even true that the *general* level of wages has become a monetary question. So long as wages were being determined within a *given* monetary framework, there was some sense in saying that there was an 'equilibrium wage,' a wage that was in line with the monetary conditions that were laid down from outside. But the world we now live in

is one in which the monetary system has become relatively elastic, so that it can accommodate itself to changes in wages, rather than the other way about. Instead of actual wages having to adjust themselves to an equilibrium level, monetary policy adjusts the equilibrium level of money wages so as to make it conform to the actual level. It is hardly an exaggeration to say that instead of being on the Gold Standard, we are on a Labour Standard." O.E.C.D. defined incomes policy in the current meaning of the term as "that the authorities should have a view about the kind of evolution of incomes which is consistent with their economic objectives, and in particular with price stability." O.E.C.D., *Policies for Price Stability. A Report to The Economic Policy Committee by its Working Party on Costs of Production and Prices* (Paris: O.E.C.D., 1962), 23.

3. Lloyd Ulman and Robert J. Flanagan, *Wage Restraint: A Study of Incomes Policies in Western Europe* (Berkeley: University of California Press, 1971).

4. See Adolf Sturmthal, *Unity and Diversity in European Labor: An Introduction to Contemporary Labor Movements* (Glencoe, Ill.: The Free Press, 1953), 169–70.

5. E. H. Phelps Brown, "Guidelines for Growth and for Incomes in the United Kingdom. Some Possible Lessons for the United States," in George P. Shultz and Robert Z. Aliber, eds., *Guidelines, Informal Controls, and the Market Place* (Chicago: University of Chicago Press, 1966).

6. *Ibid.*

7. Statement on "Personal Incomes, Costs, and Prices" (Cmd. 7321, Feb. 1948) quoted in *ibid.*, 143–44.

8. Harold Wilson, *The Labour Government 1964–1970, A Personal Record* (London: Weidenfeld and Nicolson and Michael Joseph, 1971), 62. Obviously the civil servant in question regarded this rate of growth as an achievement. Earnings from the mid-1950s to the early 1960s, for instance, rose more than twice as fast as output per manhour; the rate of productivity growth was the lowest of any Western country.

9. Flanagan and Ulman, *Wage Restraint*, 18.

10. It is interesting to note that Gustav Cassel, who formerly had been an ardent supporter of the view that the price level could be controlled by a suitable credit and fiscal policy, after the abolition of the gold standard in England in Sept. 1931 seems to have changed his mind. As gold has now been abandoned as a standard of value, he wrote in an article, "Arbetslöner och penningvärde," *Svenska Dagbladet,* Oct. 18, 1931, 4, it was necessary to decide which price level ought to be maintained. And he continued: "When it has been decided to maintain a certain price level it becomes necessary to adapt wages to this level. However, if a country has a strong trade union movement this adaptation of the wage level cannot be realized without the co-operation of the trade unions. It then becomes a natural procedure that the monetary policy of the nation should ensure this consent in advance. In this manner a state of affairs gradually develops in which monetary policy could only be executed in co-operation with the Amalgamated Trade Unions so that this organization in monetary matters stands out as an authority on an equal footing with the central bank. Perhaps in the future we shall experience that such an arrangement is considered as normal." This was written more than fifty years

ago, and, if it has not yet materialized very clearly, there are signs that the time when it will is not very far off. It should be added that Cassel based his vision on an institutional fact: the existence of powerful trade unions. This note is taken from Jorgen Pedersen's article, "The Rationale of Incomes Policy," in Erich Schneider, ed., *Probleme der Einkommenspolitik* (Tübingen: J. C. B. Mohr [Paul Siebeck], 1965), 4. Lord Beveridge's reasoning along similar lines was published a decade after Cassel's article.

11. The common statement of employers, T.U.C., and government, called "Declaration of Intent on Productivity, Prices and Incomes" of Dec. 16, 1964, was George Brown's (now Lord George-Brown) crowning achievement. Wilson, *Labour Government,* 63, refers to it in glowing terms.

12. *Ibid.,* 266.

13. The relevant figures are in Ulman and Flanagan, *Wage Restraint,* 18–19.

14. It is noteworthy that in an interview of the *Financial Times* with "a high French source" the latter made clear that one of the improvements needed to permit Britain's entry into the Common Market was that "one would no longer expect there to be a sterling crisis every few months." Wilson, *Labour Government,* 250.

15. *Ibid.,* 264.

16. *Ibid.,* 651.

17. *Ibid.,* 662.

18. B. C. Roberts and Sheila Rothwell, "Recent Trends in Collective Bargaining in the United Kingdom," in *Collective Bargaining in Industrialized Market Economies* (Geneva: I.L.O., 1973), 354–55.

19. *Ibid.,* 377. It should be noted that the decision to refuse to register under the act—expression of noncooperation—was passed by a relatively small majority at a special T.U.C. meeting. The general council of the T.U.C. reported, however, that its "efforts . . . had resulted in a substantial shift of opinion amongst trade unionists against Government's proposals." T.U.C. *Report of 103rd Annual Congress, Sept. 1971* (London: T.U.C., 1971), 99. The idea of making collective agreements legally enforceable had been rejected by the Royal Commission on Trade Unions. See ch. 11 herein.

20. See ch. 11 herein.

21. Phelps Brown, "Guidelines for Growth and for Incomes in the United Kingdom," 149.

22. Phelps Brown comes to the conclusion that the supply and demand of labor had no correlation with the movement of money wages. He refers to an O.E.C.D. finding with regard "notably to Denmark" that wages could rise ahead of productivity even in the presence of quite heavy unemployment. Stagflation is thus of much older date than recent discussions in the United States would lead one to believe. An extensive discussion of British stagflation is presented by P. Sargant Florence in John M. Blair, ed., *The Roots of Inflation: The International Crisis* (New York: Burt and Franklin Inc., 1975).

23. The support of the big unions for a system by which the T.U.C. checked the appropriateness of particular wage demands was modest at best and in some cases totally lacking. For an American student of industrial relations, where the A.F.L.-C.I.O. has no power to intervene in the collective bargaining activities of affiliated

unions, the British experience offers no surprises. See also Jon Clark, Heinz Hartman, Christopher Lau, and David Winchester, *Trade Uions, National Politics, and Economic Management. A Comparative Study of the TUC and the DGB* (London, n.d.).

24. Smith, *Incomes Policies*, 131.

25. John P. Windmuller, *Labor Relations in the Netherlands* (Ithaca, N.Y.: Cornell University Press, 1969), 275.

26. It should be noted that except for the chairman, who had a government salary, the board consisted of unpaid members. For extension of agreements, see ch. 12 herein.

27. Windmuller, *Labor Relations in the Netherlands*, 285–86.

28. *Ibid.*, 318.

29. W. Albeda, "Recent Trends in Collective Bargaining in the Netherlands," in *Collective Bargaining in Industrialized Market Economies*, 315.

30. *The Economist*, Apr. 28, 1979, 94.

31. Henry C. Wallich, *Mainsprings of the German Revival* (New Haven: Yale University Press, 1955), 299. Wallich regards wage restraint as a key factor in the rapid German recovery after the war.

32. Ulman and Flanagan, *Wage Restraint*, 173.

33. *Collective Bargaining in Industrialized Market Economics*, 259.

34. *Ibid.*

35. The rate of inflation in 1978, measured by an index of consumer prices, was 2.6 percent. Unemployment was reduced to 4 percent and gross national product grew by about 4 percent—all excellent results compared with the data for almost all Western industrial nations.

36. See ch. 11 herein.

37. Hannes Suppanz and Derek Robinson, *Prices and Incomes Policy. The Austrian Experience* (Paris: O.E.C.D., 1972), 10.

38. A radical change in the leadership personnel on both sides—Socialists and members of the People's party, the successor to the former Christian-Social party—helped bring about cooperation of former enemies. See also the excellent history, William B. Bader's *Austria between East and West, 1945–1955* (Stanford, Calif.: Stanford University Press, 1966).

39. Fritz Klenner, *Die Österreichischen Gewerkschaften* (Vienna: Verlag des Osterreichische Gewerkschaftsbundes, 1953), 2:1593ff.

40. E.g., fourteen monthly salaries, one each as holiday pay and as Christmas bonus, are the rule.

41. Suppanz and Robinson, *Prices and Incomes Policy*, 28–31. In 1968 wage drift was negative, mainly as a result of a short-lived recession.

42. An interesting presentation of the new spirit of the Austrian union leadership since 1945 can be found in Klenner, *Die Österreichischen Gewerkschaften*, vol. 2.

43. Immediately after the war wages were controlled, collective bargaining was permitted only on working conditions, and prices were, in practice, free of controls. In May 1950, as was reported in an earlier chapter, legislation was passed permitting collective bargaining on wages as well. For the variety of techniques used to control prices from about 1952, see Jacques Delors, "L'experience fran-

çaise de Politique des Revenus," paper presented at the Twelfth Study Conference of Economics and Policies, Fiuggi, Italy, May 1966.

44. The Constat de Grenelle, which settled the strikes of 1968, provided for two steps of wage increases in that year, substantially exceeding the rate of increase of the preceding period. Real wages went up 10 percent between Oct. 1967 and Oct. 1968, compared with a rise of less than 3 percent in the preceding twelve months.

45. The inspiration for these contracts came from Jacques Delors; see note 43 above.

46. Jean-Daniel Reynaud, *Les Syndicats en France* (Paris: Editions du Seuil, 1975), 1:233.

47. In technical terms, they aimed at shifting the Phillips curve downward.

48. Ulman and Flanagan, *Wage Restraint,* 93. K. O. Faxen, "Incomes Policy in Sweden; Problems and Developments," *British Journal of Industrial Relations,* II (Nov. 1964).

49. The Swedish government itself stated in July 1965 that it "has little confidence in the usefulness of a direct incomes policy as an instrument of price stabilization, irrespective of whether this policy be executed by exhortation or by a special machinery set up for the purpose." Quoted in Smith, *Incomes Policies,* 151.

50. See the discussion later in the chapter.

51. Bent Hansen, "Wage Negotiations and Wage Policies in Sweden," *International Labour Review,* LXXX (Nov. 1959).

52. T. L. Johnston, "Wages Policy in Sweden," *Economica,* XXV (Aug. 1958), 225.

53. Ulman and Flanagan, *Wage Restraint,* 108; Nils Elvander, "Collective Bargaining and Incomes Policy in the Nordic Countries: A Comparative Analysis," *British Journal of Industrial Relations,* XII (Nov. 1974); Hermod Skanland, "Incomes Policy: Norwegian Experience," *ibid.,* II (Nov. 1964), 309–21.

54. A Swedish observer described this as cheating the Phillips curve.

55. Cost-push explanations that produce moral arguments are highly popular, even though they rarely meet the requirements outlined above. The study by William Fellner *et al., The Problem of Rising Prices* (Paris: O.E.E.C., 1961), stressed cost-push factors without meeting the objections raised above.

56. Ideas of this kind have been put forward in British discussions.

57. Ulman and Flanagan (*Wage Restraint*) call this the "theory of expected loss."

58. There has been discussion about differences in the method of measuring and even more of reporting the rates of inflation in, e.g., West Germany as compared with the United States. Nevertheless, there is little doubt that a substantial real difference in the rate of inflation remains. See the *New York Times,* June 9, 1980, D1, D6.

59. A comparison of consumer price indices, even though they are constructed differently in various countries, is instructive. Setting 1970 at 100, the index for 1978, according to the I.L.O. *Yearbook,* shows the following results: Austria, 172.1; West Germany, 156.7; Sweden, 198.1; France, 219.3; Italy, 265.3; United Kingdom, 269.6. In unemployment, the rates (again measured according to the rules of each country's statistical office) show: Austria, 1970, 2.4 percent, 1978,

2.1 percent; West Germany, 1970, 0.7 percent, 1978, 4.3 percent; Sweden, 1970, 1.5 percent, 1978, 2.2 percent; Italy, 1970, 3.2 percent, 1978, 7.2 percent; United Kingdom, 1970, 2.6 percent, 1978, 6.1 percent.

60. E.g., the president of the Austrian trade union confederation is also president of Parliament.

14

Labor and the European Economic Community

THE EUROPEAN ECONOMIC COMMUNITY (E.E.C.) that came into being with the treaty of Rome in 1957 was intended to be more than a mere customs union. Jean Monnet, the great advocate of the idea, saw in it the germ of a united states of Europe that could negotiate on equal terms with the two superpowers and perhaps even prevent a clash between them. The ultimate goal of the most ardent supporters of the E.E.C. was (and perhaps remains, in spite of growing difficulties) political unification.

Movements for some form of a federation of European nation states had manifested themselves as early as the latter stages of World War II. The administration of the U.S. Marshall Plan had led in 1948 to the founding of the Organization for European Economic Cooperation (O.E.E.C.), which later, with the inclusion of the United States, Japan, and other non-Communist industrial nations, was transformed into the Organization of Economic Cooperation and Development (O.E.C.D). The European Coal and Steel Community was set up in May 1950. These organizations prepared the ground for further steps of economic cooperation and, at the same time, organized the West for the cold war.[1]

On the political front events moved fast. The setting up of the Communist Information Bureau (Cominform) in September 1947, Communist pressure on Greece and Turkey, the enunciation of the Truman doctrine promising support to countries threatened by Communists, the destruction of the non-Communist parties including the Socialists in Eastern Europe, and finally the Communist *coup d'etat* of February 1948 in Prague and the Berlin blockade by the Soviet Union in 1948–49 all led to the organization of the North Atlantic Treaty Organization (NATO). This alliance with the United States was then strongly supported by the British Labour party, but it was questioned by Kurt Schumacher and the German Social Democrats (S.P.D.) because it would make German unity impossible. The formal NATO treaty was signed in April 1949.

Further progress toward European unification was made difficult by growing Anglo-continental (especially French) disagreement about the nature of the structures to be established. Thus, when earlier in 1950 the Coal and Steel Community was set up, the French Foreign Minister Robert Schuman stated that the community should be headed by a High Authority "entrusted with the whole system (which) will be composed of independent persons designated by governments, on a basis of party . . . affiliation. Its decisions will have the force of law in France, in Germany, and in the other member countries." This was unacceptable for the British Labour government for reasons in which Socialism and nationalism formed a tight mixture. Since coal was already nationalized in the United Kingdom and steel about to be, the British were not willing to give too much authority to a foreign body[2] strongly influenced by German and Italian Christian-Democrats. On the other hand, the unions were directly represented on the High Authority, a power they lost when the Coal and Steel Community later was merged into the wider E.E.C.

This set the tone for two decades in which non-Communist Europe went two separate paths: one followed by the six countries that were to set up the E.E.C. (France, West Germany, Italy, Holland, Belgium, and Luxembourg), the other led by the United Kingdom and followed by six other, mostly smaller, nations: Sweden, Norway, Denmark, Switzerland, Austria, and Portugal. The latter formed the European Free Trade Association (E.F.T.A.) in 1960. While it is true that France saw in the E.E.C. a means of keeping Germany in check and Germany saw a way of regaining its status as a major factor in European affairs, they shared a willingness to abandon parts of their sovereignty, which the United Kingdom and especially the British Labour party was not prepared to do.[3] (Austria and Switzerland were motivated by their neutrality.)

There were internal differences among the nations that established the E.E.C. as well. Charles de Gaulle and the French Communists were united in questioning the desirability of the dependence of the six on the United States; the German S.P.D. under Schumacher and for a while under his successor, Erich Ollenhauer, regarded the organization of Western Europe as a threat to German reunification; Italian Communists and the Socialists, under Pietro Nenni's leadership, but not Giuseppe Saragat's Social Democrats, opposed an organization that they viewed as dominated by U.S. capitalism.

By late 1955, however, the attitude of many Socialists toward European unification had clearly changed. When Monnet formed his Action Committee for the United States of Europe in October 1955, both Ollenhauer and Guy Mollet, the leaders of the German and French Socialists, respectively, joined and turned what had been in danger of being a Christian-Democratic initiative into a broad popular movement. It led straight to the treaty of Rome and the formation of the E.E.C. and indirectly to the founding of the E.F.T.A.

The negotiations to prevent this split of Western Europe into "Sixes and Sevens"[4] dealt principally with issues of trade deflection, which was involved in the formation of the two blocs, but this barely concealed the underlying, far more important, issues. We shall limit ourselves here to the role of labor, particularly of the British Labour party, in these negotiations and the later developments. However, a brief reference to some other problems may be necessary to provide the background, especially for the issue of British Labour's attitude toward the E.E.C.

French policy under de Gaulle was clearly designed by the mid-1950s to use the E.E.C. as a framework for Franco-German collaboration to keep Britain and the United States as much as possible out of European affairs. Moreover, the E.E.C. was to be strictly limited in its activities and no supernational tendencies were allowed to develop. This, however, still permitted the European community to progress significantly in a number of directions, such as the design in 1958 of a joint system of social security for migrant workers. Given the large number of such workers, especially in France and West Germany, this was a major achievement. Free movement of citizens of the six countries within the E.E.C. was adopted "in principle" in 1961, though the implementation of the principle proceeded rather slowly. The elimination of quantitative restrictions on trade among the six in industrial products was carried out almost completely by the end of the same year.[5]

Even the painfully difficult problem of a common agricultural policy was resolved—after a fashion—in 1962 after prolonged negotiations, only to return much later to plague the E.E.C. What remained to hinder the further development of the organization were two basic issues: one, the supernational ideal of some of the member states as opposed to the French insistence on having the E.E.C. remain an intergovernmental organization and, second, the relationship of E.E.C. to E.F.T.A. and, in particular, to the United Kingdom. The two issues combined in the discussions on the British application to join the E.E.C., when the French, to all appearances illogically, opposed Britain while sharing its view that E.E.C. should remain a loose essentially intergovernmental institution. It was in these negotiations, following Prime Minister Harold Macmillan's application for E.E.C. membership in 1961, that British labor played a large, at times decisive, part.

The Conservative government's arguments for this reversal of British aloofness were manifold. First, there was the rapid economic growth of the six in sharp contrast to the sluggish performance of the British economy. Participation in the community might give the British economy needed impetus. Next came the increasingly convincing experience of British inability to play a significant role on the world stage, combined with the hope that within the E.E.C. the United Kingdom might have a larger role. And, finally, the United States under President John Kennedy clearly had "less patience with Britain's attempt to keep aloof from Europe than had been shown by

President Eisenhower."[6] Paradoxically, U.S. support for Britain's joining the six had at first the opposite effect from the one intended. It reenforced de Gaulle's conviction that Britain was an agent for U.S. control over Europe, and in January 1963 he broke off all further negotiations with London. A radical change in French policy toward E.E.C. and British affiliation occurred only in the late 1960s, partly as a result of a change in French leadership—Georges Pompidou having replaced de Gaulle—and partly owing to French fears that the enhanced position of West Germany would give it rather than the French the leadership in E.E.C. Great Britain might serve to offset the growing influence of West Germany. Thus at the end of 1969 France consented to the reopening of negotiations with Britain.

The evolution of the British attitude toward the E.E.C. was to a large extent also the evolution of the thinking of the Labour party and the unions. Most of the remainder of this chapter will be devoted to this subject.

After World War II Britain rejected with disdain the idea of joining France in any union. I remember a discussion with a leading officer of the research department of the Trades Union Congress (T.U.C.) at the time. With some asperity he stated: "You could not expect us to join the mess over there." Indeed, in 1951 the Labour government rejected entering the Coal and Steel Community, then in the process of formation. There followed a long period during which the French and the British governments alternated in rejecting British entry in the E.E.C.

A first decisive step occurred in 1967 when a new British approach to the E.E.C. was made. The general council of the T.U.C. prepared a lengthy document outlining the expected advantages—sharing in the dynamism of the E.E.C. economies—and disadvantages of a British affiliation with E.E.C. Among the latter, two items that reoccurred in later discussions stand out: the loss of Commonwealth preferences for British trade and the agricultural policy of the community. The second would involve higher food prices for the British consumer, the end of the key role of the British currency in the so-called sterling area, and substantial British contributions to the E.E.C. fund for agricultural purposes. In later discussions this last item emerged as far more burdensome than originally estimated.

The tone of the T.U.C. document was dispassionate. Although further discussions with Brussels were required, the T.U.C. seemed inclined to view the prospects favorably. In the internal T.U.C. debates a far more critical note was sounded by Frank Cousins, speaking for the giant Transport and General Worker Union; T. Hayday of the National Union of General and Municipal Workers supported joining E.E.C. The problem was finally referred to the general council of the T.U.C. for further study, since no decision was yet necessary.

On May 8, 1967, Prime Minister Harold Wilson spoke before the House of Commons and presented at great length the considerations for British entry into the Common Market. His almost dramatic speech concluded with an appeal to the house to "take a historic decision" in favor of joining the E.E.C. His views were reflected in a statement "Labour and the Common Market" adopted by the party conference in October 1967.

Another French veto followed, but both Britain and the five other members of the E.E.C. persisted in looking for ways to circumvent the effects of the veto. The European Community Trade Union Secretariat expressed its opposition to the French veto. Nevertheless, it was only after de Gaulle's resignation as president of France in August 1969 that the British application "became a live issue once more."[7] This led to extensive discussions between the T.U.C. general council and the prime minister in which a common attitude of delay in judging the likely consequences of Britain's entry into E.E.C. was established.

At the Labour party conference of 1969, Jack Jones, the leader of the powerful Transport and General Workers' Union, submitted a resolution that summarized the objectives of the E.E.C. opponents as follows:

> This conference calls upon the government in any negotiations for membership of the European Economic Community to insist on adequate safeguards for Britain's balance of payments, cost of living, National Health and Social Security systems, and power of independent decision in economic planning and foreign policy.
>
> Conference further rejects the proposal for a nuclear-armed Federal European State, including Britain.[8]

In fact, this resolution was an ill-concealed expression of opposition to Britain's joining the Common Market. One of the difficulties of the debate was precisely the tendency of E.E.C. opponents to veil their objections as conditions rather than to state their clear "no."[9]

Yet, when in 1971 the Conservative government indicated its willingness to join the three communities (Coal and Steel, Euratom, and the E.E.C., later combined into one) on the terms negotiated by the government, both the T.U.C. and the Labour party expressed opposition. The T.U.C. at its congress asked for a general election before a definite decision would be taken and organized a campaign against entry. It centered on three issues. (1) The United Kingdom would have to pay 25 percent of the budget of the three communities but get only 6 percent back. (2) The balance of payments costs by reason of the loss of Commonwealth preference, greater accessibility to imports from the continent, and contributions to E.E.C. would run between 500 to perhaps 700 million pounds sterling a year. This would necessarily be reflected in unemployment in the United Kingdom. (3) Joining E.E.C.'s common agricultural policy (C.A.P.) would inevitably lead to substantially higher food prices.

These objections were reenforced by clause 2 of the bill that the government submitted to Parliament. It provided that E.E.C. regulations affecting the internal life of the member countries would directly, without parliamentary vote, become law in Britain. And finally, the devaluation of the pound sterling, following the government's decision in July 1972 to float the pound, raised the weight of British contributions to E.E.C.

The T.U.C. campaign was undertaken jointly with the Labour party, which in its "Program for Britain" had also come out against joining the E.E.C. on the terms negotiated. The spirit of some elements of the T.U.C. opposition can be illustrated by quoting one of the speakers at the 1972 T.U.C. conference who referred to the E.E.C. as "this shabby, second-rate empire." The strange combination of Socialism—rejecting the predominance of Christian-Democrats in E.E.C.—and nationalism unwilling to abandon Britain's former worldwide role emerged clearly in the debates, though not in Labour's official documents. [10]

Ten years after the British Parliament had first requested entry into the E.E.C., the House of Commons on October 28, 1971, approved by a large majority (356 to 244 votes) the principle of entry. In 1963 de Gaulle had vetoed Britain's admission; in 1967 Wilson as Labour prime minister had renewed the application. When the vote was reached, Edward Heath, leader of the Conservatives, was prime minister.

A majority of the Labour members voted against entry and exerted heavy pressure on the pro-E.E.C. minority led by Roy Jenkins, deputy leader of the Parliamentary Labour party (Labour's group in the House of Commons). No fewer than 101 Labour members sent a letter to Jenkins asking him not to vote with the prime minister. Since the latter lost forty-two votes (thirty-nine Conservatives voting against and three abstaining), the support of sixty-nine Labourites (with another twenty abstaining) became highly important for the outcome. Indeed, if the sixty-nine had voted against the motion, it would have lost. The main spokesman of the anti-E.E.C. group was Tony Benn, who emerged more and more as the leader of Labour's left wing.

Jenkins, earlier regarded as the "coming man" in the Labour party, responded that he did not vote for the Conservatives but for European Socialism. A Socialist group of the original six E.E.C. members had indeed asked British Labour to support the community. Still, for the time being at least, Jenkins's role in British Labour came to an end, and he transferred his activities to membership in the E.E.C. commission. There he soon played a leading part. He later reappeared on the British scene as a member of the "gang of four" that founded the Social-Democratic party.

The vote, however, did not end the problems raised by Labour. The 1972 Labour party conference took a new decision on the issue. If negotiations about the conditions under which the United Kingdom was to join were successful, the conference stated, "the people should have the right to decide the issue through a General Election or a Consultative Referendum. If these two tests are passed, a successful renegotiation and the expressed approval of the majority of the British people, then we shall be ready to play our full part in developing a new and wider Europe."

The renegotiations then undertaken concerned the E.E.C. budget, the Monetary Union established by the E.E.C., the powers of Parliament, Commonwealth interests, and the harmonization of the Value Added Tax, which required a substantial increase in British indirect taxation. The government, acting on the results of these negotiations, recommended that Britain should continue as a member of E.E.C. A majority of the executive committee of the Labour party disagreed and opposed Britain's continued membership. However, both the Labour government and the party decided that on this question party discipline should not be enforced. In Norway a referendum on joining E.E.C. in September 1972 rejected membership. In the United Kingdom public opinion polls indicated a majority of the people opposed to joining. Yet the British decision in favor of E.E.C. was maintained.

The T.U.C., at the beginning of 1973, issued a statement of its general council on the occasion of the United Kingdom's joining the Common Market. The unions did not conceal their worry about the effects of this event on the cost of living and added that entry had been decided without the express consent of the British people. Consistent with this objection, the Labour party refused to nominate representatives for the Strasburg parliament of the E.E.C., and the T.U.C. did the same with regard to the Common Market institutions in which the unions were represented. This noncooperation was to be maintained, according to a resolution adopted by the Labour party conference in 1973, until a referendum had decided whether Britain was to continue its membership. Again, as Clive Jenkins of the Association of Scientific, Technical and Managerial Staffs, indicated in seconding this resolution, this was a way of expressing hostility toward the E.E.C.[11]

A Labour government took office in 1974 and, following a commitment made in the election manifestos prior to the two elections held in February and October of that year, arranged for a consultative referendum. It was held in June 1975. Sixty-five percent of the electorate voted; 17.4 million voted yes, 8.5 million voted no. This vote, however, did not settle the issues, as the British demands for a renegotiation of the terms of its membership demonstrated.

The main issues now were the size of Britain's contribution to the E.E.C. budget and Britain's receipts from the E.E.C. monies. Some 70 percent of E.E.C.'s budget goes to farm supports. Of this amount Britain with its small agricultural output and large imports receives so little that the gap between what she pays to E.E.C. and what she receives from it (the net British contribution) is expected to amount to £1.18 for 1980 (about $2.2 billion), by far the highest of any E.E.C. member. Since the British gross national product per head of its population ranks quite low in the list of E.E.C. members, this disparity is hard to accept for the British, and most other member countries are slowly and reluctantly acknowledging the justice of London's claim for a remedy. Even if Britain were not to complain, the growing burden of the agricultural support policy[12] would demand rapid reforms. Huge food reserves are being built up by the community and the "butter mountain" that it hoards has become proverbial. Moreover, if subsidies continue to grow at the present rate, the financial resources of the community will soon be insufficient to maintain them. The most immediate issue, however, is the British demand that reforms reduce British contributions and increase British receipts; the United Kingdom thus wants the problem to be tackled from both sides and the changes to be permanent, not merely stopgap measures.

The commission, trying to avoid politically dangerous ground by reducing supports for the strong farm bloc in the member countries, looks for a practical solution in an increase of E.E.C. revenues. The C.A.P. is to be revised, but this is a long-term project. In the meantime, the E.E.C. meetings at the end of 1979, during which the new Conservative prime minister, Margaret Thatcher, presented British complaints, ended in failure. The continental powers offered a reduction of the British payments gap of some $700 million, far less than Britain expected. So far the fears of the opponents to the E.E.C. among the Labourites appear to have been justified. Talk of a possible break-up of the community may be part of bargaining strategy, but there is little doubt that the community is confronted with a serious crisis. Moreover, the continental nations, even those recognizing some justice in the British demands, feel that Britain's solidarity with its partners in the E.E.C. is shaky and limited. Thus the United Kingdom did not join the community's monetary system and did follow the leadership of the Organization of Petroleum Exporting Countries in pricing North Sea oil.

Labour's reluctance to commit itself to support of E.E.C. was manifested again on the occasion of the first direct elections to the European parliament. The Labour party conference recommended abstaining from participation in the elections, with the result that the Labour and Social Democratic faction in the parliament was weakened, and Conservatives relatively overrepresented. The continued hostility of the left wing of British Labour to membership in the E.E.C. was one of the main issues that led to growing dissension within the movement and finally to a split. The Social Democrats, which became rapidly a powerful force on the political scene, strongly support membership in the E.E.C..

NOTES

1. As is well known, the Czechs and Poles had originally planned to participate in the Marshall Plan but were "induced" to change their stand after the U.S.S.R. withdrew. Foreign Minister V. Molotov had participated in preparatory talks during 1947 but changed his views.

2. British mines at the time produced almost as much coal as the rest of Western Europe.

3. A contemporary observer of French politics described the French attitude— which many Socialists and trade unionists shared—as wishing for a German armed force strong enough to deter the Russians but not larger than the French, a somewhat difficult, because contradictory, objective to achieve.

4. The expression is Emile Benoit's in his *Europe at Sixes and Sevens: The Common Market, the Free Trade Association, and the United States* (New York: Columbia University Press, 1961).

5. Roger Morgan, *West European Politics since 1945. The Shaping of the European Community* (London: B. T. Batsford Ltd., 1972), 198.

6. *Ibid.*, 202.

7. T.U.C. *Annual Report for 1970* (London: T.U.C., 1971), 468.

8. This proposal was never taken up again, and it is doubtful whether it was ever intended to be taken seriously.

9. This was pointed out rather frequently. One of the clearest statements was by Brown at the party conference of 1969. See Report, p. 320.

10. "The insular outlook of many union leaders suggests the residue of nineteenth-century-style nationalism has found its resting place on the left of the Labour movement. . . . chauvinism is a strong emotional force among many British trade unionists, who scorn the peculiar habits of their Continental colleagues and look with deep distrust at other Western trade union movements." Robert Taylor, *The Fifth Estate. Britain's Unions in the Seventies* (London: Routlege and Kegan Paul, 1978), 155.

11. Clive Jenkins concluded: "I invite you to join with me in voting for this motion and saying, 'We cannot do it in the Market; we will accomplish it victoriously outside the Market.' So let's withdraw now." *Congress Report for 1973*, p. 283.

12. C.A.P. guarantees profitable prices for agricultural products. The E.E.C. buys surpluses that might depress the price, out of import duties and a share of the sales tax proceeds of member countries. This amount is less and less adequate to finance C.A.P. as the high prices guaranteed the farmer encourage increased agricultural production. Next to the United Kingdom, West Germany is among the losers under C.A.P.

15

Euro-Communism

THE RISE OF apparently independent movements within the Communist parties of Italy and Spain and later France was intended to create the impression that one of the fundamental objections to the reception of Western Communists into the national communities and possibly even into the governments of democratic countries had disappeared. It does not appear to have succeeded. The entry of four Communists in minor jobs in the French cabinet in 1981 had nothing to do with Euro-Communism, which is especially weak in France. It was primarily designed to keep the Communist-led unions of the Confédération Generale du Travail (C.G.T.) in line and to pay off election debts to the Communist party.

It is difficult, if not impossible, for the outside observer to test the sincerity and permanency of this new development. Clearly if it were sincere and permanent, it would represent a historic event that could change the evolution of political and social structures in a number of Western countries in which the Communist party and the unions related to it represent strong political and social forces. It is of tremendous importance to follow this evolution with care, taking into account the vast implications of such a conversion but also the dangers of a potential deception. Later in this chapter I shall present my view that the question of the sincerity of this conversion as it is usually formulated is not the most relevant way of analyzing this issue. Still, it is the most widely asked question and, therefore, deserves consideration.

As a partial contribution to such an evaluation, it may be useful to recall much earlier statements of Communist leaders that have a strange resemblance to the current ones and to remember the passing character of these conversions. Nothing ensues of necessity from the fate of these earlier events; the failure to follow up on them may have resulted from the specific circumstances of the period, especially the outbreak of the cold war. Yet, it would be foolish not to take into account these earlier incidents. Caution and perhaps even distrust appear reasonable in the light of this earlier history.

Older observers of the European scene will remember the almost desperate offers of alliance, cooperation, and moderation, especially on the part of the French Communists, in the period between about 1934 and the conclusion of the German-Russian pact in 1939. The offer was addressed to the proverbial "water front" reaching from the Socialists to the pope, indeed, to almost anyone who could conceivably be recruited into a united front to combat the Nazis and defend the Soviet Union.

This policy and its sudden reversal in August 1939 may be regarded—and possibly excused—as an act of desperation in the face of the overwhelming Nazi threat and the foot-dragging of the Western powers in their negotiations with Moscow about an alliance. Yet a different motivation must be assigned to some peculiar, but nowadays familiar, expressions of Communist policy changes toward the end of World War II and shortly afterward. Thus the Italian Communist party spoke of an "elastic policy" after its legal reconstitution at the end of World War II; various other Communist parties stressed the need for a road to Socialism adjusted to the specific conditions of their country. Even the East German Communist party, known now as one of the most orthodox and Moscow-oriented of all Communist parties in the world, had its East Berlin leader, Anton Ackermann, remark: "We are of the opinion that the method to force the Soviet system upon Germany would be erroneous."[1] And the appeal that the newly established Communist party of Germany (K.P.D) addressed to the German people on June 11, 1945, stated: "We are of the opinion that the idea to force the Soviet system on Germany, would be wrong because this road does not correspond to the existing conditions of the development in Germany."[2]

However, with the introduction of the Marshall Plan by the United States, the language rapidly and radically changed. The Soviet Union reasserted its domination over the Communist parties of the world. The Comintern, having been dissolved in May 1943 as a sacrifice to the wartime alliance with the United Kingdom and the United States, was reestablished in a slightly modified form under the name of Cominform (Information Office of the Communist and Workers' Parties). It was officially dissolved in 1956 as part of the "de-Stalinization" process introduced by Nikita Khrushchev's famous revelations about Joseph Stalin's terror at the 20th Communist party congress. Whether any of these maneuvers changed very much Moscow's claim to control the Communist parties outside the Soviet Union is highly doubtful.

In the meantime both Josip Tito's Yugoslavia and Mao Tse Tung's China had thrown off Moscow's control. Romania, while Stalinist in its internal policy, embarked on an independent course in foreign affairs, and Albania looked until 1978 toward Peking rather than Moscow for support. After 1978 it remained in "splendid isolation." Even the formerly loyal servants of Moscow in Italy, France, and Spain were manifesting signs of increasing independence, though in different degrees. While Moscow attempted to reestablish various institutions to influence and if possible control the party officers beyond the area under Russian army domination, the signs of rebellion multiplied, especially after the Russian suppression of the movement to introduce a humanitarian Communism in Czechoslovakia.

In Moscow an "International Department" of the Secretariat of the Party Central Committees (Z.K.) exists under the direction of Boris Ponomarjev. Every Soviet Embassy has employees whose special assignment it is to maintain contacts with the Communist party of the countries to which they are accredited. The trade representatives see that the various Communist parties act as trade agents or at least get a share of the commercial transactions between the Soviet Union and the different countries. In this way Moscow maintains a degree of financial control over its fraternal parties.

However, the 20th party congress with its revelations about Stalin's terror regime broke the spiritual spell in which Moscow held the former affiliates of the Comintern. Moreover, the majority of the Communist party leaders in the capitalistic countries began to realize that as recognized agents of Moscow[3] they could never expect to obtain political power in their countries. They were enclosed in a ghetto into which their enemies could not break, but from which the Communists could not break out to get closer to the seat of power. It looked more and more like an eternal stalemate in which some of the leaders felt quite comfortable, while others, more ambitious or more gifted, were eager to find a way for a radical change in the situation.

One of these, Enrico Berlinguer, leader of the Italian Communist party as successor of Palmiro Togliatti, became the main spokesman of the so-called Euro-Communists. The Spanish leader, Santiago Carillo, and, slowly and reluctantly, the French Communist General Secretary Georges Marchais followed Berlinguer.

The degree of independence from Moscow asserted by the different parties varies a good deal. And especially varied is the degree of confidence that various observers in the West have in the conversion. Three kinds of tests have been advanced by serious students (no evidence except suicide of the Communist leaders could convince veteran cold war warriors, especially those who were Communists themselves in their youth).

One: how far does the conversion go? Is abandoning the formula of the dictatorship of the proletariat and similar traditional incantations sufficient evidence of an acceptance of the democratic rules of the game? Will—as happened after World War II—the party leaders, once installed in ministerial offices, abandon them if the democratic system should so demand? Even assuming that the present Communist party leaders are sincere in their acceptance of democratic legality, will their party follow them once it has achieved its objectives, or will a palace revolution—perhaps inspired by Moscow—put a new team in their place that will not feel committed to the new faith its predecessors accepted and proclaimed? There are no signs that Moscow is willing to abandon control over world Communism.

Two: what is the internal organization of the Communist party like? This relates to what has been euphemistically called "democratic centralism." It may be comprehensible that under the conditions of czarist oppression—mild as it may appear compared to twentieth-century totalitarianism—an open, democratic mass organization after the pattern of the German Social Democratic party in the post-Bismarck period was impossible. An effective political party aiming at a radical change of the economic, political, and social system under the circumstances of the czarist system was probably compelled to have some of the characteristics of a conspiracy or of a military organization, emphasizing discipline and unity rather than freedom of expression, prolonged discussions, and democratically arrived at decisions.

But that merely indicated the backwardness of the society in which V. I. Lenin's party had to operate. To transfer the same principle of organization to the West meant creating a party organized differently from the political parties of the West and poorly adapted to western conditions. The mass organizations of the British Labour party, the German Social Democrats (S.P.D.), or the Austrian Social Democrats, regardless of their programs and their slogans and symbols, were operating in countries quite different from the underdeveloped, authoritarian countries of Eastern Europe with a numerically and organizationally weak industrial working class and a huge, illiterate peasantry. It is no accident that the only Western countries in which Lenin's ideas had found substantial and permanent support—beyond the brief first period when they could derive their strength from the prestige of the Russian revolution—were France and Italy, then among the industrially most backward countries of the West. Karl Marx and Lenin both had understood the special situation of backward nations, even while they were firmly convinced that what they were witnessing was the last stage of capitalism in the West.[4]

Basically, the main deviations from the democratic revolutionary, even if utopian, tradition in which Marx's philosophy was founded, followed from Lenin's illusions about the coming revolution in the advanced industrialized countries of the West. The fundamental error was the expectation of a Socialist revolution in Germany. What happened in 1918 was the consequence of the military defeat, not of a profound anticapitalist longing among the vast majority of the German working class. And in the victorious nations of World War I in Europe conservative governments prevailed.

This may help explain the reason why Lenin turned Marx upside down—to use a phrase that Marx employed in describing his own relations to Friedrich Hegel's philosophy: the economic and social structure of the country had to be adjusted—nay, revolutionized at top speed—in order to respond to its political system, the opposite to Marx's thesis that the political and social superstructure depended on the economic fundamentals. In this endeavor, Lenin and even more Stalin have been quite successful. At the cost of fantastic sacrifices of human life and dignity, a rapid industrialization process was carried out. Extreme emphasis was placed on developing heavy industry at the expense of the production of consumer goods. The shortage of the latter caused mass misery and starvation. However, the record in the area of armaments was impressive: the Soviet Union emerged as a rival of the United States in military power. And so far as Russian armaments insured a Communist victory, the Soviet example proved irresistible, far less because of its ideological attraction—which was surely minimal in countries like Poland— than because of Russian military power. Tito's independent Communism was followed by China, where after an unsuccessful attempt to adopt the Soviet model independent policies were developed. This gave a major impulse to the break-up of Moscow-dominated Communist internationalism that Tito's break with Moscow had initiated.

From this follows the third test to which the sincerity of a Communist party's break with Soviet domination may be subjected. If the shortcomings or crimes of the Russian system, after the Russian defeat of the Hungarian uprisings and of the Prague spring could no longer be excused as the product of Russian backwardness or of the cult of personality long after Stalin's death, then could the Soviet Union serve any longer as a model for the proletariat of the West? Do the Communists of the West owe any more allegiance to Moscow than to any other capital perhaps even including Washington? Would they in a conflict between the superpowers act as Soviet agents regardless of circumstances, or would they at least adopt a position of neutrality, even though they might still regard the Soviet Union as the lesser evil compared with the United States? This last test may prove decisive in the light of the history of the relations between Moscow and its affiliates in the West.[5]

The failure of Lenin's expectation of the Socialist revolution in the West, especially in Germany, caused him and his successors to transform the Communist International first into an instrument of indoctrination of its affiliated parties and then increasingly into a tool of Russian foreign policy. The patently obvious subservience of the Western Communist parties to Moscow's direction prevented them from following independent policies appropriate to each party's particular situation and was a major factor in changing them into sects of unquestioning supporters. This became painfully clear to everyone but the hopelessly indoctrinated in 1939, when the Soviet Union suddenly reversed its policy toward Nazi Germany and the overwhelming majority of the Communist parties followed Moscow's instructions.

In the West Communism exerted major influence only in countries in which industrialization had not gone very far or in which economic growth was particularly slow: France, Italy, and possibly Spain and Portugal. However, since World War II was followed by a stage of rapid economic growth in France and Italy, the official party line was increasingly inappropriate for the social and economic situation in the two countries. Undying loyalty to the Leninist dogma pushed the Communist movements into a ghetto. For the faithful party member, the ghetto was quite liveable. The movement—similar, but only in this respect, to the German and Austrian Social Democrats of the interwar period—became a home that provided for most of the needs of its followers. It thus fulfilled in many ways a useful social function, but it was not an effective political organization; its results were negative rather than positive. It prevented the working class from exerting a creative influence on events. It could at times prevent developments, but not call them forth.

It is remarkable how long this purely negative role toward the community at large could be combined with the maintenance of a fairly stable core of followers. Undoubtedly the prestige of the Soviet Union as a victorious anti-Nazi force and agent of rapid industrialization, as well as the apparent harbinger of a new society of plenty, equality, and social harmony, played a key role in enabling the Communists to maintain their control over a core of ardent supporters in the unions and among a substantial body of prestigious artists and intellectuals. But, unlike the Bolshevik revolution in Russia, Western Communism could never derive even the shadow of success from furthering and speeding up the process of industrialization and modernization. This, as the growth rates of gross national product suggest, was done quite effectively by capitalism or the mixed forms of capitalist and noncapitalist institutions that developed in France, Italy, and some other countries with or without relatively strong Communist labor movements.

The Soviet invasion of Czechoslovakia and the revelations of Stalin's terror system produced a profound shock among the Communist parties of the West. In Italy especially, where the party felt government office within its reach, the violent events leading to the ouster and death of President Salvador Allende in Chile induced a rethinking of the leftists' strategy. A fifty-one percent majority was not regarded as sufficient to guarantee implementation of their program. The Italian Communist party was the first to rebel against Moscow's directives that had doomed the party to isolation and the role of the eternal opponent.

In part this development may be related to the authority of Antonio Gramsci, an early theoretician of the party, who rejected the concept of the dictatorship of the proletariat, replaced it with the more modest "hegemony" of the working class, and coined the idea of a "civilian society" as distinguished from the state. Later party leaders, especially Palmiro Togliatti, however, became faithful servants of the Kremlin bureaucracy.

Under Berlinguer's leadership the Italian party set the pace for declarations to mark its independence from Moscow. It stated its willingness to recognize the principle of majority rule in a parliamentary system and, consequently, to abandon power if in a free election it were to lose its legitimate claim to governmental positions; it promised that it would guarantee basic democratic freedoms, especially the existence of a multiparty system; it accepted a market-oriented economy with both private and public enterprises;

and, finally, it pledged itself to reject the claim to leadership on the part of the Soviet Union.

The Italian trade union movement as it was described earlier in this study made attempts to overcome its threefold ideological division. Pushed forward by the metal workers, the three trade union centers, after prolonged and fruitless talks about a merger, formed a superfederation to ensure concerted action. The C.I.S.L., the Communist-led confederation, left the W.F.T.U. (World Federation of Trade Unions) to become acceptable as a member of the European trade union confederation, which is loosely connected with the International Confederation of Free Trade Unions and dominated by non-Communist unions.

In the words of the German S.P.D. leader, Horst Ehmke:

> All those Communist parties—the Italian, the Spanish, and even the French—accept that ideological, political, and social pluralism should be maintained even during the process of building up socialism, and have declared that they would be prepared at any time to bow to the decision of the electorate. Much of this is a question of tactics. But nevertheless it is of some importance in the long-term that even Communists now admit the inherent value of the basic rights and political freedom of bourgeois democracy. . . . Whether this will lead to a genuine and final change of heart on the part of the Western Europen Communists is impossible to predict. But the process alone represents a turning point in the history of the Communist parties which is well worth our careful consideration.[6]

While the Italian Communist party was the first to embark upon what had come to be known as Euro-Communism—an ill-defined concept—and has gone perhaps farther along in the direction of independence from Moscow, the French have been the last and the most hesitant to do so.[7] Spain's Carillo has used the strongest language in asserting his independence, but his party's modest support among the Spanish electorate reduces the political importance of his stand.

Still, the attitude of these parties has had its effect, primarily as far as the language and the statements of objectives of Western Communists are concerned, and ultimately called forth an official international Communist reaction. After almost two years of negotiations, mainly about the role of "proletarian internationalism, one of the main principles of Marxism-Leninism"—i.e., the degree of Moscow's control of the parties formerly affiliated with the Cominform that was dissolved in 1956—a conference of representatives of twenty-nine European Communist parties was finally held in East Berlin in the summer of 1976. They agreed on a compromise formula that referred to "voluntary international collaboration and solidarity on the basis of the sovereign independence of all parties."[8] In addition, the conference abandoned the traditional reference to Marxism-Leninism in favor of "the ideas of Marx, Engels, and Lenin."[9] Moscow demonstrated its unhappiness with the conference results in a variety of ways. So great was the pressure upon the recalcitrant fraternal parties that they finally recognized that a special relationship existed between them and the Soviet Union. The Western parties rationalized their concessions by describing them as the only way by which they could exert any influence upon the treatment of dissidents in the Soviet Union.

However, these concessions strengthened the powerful elements within the French Communist party that resisted any departure from tradition and dogma. The French party was the slowest of the three major Latin-European Communist parties to embark upon the course of Euro-Communism, and the first to depart from it. Having been abandoned by the bulk of its intellectual supporters after the Russian invasion of Czechoslovakia, the party machinery continued to function as bureaucracies in general tend to do when they are not pressured by unorthodox minds, which means it continued as if nothing had changed. Indeed, for a long time the democratic freedoms of the West were regarded as bourgeois institutions, and internal party democracy—as opposed to the authoritarian system of democratic centralism—was described as characteristic of a "parlor party such as the Socialists."[10] It is true that the French Communist party permitted its official organ in the late 1960s to publish an article by one of the favorite party intellectuals, Louis Aragon, criticizing the Soviet Union for prosecuting two Russian oppositionists, Sinjievski and Daniels, who had published abroad articles critical of the Soviet regime. But the Russian invasion of Czechoslovakia saw the French Communist party more concerned with the wave of anti-Communist criticism that these events provoked than with the invasion itself.[11] And as late as 1970 Roger Garaudy, member of the Politbureau of the French Communist party, was expelled for having criticized the Marxian theory of the state. Even when the party at its 22nd congress finally rejected the traditional and once sacred demand for the dictatorship of the proletariat, this fundamental revision of the party ideology did not result from a prolonged discussion in the party ranks but was simply proclaimed by the party leader, Georges Marchais.

In 1972 the decisive change in the party ideology and strategy seemed finally to have arrived. Apparently eager to break out of its ghetto (where it garnered only 15 to 20 percent of the vote), the Communist party formed an alliance with the Socialist party, itself torn apart by internal quarrels and divisions. A carefully worked out common program was accepted. Within the span of two years, this union radically changed the political scene in France. A government of the left became a distinct possibility. In 1974 the Socialist leader François Mitterand came close to winning the presidency. However, the alliance began to falter when it became clear that the Socialists rather than the Communists were the main beneficiaries. Negotiations about updating the common program, earlier expected to be fairly simple, turned into a major battle. Socialist proposals about the list of enterprises to be nationalized were sharply rejected by the Communists, just as the public opinion polls indicated a clear victory for the left. The Communist paper, *L'Humanité*, openly and sharply denounced the Socialists in very much the same terms that it had used in pre–Euro-Communist days.

Some commentators interpreted the sudden changes as the result of a command from Moscow, which in its international dealings is said to prefer the "bourgeois" Valery Giscard d'Estaing to François Mitterrand.[12] Since once again a major policy decision had been taken by the party leaders without previous discussion among the rank and file, one can only guess at the reason. A prolonged debate within the central committee of the party ended with a decision not to allow an open discussion of the party's policy among the members at large. "We are a democratic party, but not a discussion club," proclaimed Marchais. In any case, the cause of Euro-Communism in France had been dealt a terrible, possibly deadly blow.[13]

A postelection debate has nevertheless taken place within the Communist party but, significantly, not within the pages of *L'Humanité*. Instead the highly respected non-Communist daily *Le Monde* has opened its pages to critical articles. Referring to the BBC broadcasts addressed to the French people during the Nazi occupation, a French Communist said: "Now *Le Monde* is our BBC." That such a debate can take place at all shows that things have changed in the French Communist party. That it must take place outside the party publications indicates the limits of the change.

As the election of 1981 approached, the pressure of rank and file upon the leadership of the Communist party increased to the point that the majority of the leaders feared they would lose control of the party and their voters if they refused to support the Socialists in the elections. They were compelled to adopt a policy, once traditional on the French left, that the candidate on the left who had the better chances of defeating the rightist opponent had to be supported. In fact, Communist voters were ready in large numbers to support the Socialists. The election results of 1981 indicated for the first time since World War II that even the core of the Communist support was no longer a secure haven for the traditional party leaders. Heavy Communist losses gave the Socialists the dominant role in the left coalition. Not to be totally isolated, the party accepted the conditions and inferior role that Mitterrand imposed upon them in the government. However, as long as the Communist party controls the largest trade union confederation, its hopes for a future revival— if not in the immediate future—are not unreasonable.

The most decisive turn away from Moscow's domination (next to Italy's) has been taken, at least verbally, by the Spanish Communists under the leadership of Santiago Carillo.[14] In the early 1960s Carillo was an ardent supporter of Moscow. In 1964, for instance, he was instrumental in expelling from the Spanish Communist party the Marxist theoretician Fernando Claudin for defending the moderate policy that Carillo later adopted.[15] By 1968 Carillo's conversion had already occurred, as demonstrated by his sharp criticism of the Soviet invasion of Czechoslovakia. For awhile the Soviet Union responded by giving support to a rival Spanish Communist party headed by Enrique Lister, a hero of the Spanish Civil War, but this organization remained miniscule. However, while opposition to Carillo's new line persisted, it remained ineffective even though the venerable Dolores Ibarruri, known as La Passionaria from Civil War days, supported it. A sharp attack on Carillo in the Soviet foreign affairs weekly, the *New Times,* was rejected by the Spanish party and its central committee, which pledged continuance of its Euro-Communist independence from Moscow. "For Spain," the statement said, "and for other capitalist societies with similar characteristics, the way called Euro-communism offers the only valid alternative for the advance to socialism." Further on, the document continued, "The so-called 'real socialism' that exists in nations like the Soviet Union cannot be presented as an ideal model of a socialist society."

The Soviet invasion of Afghanistan has widened the split between the French Communist party leaders, on one hand, and Berlinguer (Italy) and Carillo (Spain), on the other; and between the Italians and Spaniards and Moscow. Giancarlo Pajetta of the Italian Communist party made it plain that Moscow's attack on Afghanistan was a "gross violation of national sovereignty and independence." And the party paper *Unita* described the "Soviet intervention as the latest serious aggravation of political and military acts of force which endanger world peace." Still, the paper also criticized U.S. reaction as "disregarding any attempt at negotiation." Carillo, after some hesitation, finally came out with a statement in support of his Italian colleagues. Marchais, however, in a broadcast from Moscow, on January 11, 1980, declared that one had to choose sides: "Either the side of imperialism or that of the international revolution." Thus no united front of Euro-Communists exists any more.

The break among the three previously united—or apparently united—Euro-Communist parties had become inevitable since Marchais had failed to win Berlinguer over to participation in a "Pan-Communist meeting at the highest level regarding the problems of Disarmament" as proposed by then Polish party chief Edward Gierek. Still, a meeting planned for January 16, 1980, between Willy Brandt (as head of the Socialist International) and Berlinger was postponed indefinitely, perhaps more in the interests of the Italians than of the Germans, to disarm those critics of Euro-Communism who see it clearly marching toward a pact of friendship with the S.P.D.[16]

Carillo has made an attempt[17] to define the policy described as Euro-Communism, without too much success. According to him, Euro-Communism, unlike Social Democratic currents and parties, aims at "transforming the capitalist society, but not to administer it; to develop a Socialist alternative to a system of state-monopoly, not to integrate itself in it and to be one of the varieties of its governments."[18] The Communist parties, he says, are undergoing a process of rethinking their policies and strategies. If the Socialists were to do the same, there would be "no reason why the split of 1920 could not be overcome."[19]

All this, of course, does not tell us very much about what Euro-Communism is. There are some elements of greater independence from Moscow, though criticism of the Soviet Union is almost always accompanied by assertions of friendship and admiration. Parliamentary democratic institutions are to be recognized, even if they would force the party out of power. The traditional formula of the "dictatorship of the proletariat" is abandoned in favor of demands for even greater democracy than now exists or a vague formula of proletarian "hegemony." Carillo speaks positively of a mixed economic system combining nationalized and privately owned and managed enterprises. Foreign capital is to be welcomed. Spain's armed forces are to be independent from the United States as well as from the Soviet Union and preserve their national character.[20]

The events in Poland in 1981 have created severe embarrassment for the French Communists. While the party leadership under Marchais put the blame for the Polish military coup upon the excesses of the union, the four Communist cabinet members claimed that they agreed with their Socialist colleagues on their judgment of the Polish events. Mitterrand condemned the military takeover in no uncertain terms, and his party supported Solidarity enthusiastically.

Foreign policy issues had been among the most difficult questions that threatened to make impossible the Socialist-Communist coalition that formed the government in 1981. The Socialists at the time forced the reluctant Communist leaders to accept—even if not explicitly endorse—the Socialist pro-Western line on Afghanistan, Euro-missiles, and related issues. It is, therefore, unlikely that while opposing Euro-Communism the French Communists would break up their alliance with the Socialists over foreign policy issues. If they did, the internal tension over the submissive role of the party leadership in its relations with Moscow might endanger the unity of the party. Moreover, withdrawal from the government coalition by the seriously weakened Communists—they lost 1.5 million votes in the elections of 1981—would not force the Socialist government to resign.

For the Italian Communists the events in Poland merely reenforced their Euro-Communist views. They condemned the military coup in no uncertain terms. Yet the events could not fail to weaken the Communists in favor of the Socialists, now led aggressively by Bettino Craxi, and of the left, where terrorists rejected the "conciliatory" attitude of the Communist party.

What should the non-Communist left think of these developments? Clearly, the sudden shift toward the traditional Stalinist line by the French Communists shortly before the election of 1978 has made the problem of less immediate importance in that country, and the outcome of the 1981 elections has made the issue at least temporarily of even less weight. True, there are internal conflicts in both the Communist and the Socialist parties that may present the question in the future in a new light and under new circumstances. Given the small size of the Spanish Communist party, it, too, does not seem to present a pressing question. This leaves only the issue of the Italian Communist party.[21]

Its concessions to a non-Soviet oriented Communism are manifold. Togliatti, toward the end of his life, paved the way by describing a "new democracy" as a stage of peaceful transition to Socialism. In his testament, the Yalta memorandum of 1964, he proposed a more conciliatory attitude toward the Roman Catholic church. After the revelations of the 20th congress of the Soviet Communist party in 1956, the idea of "polycentrism"—of providing for a high degree of independence from Moscow—became popular in the Italian party. Still it supported the Soviet intervention in Hungary and associated itself with international Communist statements in 1957 and 1960; only in the late 1960s, especially after the invasion of Czechoslovakia, did it dare to utter criticisms of the Soviet Union. The fiasco of the Allende regime in Chile finally compelled the party to look for allies beyond the 51 percent of the parliamentary vote, i.e., even within the "bourgeoisie." Only the uppermost groups of that class—monopoly capital, big business, and multinational corporations—remained the enemy. From this followed the idea of the "historic compromise": an alliance between the Communist party and at least substantial parts of the Christian Democratic party was to be the way for the Communists to gain a share in the government.

For a long time, the Communist party was satisfied with being a part of the parliamentary majority supporting a Christian Democratic government without being represented in it. Late in 1978, however, Berlinguer became impatient and, by insisting on government participation, brought the government down. His only success, however, was that for the first time the prime minister was not a member of the Christian Democrats.

What is missing in the apparent conversion of the Communist party of Italy? Usually that question is being discussed from the angle of the sincerity of the Communist conversion. That, I believe, is a somewhat naive way of looking at it. Assuming the genuineness of the Italian Communist party leaders' turn toward democracy, there is, of course, no guarantee that, given different internal or external circumstances, a new leadership with old ideas might not take over. This might become more difficult as time passes but cannot be excluded. The only relevant questions to be asked concern the present and the immediate future of the party's policy.

As far as its internal system goes, the observer may raise the issue of democratic centralism, the organizational principle of all Communist parties. This may well be described as a misnomer. The system is centralized to a point where it is not democratic. Major policy decisions including the turn toward Euro-Communism were proclaimed by the party leadership but only very recently discussed by the membership, and even then after the event. This certainly contributes to the feeling of distrust in the permanency of the conversion, and the sudden changes in the French Communist party line in the 1970s are good examples of what democratic centralism means in practice. Thus, since major policy decisions are not anchored in an expression of rank-and-file sentiment, they are easily reversible. The Italian party appears to have gone further than its French counterpart in developing a mass organization rather than a cadre party and in mass discussions of contradictory opinions, but has it gone far enough to warrant placing confidence in the genuineness of its new stance?

Related to this is the question of the Euro-Communists' attitude toward NATO. Is it possible that Italian Communists in a conflict between the United States and the Soviet Union will side, under any circumstances whatsoever, with the first against the second? The party has been less critical of the Soviet Union than of the United States on foreign policy issues; the stereotype of imperialism applied to Western policies is still far more acceptable than a reference to Soviet expansionism. Yet Berlinguer has indicated "that he would feel safer with Italy inside NATO than outside it"; but how firmly this view is held in the party itself is less clear.[22] Toward the European Economic Community the party has shown distinct sympathy and has supported the inclusion of Spain in the organization.

Yet, when all is said and done, the West would feel ill at ease with Euro-Communist members, even from the Italian party, in their respective governments and perhaps familiar with NATO secrets, policies, and actions; even more reluctantly would Western public opinion admit Euro-Communist cabinet members into a position to influence decisions on NATO and defense matters in general. Thus, ambivalence toward Euro-Communism is likely to persist in the West for some time and to delay policy shifts on domestic issues of growing importance at a time when radical changes seem urgently called for. The setback of the Italian Communist party in the elections of June 1979 may well prevent for some time a decisive shift in the Italian party alignment or make the issue lose most of its urgency.

NOTES

1. Quoted in *Der Spiegel,* 31 (May 30, 1977), 154.

2. *Ibid.*

3. Not all of the older French people have forgotten the period of Nazi-Communist collaboration between 1939 and 1941.

4. Lenin's farewell letter to the Swiss workers, written when he left Switzerland to return to Russia after the first revolution of 1917, indicates that he had few illusions about the backwardness of Russia. It is worth quoting from this document, whose importance for an understanding of Lenin and the Russian revolution has been greatly underestimated. "To the Russian proletariat has fallen the great honor of beginning the series of revolutions which the imperialist war has made an objective inevitability. But the idea that the Russian proletariat is the chosen revolutionary proletariat among the workers of the world is absolutely alien to us. We know perfectly well that the proletariat of Russia is less well organized, less prepared and less class-conscious than the proletariat of other countries. It is not its special qualities, but rather the special conjuncture of historical circumstances *that for a certain, perhaps very short,* time has made the proletariat of Russia the vanguard of the revolutionary proletariat of the whole world. . . . Russia is a peasant country, one of the most backward of European countries. Socialism cannot triumph there directly and immediately. But the peasant character of the country, the vast reserve of land in the hands of the nobility, may, to judge from the experience of 1905, give tremendous sweep to the bourgeois-democratic revolution in Russia and may make our revolution the prologue to the world socialist revolution, a step toward it." *The Collected Works of Lenin,* tr. from the 4th edition by M. S. Levin *et al.* (Moscow: Progress Publishers, 1964), 23:371.

5. Santiago Carillo, leader of the Spanish Communist party and perhaps the most outspoken Euro-Communist, views the Soviet Union as in an intermediate stage between a capitalist and a genuine Socialist state. See his book, *Eurocommunismo y Estado* (Barcelona: Grup Editorial Grijalbo Critica, 1977), published in Germany as *Euro-Kommunismus und Staat* (Hamburg–West Berlin: VSA, 1977). (References are to the German edition.) But this view would also apply to a number of Western European countries that have the added virtues of freedoms of speech, organization, and opposition. Logically, then, these countries, compared with the Soviet Union, might easily be classified as the lesser evil. The collectivist property relations of the Soviet Union can hardly be sufficient to offset all the democratic and Socialist elements in Western European societies. The only refuge for Euro-Communists is in "the notion that the Soviet model might have been appropriate at a certain historical stage for societies as backward as the U.S.S.R., but that in terms of world socialist perspectives, the extension of Soviet 'socialism' to the advanced West European societies would be a reactionary step backward." Bogdan Denitch, "Eurocommunism and 'The Russian Question,' " *Dissent,* Summer 1979, 329.

6. Quoted by Irving Howe, "Euro-Communism—Reality, Myth, Hope, or Delusion?" *Dissent,* Winter 1978, 27.

7. While the French Communist paper *L'Humanité* printed some critical articles about Stalin on the occasion on his 100th birthday in Dec. 1979, it is significant that until then only references to Khrushchev's revelations of 1956 had been published in the French Communist press. The full text of this historic and shocking report at the 20th congress has never been published in the French Communist press. Resolutions dissociating the French party from Stalin were passed as late as twenty and twenty-three years after Khrushchev's speech. Somehow the French Communist party regards this late and partial repentance as convincing evidence of its present democratic virtue and appears to expect public recognition of its con-

version to democratic ideas. The result of the 1981 elections may indicate that a substantial part of its following did not have much faith in this late conversion. It is more likely, however, that the Communist setback was related to issues of domestic policy.

8. My translation from the German text as printed in *Der Spiegel,* 32 (1978), 154. This is from part III of the series on "Kommunismus Heute."

9. The Communist party of Japan went further and used the term "scientific socialism."

10. René Andrieu, editor-in-chief of *L'Humanité.*

11. Jean Elleinstein, *P.C.F.* (Hamburg–West Berlin: VSA, 1977), 33–34. A French edition was published in Paris by Grasset et Fasquelle in 1976.

12. Stanley Plasternik, "Socialists vs. Communists in France," *Dissent,* Winter 1978, 21.

13. Significantly, while the Italian C.G.I.L., though close to the Communist party, has been accepted as a member of the European trade union confederation, the French C.G.T. has been rejected. Among the reasons given for this distinction is that at least two C.G.T. leaders, Marchais and Henri Krasucki, are members of the central committee of the French Communist party, and a third, Michel Warcholack, was due to be elected to the latter.

14. See, for instance, his book, *Euro-Kommunismus und Staat.* Since then Carillo has lost the leadership of the party. However, his successor, Gerardo Iglesias, seems ready to continue the Euro-Communist line of his predecessor.

15. *New York Times,* June 27, 1977.

16. Both Romania and North Korea have refused to defend the Soviet action in public, and Romania regarded the moment as propitious to be the first Communist state to come to an agreement with the European Economic Community.

17. In *Euro-Kommunismus und Staat.*

18. *Ibid.,* 112.

19. *Ibid.,* 113.

20. *Ibid.,* 118.

21. In the course of 1979 a sharp conflict developed between the Spanish Socialists and Communists. Felipe Gonzalez, the Socialist leader, rejected Communist claims that he received financial support from West Germany and in turn accused Carillo of receiving funds from the East for his daily, *Mundo Obrero.* In any case, Carillo has ceased his criticism of the Soviet Union, attacks NATO, and seems to be once again on good terms with Soviet leaders.

22. Richard Kindersley, "Eurocommunism," *The Ditchley Journal,* 5 (Autumn, 1978), 78.

16

The Evolution
of the Internationals

FROM ITS VERY beginnings the International Confederation of Free Trade Unions (I.C.F.T.U.), while at first strongly anchored in the colonial areas, particularly those of the British empire, had its centers of gravity in the United States and Europe, the leading industrial areas of the world. In this first period these unions were united primarily in their resistance to totalitarian ideas, especially Communism. Their main international rival was the World Federation of Trade Unions (W.F.T.U.), whose dominance by Communists and their sympathizers could hardly be concealed. A third international union organization, the World Confederation of Labor (W.C.L.), essentially Christian in inspiration, was too small to be an effective competitor.[1]

Next to these international organizations of trade union centers, there have existed since the latter part of the nineteenth century the international trade secretariats (I.T.S.), international organizations of unions in different countries that enrolled workers in the same or similar industries; examples were the I.T.S. of the transport workers and that of the metal workers. All of these in the post–World War II era worked in harmony with the I.C.F.T.U., even though they were independent of it. However, their membership consisted in the past, but no longer at present, of unions that through their national confederations were I.C.F.T.U. affiliates.

From the early days of the I.C.F.T.U. the relationship between the unions of America and Europe was not without problems, some transitory, some permanent. The U.S. unions, operating in a country of unequalled prosperity and expanding capitalism, were concerned with shorter working hours and more equal income distribution. They accepted and endorsed the system of "free private enterprise" and, though some of its leaders, especially Walter Reuther, had sympathies for democratic Socialism, the great majority of the U.S. labor leaders refused to make any concessions to Socialism, many identifying it with Communism. For most of them, the main problem was distribution of the national product rather than its growth, which they took for granted. For most European unions, emerging from the devastation caused by the war, it was precisely the growth of production that was the immediate problem. Beyond that, they rejected a return to the unfettered system of capitalism, which in their view had given rise to Fascism and Nazism.

Once economic reconstruction was well underway, another problem emerged as dominant: the disproportionate weight of the big and rich U.S. unions and their persisting demand that the bulk of the attention and of the resources of the I.C.F.T.U. be devoted to the struggle against Communism. But after the failure of the United States to intervene in the anti-Communist rebellions in East Germany, Hungary, and Czechoslovakia, its acceptance of the Berlin wall, and ultimately its withdrawal from South Vietnam, the Europeans realized that they had to come to some terms of coexistence with their Communist neighbors. While for Americans Communism was a distant danger, the Europeans live within the range of the missiles of the Red army. The former heroes from overseas who had broken the Berlin blockade now appeared unwilling or incapable of liberating the countries of Eastern Europe whose population was so clearly anti-Communist. Would the United States be willing to engage in a third world war—probably fought on both sides with nuclear weapons—to defend non-Communist Europe? Was it not wiser to come to some form of arrangement with the Communist powers to preserve one's independence?

The labor movements of the European continent, with few exceptions, were no longer dependent, as reconstruction progressed, upon the material help of U.S. unions and increasingly resented the latter's efforts to control their foreign relations. While the Europeans, who at first expected a radical social transformation of their countries to follow the end of the war, institutionally and ideologically assimilated a good deal of American thinking, their geographic situation and traditions induced them to adopt a less principled— or more realistic—attitude toward Communism; in some cases, realism meant something close to fraternization.

For a long time, these divergences could be covered up by clever phrases. But when the internal conflicts of the U.S. unions were added to the transatlantic strains, open rift could no longer be avoided. It manifested itself both regionally and worldwide.

From its inception the I.C.F.T.U. organized a number of regional groupings of affiliated trade unions. The two largest among them were the European (E.R.O.) and the Latin-American (O.R.I.T.) organizations; O.R.I.T. included the U.S. and Canadian affiliates without whom the financial basis for the regional grouping would have been exceedingly feeble.

E.R.O. had a difficult fate. Next to it arose, beginning in 1952 in a Committee of 21, a special organization of the I.C.F.T.U. affiliates in the Common Market (E.E.C.) and later another for those of the Free Trade Association (E.F.T.A.). The union organization of E.E.C. was called at first the European Trade Union Secretariat and later the European Confederation of Free Trade Unions (E.C.F.T.U). While its membership continued at first to be limited to union confederations affiliated with the I.C.F.T.U., it is noteworthy that the founding congress of the E.C.F.T.U. in 1973 rejected a proposal of the French Force-Ouvrière (F.O.) to keep the membership permanently limited to I.C.F.T.U. affiliates.[2]

The union centers in E.F.T.A., led by the British Trades Union Congress (T.U.C.), took much longer to develop their own organization, partly because E.F.T.A. itself was a far less ambitious enterprise than E.E.C., partly because the T.U.C. had only a modicum of interest in a supportive international union organization. Thus it was only in 1968 that this group came into being, and it was rather feeble. Its founding coincided pretty closely with British government's renewed attempts to join the E.E.C.[3] There were thus three European trade union confederations in existence—all connected in some ways with the I.C.F.T.U.

An intricate series of international labor diplomatic maneuvers led finally, after the admission of Britain and some other E.F.T.A. members to the E.E.C., to a decisive new step. Another European trade confederation was set up which included not only I.C.F.T.U. affiliates from all countries in Europe that belonged to E.E.C. or E.F.T.A., but also the European affiliates of the Christian W.C.L.—i.e., essentially the Christian unions of France, Italy, Holland, and Belgium plus the unions of Malta and Spain and later the Italian Communist-led Confederazione Generale Italiana del Lavoro (C.G.I.L.). This new or greatly modified organization—number four in our list—was called the European Trade Union Confederation (E.T.U.C.). In view of the breaking away of the main bodies of the U.S. unions from the I.C.F.T.U. discussed below, the relationship of E.T.U.C. to the I.C.F.T.U. and to the E.R.O. became a vital issue for the survival of the latter two bodies.

The founding in 1973 of the E.T.U.C. with its more than 25 million affiliates created a situation full of problems. While the U.S. unions in the earlier stages of the I.C.F.T.U. favored greater European unity as a device to strengthen resistance to Communism, in the late 1960s and early 1970s European unity also meant greater independence from the United States. In the union grouping of the E.E.C. considerable cohesion had been obtained: binding decisions of the congress and of the executive committee could be arrived at by a two-thirds majority, which was a basic departure from the traditional insistence on national sovereignty within most international labor organizations.[4] Another new departure was the decision of the organization, after prolonged debates, to come out in favor of workers' participation in the directing bodies of the new European corporations whose statute the E.E.C. worked out. Then the principle of the two-thirds decision was transferred to the wider E.T.U.C. itself. After internal crises in 1965 and 1966, the European Council of Ministers, however, insisted on unanimous decisions for the E.E.C., thus maintaining the principle of national sovereignty.

An element of crucial significance in the development of E.T.U.C. was the participation of the British. The British T.U.C. had been dragging its feet when the organization of the unions of E.F.T.A. was under consideration. With some ups and downs, British trade union policy as a rule vigorously opposed the creation of authoritative European economic bodies, the adoption of European-wide policies in social and labor affairs, and any measures that conceivably might have reduced the domestic autonomy of individual T.U.C. affiliates.[5] The election of Victor Feather, general secretary of the T.U.C., as the first president of the E.T.U.C. was symbolic of the efforts of the continental unions to obtain the active cooperation of their British colleagues.[6]

Another new feature of the organization was the decision to sponsor or encourage the formation of trade union industry committees, inter-European union organizations of the same industry or profession, similar to the I.T.S., but with membership limited to Europe. A rather curious conflict—which concealed rather than revealed the real issue—concerned the name to be given to the new organization. The apparent problem was whether in the designation of the new confederation the term "free" trade unions should be retained as the German Trade Union Confederation (D.G.B.) advocated or abandoned as the T.U.C. demanded. What was really at stake was the relationship of the European organization to the I.C.F.T.U. and whether the new organization should accept Communist unions as members. By a vote of eleven to five the British proposal to strike the word "free" was adopted. With the admission of seven Christian unions in March 1974, a further step away from the I.C.F.T.U. was taken. A by-product of this decision was the dissolution of the European organization of the W.C.L.

Finally under the pressure of the T.U.C. and the two Italian I.C.F.T.U. affiliates (the Confederazione Italiana Sindacati Lavoratori [C.I.S.L.] and the Unione Italiana del Lavoro [U.I.L.]) the C.G.I.L.I., the largest of the Italian union confederations, was admitted to the E.T.U.C. This resulted partly from the progressive cooperation of the three Italian confederations. To facilitate the admission of C.G.I.L. the W.F.T.U. even introduced, against the opposition of the French Confédération Générale du Travail (C.G.T.), but with the approval of the Soviet trade unions, a new membership category. This was called "associate membership" and indicated a looser connection and a less firm ideological commitment. Later the Italians left the W.F.T.U. altogether.

Nevertheless, there was considerable opposition to accepting C.G.I.L. among a group of overwhelmingly anti-Communist unions. Still, the vote in the E.T.U.C. executive produced a majority of twenty-one to seven in favor of admission. Altogether this produced an organization of thirty affiliates with about 37 million members.[7] The only major organization left out then and still remaining out is the French C.G.T., whose Communist control is not only difficult to dispute but whose views are much closer to those of the Soviet Union than are the views of the Italian C.G.I.L.

The ambivalent attitude of the T.U.C. toward the E.E.C. was reflected in the fact that until 1975 the majority of the British unions were either hostile or lukewarm toward E.E.C. "while nevertheless playing a major role in the European Trade Union Confederation, labor's chief lobby in the E.E.C."[8] This contradiction did not altogether cease, but was weakened after the pro-market outcome of the referendum in Britain in July 1975. As if these diffi-culties were not enough, the European issues merged in a rather confusing fashion with internal U.S. trade union conflicts. Relations between George Meany and Walter Reuther, the leaders respectively of the A.F.L. and the C.I.O., had been strained since the two organizations had merged. There was personal friction: Meany has never been accused of possessing personal grace and charm and he did not attempt to conceal his dislike of the younger, more aggressive, and more impressive, but also more leftish leader of the C.I.O. Even at the merger congress itself, he as the president of the new organization did not see fit to address any pleasant words to the man who gave up the presidency of the C.I.O. to make the merger possible. On the other hand, Reuther and his associates made no effort to conceal their critical feelings toward the conservative, slow-moving chief of that wing of the labor move-ment that saw itself as a special interest group rather than a social reform movement.

The withdrawal of Reuther's United Automobile Workers (U.A.W.) from the A.F.L.–C.I.O. in 1968 caused the U.A.W. to apply to the I.C.F.T.U. for separate membership. There was a kind of precedent for this action: the United Mine Workers had joined the I.C.F.T.U. on their own as a result of their previous separation from the mainstream of organized U.S. labor. Since the U.A.W. was far closer in its general philosophy to the majority of the I.C.F.T.U. leadership and—probably—also of its membership, Reuther and his colleagues expected clear sailing for their request. Instead, they met prolonged and embarrassed procrastination on the part of the I.C.F.T.U. Meany made it plain that the A.F.L.–C.I.O. would not tolerate the acceptance of Reuther within the ranks of the international organization. The precedent of the United Mine Workers and other cases of multiple affiliations from one country did not really apply in his view, since the admission of a recently split-off organization should be described as a different situation from that of admitting organizations that had existed independently for a long time prior to the founding of the I.C.F.T.U. In the end, the I.C.F.T.U. alienated both sides to the dispute. The U.A.W., disappointed at not being admitted with open arms, withdrew its application and intimated that in the future it would channel its international activities through the International Metalworkers'

Federation headquartered in Geneva with which it had been affiliated for a long time. There it did not encounter Meany's objectionable philosophy. Meany, in turn, offended that the I.C.F.T.U. had not rejected the U.A.W. application instantaneously and shocked by the increasingly frequent contacts between I.C.F.T.U. affiliates and Communist unions, announced that the A.F.L.-C.I.O. was withdrawing from membership in the I.C.F.T.U.

Developments since then sharpened the tension between U.S. and European non-Communist labor. Indeed, if anything, the relations deteriorated further as the European unions sought for an accommodation with the organizations in the Communist countries while the A.F.L.-C.I.O. rejected any semblance of fraternal relations with organizations that it refused to regard as bona fide trade unions.[9] However, the retirement of Meany and his subsequent death as well as the death of Reuther have made possible a reappraisal of the situation. The deterioration of the economic and political situation in the Western world as well as the disappearance of the protagonists on both sides caused the U.A.W. to return to the A.F.L.-C.I.O. and the latter to reaffiliate with the I.C.F.T.U. in 1981.

The European trade unions were directly affected by the growth of the E.E.C. and subsequent political changes. These expressed themselves at first in an increasing volume of violations of the I.C.F.T.U. ban of contacts with the unions in Eastern Europe. A growing number of exchanges of union delegations between East and West occurred, especially following the change in the eastern policy of the West German government. Strangely enough, however, the main pressure for contacts with Soviet leaders came from the British T.U.C., while the Germans, though willing in principle, were in practice less enthusiastic about the developing character of East-West ties.

Radical changes in the attitude of the British T.U.C. toward the Soviet organizations played a significant, if not decisive part in this development. After World War II, the leading British union officials were among the most outspoken anti-Communist members of the international labor movement. By the 1970s this had changed into a pro-Soviet groundswell, made possible mainly by the fact that international relations as a rule were regarded as marginal issues for the T.U.C. Thus the personal leanings of a few union leaders could prove decisive, and, as the personnel at the top of certain unions such as the Transport Workers had substantially changed during the two decades following the end of the war, this was reflected in the "increasing willingness among many T.U.C. leaders to turn a blind eye to the odious behaviour of the Soviet Union and its satellites in Eastern Europe."[10]

In April 1975 the former head of the Soviet secret police, Alexander Shelepin, elevated or demoted to the rank of head of the Soviet trade unions, even visited England as a guest of the T.U.C. This visit ended so disastrously (producing criticism in Britain and elsewhere) that Shelepin lost his job after his return to the Soviet Union. At the same time the British unions continued to attack trade union persecution in other countries outside the Soviet bloc. While the German unions accepted contacts with the Soviet organizations as a bitter necessity to improve the situation of their compatriots in East Germany, the British, without any similar motivation, refused to engage in what one of the union leaders described as "cold war stuff, ten to fifteen years old."[11]

In 1970 the I.C.F.T.U. was still strong enough to prevent the organization of an East-West European union meeting on security matters, to be sponsored by the international union organizations. Three years later, it could no longer stand in the way of a meeting on the same subject, to be sponsored by the T.U.C., the German and Swedish unions, the unions of the Soviet Union, East Germany, and Hungary, "within the framework of an already scheduled Regional European Conference of the International Labor Organization (I.L.O.)."[12] In spite of various reservations, this meeting took place in January 1974 in Geneva, to be followed by a second such gathering in February 1975. Then, the steam seemed for a while to have gone out of this urge for East-West cooperation, perhaps because of the unbending attitude of the East German trade union leaders who refused even minor concessions of a humanitarian nature. Still, after a two-year interval another conference of the European trade unions took place on March 5 and 6, 1977, in Geneva. Forty-two trade union confederations from twenty-eight countries in West and East Europe were represented. As in the past, the conference was called by the labor representatives from European countries on the governing body of the I.L.O. In 1977 these countries were Great Britain, Sweden, West Germany, and the Soviet Union.[13]

The official conference subjects were humanizing industrial work and safety on the job—both topics discussed at the 1975 conference—as well as trade union education and formation. Most of the discussion was quiet and nonpartisan. However, there were some surprises. A delegate from Hungary proposed that a statue be erected to honor that unionist who could say in good faith that no cases of social injustice occurred in his country. What was remarkable about that statement was that the Communist speaker did not exclude the Communist countries from his sweeping indictment. More interesting still was the proposal of George Séguy of the French C.G.T. that on the agenda of the next conference be placed the topic trade union rights of the workers and freedom of trade union organization. When asked by reporters about details of his proposal, Séguy admitted that he had in mind the situation of the unions in East and West and that his proposal would certainly not be received too happily everywhere.

Most observers regarded this as a remarkable event. A Communist trade union leader dared, even if only by implication, to question the Soviet trade union system in the presence of the man whom the Soviet Polit-Bureau had just designated the new head of the Russian trade unions and of trade union representatives of the Eastern bloc nations. Oddly, Séguy's proposal was not followed up. No one took it up for further discussion, perhaps because everyone was afraid the conference would break up if such delicate ideological issues were to be pursued.

These contacts led to a sharpening of the differences between the A.F.L.-C.I.O. leadership and that of the European labor unions. An earlier exchange of letters between Meany and Heinz Oskar Vetter, president of the German D.G.B., illustrated these divergences.[14] While Vetter justified the new international policy of the D.G.B. as part of the effort to maintain peace and to establish halfway decent human relations between both sides of what used to be called the Iron Curtain, Meany questioned whether any new element had arisen to justify a change in the previous rejection of East-West contacts.

Vetter stressed that the Germans "live next to the states and peoples of East Europe. This unavoidable proximity to the social systems existing there forces us, whether we like it or not, to seek a meeting and intellectual confrontation with the people and ideas of the Soviet Union and her allies. . . . More than any other group of German society, the trade unions are committed to lasting detente and a stable peace. This is the principal reason of our Ostkontakte." Meany responded that the geographic facts were not new and had not prevented the German unions from voting in December 1955 for an I.C.F.T.U. resolution rejecting all contacts with the so-called Soviet trade union leaders who, in fact, were appointees of the Soviet Communist dictatorship. Protests against the terrorist regime in Chile would gain in impressiveness if equal protests were directed against the large-scale suppression of all freedoms in the Soviet Union. "The record shows," Meany added, "that the six-year-old policy of Ostkontakte has brought no benefits to the D.G.B."

It is of some interest to observe the usually practical U.S. trade unions committed to a heavily ideological policy whose loyalty to the principles of free trade unionism cannot be disputed. On the opposite side are the German unions, usually far more committed to ideological principles but obviously motivated by easily understandable pragmatic considerations.

What did prove most persuasive, at least in the short run, is Meany's last point that the *Ostkontakte* had failed to produce any significant changes in the attitudes and policies of Eastern unions and their governments. In any case an East-West union conference originally scheduled for 1976 did not take place until 1977, and there has been none since then.

In Italy and Holland laborious discussions about closer collaboration or even merger of the ideologically divided trade union confederations of these two countries were begun, with some partial results.[15]

What all this complicated maneuvering amounted to was the beginning of a new relationship between non-Communist and Communist unions. This resulted partly from the new *Ostpolitik* in Germany under the guidance of Willy Brandt and a shift to the left by the British T.U.C.[16]

While these developments were occurring, joint meetings of the three trade union internationals themselves (I.C.F.T.U., W.F.T.U., and W.C.L.) took place in 1973. At that time their representatives met in Chile—then under the presidency of Salvatore Allende—for a discussion of the problems raised by multinational corporations. While other joint meetings were later held under the auspices of the I.L.O., no steps were taken toward unification, since both I.C.F.T.U. and W.C.L. continued to regard the W.F.T.U. as an agent of Moscow, a view strengthened by the presence of Shelepin as president of the Soviet central council of trade unions.[17] Moreover, at least some of the T.U.C. leaders realized that by going too far in their efforts to collaborate with the Communist unions, they might endanger their cooperation with the A.F.L.-C.I.O. and some of their Western European allies. The election and reelection of Vetter as president of the E.T.U.C. and the election of Mathias Hinterscheid of Luxembourg, known as a cautious man, as general secretary pointed in the direction of slow and prudent progress. Still, the evolution of the E.T.U.C. marks a new chapter in the history of the international labor movement.

While the founding of E.T.U.C. was a severe blow to the I.C.F.T.U., a decision to have the two general secretaries sit on each other's executive boards softened the impact. Still, the establishment of the E.T.U.C. as a fairly independent body and representing so large a part of the I.C.F.T.U. membership greatly tended to undermine the latter's authority.[18] A slightly less dangerous process threatens the I.T.S. The largest of them, such as the International Metalworkers' Federation (I.M.F.), have several million members. Many have retained their U.S. affiliates even while the A.F.L.-C.I.O. was not in the I.C.F.T.U. Close collaboration nevertheless still continued between the I.T.S. and the I.C.F.T.U., as had been the tradition. Then the E.T.U.C. began to set up its own industry committees, more or less after the pattern of the I.T.S., but limited to European unions. As a result, friction between them and the I.T.S. was unavoidable. Some of the industry committees on the European scale seek the cooperation or affiliation of the corresponding W.C.L. and Communist unions as do the worldwide I.T.S., which have accepted Catholic unions as members.[19] Moreover, since one of the main subjects with which both are to deal is the multinational enterprises, many with headquarters in the United States, the organizations that can count upon U.S. membership or support seem to have a decided advantage. Moreover, the differences of tradition, ideologies, and political influence among the European unions tend to make unified policies of the European industry committees extremely difficult to work out.

On one hand, then, contrary to the economic trend toward a worldwide economy, the international trade union movement has tended to divide and subdivide into regional fragments, each with increasing independence. On the other hand, it is true that with the breakdown of the international monetary system established in Bretton Woods, regional blocs have taken on growing importance in economic matters. In both economics and industrial relations the future of international organizations and of worldwide cooperation is increasingly difficult to predict.

The return of the U.A.W. to the A.F.L.-C.I.O. and the reaffiliation of the latter to the I.C.F.T.U. in 1981 have given new strength to it. While the powerful conservative trend in the United States has weakened the influence of U.S. labor in the international field as well as at home, the I.C.F.T.U. with its newly acquired affiliates represents a force that, though temporarily eclipsed, has the prospect of reemerging in due course as an influential factor in international affairs. The events of 1980–81 in Poland have indicated not only the possibilities but also the limits of trade unionism as a social force in dictatorial regimes.

Radical changes have occurred in what has been called the Third World. This had been for a long time the main battleground between I.C.F.T.U. and the W.F.T.U. Since the industrially advanced core of the two international organizations seemed unshakable, Italy being an exception, their rivalry has inevitably focused on the newly emerging unions in Asia, Africa, and Latin America. The Third World became the main battlefield between the two main trade union internationals as well as the W.C.L.[20]

The attention that the I.C.F.T.U. and the W.F.T.U. devoted to the Third World unions paid off very badly. In Africa almost all of the original affiliations of the I.C.F.T.U. were lost in the course of the 1960s when the African unions decided to form their own federation, the African Trade Union Unity (O.A.T.U.U.). What this loss really amounted to in terms of membership is difficult to determine. The official membership figures, when published at all, are undoubtedly highly fictitious. Not is it clear whether under a strict application of I.C.F.T.U. statutes many of the African unions really qualified for international membership; their dependency on mostly dictatorial government control and financing is in most cases close to complete. A new regional affiliate of the I.C.F.T.U. in Africa has been established in the early 1970s, but it remains to be seen what influence it can exert on events.

Not quite as catastrophic was I.C.F.T.U.'s loss of membership in Latin America, although there, too, the progress of dictatorships wiped out several I.C.F.T.U. affiliates, and the free independent nature of some of the remaining affiliates can be questioned. Even the official reports of the I.C.F.T.U. indicated a decline of some 4 million members in Latin America and the Caribbean between 1965 and 1975.[21]

A victim of these conflicts and changes appears to be not only the I.C.F.T.U., which has shown remarkable elasticity in disregarding its rules of organization, but also the Communist-controlled W.F.T.U. Having lost in 1966 its Chinese and Albanian affiliates who opposed the Russian domination of the organization, it had to permit its Italian affiliate first to assume an ill-defined associate status and then, in 1978, complete disaffiliation. However, it—and through it, Moscow—exerts considerable influence in the Third World. Although in size of membership, the W.F.T.U. is probably still the largest international labor organization, one has to remember that union membership in Communist-dominated countries is hardly voluntary and most often simply coincides with membership in the industrial labor force.

The Socialist International

While the seat of Secretariat of the Socialist International (S.I.) has remained in London and its membership relatively constant (forty-seven member parties, of which twenty-two are in Western Europe), its activities and their direction have undergone considerable changes. Up to the mid-1970s, the S.I. led a rather quiet life, owing primarily to its weak leadership. In 1976 Willy Brandt of West Germany was elected president to replace the ailing Bruno Pittermann of Austria, and Bernt Carlsson of Sweden took over as general secretary from the Austrian Hans Janitschek.

One of the results of this change in leadership was new forms of activity and enhanced functioning of the S.I. Special assignments were given to different leaders. Thus François Mitterrand—until his election as president of France in 1981—was in charge of human rights; southern Africa was assigned to Olof Palme, the former prime minister of Sweden; the Middle East to Bruno Kreisky, chancellor of Austria; Latin America to Mario Soares of Portugal. The close personal relationship among Brandt, Palme, and Kreisky, going back in part to the years of exile during the Nazi period, was a pillar of strength for the S.I.

Another change occurred in the emphasis of the S.I.'s policy. In the Oslo declaration of 1962, equal distance was expressed toward the "evils of capitalism and communism alike," and NATO was described as a "powerful bulwark of peace." This was fully in line with the progammatic declarations of Frankfurt at the founding Congress of the S.I. Under the influence, at least in part, of the new *Ostpolitik* of West Germany, inspired by Brandt, the S.I. embarked upon a new strategy toward the East. While loyalty toward NATO remained unchanged, the relations to Moscow were increasingly based on Brandt's slogan "change through rapproachment." This is obviously a much more intricate strategy than the earlier refusal of any contact, and in fact numerous cases of Socialist-Communist cooperation occurred, especially since the late 1970s. A declaration of principles was to be worked out by a committee under the chairmanship of Felipe Gonzales, secretary general of the Spanish Socialist Workers' Party (P.S.O.E.) who had come out in favor of cooperation between his party and the Spanish Communists and who had personal contacts with leaders of the Soviet Communist party. Personal contacts were also established between Brandt and Leonid Brezhnev. The importance of these contacts, symbols of the new direction of the S.I., was highly appreciated by Moscow.

In many circles, especially in Washington but also within the S.I., the new direction of S.I. policy was viewed with a jaundiced eye as a rapprochement to Moscow—which it was. Some manifestations of this trend were indeed disturbing to members of the S.I. as were the parallel developments among the unions. Attempts at fraternization were made. Some modest steps toward a more humane treatment of the citizens of East Germany were obtained, but no basic change occurred in the oppressive system. A balance sheet of the new policy would probably show a surplus of benefits for the Soviet Union in the form of a less aggressive attitude of the S.I. These benefits, however, were more than offset by the public reaction to the Soviet aggression in Afghanistan and the destruction of Solidarity in Poland. In any case, "change through rapprochement" has had only little success.

The best argument for *Ostpolitik* is probably that the alternatives of the past did not work even as well. The Iron Curtain has not been pushed back. None of the popular rebellions in the eastern countries has had more than verbal support from the West. Thus the main hope lies with internal developments in the Soviet Union. The example of China may be cited to show that such an evolution toward a less oppressive and less aggressive regime is not impossible. Increased contacts with the West may strengthen the forces making for reform in the Soviet Union.

The new policy has not prevented, though surely softened, criticism of Soviet aggression by some of the leaders of the S.I. At the same time their opposition to U.S. intervention in Central America has become outspoken, particularly on the part of Mitterrand. In Nicaragua, Guatemala, and El Salvador Socialist action and voices were clearly in contradiction to President Ronald Reagan's policies.

NOTES

1. Relations between I.C.F.T.U. and W.C.L. have become increasingly friendly, and one of the most competent observers of the international labor scene, John P. Windmuller, regards a merger as one of the future possibilities. See "Realignment in the I.C.F.T.U.: The Impact of Detente," *British Journal of Industrial Relations,* XIV (Nov. 1970). In Europe the merger has already been almost completely accomplished since 1974; there has, however, been some cooling off between I.C.F.T.U. and W.C.L. recently.

2. John P. Windmuller, "European Regionalism: A New Factor in International Labour," *Industrial Relations Journal,* 7 (Summer 1976); this excellent article provides much of the material for this section.

3. Both the W.C.L. and the Communist-dominated union confederations of France and Italy set up groups designed to influence European governmental organiza-

tions. However, they were only officially recognized in 1969 by the European Commission of E.E.C.

4. Heinz O. Vetter, "Zwanzig Jahre europäische Gewerkschafts—Politik," *Gewerkschaftliche Monatshefte,* 4 (1973), 203.

5. Windmuller, "European Regionalism," 40.

6. To some extent, British resistance to inclusion in the European institutions in general may have its origin in the desire to retain a "special relationship" to the United States. This also extended to the fairly intimate and traditional relations between the A.F.L. and later the A.F.L.-C.I.O. and T.U.C.

7. *Ibid.,* 44.

8. *Ibid.*

9. In 1977 Meany's influence succeeded in preventing the issuance of entry visas to Soviet trade union delegates invited to attend the convention of the U.S. West Coast Longshoremen's Union. At an earlier stage, this official A.F.L.-C.I.O. policy was greatly facilitated by the provocative fact that Alexander Shelepin, former head of the Soviet secret police, had been appointed the chairman of the Soviet Trade Union Confederation.

10. Robert Taylor, *The Fifth Estate. Britain's Unions in the Seventies* (London: Routledge and Kegan Paul, 1978), 148.

11. Quoted in *ibid.,* 149.

12. Windmuller, "Realignment in the I.C.F.T.U.," 255. The I.L.O. is a governmental organization set up in 1919, with labor and employer participation.

13. *SMUV-Zeitung,* Mar. 16, 1977.

14. See *AFL-CIO Free Trade Union News,* 28 (Dec. 1973) for all of the quotes cited in this exchange.

15. See ch. 13 herein.

16. B. C. Roberts and Bruno Liebhaberg, "The European Trade Union Confederation: Influence of Regionalism, Detente and Multinationals," *British Journal of Industrial Relations,* XIV (Nov. 1976).

17. *Ibid.* I follow this article rather closely in this part of the discussion.

18. The European regional organizations of the I.C.F.T.U. and of the W.C.L. have ceased to exist. Heinz O. Vetter, "Gewerkschaftseinheit für Europa," *Gewerkschaftliche Monatshefte,* 5 (1979), 259.

19. The European industry committees have developed in different ways with regard to their relationship to the I.T.S.

20. Windmuller, "Realignment in the I.C.F.T.U." Also see Efren Cordova, "The Changing Character of the Christian International," *Industrial Relations,* 23 (Jan. 1968).

21. Windmuller, "Realignment in the I.C.F.T.U.," 249. For the doubtful nature of Latin American union membership figures, see his Table 3 on p. 250.

PART V
Assessments

17

A Study in Contrasts

THE EVOLUTION of the trade union and political labor movements in Western and Central Europe after World War II offers bewildering contrasts. There appears to be a fairly sharp North-South differential in the degree of Communist influence. While Britain, Scandinavia, West Germany, Austria, Switzerland, Belgium, and Holland have virtually nonexisting Communist parties, France and Italy have powerful Communist movements. Spain and Portugal are exceptions to this rule, but it is rather early to have more than a provisional impression of the future evolution of the labor movements in these countries since their dictatorships have so recently been ousted. Some brief comments on the trend of the Spanish movement will be made below. Another fairly clear division separates the British from the continental labor movements of Western and Central Europe. As has been said many times, the British movement stands part way, not simply in geography but also in ideology and practice, between the continental and the American traditions.

Anthropologists have attempted to find an explanation of these contrasts in national characteristics. I have made an effort to do so in an early study,[1] and I have little doubt that prolonged behavior patterns of different labor movements in different countries or even in different regions of the same country exist and that one possible way of explaining them might be found in the methods of anthropology. However, no one is likely to claim that anthropology is the one and only method of analysis for such different behavior patterns, even though this way of thinking may have a good deal to contribute. There still remains a large area in which other methods of analysis may provide fruitful insights.

Thus, it is fairly easy to relate the North-South differentiation to different stages of economic development and perhaps even more to different rates of economic growth. Even a superficial glance at an economic map of Europe would tend to suggest that the revolutionary or radical appeal to the workers was most successful in those areas in which the rate of economic progress was particularly low or where capitalism was in its early stages of development. Long-term growth rates of gross output for a number of countries during the period 1870 to 1960 have been collected by Angus Maddison from several sources and are summarized in Table 1.[2] Without exception growth rates since 1950 were higher than during the preceding four decades, during which France in particular showed the well-known evidence of its long-term stagnation. It should be noted, moreover, that even during the preceding fifty years France had suffered from a conspicuously lower growth rate than all of Western Europe except Italy. The higher growth rates of the 1950s in Western Europe in general—mainly reconstruction after the war—stand in contrast with the relative slackening of growth in the United States. Indeed, of the countries investigated only Belgium and the United Kingdom had lower growth rates than the United States in the 1950s. The poor performance of the United Kingdom continues up to now. However, since the mid-1970s growth rates in general have slackened.

The period from 1956 to 1961, in which the effects of the treaty of Rome (which set up the European Economic Community [E.E.C.]) might be expected to have had their first manifestation—if only in anticipation of future unification measures—offers some variety. In Belgium, France, Germany, and the Netherlands growth rates declined—particularly in Germany and the Netherlands. Italy, on the other hand, witnessed a further increase of its rate of growth, impressive even during the earlier period.

A somewhat different picture emerges when we refer to per capita output, which takes into account the different rates of population change. Table 2 summarizes the information.[3] Belgium and the United Kingdom—with low rates of population growth since 1950[4]—now appear to do relatively better than the United States, but are still behind the rest of Europe. Next to Belgium, France was the slowest growing E.E.C. country on a per capita basis during the 1950s, even though the rate of growth in France was then five times that of the earlier period. In spite—or perhaps because—of a high rate

Table 1.
Annual Compound Growth Rates of Total Output.

Country	1870–1913	1913–50	1950–60	1956–61	1958–60 to 1967–69	1967–74	1972–77	1973–80[c]
Belgium	2.7	1.0	2.9	2.5	6.1	5.3	2.6	2.4
France	1.6	0.7	4.4	4.2	6.5	6.0	3.0	2.8
Germany	2.9[a]	1.2	7.6	5.9	6.2	5.5	2.3	2.3
Italy	1.4	1.3	5.9	6.7	8.0	4.3	2.8	2.8
Netherlands	2.2[b]	2.1	4.9	3.9	6.9	5.7	2.8	2.2
United Kingdom	2.2	1.7	2.6	2.1	3.4	2.4	1.4	0.9
United States	4.3[a]	2.9	3.2	2.3	5.5	3.1	2.7	2.3

Note: Data are given as percentages.
[a]1871–1913
[b]1900–1913
[c]Percentage changes of real gross domestic product.

Table 2.
Annual Compound Growth Rates in Per Capita Output.

Country	1870–1913	1913–50	1950–60	1960–70	1970–75	1973–80
Belgium	1.7	0.7	2.3	5.3	6.1	2.2
France	1.4	0.7	3.5	5.5	4.5	2.4
Germany	1.8[a]	0.4	6.5	5.5	4.7	2.4
Italy	0.7	0.6	5.3	8.0	5.3	2.2
Netherlands	0.8[b]	0.7	3.6	5.0	n.a.	n.a.
United Kingdom	1.3	1.3	2.2	—— 3.8 ——		0.9
United States	2.2[a]	1.7	1.6	2.5	1.3	1.3

Note: Data are given as percentages.   n.a. = not available.
[a]1871–1913   [b]1900–1913

Table 3.
Annual Average Compound Rates of Growth of Output per Manhour.

Country	1913–38	1938–60	1950–55	1955–60	1960–80[a]
Belgium	1.5	1.9	2.4	2.6	3.5
France	2.3	1.8	4.2	3.6	4.1
Germany	1.3	2.8	6.0	5.9	3.8
Italy	2.6	2.0	4.0	4.1	4.3
Netherlands	1.5	1.9	4.1	3.4	3.4
United Kingdom	2.1	1.5	1.6	2.3	2.2
United States	3.0	1.7	2.8	2.0	1.5

Note: Data are given as percentages.
[a]Real gross domestic product per person employed.

of population growth by Western standards, Germany had the highest growth rate per capita in the West, closely followed by Italy. With the exception of the United Kingdom, all Western countries achieved record growth rates up to the mid-1970s.

One of the keys for an understanding of these figures can be found in an analysis of growth rates of output per manhour (Table 3). More subdivisions of time periods are available for these estimates.[5] The average rate of productivity growth in the West during the period between 1870 and 1913 was a little short of 2 percent; it dropped to 1.7 percent during the era from 1913 to 1950—two world wars and a great depression. Germany, in particular, lagged during this period with 0.9 percent (while U.S. productivity growth was above average, at 2.4 percent). During the 1950s the average rate was unusually high—3.5 percent. Yet Germany, making up for the lag during the earlier period, and Italy exceeded the high average by a considerable margin.

If we consider especially the period 1955–60, comparing it with 1950–55, we find no clear-cut difference between E.E.C. members and nonmembers. Some of the E.E.C. countries maintained or even improved their rate of advance: Belgium, Italy, and, for all practical purposes, Germany. But so did a number of European non-E.E.C. countries: Denmark, whose rate of productivity growth jumped from 1.0 percent in the earlier quinquennium to 4.8 percent; Norway, from 3.6 to 4.3; Sweden, from 3.3 to 3.7 percent; the United Kingdom, from 1.6 to 2.3 percent. Other E.E.C. countries registered a drop: France fell from 4.2 to 3.6 percent.

It should be kept in mind that the starting levels in the various countries listed were drastically different. This appears most clearly in a comparison of indices of per capita gross national product (G.N.P.). With the United States set at 100 and using U.S. price weights, a study by the U.S. Bureau of the Census shows that all of these countries improved their position relative to the United States (Table 4).

While the growth records of the postwar period in Italy and France are impressive, there is evidence that a far greater income inequality exists in the Latin countries. This, of course, strengthened the feeling of social injustice, especially as postwar migration has made millions of workers and, in Italy, peasants and farm workers aware of the living standards of their more favored compatriots in other parts of their own country or in other Western countries. Whether or not related to the material inequality, social discrimination is equally conspicuous in the Latin countries, including, and perhaps even in a more drastic way, Spain and Portugal.

The growth rates used earlier are based on the absolute values of the starting year. No reliable and comparable figures are available for these so that accurate computations are impossible. We must rely on the estimates of experts who, fortunately, seem to be in agreement. Thus, Charles Kindleberger points out that "there can be no doubt that income per capita in France was well below that of Britain in 1851, as it was in 1940 when the question was submitted to careful measurement. Britain had been growing faster than France from 1760 to 1850, possibly earlier, and its lead was extensive."[6] Moreover, since economic growth in Britain seems on the whole to have proceeded faster between 1851 and 1873 than in France, the starting point for the growth rates listed above must have been substantially lower in France than in Britain.[7]

Table 4.
A Comparison of Indices of Per Capita Gross National Product.

Country	1950	1964	1970	1980[a]
United Kingdom	62	70	n.a.	87
Germany	44	76	80.3	107
Italy	30	48	53.5	82
France	53	69	81.8	103

Note: n.a. = not available.

[a]Source: O.E.C.D., "National Accounts," per gross domestic product, in purchasing power activities. OECD = 100.

Thus for most of the period when the labor movements came into being—in both their political and economic branches—not only living standards but also the rates of progress in France were conspicuously low. The same seems to apply to Italy. The slow increase in G.N.P. did not permit any significant increase in living standards when population increase is taken into account. Indeed, it is probable that there was a deterioration in living conditions, which fits well into the framework of the Marxian theory of the "increasing misery" of the working classes. However, in both countries it was not Karl Marx but Mikhâil Bakunin and other anarchists who made the greatest impact on the workers' minds. It is this and related facts that make a comparison of the evolution of the labor movements in the two countries particularly instructive, at least for raising important questions.

There is no obvious explanation for the power of anarchism in these countries, especially since the membership of the Bakunin-inspired anarcho-syndicalist organizations consisted largely of the better-paid skilled workers rather than the most oppressed and worst-paid groups. It is, of course, plausible that in the middle of the last century or even its last quarter, the worst-paid workers were unable financially, morally, and educationally to set up their own organizations, especially against the ferocious resistance of both employers and the state. Indeed, in most countries in the earlier stages of industrialization, it was the skilled workers, often considering themselves artisans, who set up the first friendly societies or trade unions. This may lead to the hypothesis that it is less the absolute living standard but rather its rate of improvement (or lack of improvement or even its deterioration as a result of competition with more capitalistic production methods), the dangers to the social and political status of the workers, and the rise or decline of status that motivate the spirit in which the labor movements operate, appeal to the workers, and educate their members. These considerations may apply especially, though not exclusively, to the early formative stages of the movement. Some of these early unions carried on a pronounced defensive activity in spite of their violent language and slogans.

In these respects the contrast between Britain, on one hand, and France and Italy, on the other hand, in the crucial period in which labor movements were formed is indeed conspicuous. True, the rate of per capita G.N.P. growth in Great Britain and in France during the period 1870 to 1913 is slightly in favor of France, while the growth of total G.N.P. shows a conspicuously high rate in Britain. Two factors have to be taken into account in evaluating this picture: the gradual absorption of the skilled workers in Britain into a respected middle class with the right to vote (which was still denied the low-skill or unskilled workers) and the increased willingness of employers, especially after the turn of the century, to deal with the organizations of skilled workers. At the same time, income differentials in France appear to have remained exceedingly large,[8] and the social and even physical distance separating the middle class from the workers, including the skilled workers, stayed high. As late as February 1899 Fernand Pelloutier, the leader of the anarcho-syndicalists, then dominating one influential wing of the emerging trade union movement, wrote in his *Letter to the Anarchists:* "We are rebels at all times, men truly without God, without master, without Fatherland, the unshakable foes of all moral or material despotism, whether individual or collective, i.e., of laws and dictatorship (that of the proletariat included) and the passionate lovers of culture by itself."[9]

The Italian case is comparatively simple. All of our criteria for the development of a class-conscious, rebellious working class are being met: the low level of economic development, the low workers' incomes, the low rate of economic growth, the high rate of both unemployment and underemployment, the social and political discrimination against the working class, and the existence of a large landless peasant class, depressing the living standards of the industrial workers, at least in the occupations requiring a minimal skill. These were the conditions in which the French and Italian labor movements came into being.

Later developments in France are particularly instructive as various authors[10] have pointed out; the glorification of the Resistance, the legend of quasitotal opposition to the Nazi conquerors, and the insistence upon the important contribution the French themselves made to their liberation were essential for the nation's effort to regain its self-esteem. For at least a partly factual base, this myth had to emphasize the large role that the workers played in the Maquis, the French underground movement. Charles de Gaulle himself paid tribute to the "importance of the role which the patriotism of the working class, its wisdom, its courage played in the resistance of the nation to the enemy, which they play now in its reconstruction, which they will play tomorrow in its regeneration."[11]

This enhanced role of labor was reflected in the participation of Socialists and Communists in the government and in the part the unions were given in the management of nationalized enterprises, the administration of the enlarged social security system, in the establishment of a kind of joint worker-employers plant committee (*comités d'entreprise*), the legal reestablishment of shop stewards for the handling of grievances, and in the National Economic Council, an advisory body on economic and social issues.

At the same time membership rose very rapidly, primarily in the old Confédération du Générale Travail (C.G.T.), but also in the Christian Confederation Française des Travailleurs Chrétiens (C.F.T.C.) Accepting new responsibilities and responding to the inclusion of Communists and Socialists in de Gaulle's government, the C.G.T. became the advocate of higher production and greater productivity. Maurice Thorez, the Communist leader who had deserted to Moscow at the outbreak of the war, returned to France. He joined in the patriotic appeal: "cooperation with the authorities, a powerful

national army, and economic recovery."[12] Striking workers were sharply criticized by the union leaders. At the same time, the Communist party concentrated its efforts on obtaining control of the unions. They were surprisingly
successful in this enterprise, assisted by a number of factors, mentioned
earlier and summarized here.

1. The prestige of the Soviet Union in resisting and defeating the Nazi
onslaught at the price of millions of human lives was tremendous. Forgotten
was the German-Russian pact; what was remembered was Stalingrad and the
Russian conquest of Berlin. On all sides, it was regarded as bad manners,
during the first years after the liberation, to refer to the years from 1939 to
1941, when the Soviet Union and Nazi Germany cooperated in many ways,
including the joint destruction of Poland.

2. The French Communists not only basked in the reflected glory of the
Soviet Union but also presented themselves as heroes of the Resistance.
Forgotten again the two years prior to June 1941 when the war was described
as an imperialist conflict, only to change suddenly into a war of national
freedom against a foreign aggressor. It is true, however, that from June 1941
on the Communists played a large, perhaps predominant and certainly heroic
part in the Resistance and that many Communists paid with their lives for
their anti-Nazi stand. It was this recent part of Communist strategy that was
most vivid in the memory of the French population eager to find evidence for
its own struggle against the Nazi invaders. It was almost a general consensus
to cover up one of the darkest periods in French history. The Communists
greatly profited from this conspiracy of silence.

3. To ensure their dominant position in the unions, the Communists took
advantage of the confusion in the last stages of the war to get rid of some of
their opponents in the ranks of labor. A highly incomplete list of Communist-
directed executions of such enemies—mostly former Communists, many of
whom had opposed the Nazi-Communist pact of 1939—is presented in a
study by a former Communist.[13] Yet it must be admitted that several of the
anti-Communist trade union leaders had been pacifists and as such had supported the Munich Agreement of 1938 that in effect had handed Czechoslovakia over to Adolf Hitler, in the illusionary belief that this would be the end
of his territorial demands. These men were often identified with the Vichy-
regime of Marshall Henri Pétain, the symbol of French collaboration with the
enemy. Contrary to what happened to the Communist party the sins of these
men were not forgotten, and they provided excellent propaganda material for
the Communists. Trade union purge commissions eliminated not only those
identified with Munich or the Vichy government but also a great many anti-
Communists by equating them with collaborationists.

In 1943, at the reunification, the Communists were given three out of
eight seats on the C.G.T. executive board. In March 1945 they obtained parity
with the non-Communists. In fact, they had already a clear majority: Pierre

LeBrun, who labeled himself a Radical Socialist, voted consistently with them, and Louis Saillant, originally a right-wing Socialist, moved steadily to the Communist side.[14] He was to end up as secretary general of the Communist-dominated World Federation of Trade Unions (W.F.T.U.).

By September 1945 the Communists, in full control of the C.G.T., named Benoît Frachon co-secretary general of the C.G.T. together with the non-Communist Léon Jouhaux, whose absence because of his belated return from a Nazi camp in Austria greatly weakened the non-Communist wing of the confederation. A few months later, at the first postwar convention of the C.G.T. in April 1946, the Communists had a majority of four to one.

4. Perhaps the decisive fact in this process was the unity of the Communists, their discipline, and their realization that getting control of the C.G.T. was vital. By contrast, the Socialists were divided into factions and often regarded their family quarrels as more important than the march to power.[15] The Socialist party and union action were separate and uncoordinated, following the sacred syndicalist tradition, in contrast with the strict unity of action and purpose of the Communists, party and union leaders alike. There was a core with iron discipline that had held together throughout all the gyrations of Communist policy, enlarged by newcomers who were hardly aware of these swings, but attracted by Communist heroism during the Resistance.

Perhaps the clearest expression of the new era came in 1946, when the incompatibility of political and trade union offices—one of the main ideas of the Charter of Amiens, the almost sacred document adopted by the 1906 congress of the C.G.T.—was abolished. This added to the efficiency of the Communists, who could now use political and union tactics together more easily. Thus the party acquired the reputation of "getting things done," in contrast with the argumentative, talkative, and inactive Socialists. Even though part of the government, the Communist party attracted voters who were dissatisfied with the deprivations that war, occupation, and reconstruction made inevitable. The reason simply was that they were regarded at first as the party farthest to the left; joining the opposition of the extreme right was regarded morally impossible by most workers, for it was identified with collaboration with the Nazis.

Sacrifices were indeed the rule. True, large increases in wages and social benefits were granted after liberation, but as early as March 1945 wage increases were tied to price rises. Black marketing was the order of the day, especially in essential food items and tobacco.[16] Since selling food on the black market had been a patriotic deed during the occupation, the farmers simply continued the practice after liberation, especially since the government-regulated food prices provided little or no incentive to do otherwise.

Hand in hand with the spread of the black market, which made life intolerable for low-income groups, went the sharp class divisions of French society.[17] While the wage structure was compressed, the real income differentials between the top nonwage earners and unskilled workers reached hardly tolerable dimensions. This made the situation difficult even for the well-disciplined Communists. Part of the government, they tried but did not always succeed in being also critics and oppositionists. The anarcho-syndicalists who had accepted Communist domination of the C.G.T. in the mistaken belief that their two ideologies were fairly well compatible soon discovered that they were at opposite ends of the scale, at least as far as the principle of authority was concerned. The Communists were shaken up by strike movements—wildcat strikes against the expressed will of the Communists union leaders—during the summer of 1946. Communication workers led by Socialists, Trotskyites, and syndicalists left the shops. The strikes succeeded and led to the founding of an independent union, which was recognized by the employer, the non-Communist minister of post, telegraph and telephones. A further serious warning to the Communists was the outcome of the social security elections in April 1947, which was to designate the members of the administrative organs of the system. While the C.G.T. claimed some 6 million members, its list obtained slightly more than 3 million votes. The C.F.T.C. obtained almost half that number, a surprisingly high vote, the more so as they claimed only 800,000 members.

All this and two other major events led to a sudden reversal of Communist strategy. One event was the small but growing influence of the weekly *Force Ouvrière* (Labor's strength), a successor to the underground paper, *Resistance Ouvrière,* published during the occupation. Its best-known spokesman was Jouhaux, C.G.T. general secretary and its undisputed leader in the prewar era. The group, internally diverse, was united in its opposition to the Communist party. More direct in its immediate impact was yet another wildcat strike, called by Trotskyites in one department of the large and nationalized Renault automobile plant. All official C.G.T. attempts to stop the strike failed, and it spread throughout the plant.

This action compelled the C.G.T. to reverse itself and to attempt to wrest the leadership of the strike from the Trotskyites. Contradicting their constant propaganda, they came out for general wage increases. They also voted in Parliament against the government's wage policy. The next day (in May 1947), they were dismissed from the government.[18] From then to the elections of 1951, the government relied for its majority on the Socialists, a Catholic leftist party (the M.R.P.), the remnants of the old Radical party (misleadingly called Radical Socialists), and a few minor parties.

This ended participation in the government by the Communist party and stopped any threat of a Communist takeover in France. That something similar happened in Italy at about the same time was again more than a coincidence. The cold war had started in earnest; but the Communists, by their rapid turnabout, had retained control of the majority of organized workers.

Yet as the French economic miracle occurred, the Socialists, rising out of their disintegrating party, took the lead on the left. Under François Mitterrand's leadership, as we have seen, they were still clinging to an alliance with the Communists, with whose assistance they hoped to obtain a majority in the French Parliament. While this alliance was facilitated by the allegedly growing independence of the French Communists from Moscow, it did involve adherence to traditional Marxian slogans, in words, if not in deeds. Yet the failure of this alliance in 1975, due to the last-minute rebellion of the Communist party leadership against Socialist superiority, put a progressive revision of the Socialist ideology and leadership on the agenda. The modernization of the French economy and the decline of the number and proportion of the family peasant enterprises and the small shops make it likely, if our hypothesis is correct, that the French Socialists will find their way into the third phase, that of acceptance of a mixed market economy even if the public sector were still to be expanded.

Undoubtedly the achievements of Mitterrand in reconstructing an almost destroyed party and leading it to power in 1981 were remarkable. They allowed him to relegate to the second rank his rival, Michel Rocard. Even more important are the tasks ahead. The most urgent is to free the bulk of the French working class from Communist domination. A new ideology will have to emerge from the new government under Socialist control. This will not be a copy of the German Godesberg program, but its equivalent—French style! One difference became clear from the beginning of the new government: its sharp opposition to the Soviet regime differs from the German *Ostpolitk*.

The Italian evolution leading into the cold war has been described in an earlier chapter. The parallels with France are striking—with one major difference. While in France the Socialists separated themselves rather early from Communist domination, the bulk of the Italian Socialists under Pietro Nenni maintained their alliance with the Communists for many years and only in the late 1970s asserted a higher degree of independence from the Communist party.

Nenni had been a consistent follower of the Austrian Socialist leader and theoretician Otto Bauer during the interwar years. He shared his faith in the ultimate reconstitution of working-class unity and in the expectation of an impending Socialist revolution in Europe.[19] Nenni maintained this basic attitude for many years after World War II. His authority, fortified by his consistent struggle against the Fascists, was tremendous. Even Giuseppe Saragat, though the favorite pupil of the immensely popular Filippo Turati, was unable to diminish Nenni's personal appeal. On the Communist side, Palmiro Togliatti and Giuseppe di Vittorio demonstrated great ability, which attracted a large number of distinguished artists and intellectuals.

However, while the role of individuals mattered a good deal in this factional struggle, it was only a part, perhaps even a relatively small part, of the story. More basic, as Italian statisticians have pointed out, was the high proportion of young people voting for the parties of the left, especially the Communists.[20] Still more significant was the north-south differential in voting. While in the heavily industrialized north, the combined left obtained more than 50 percent of the vote in 1946, it lost about 1.5 million votes two years later, and, though it recovered some of this loss, the combined left—with the Communists and Socialists cooperating—had reached a stable, strong minority position. In 1946 the Communists fell behind the Socialists, but this was the only time this happened in Italian elections.

Quite different was the evolution in the underdeveloped part of Italy, the south. There the first reaction of the poor peasants to the fall of the Fascist regime was a turn toward a new party, the *Uomo Qualunque,* or Common Man party, right-wing in character, but playing on the cynicism of the uneducated peasantry, with its slogan: "We're better off when we were worse off."[21] It attracted more than 1 million votes but could not hold onto them. The party's appeal for a combination of work and order did not go well with the skepticism toward all institutions that it preached at the same time. "The Communists stepped in to fill the void with their propaganda. In the seven years between 1946 and 1953 the Left vote increased by nearly a million (from 1,350,000 to 2,345,000) rising from 21.75 to 30.21 percent of the total Southern electorate. This was the result of a clear-cut policy, for the Communists immediately after the War had been quick to grasp the immense possibilities of winning adherents for their cause in the neglected South."[22] The focus of Communist propaganda changed on the basic issue of land reform, as soon as this was introduced by the government in 1950. At first, the Communist party was its champion. Then the attack was directed at its inadequacy. While the right wing criticized the government for having introduced the reform at all, the Communists concentrated their objections on the reform's shortcomings.

Needless to say, that neither French nor Italians were witnesses to the frightful events accompanying the advance of Russian troops through Eastern and Central Europe enabled the Communist supporters to accept the idea that Communism in France or Italy would be what the propaganda of the party made it out to be. "It has to be remembered that there is a wide gulf between the average Italian worker's conception of a Communist state and the state which the Moscow-trained or -influenced leaders of the Italian Communist Party have in mind to impose."[23]

Some of the most intriguing issues are raised not only by international comparisons but also by interregional ones, such as in France and Italy. There is, for instance, the contrast between the anarcho-syndicalism of the small minority of organized high-skilled workers, especially in the Paris area prior to 1914, and the success of the Marxian appeal among the coal miners of the north and the steel workers of St. Etienne. This contrast was also reflected in the dual organizational patterns followed by the unions, more or less according to their ideological preferences. The anarcho-syndicalists emphasized local craft unions based on different occupations (*syndicats de métier*) combined in an interunion local, while the Marxist-oriented organizations preferred large industrial unions that included unskilled workers. Indeed, the C.G.T. was formed by a simple addition of craft and industrial unions. It was the relative scarcity of skilled workers based largely upon intricate apprenticeship rules that gave their unions their bargaining power, while their large unskilled and semiskilled membership provided the weapons of the industrial unions.[24] In the same way the Italian unions preserved their *Camere del Lavoro,* interunion locals, until industrial development in the north led to the formation of powerful industrial unions.

Still in spite of some parallels between the labor movements of the two countries, their evolution in the ten years since the end of the 1960s has been different. The most widely known difference is in politics. The French Communist party, after a belated and feeble attempt at showing some semblance of independence from Moscow, has returned to the fold. Once again, it follows slavishly the directions coming from the Soviet Union, even—as was shown in Chapter 14—at the price of considerable internal conflicts and a sharp drop in its vote and prestige. The Italian Communist party, though unsuccessful so far in its effort to enter the government and increasingly outmaneuvered by the Socialists under Bettino Craxi, has persisted in a course of relative independence, which was accentuated by the repression in Poland in 1981.

There are other significant differences. The Italian unions of different ideologies have moved together and now cooperate effectively. The fratricidal war among the French unions continues, in spite of occasional, though highly temporary, alliances. Italian unions not only traditionally speak in behalf of the working class as a whole; they have, by their high degree of cooperation, acquired far more than a mere semblance of the right to do so. An impotent official government, administration, and political system have, moreover, created a wide gap that unions acting in unison have been able, to some extent, to fill. The French C.G.T., having withdrawn once again into its ghetto, could until 1981 only stealthily take part in public policy-making.

Nor are the differences between the two Communist movements now limited to general ideological or strategic issues. While the French party made its demand for an extended list of nationalization measures the pretext for its break with its partners in the common leftist front and emerged greatly weakened from the elections of 1981, the Italian unions and Communist party have shown little interest in further nationalizations *per se.* They attach far more importance to enhanced information rights for the unions, to their influence on investment decisions, and to controls of the work process. They are for codetermination, though not necessarily after the West German pattern.

The heavy emphasis of the Italian unions on collective bargaining at the plant level by way of the factory councils needs only be mentioned here; it was discussed earlier. At this stage, I only wish to point out the contrast with a much less developed trend in France. The discrepancy in the evolution of the two political movements reached its climax in 1981, when Mitterrand led his party to a tremendous success while the Italian left continues to be a minority. This difference becomes even more interesting if it is kept in mind that the factors suggested in an earlier chapter that led the French left to victory appear to be at variance from the traditional issues that motivate leftward moves of the electorate. The Italian left, though not at all hostile to new strategies, seems to have had less success in sensing the new mood of the electorate. Or could it be that the motivations of the voters on the two sides of the French-Italian border are fundamentally different?

At attempt to explain this parting of the ways in the last decade or so thus runs into great difficulties. Intellectual traditions such as that of Antonio Gramsci in Italy may have played a part, though this explanation fails to make understandable the delay of its effectiveness until the 1970s. The failure of a great personality on the conservative side to emerge in Italy after the departure of Alcide de Gasperi contrasts with the impressive French list from de Gaulle via Georges Pompidou to Valéry Giscard d'Estaing. The class distinctions in France seem to this observer more pronounced than in Italy and the intellectual quality of the recent generation of the Communist party and most union leaders in France less impressive than that of the corresponding generation of Italian leftist leaders. Perhaps the passage of time will permit singling out the decisive factors in the different evolutions of the two labor movements.

Another Latin country that challenges the analytical ability of the social scientist is Spain since the end of the Francisco Franco regime. At its centenary congress in 1979, held not long ago after the peaceful end of the Franco dictatorship, ideological conflicts came out into the open, after a long period of internal disputes. Felipe Gonzales, the young, highly popular, and successful general secretary, resigned after he had vainly attempted to present the Western Social Democratic parties in their adjustment to a prosperous mixed economy as the model for the Spanish Socialists. As if repeating the Godesberg formula of the German Social Democrats, he described Marxism as a useful tool of social analysis but rejected it as a dogma. He referred to the misuse of Marxist slogans by Bolshevik totalitarianism, which has crushed freedom just as the totalitarians of the right had done. He was defeated by some 60 percent of the delegate vote at the party conference,[25] which then set up a temporary commission to govern the party for six months. Then a new congress was to elect a general secretary. At that congress Gonzalez under whose leadership the party had won 182 seats in the two Houses of Parliament and gained 200,000 members was triumphantly reelected.

That the opposition against him counted among its leaders the outgoing president of the party, Professor Tierno Galvan, added to the sharp cleavage in the party. Tierno, once an ardent supporter of the Libyan dictator, had been elected mayor of Madrid with the support of Communist votes. Quite conceivably, Gonzalez had undertaken to lead his party into the third phase of the postwar evolution of Western European labor, perhaps too soon, given the state of Spanish modernization. But that he emerged the victor after a relatively short battle gives testimony to the rapid progress of the Spanish economy, if it is indeed the latter factor that determined, to a large extent, the moderation of the Socialist parties of the West.

While we have been dealing with the North-South differential in the economic development and the ideological orientation of Western European labor, a cleavage of a somewhat different kind exists between British and continental labor. The most obvious fact to which these differences appear to be related is the origins of the British movement as contrasted with those of the continental organizations. In Britain unions historically preceded the founding of the Labour party, and a further interval separated the emergence of the party from its adoption of a Socialist program. Indeed, the party came into being by the efforts of unions and as their instrument in a battle that threatened the very survival of the unions. On the continent or at least most of the continental countries, the sequence was the reverse. Socialists created most of the early unions, and even after unions of different persuasions came into being the Socialist-led unions remained the strongest and leading group. While in Britain the party had to strive to assert its own status toward the unions in order to attract support from nonunionized individuals, it was the unions on the continent that had to obtain by their own effort equality of status with the party. France and to some extent Italy formed groups of their own, since, under the influence of anarcho-syndicalism, unions and Socialist parties for a long time went their separate ways, not necessarily in conflict with each other, but also not in alliance.

These differences had their impact not only on the organizational structures on the two sides of the English channel but also on the ideologies guiding the movements. The collective affiliation of most of the unions with the British Labour party inevitably led to powerful union influence on the party. In most continental countries the unions, though clearly acquiring increasing stature within the political organization, were led by people of Socialist persuasion and derived a good deal of their intellectual apparatus from party members.

Beyond this, the British evolution throughout the nineteenth century led to the absence of a main element in the makeup of continental labor movements: class-consciousness. While in Germany or Austria-Hungary, Belgium, Scandinavia, and many other countries the bulk of the workers were refused political and social equality, openly and legally, British workers acquired higher political status in stages and by subgroups. In the 1870s and then again in the 1880s skilled workers acquired the right to organize unions and obtained higher incomes and the right to vote, leaving the unskilled workers behind for decades. The means by which the skilled workers defended their improved status were exclusionary; their unions restricted the access to their occupation by a variety of means to reduce or limit the supply of their particular type of labor. Such methods were by no means completely lacking on the continent, but the bulk of the discriminatory measures was directed from above against the workers as a class, distinct from other classes, while the British process tended to subdivide the working class.

Though legislation paved the way for some of the union activities and later helped or at times hindered union development, the bulk of what unions in Britain do or not do, and in particular their collective agreements, have been generally free of state intervention. The Industrial Relations Act of 1971 was the first major piece of legislation enacted to change this state of affairs and to substitute the power of the state and the authority of the law for voluntary collective action. Neither employers' federations not the great majority of the unions were willing to make this fundamental change, which would have brought British industrial relations nearer to the U.S. model, and the unions, as we have seen, succeeded in defeating this attempt.

British unions attach tremendous importance to their autonomy. The authority of the Trades Union Congress (T.U.C.) is quite limited. Even in the great struggle against the Industrial Relations Act of 1971, the unions were anxious for the T.U.C. not to control their actions of resistance. Thus affiliated unions were to be "strongly advised" not to register according to the provisions of the act, and if they nevertheless did the general council of the T.U.C. would make "observations" on each case. As one unionist remarked: "What is going to happen if a union before it decides to remain on the register goes to the General Council and says, 'Yes, we have terrible problems. We are going to register.' The General Council then raises its finger and says: 'No, no. Naughty, naughty!' and the union goes and registers. What would happen then?"[26]

One need only compare this with the German trade union confederation, the D.G.B., with its own full-time executive committee, large research organization, and substantial finances, or with the powerful Swedish L.O. (manual workers trade union confederation) to sense the contrast. Even more extreme is the case of the Austrian trade union confederation, whose centralism goes so far that its affiliated unions have only delegated powers and officially no legal existence.[27]

It is true that in Germany since the founding of the D.G.B. the autonomy of the individual unions has substantially increased, especially during the last two decades and that class consciousness has perhaps correspondingly declined. But this is no decisive argument against the reasoning presented here. Clearly, as the memory of earlier class discrimination recedes, the sense of class solidarity and class consciousness diminishes. Nor should the argument be overstated: there is in Britain a vague but still real feeling of belonging to "Labour," and there are increasing signs of rebellion against "excessive" egalitarianism and class solidarity on the continent. The success of the British Social Democrats would tend to confirm the weakness of class solidarity in Britain: the new party refuses to accept the collective affiliation of unions.

It follows that the familiar question asked by most Americans—how do they do this or that in Europe—produces diverse answers. While there are common themes in many European labor movements and industrial relations systems, the variations and differences in union, management, and public thinking and behavior, in law, in traditions, and in circumstances are so wide that a general answer is likely to be vague. There is "Unity and Diversity" (a title I gave to an earlier book) in European labor. But there is less unity and more diversity between the movements and systems of the countries of Europe today than earlier. It requires a very high level of abstraction to make statement of general or even fairly widespread validity. Below this level, however, there is a wide range of questions of great significance and interest. And it is precisely in this area that we encounter the high degree of diversity that is of most interest to the intelligent observer.

NOTES

1. "National Patterns of Union Behavior," *Journal of Political Economy,* LVI (Dec. 1948).

2. Angus Maddison, *Economic Growth in the West: Comparative Experience in Europe and North America,* Appendix A (New York: 20th Century Fund, 1964). See also U.S. Bureau of the Census, *Long-Term Economic Growth 1860–1965* (Washington, D.C.: Government Printing Office, 1966). For 1967–77, Department of State, Bureau of Public Affairs, Special Report no. 41.

3. Maddison, *Economic Growth in the West,* and U.S. Bureau of the Census, *Long-Term Economic Growth.* For 1960–75, National Center for Productivity and Quality of Working Life, *The Future of Productivity* (Washington, D.C.: GPO, 1978), 100, 115.

4. 0.6 and 0.4 per cent, respectively, compared with 1.1 for Germany, 0.9 for France, and 1.7 in the United States.

5. Maddison, *Economic Growth in the West,* and U.S. Bureau of the Census, *Long-Term Economic Growth.*

6. Charles P. Kindleberger, *Economic Growth in France and Britain* (Cambridge, Mass.: Harvard University Press, 1964), 9.

7. *Ibid.,* 13.

8. Which, according to the studies of the U.N. Economic Commission for Latin America, they still are, compared with those of other advanced industrial nations.

9. Jean Montreuil, *Histoire du Mouvement Ouvrier en France des Origines à Nos Jours* (Paris: Aubier, Editions Montaignes, 1946), 162.

10. E.g., Val R. Lorwin, *The French Labor Movement* (Cambridge, Mass.:

Harvard University Press, 1954); Alexander Werth, *France, 1940–1955* (London: Robert Hale Ltd., 1956).

11. Speech to the Consultative Assembly, Mar. 2, 1945, quoted in Lorwin, *French Labor Movement*, 100.

12. *Ibid.*, 106.

13. A Rossi, *Physiologie du Parti Communiste Français* (Paris: Editions Self, 1948), 443–45. This, while clearly biased, contains a large number of reliable and verifiable facts.

14. Lorwin, *French Labor Movement*, 108n31. See also ch. 7 herein.

15. Lorwin quotes one of their sharp debates over the "issue" of whether to talk in the party preamble of "class action" instead of "class struggle." Moreover, as we have mentioned, some of the ablest Socialist trade unionists preferred a political career to trade union work: Albert Gazier, Robert Lacoste and Christian Pineau. See ch. 7 herein.

16. This part follows closely Lorwin's excellent book, *French Labor Movement*.

17. Attempts to measure earnings in 1946–47 are reproduced in *ibid.*, 113.

18. This coincided, more than accidentally, with the beginnings of the cold war.

19. Otto Bauer died in 1938 as an emigre in France.

20. Elio Carante, *Sociologia e statistica delle elezioni italiane nei dopoguerra* (Rome, 1954), 120.

21. Muriel Grindrod, *The Rebuilding of Italy: Politics and Economics, 1945–1953* (London: Royal Institute of International Affairs, 1955), 19.

22. *Ibid.*, 93. An extensive analytical discussion of the dual economy is presented by Vera Lutz in *Italy—A Study in Economic Development* (London: Oxford University Press, 1962) and in various publications by P. N. Rosenstein-Rodan.

23. Grindrod, *Rebuilding of Italy*, 95–96.

24. Michel Collinet, *L'Ouvrier Français. Esprit du Syndicalisme* (Paris: Editions Ouvriéres, 1951).

25. *The Economist*, May 26, 1979, 44.

26. Quoted in Michael Moran, *The Politics of Industrial Relations. The Origins, Life and Death of the 1971 Industrial Relations Act* (Loncon: Macmillan, 1977), 129.

27. Obviously, in the latter case, the size of the country is one factor among others in making possible the high degree of centralization. On the relative authority of British and German trade union confederations, see John P. Windmuller, "The Authority of National Trade Union Confederations: A Comparative Analysis," in David B. Lipsky, ed., *Union Power and Public Policy* (Ithaca, N.Y.: I.L.R., 1975), ch. 5, and Tom Clark *et al.*, *Trade Unions, National Politics, and Economic Management. A Comparative Study of the TUC and DGB* (London and Bonn: Anglo-German Foundation for the Study of Industrial Society, 1980).

18

Ideological Evolution

No one can doubt that the Western labor movements—including even some of the Communist-led organizations—have undergone a tremendous change in their character and philosophy since World War II. It is sufficient to summarize here some of the main facts, stated earlier in this volume, that refer to the direction, the spirit, the composition of the movement, and the dominant qualities of its leadership.

One of the most obvious examples is the attack on clause IV of the introduction of the British Labour party constitution adopted in 1918 under the influence of the Fabian Society. That clause described one of the objectives of the party as follows: "To secure for the workers by hand or by brain the full fruits of their industry and the most equitable distribution thereof that may be possible, upon the basis of the common ownership of the means of production and the best obtainable system of popular administration and control of each industry and service." It should be added that though Hugh Gaitskell's attempts to drop this clause from the party statutes failed, as we have seen, this failure just widened the gap between words and deeds of the movement.

Two other examples deserve to be mentioned. One is the fundamental changes in the program of the German Social-Democratic party at the party congress held in Godesberg in 1959. This was a particularly remarkable transformation of the party that once was regarded as the model of a Marxian class party and that was held up as ideal by no less a leftist leader than V. I. Lenin himself.[1] The other is the change in the Austrian movement, once the stronghold of "Austro-Marxism," led by men in the intellectual mainstream of Marxian theory such as Victor and Friedrich Adler, Otto Bauer, Max Adler, and many others. Now the party under the highly successful leadership of Bruno Kreisky has a minimum of theoretical foundation and a maximum of electoral appeal.

On the union side, the change has been somewhat more complex and perhaps more interesting because of this complication. It is, first, a change of

different nature in different countries, and second, it culminates in some countries in programmatic ideas of highly diversified character.

In the defeated countries the predominant trend of the unions went from the expectation of radical social change following the end of the war to the acceptance of a mixed but predominantly capitalist economy and the progressive elaboration of codetermination programs. In the victorious countries some robust facts of a new social order were set in the nationalization measures and the developed social security systems. All these were welcomed and supported by the unions. This period was followed by a gradual and in several countries delayed adjustment of the collective bargaining system to full employment.

Out of the realization of the new problems that this state of affairs raised was born the second great change: the recognition, delayed and often incomplete, that collective bargaining could no longer be regarded as a private matter of concern only to unions and management. Public interest was in some ways—differently defined in different countries—to be represented in the bargaining process. More and more, the unions had to integrate their goals as representatives of interest groups with the concerns of the community at large. This process was reflected—again in different forms and to widely different degrees—in the Socialist parties as well. From a class party to a people's party, that was the slogan under which this adjustment proceeded.

A good deal of this had its beginnings long before 1945, but it was only after that date that fewer and fewer attempts were made to conceal the contrast between the ideas of the origin of the movement and its behavior. The open recognition of this radical change occurred in very different ways in two of the leading movements in Western and Central Europe, in West Germany, and in the United Kingdom.

The change of the party from the traditional class party committed to wholesale nationalization, defense of union interests without reservation, and representation of the working class to a people's party integrating the workers into the national community, accepting a mixed economy, and aiming primarily at full employment occurred relatively easily in West Germany. At first this may appear most startling, since the German Social Democratic party (S.P.D.) had traditionally appeared as the guardian of the Marxist legacy. During the Great Depression of the 1930s this was expressed in the passionate arguments over the issue of whether the labor movement was to be the doctor or the heir of the sick and paralyzed capitalistic society. The post–World War II movement now came out unreservedly for the medical role. The inglorious defeat by the Nazis, the reformist mood of the working class gratified by the progress made in the West German Republic, and the horror felt for a long time at the cruelties committed at the end of the war by the neighbor in the East made that transformation relatively easy, the more so as the attempt to retain Marxist slogans at least in the language of the movement was consid-

ered to have been one of the root causes of the rejection of the party by the
great majority of the West Germans in the early postwar elections.

Quite different was the experience of the British movement, which had
never been greatly influenced by Marxism. The resistance to radical change
in the party program had little or nothing to do with the persistence of a
powerful revolutionary Marxian tradition but rather with a number of other
factors not the least of which was a mixture of trade union conservatism and
British nationalism. Both were strongly reenforced by the decline of the
power and the international standing of the United Kingdom and the sharp
deterioration of the economy of the country in the post–World War II era,
both changes that ran counter to the established order that the unions anxiously guarded. Given the dominant role of the unions in the life of the party,
their conservatism and defensive attitude greatly influenced thought and strategy of the movement as a whole. Still, it is curious to observe that the
workers' party that was last in Western Europe to adopt a Socialist program
(after World War I) showed now the greatest reluctance to abandon or revise
its established stance. It seems plausible to explain the difference in the
behavior of the British and continental movements by referring to the different
fate of the two economies in the post–World War II period, one in almost
continuous stagnation, the other progressing at an amazing speed.

In West Germany the adoption of the Godesberg program proceeded, as
was pointed out, without significant outward signs of opposition. Even later
the leftist opposition in the party focused on nuclear power and weaponry as
their objects of rejection rather than on the traditional social or economic
issues of the movement. In the United Kingdom, resistance to anything that
appeared to be a compromise with the existing economic order met with
powerful resistance.

Attempts to bring about some changes were made as early as the 1950s
and 1960s by Gaitskell and his friend and follower Anthony Crosland. Gaitskell proposed in 1959 that the party drop its commitment to wholesale
nationalization of the economy and reject its demand for unilateral disarmament. He was defeated on the first issue, but in the area of foreign policy he
returned to the battlefield the following year and won. Crosland, who became
Gaitskell's successor in the self-assigned task of modernizing the movement,
showed greater tactical skill. In his numerous publications and speeches he
helped to prepare the ground for Harold Wilson's highly pragmatic style of
governance. The search for compromise and gradual adjustment helped to
maintain party unity. After the failure of industrial relations reform as advocated by Barbara Castle during the Wilson government—the proposal contained in "In Place of Strife"—James Callaghan as Wilson's successor kept
the unions close to the center of the party. Crosland's premature death deprived the party not only of a highly promising leader, who might have taken
in due course Callaghan's place, but also of a moderate spokesman, who

combined his wish for a change in the party's strategy and objectives with a recognition of the vital importance of keeping the party united.

A crucial issue in this respect was the relationship of the party to the unions. Having been created by the unions, the British Labour party was traditionally and primarily their spokesman and defender. But, increasingly, the public and some of the party leaders themselves realized that union structure and the philosophy of many union leaders and rank and file prevented the unavoidable adjustment of the British economy to the conditions of the late twentieth century. Moreover, given the changes in the structure of the working population, it was imperative for the party, in that view, to become a people's party rather than to remain a class party.[2] This view, however, met sharp criticism and resistance within the unions and the party.[3]

But it was not only the union affiliation but also the verbal radicalism of the individual membership or at least of the activists among them that aroused the opposition of the moderates. Withdrawal from the Common Market, unilateral nuclear disarmament, further nationalization measures, and changes of the party constitution were the objectives of many of the activists. The modifications of the constitution would have transferred the direction of the party away from the Labour members of Parliament to the usually left-wing–dominated constituency organizations. To what extent tactical rather than philosophical considerations prevailed in this conflict is not clear to the observer.[4]

Just as with the Godesberg program of the German S.P.D., its British counterpart (the newly formed British Social Democrats) does not aim at large-scale nationalization measures. Indeed, apart from their support for the European Economic Community and national defense, the Social Democrats are better known so far by what they reject in the Labour party's program than by positive objectives. Working these out in concert with the Liberal party with which they are allied may prove rather difficult. Undoubtedly the Social Democrats favor a mixed economy and oppose the strong concentration of capital, which they hope to combat by measures favoring small business.

A further element illustrating the changing character of the Western European labor movements follows from the gradual change to a people's party. Quite clearly, this must affect the relationship between unions and party. One fact determining the nature of this change was the achievement of a high degree of unity in the previously divided trade union movement of several countries; another was the refusal of the new British Social Democrats to accept the collective affiliation of trade unions—in contrast to the organizational structure of the Labour party.

What factors are responsible for these and other changes in the character of Western European labor and where are they likely to lead in the future?

Marxian tradition would require that economic factors be put at the head of the list. Undeniably, they played an important role; whether they were dominant, especially everywhere in Western and Central Europe, is less obvious. Undoubtedly the rate of economic expansion in Western Europe until after 1974–75 was extraordinarily high, compared not only with the gloomy interwar period but most probably also with the relatively prosperous era from 1895 to 1914.

Uncertain as our knowledge about earlier growth rates is, it seems at least highly probable that the period under consideration was one of the most prosperous in modern history, as far as the industrialized countries of Western Europe were concerned. Annual growth rates of 2 to 3 percent were characteristic of that earlier period, not to mention the sharp decline of G.N.P. in Europe in the 1870s and in all of the Western world during the Great Depression. Undoubtedly, also, the twenty-five or thirty years following the end of World War II led to an unparalleled rise in average living standards.

This in itself wreaked havoc with one of the basic assumptions of the Marxian theory. As early as the turn of the century, Eduard Bernstein had questioned the validity of the theory of "growing misery" of Karl Marx and Friedrich Engels. The attempt to salvage it by turning it into a prediction of relative rather than absolute decline in working-class living standards would have helped very little, even if it were accurate. Why should workers engage in revolutionary adventures for economic reasons when their life became easier, even assuming that that of the upper classes improved more? But the underlying factual assumption could only rarely be supported by evidence. At the most, it could be demonstrated that while living standards were rising more rapidly than ever before in modern history, inequality of incomes and even more of wealth in most industrialized countries did not noticeably shrink or disappear.

In any case, the rapid recovery from the ravages of the war and the prolonged prosperity of the 1950s and 1960s created a new climate in which the labor movement could operate. Low rates of unemployment, indeed acute labor shortages in most industrialized countries of the West, the near-exhaustion of the almost eternal excess labor supply in Italy and most other Southern European countries and Turkey combined with rising living standards, improved social services, and almost constantly rising wages to make obsolete most of the traditional appeal of the labor movements in the West. The "oppressed and exploited" proletariat gave way to skilled or semiskilled workers owning their homes, driving their own cars, watching television, and engaging in sports that previously had been the privilege of a small minority of wealthy citizens.

At the same time, the political and economic influence of labor, though fluctuating, was always significant enough to give the movement a major voice in the government's general direction. When labor did not form the government, it was and remained at least the leading opposition during most of the post–World War II era in Western and Central Europe.

True, there were working-class groups that shared only to a modest extent in the new economic, social, and political status of the workers. The "guest workers"–foreign workers imported for limited periods—were far from fully sharing in the new "golden age" (as far as it went), just as only a small portion of the blacks and of the Spanish-speaking immigrants in the United States did. They were usually employed in the lowest paying, most disagreeable, and least healthy jobs. Still, for most of them even these jobs that few of the native workers were willing to accept were a tremendous improvement over the miserable situation that faced them at home. The millions of foreign workers whom France, West Germany, Switzerland, Sweden, and Austria imported regarded their jobs, poor as they were, as salvation from the terrible lot they had at home.

Many of the unorganized native workers also found their progress lagging behind that of their unionized brethren. But rising minimum wages and the fairly widespread system of extending by law the terms of collective agreements to unorganized firms and their workers often reduced the difference between the two rates of economic and social advance. Even more important was the persistent labor shortage that compelled employers to compete even for scarce unskilled labor. All in all, the great majority of the inhabitants of the Western countries enjoyed living standards and comfort and a high social and political status far beyond their fondest dreams of a few decades before.[5]

This trend was reenforced by the almost universal tendency in the West for the occupational composition of the working class to change in the direction of white-collar work. Although the classifications vary from country to country, the general direction of the change is clear. An increasing proportion of the dependently employed persons entered white-collar occupations. In some countries the majority of the employed persons are engaged in these occupations. This does not necessarily in all cases involve an improvement in earnings, but quite commonly did improve social status. While in the traditional Marxian analysis this need not matter—an employee is still someone who sells his labor power and is therefore the victim of exploitation—the analysis of the German sociologist Max Weber demonstrated the importance of status or standing in society. In this respect, too, the post–World War II era brought tremendous progress.

The growth of white-collar occupations is most conspicuous. The decline of the proportion of unskilled or low-skilled workers is an equally universal phenomenon of the Western world. Mechanization is a factor in this process, but frequently there is also a powerful trend to transfer the lowest occupation on the pay—and prestige—scale to guest workers in Europe and legal or illegal migratory workers in the United States. In agriculture a double transformation is taking place: the replacement of the independent peasant by the market-oriented farmer and a rapid shrinkage of the working population in agriculture altogether, due to mechanization and the introduction of scientific methods by what used to be the most conservative part of the European population.

The two most rapidly growing groups in this internally increasingly diverse working class are white-collar workers and public employees. While neither of these overlapping groups, owing to their diversity, can be called a class in the traditional (Marxian) sense, they are sufficiently distinct in social status and self-recognition from other dependently employed groups to cause us to expect differences in their political behavior and social outlook. Finally, there are rapidly growing numbers and proportions of professionals and technicians—a significant characteristic of modern industrial societies. The working class, Marxian style, thus evolved into a loose conglomeration of diverse social groups, differentiated not so much by earnings, but by status, education, and, to some extent, life-style.

A further factor to which reference has been made is the social integration of the working class. The recognition of the workers as citizens of equal rights was no longer questioned by any significant part of the population of the West. While officially and legally this historic event had occurred all over Western and Central Europe at the latest right after World War I, it was reluctant recognition, and substantial parts of the upper and middle classes then harbored the hope that it was temporary. In due course an opportunity would present itself to put the workers "in their place," i.e., at the margin of the national community.[6] Friedrich Ebert had been for many Germans both an abnormality and a ridiculous figure as president of the Weimar Republic, and Jimmy Thomas had thought that the social revolution had been victorious the day he, the proletarian and son of a proletarian, was appointed to His Majesty's cabinet. Now the rise of the working class was accepted as an irrevocable, even if a regrettable, fact. Neither the British Labour government that came into office in 1945 nor the election of the Social Democrat Karl Renner as president of the Austrian Republic appeared to the great majority of the contemporaries as strange and as part of a passing tide in history. Charles de Gaulle accepted Socialists and Communists in his cabinet. It is significant that in this period even the German Christian Democrats, later the bulwark of conservatism, recognized that a new era in the political and social life of the German nation had arrived. Witness their progressive "Ahlener Program," adopted shortly after 1945, which many Social Democrats now would find quite acceptable.[7]

It is, therefore, not surprising that gradually during the three decades following the end of World War II a voluminous debate developed all over Western Europe; the main issue was the question of "working class embourgeoisement," the extent to which Socialist parties and their allied trade unions had become part of the existing social system. They may have modified it to their benefit, but they had not abolished and replaced it with a social order of a fundamentally different nature. Under a different slogan, the same debate arose in the United States. There Daniel Bell spoke of "the end of ideology." To some extent, but surely not altogether, the questions were of a semantic nature or based upon comparisons of a doubtful nature. Thus "embourgeoisement" and "affluent worker," another term used in this debate, refer to the same evolution. As David Butler and Donald Stokes see it, this is "a process of conversion whereby the prosperous working class acquires the social and political self-images of the middle class as it acquires middle class consumption patterns."[8]

In Britain this discussion was in part a reaction to the three successive election defeats of British Labour during the 1950s and up to 1964 when Labour returned to power. As the undeniable improvement of the material condition of most workers contradicted basic forecasts of the Marxian theory, most participants in that debate established a close connection between this improvement and the weakening support the workers gave to the Labour party or to radical ideas on the continent.

Quite conceivably, in the case of Britain and perhaps Germany this stress on economic factors to the neglect of others may be related to the acceptance of a stratified social structure by large parts of the working class. This would contradict the alternative thesis, which stressed the importance of social equality. Yet, the deep-seated class feeling that permeates British society is well known, as is the "knowing one's place" in this structure by almost the entire population. John H. Goldthorpe's various studies[9] have documented the acceptance of authority based on one's status in the class system and of the "right of certain groups of people to wield that authority." Eric A. Nordlinger[10] provided data on social deference and the British political system. "Even among those workers who . . . are prone to be critical of various aspects of the social stratification system, there is a hearty respect and admiration for high born, well-bred and exclusively educated men as political leaders." An educational system that makes for early segregation provides a "correspondence between an individual, adult occupation, status and authority position."[11] The German respect for social status and titles is well known and, though perhaps weakened by the destruction of traditional hierarchies by the Nazis, is far from abolished.

Still, no one can seriously doubt that the long period of rapidly rising real incomes has had a powerful impact on the way labor sees itself and its role in society. But has this totally abolished the class structure of Western society and conflicts among classes—or at the least among "interest groups"? Ralf Dahrendorf, a sharp observer, sees the basis of class opposition in the uneven distribution of authority rather than of property in society.[12]

The importance of property rights has been increasingly questioned during the period we are investigating. While Marx and Engels saw the basis of power in the property system, A. A. Berle and G. Means,[13] forerunners of New Deal thinking, drew our attention to the growing separation of property and management and the increased importance of the latter. This was later reenforced by the continuing social conflicts in the nationalized industries in several countries involving management, in spite of the absence of private owners. The decline in the importance of property rights, even beyond the area of industrial relations, emerged also more and more clearly as various experiments in macroeconomic planning were undertaken. The frequent disappointment with public ownership in part because of continued labor-management conflicts and in part resulting from financial difficulties was not altogether a fair judgment of the system itself. As Roy Jenkins has pointed out, "Among the electorate at large, nationalization has become an unattractive label, with highly emotive overtones (witness the very different reaction to the synonym 'public ownership'). This antipathy to nationalization can largely be traced to its identification in the public mind with the problem industries, coal and the railways. Ironically, successful state-run industries tend not to be thought of as 'nationalized' at all."[14] While this is to a considerable extent a correct observation, it does not explain the almost universal phenomenon of the decline of the mythos of nationalization. Thus, contrary to a widespread opinion, wages in most nationalized industries in the United Kingdom have risen less than in the private sector,[15] and the principle of free collective bargaining in the public sector has often remained a legal fiction, even in Britain. At the least, consultations between board chairmen and ministers have taken place; and in France, apart from the case of the individual nationalized firms to which the same industry agreement applies as to the privately owned firms in the same industry, government supervision of nationalized industries is the rule rather than the exception.

Most important, however, is that nationalization per se—once a cornerstone of the Marxian system—has remained without any visible impact on workers' attitudes or productivity. "[The nationalized industries] have tended to take their tone from private industry. They have not been very successful in pioneering new forms of managerial control or techniques, or in creating a public enterprise *esprit de corps*. Their freedom of manoeuvre in such things as wage and price policies has been strictly limited. Relations with the consumer—and therefore the general public—have been less happy than they could have been."[16]

The inclusion of nationalization measures in the program of the French Socialists is a distinct exception from the general trend in the thinking of Western labor. Part of the explanation may be found in the need of the Socialists for Communist support. This could be obtained only by the establishment of a nationalization program. Indeed, the alleged insufficiency of the Socialist list of enterprises to be nationalized had served earlier as an argument for the Communists to liquidate their alliance. The left wing of the Socialist party may also have played a role in the decision for further nationalization measures, which may be related to the laggard evolution of the

French industrial relations system, with some French employers still resisting practices that in other European countries have long been accepted.

If Western labor movements have become practical in their rejection of expropriation, then the proper question to ask is what have they accomplished for the workers. This is the formulation of Frank Parkin in *Class Inequality and Political Order*.[17] He uses three social indicators to compare the situation in Western countries with a long history of Socialist governments with those who had no governments of Socialist orientation for any length of time. His first group consisted of Norway and Sweden, the second of Britain and France.[18] The indicators chosen were rates of social mobility, educational opportunity, and the distribution of wealth. For the first two he discovered differences in favor of the Socialist government countries; for the last, however, he failed to see any Socialist success in combatting inequality. These results do not at first sight coincide with those of Seymour Martin Lipset and Reinhard Bendix.[19] However, Lipset and Bendix point out that "there may be more mobility in one country than in another, and yet less equality of opportunity." Reservations must be made with regard to the variety of statistical methods used,[20] and differences of the social and economic structures of the countries influenced the results. Thus, according to the methods of measurement used, if the proportion of nonmanual jobs increases, upward mobility is enhanced, regardless of whether this means greater material equality or material improvement. Lipset and Bendix also note that

> when the various national labor movements began to rise to political power in the Western world their leaders were largely persons from the middle or upper classes, and workers were thus afforded little chance to attain positions of political power and prestige. But labor movements old enough to have a second or third generation have usually recruited leaders from their ranks, and given them an opportunity to advance socially and occupationally via the political ladder. . . . Since at least ten percent of the members of trade unions have held some union office—paid or unpaid—it is probable that this one form of power mobility plays an important role in the dynamics of social mobility. . . . In Europe, the labor and Socialist parties undoubtedly give many lower-class persons an opportunity to secure power and status far greater than that which their economic position could give them.[21]

This would tend to confirm Parkin's conclusion regarding the first and probably also the second of the indicators mentioned above.

While Parkin's way of raising the question has the advantage of moving the discussion from the realm of high abstraction, it can easily be convicted of oversimplification. There are many other factors in addition to the political color of the government that influence the indicators he chose. Full employment and modernization are two such powerful factors, and in the 1960s these were common phenomena of many Western countries, regardless of the ideological orientation of their governments. Conservative France and Switzerland shared this trend with Socialist Sweden and Austria. Another factor might be inflation, and there again Socialist governments in Austria and later West Germany rank with conservative Switzerland among the most successful in combatting the deterioration of their national currencies and keeping down the rate of inflation.

The data about the social background of labor leaders are likely to be misinterpreted. Earlier discussions, as for instance, Selig Perlman's classic study,[22] spoke of the intellectual leaders of labor as outsiders whose duty it would be to withdraw from their positions in the movement as soon as qualified working-class leaders emerged. This, however, manifests itself in an unexpected way, namely, in the appearance of university graduates out of the working class among the labor leaders so that the difference between the early and the later stage of the movement is obscured. Thus social mobility within and outside the movement has increased, and this has affected the spirit of the movement, contributing to its ideological change and the corresponding revision of its operative program.

For the United Kingdom the figures regarding the educational level of the labor leaders are particularly impressive. While in 1945 no fewer than 72 percent of the members of the Labour group in Parliament consisted of workers and only 15 percent were university-educated, twenty years later the proportion was reversed. The proportion of workers had dropped to 30 percent and that of the university graduates had risen to 51 percent, an increase of more than threefold.[23] With this change came alterations in the personal style of the movement. In the German S.P.D. a symbolic expression of the change was the abandonment of the traditional term "comrade" in favor of "Mister" or, at best, "friend." But perhaps the most significant symptom of the change from a class to a people's party was the failure in Germany and Austria to reconstitute or to maintain the gigantic network of auxiliary organizations—from the Red Falcons to the workers' philatelic clubs—that created an entire working-class society within the community at large. If the community excluded the workers, the labor movement responded—as late as the 1920s—by creating a world of its own. The division of the classes was thus reflected in the separation of the workers in all phases of their life from a community that looked down upon the "lower classes." That these organizations that had flourished in the Weimar Republic, in Austria, and several other nations in the first third of this century[24] either did not exist or were of minimal importance after World War II marks a milestone in the evolution and transformation of European labor. The only exception is the "Jusos," the young Socialist organization that plays a not unimportant part in Germany, and the Socialist student organizations. But even these do not express what the former cultural working-class groups had done: the exclusion of the workers from equal status and participation in the national community; they are now simply ideologically oriented age groups. These changes were reenforced by the rapid evolution of the occupational structure pointed out earlier. They implied a shift toward higher educational levels within the employed population, a greater diversity among the people, and generally higher educational achievements of the great majority of workers.

This process creates everywhere in the West a change of gigantic proportions in the numbers of educated individuals. There are without doubt still significant differences in the educational prospects of a child according to the social status, the tradition, and the financial means of the family into which it was born. But the trend is clearly in the direction of reducing these differences. Thus, for Austria, a country with a strong tradition of mainly socially determined separation in the educational system, the occupational mobility over four generations has clearly increased, even though for men there are indications that the trend is leveling off while for females it is continuing.[25] Still, Austria is one of the Western countries in which optimism about intergenerational mobility is lowest. Undoubtedly the tightness of the labor market during most of the postwar era made a contribution to this speed-up in upward social mobility, as did the rapid growth of the economy, the general rise in living standards, and the growing political influence of labor.

What appears to be, on closer examination, the main success of the Social Democratic labor movements is the greater opening of educational opportunities and consequent mobility of talented people—"meritocracy" rather than egalitarianism. This is perhaps most clearly demonstrated in the universal or almost universal acceptance of the ideas underlying meritocracy and the concomitant rebellion of minorities against systems of discrimination that interfere with the advancement of talented men and women from minority ranks. In some sense the main achievement of the labor movements in the West is another step in the direction of a wider concept of democracy, interpreted as equality of opportunity.

Yet it can be shown that greater social mobility is likely to increase inequality in any hierarchically organized society.[26] At the least, the frequently made assumption that a society of high social mobility would also be a more egalitarian society must be questioned. Moreover, the same process can also be described as a further strengthening of the existing social order. By permitting the social advancement of the more talented and energetic people among the "lower classes" and, we may add, the minority groups, the reform movement has often deprived the very same groups of many of their natural leaders. Quite often leadership of those discriminated against has served to raise the status of the spokesmen themselves, not necessarily the deprived groups. Nevertheless, universal basic education and easier access to higher schools and training institutions will be rejected only by the most conservative or reactionary elements in society, those who still assert, as a French statesman once did, that "whoever has not lived before 1789 has not known the sweetness of life."

Thus what the Socialist movement has achieved, in the light of this reasoning, is primarily, though not as exclusively as some critics seem to think, greater equality of opportunity, perhaps—though this may be the result also of other factors—a higher degree of social mobility, and a further extension of democratic rights, but not Socialism. In this sense it is not far from the truth to speak of the "embourgeoisement" of the workers. From this recognition of the facts, it is only a short step to the kind of reasoning expressed in Daniel Bell's challenging essay, *The End of Ideology in the West*.[27]

"These ideologies," he says, referring to Marxism as well as to classic liberalism, "are exhausted. The events behind this important sociological change are complex and varied. Such calamities as the Moscow trials, the Nazi-Soviet pact, the concentration camps, the suppression of the Hungarian workers, form one chain; such social changes as the modification of capitalism, the rise of the Welfare State, another. . . . This is not to say that such ideologies as communism in France and Italy do not have a political weight, or a driving momentum from other sources. But out of all this history, one simple fact emerges: for the radical intelligentsia, the old ideologies have lost their 'truth' and their power to persuade." He then goes on to point out that the belief in "blueprints" and "social engineering" as a means to "bring about a new utopia of social harmony" is now being held by "few serious minds." The same applies to the older "counter-beliefs." "Few 'classic' liberals insist that the State should play no role in the economy, and few serious conservatives, at least in England and on the Continent, believe that the Welfare State is 'the road to serfdom.' In the Western world, therefore, there is today a rough consensus among intellectuals on political issues: the acceptance of a Welfare State; the desirability of decentralized power; a system of mixed economy and of political pluralism. In that sense . . . the ideological age has ended."[28]

There is an important though often silent assumption underlying this kind of reasoning, namely, that there was what Tom Forrester calls a "golden age," some time in the past, in the early stages of the labor movements.[29] Then the working class or the labor movements were dedicated to the cause of social transformation by revolutionary means, whole-heartedly devoted to Socialism, uncompromising in their stand against the capitalistic system. In the case of Great Britain this is obviously incorrect. The bulk of organized labor did not officially accept a Socialist program until 1918, when Sidney Webb's clause IV was adopted.[30] The most influential among the early British Socialist societies, the Fabians were, as their name and their pronouncements indicate, in favor of a slow and gradual transformation of society. Even the

Independent Labour party (I.L.P.), a receptacle for individuals favoring Socialism who could not join the Labour party by way of a union, as long as it was a "holding company" of organizations rather than individuals, was hardly a radical group, except perhaps in its pacifism.

The situation was different in most countries on the continent. There the unions were, in most cases, organized by Socialists or anarchists—the reverse of the British development. In the struggle against the official, constitutional discrimination against the workers, embodied, for example, in the Prussian three-class parliament and varieties thereof in other countries, the early Socialists were indeed using the Marxian concepts of class struggle and social revolution and in some cases making references to the necessity of armed rebellion to gain power.[31] In contrast to Britain, where the unions founded the Labour party, on the continent, with the exception of France, it was the party or party activists that helped to set up most of the important labor unions. As a result, the union leaders followed the guidance of the Social Democrats. Thus, at the German Social Democratic party congress in Dresden (1903), the union representatives voted against Bernstein and his revisionism. In practice, however, they were "revisionists" and did exactly what unions in general and especially at present, in the nonideological stage do— negotiate collective agreements, improve wages and working conditions, and make life more tolerable or even enjoyable for the German workers rather than prepare them for the social revolution. That for a while they accompanied these reformist actions with revolutionary language should not mislead anyone into believing that Theodor Leipart, the leader of the free (Socialist) German union confederation (A.D.G.B.), was a revolutionary. He and his comrades voted for the Social Democratic candidates to the German Reichstag—the All-German Parliament where universal one-class manhood suffrage existed. They also contributed money to the party, but in fact neither they nor the Party seriously prepared for a revolution. They endorsed the war in 1914. When the revolution came in 1918, it was the result of military defeat, not of a working-class rebellion against capitalist exploitation. And it led, not to the establishment of a Socialist state, but rather to the establishment of a weak democratic and capitalistic regime. The end of the Marxist ideology in the West had arrived by the turn of the century, long before it expressed itself semantically and was discovered by the sociologists.

In any case, to speak of a "golden age" in the history of the labor movement makes considerably more sense in the case of the continental movements than it does for British Labour. The founding fathers of the continental movements were indeed a dedicated elite, fully convinced of the truth and the beauty of their cause, and in many cases they devoted their lives to these ideas and the movement. They were prophets with a single-minded devotion. But they were only a small elite. If what is now referred to as the "embourgeoisement" of the Socialist movement is being measured in terms of the dedication to the idea, there is no question that much of today's movement has lost most of the old-time religion. In both their symbols and their actions the contemporary movements show little of the old spirit. Is this, however, a meaningful comparison? Most of the early labor organizations were of necessity small. Not only were they hampered in their recruiting efforts by the combined resistance of employers and state, both most often endowed with semidictatorial powers, but they also ran into the enmity of the church—especially the Roman Catholic church on the continent—and, even more important, the indifference of the great majority of workers. The expansion of the organizations when it finally came was bound to bring in large numbers of less dedicated or even indifferent members, diluting the spiritual contents of the movement.

Given the widespread illiteracy or at least low level of education of the workers, it was inevitable that the intelligentsia played a decisive role in setting up the budding labor organizations and retained the leadership for many years until new leaders could be recruited and trained from among the workers. It is in the nature of the intelligentsia to find ideas and causes of more interest than apparently insignificant or, to those not familiar with manual work, unknown matters such as the order, safety, and cleanliness of the workplace, the arbitrariness of the foreman, or the speed of the work process. Inevitably, therefore, as with increasing experience and education leaders arose out of the ranks, priorities shifted in favor of ideologically less but materially more significant demands. For the outside observer this change could easily appear to be one of abandoning long-cherished ideas. And, indeed, in many cases it was. The new leaders often became so involved in the issues of the daily work life that the ultimate objectives of the movement—its "mythology"—were lost or, worse still, became simply incantations in a semireligious ritual.

To summarize our argument so far: the diminution of political tensions in post–World War II Europe and the rise of living standards and the other changes described earlier have been variously labeled and discussed.[32] The question is, however, less that of the correct labeling of the phenomenon, but rather what it implies for society and its future. It is fairly obvious that there is little, if any, pressure for revolutionary or even simply radical changes coming from organized labor. Even the great social explosion of 1968 had its origin in the student and intellectual groups, rather than labor, and the French union movement that came closest to establishing contact with the rebellious youth was the C.F.D.T.—an ally of the Socialists—and not the Communist-inspired venerable and tradition-bound Confédération Générale du Travail (C.G.T.).

Codetermination rather than far-reaching nationalization programs, full employment, lessened income differentials, a developed social security system, greater educational opportunities for the children of low-income families, a meritocracy, a mixture of public and competitive private enterprise, democracy in as many areas of life as can reasonably be introduced and maintained, and an international policy aiming at the peaceful solution of conflicts combined with measures to achieve decolonization and a reduction of the international income differentials—these seem the common aims of the non-Communist labor movements of Western and Central Europe. Some of these objectives are not easily combined, especially if a stable price level and significant economic growth rates are added to the list. But what matters in our context is that these objectives could also be included in the program of a progressive democratic party whose ancestry cannot be traced back to the Socialist ideas of Marx and Engels and perhaps not even the Webbs.

The "end of ideology" has been related in a large part of the literature to the economic improvement of the workers' lot, or to their "official" reception into the national community in law and to a large extent in fact, or, finally, to a combination of both. It is the thesis of this book that while these processes have undoubtedly been going on in the industrialized countries of the West, and have unquestionably reduced and rendered civilized the expression of the social tensions, these facts should not be identified with the elimination of social conflict. As long as there are organized societies, there are people with more authority than others and inevitably some submit to the temptation to use their power arbitrarily or to personal advantage. Even in the absence of this last element, there is a need for offsetting power, which means for organizational pluralism. And that implies conflict. The "end of ideology" does not mean the end of social conflict. It turns the struggle into pragmatic strife in which the issues are less exciting for the historian of ideas, but no less consequential in terms of human lives and the penalty for strife.

The search for a society without conflict—one of the great inspirational ideas of Marx—is not only aiming at an utopian objective, as far as free societies are concerned, but also at one that on closer examination proves undesirable and dangerous to the very idea of freedom that the harmonious society is supposed to serve. Total or quasitotal harmony between employees and employers, those that are being managed and their managers, can probably be established but most often at the price of a joint conspiracy against the consumers, against society at large. Obviously, a society in continuous conflict, especially one using those forms of conflict that are or appear intolerable to large parts of the community, will rarely succeed in the long run in maintaining freedom of organization or freedom of individuals to pursue their interests. Thus a balance between conflict and harmony seems an indispensable condition of a free society. Neither the advocates of permanent social peace nor those proclaiming the need for eternal warfare among the social groupings within a given community are, whether they know it or not, friends of democracy and freedom.

It is, therefore, not only inevitable but also desirable that in a free society with differences of status, i.e., in any organized society, conflict and harmony coexist. Unfortunately, it is not possible in the present state of our knowledge to indicate the proportions of the two elements that are required to maintain a free and democratic society. We must limit ourselves to reject the extreme positions: perfect and permanent harmony, on the one hand, and irreducible class conflict, on the other. The desire for a perfectly harmonious and orderly society is illusionary and its aim not even an attractive utopia. In pluralism, in stress and strain and occasional disorder—again within ill-defined limits— does freedom find room for its survival.[33]

With the decline of the cohesive force of class discrimination and consequent class consciousness, a process of disintegration of class-based organizations was inevitable. They tended to become coalitions of smaller interest groups. Within the context of the class movement—which weakened as time went on—they asserted the primacy of the particular group each was representing. At the same time the advance of each individual group became a challenge for others to obtain the same or even better advantages. The cohesion of society at large tended to become ever more fragile. To some extent, it was tradition rather than awareness of class or national solidarity that formed the cement binding societies together.

The disintegration of the Belgian parties into language groups, the rise of separatism even in a country like France, and similar developments in the United Kingdom, Spain, Canada, and even in Switzerland all are evidence of the disintegrating forces that run counter to class consciousness and the obvious economic advantages of large-scale economic units. This process brought problems to the fore that overshadowed in the citizens' consciousness the earlier primary importance of class issues, or, perhaps more frequently, added to the complications and the decline of the latter. Expressed in the terms of marginal utility theory, economic advance, though still desirable, lost in importance at the margin relative to social and even more nationalistic values that had been suppressed in the early days of class oppression or that had been ideologically transformed into an aspect of it. And frequently such transformation was understandable as the cases of the Poles in czarist Russia, the Flemings in prewar Belgium, and the Quebecois in Canada demonstrate.

Reference has been made to the reflection of some of these facts in the Godesberg program of the German Social Democrats. A further expression of this evolution can be found in the program of the party that during the interwar period was regarded as the shining model of a modern interpretation of Marxism, the Austrian Socialists. The draft of the new Austrian party program proclaims in point 2.3: "We are today the party of the workers in the same way as that of the white-collar workers and civil servants, of the intellectuals, scientists and technicians, as well as that of the progressive managers and writers and artists [*Kulturschaffende*] and of the independent entrepreneuers in trade, artisans, and agriculture who earn their living by their own work.

These social groups base their hopes on a new society, on social democracy." This widening of the scope of the party—no longer speaking of the leading role of the industrial workers—and the decentralizing forces manifesting themselves among many movements[34] make it increasingly difficult in many democratic societies to obtain the requisite social consensus. Varying combinations of organized groups assert themselves inside the main social forces, Socialist parties and unions not the least among them, and make effective and rapidly moving governments in the democracies an almost unattainable goal of statesmanship.

It is difficult to exaggerate the problems this state of affairs creates in a world of sharp power conflicts. And one's pessimism is enhanced by the fear that a long-run economic stagnation or decline might make the world an even more dangerous place for the survival of democratic institutions. Still, there seems to be little likelihood that the non-Communist left in Western Europe could reverse the process of revision to a moderate reform policy, which it carried out in the last three decades.

NOTES

1. It is, of course, true that the Godesberg program only codified what had long been the practice of the party—at least as early as the Weimar Republic. But few until then had had the courage of stating in so many words what had long become the accepted practice.

2. David Lipsey and Dick Leonard, eds., *The Socialist Agenda* (London: Jonathan Cape, 1981), contains several references to the danger of "corporatism." This term has a distant relationship to "plant egoism."

3. It is not clear whether the disastrous results of Ramsey MacDonald's split in 1931, which also separated him from the unions, had a major impact on the events of 1980–81. Admittedly, the political and economic circumstances were then quite different.

4. Cf. Michael Rustin's interesting report: "The British Labour Party and the Social Democrats," *Dissent*, Summer 1981, 300–307.

5. Michael Harrington (*The Other America* [New York: Macmillan, 1962]) and G. Kolko (*Wealth and Power in America* [New York: Praeger, 1962]) show a considerably larger proportion of poor than the discussion above would suggest. Kolko adds the challenging finding that the share of the lowest 20 percent of U.S. income recipients dropped from 8.3 percent of national income in 1950 to 4 percent in 1959.

6. Reinhard Bendix, "The Lower Classes and the Democratic Revolution," *Industrial Relations*, 1 (Oct. 1961). See also the extensive literature quoted in this article.

7. De Tocqueville in his classic study *Democracy in America* contrasted the frequent upheavals in French society in the nineteenth century with the order and liberty prevailing in the United States. Were he alive today, he could have used Central Europe after World War II as a confirmation of his main thesis of the spread

of egalitarian ideas in society. Still, the reaction of a few conservative groups in France to the election of François Mitterrand as president had some similarity to the German attitude toward Friedrich Ebert.

8. David Butler and Donald Stokes, *Political Change in Britain* (New York: St. Martin's Press, 1969), 101.

9. E.g., John H. Goldthorpe *et al.*, *The Affluent Worker: Industrial Attitudes and Behavior* (New York: Cambridge University Press, 1968), 108–9.

10. *The Working Class Tories* (Berkeley: University of California Press, 1967).

11. *Ibid.*

12. "Social classes and class conflict are present wherever authority is distributed unequally over social positions." *Class and Class Conflicts in Industrial Society* (Stanford, Calif.: Stanford University Press, 1959), 247. Thus class conflict persists in the affluent society as well as in the so-called Socialist countries.

13. *The Modern Corporation and Private Property* (New York: Macmillan, 1932).

14. Foreword to Michael Shanks, ed., *Lessons of Public Enterprise*, a Fabian Society Study (London: Jonathan Cape, 1963), 7.

15. *Ibid.*, 73.

16. *Ibid.*, 219–20.

17. (London: Paladin, 1972).

18. The book was apparently written during the early 1960s, prior to the return of Labour to office in 1964.

19. *Social Mobility in Industrial Society* (Berkeley: University of California Press, 1959), esp. ch. 2. The quotation is on p. 27.

20. *Ibid.*, 27n24.

21. *Ibid.*, 276–77. See also the sources quoted in note 27 on 277–78 of the book.

22. Selig Perlman, *A Theory of the Labor Movement* (New York: A. M. Kelley, 1949).

23. This is, of course, related to the fact that children of working-class families now have far better chances to study at universities than in the past.

24. Some of them had branches in the United States that, significantly, either never reached anywhere near the importance of their European sponsors or were ethnic rather than political groups.

25. Herta Firnberg, "Die soziale Strukturveränderung in Wien," *Der Sozialistische Akademiker,* 20 (1967), 20, quoted in Kurt Steiner, *Politics in Austria* (Boston: Little Brown, 1972), 72. Other studies covering other countries point in the same direction. See, e.g., S. M. Lipset, "Class Structure and Politics," in Stephen R. Graubard, ed., *A New Europe* (Boston: Houghton Mifflin, 1964). Polls of the German D.I.V.O. Institute form the basis for much of the research in this area.

26. The proof for this is presented by Raymond Boudon to whose work reference is made in ch. 19. See also Heinz Hartmann, "Works Councils and the Iron Law of Oligarchy," *British Journal of Industrial Relations,* XVII (Mar. 1979), for a related discussion.

27. (New York: The Free Press, 1962), 402. Actually, that catching phrase antedates Bell's essay by several years.

28. *Ibid.*, 402–3. Whether this still held true in the late 1970s or early 1980s

may be a matter of dispute, especially in view of the heavily ideological politics of the United States.

29. Tom Forrester, *The British Labour Party and the Working Class* (New York: Holmes and Meier, 1976), 7.

30. Contrary to a widely accepted view in the United States, the British miners were far from being radical. They were among the last major unions to join the Labour party. For a long time, they voted for the less radical Liberal party candidates to Parliament, the so-called Lib-Labs.

31. Notice also the contrast with the United States, where civic antilabor discrimination was rare, and where it occurred was regarded as an aberration from the official ideology, at least since the days of Andrew Jackson.

32. Early expressions of this thought can be found in Arthur M. Ross's series of articles on European labor published in the 1960s, e.g., "Prosperity and Labor Relations in Europe: The Case of West Germany," *Quarterly Journal of Economics,* LXXVI (Aug. 1962).

33. See Jan Pen, *Harmony and Conflict in Modern Society* (New York: McGraw-Hill, 1966).

34. As I have endeavored to show elsewhere in this book, there are also opposite centralizing trends, stemming mainly from the requirements of a more effective incomes policy; that they are victorious in a small number of countries and then most often only temporarily adds to the weight of the argument advanced above.

19

Conclusion

CAUTION ACQUIRED by long experience suggests that I begin this conclusion with a reference to Sam Goldwyn's classic warning: it is difficult to make forecasts, especially about the future.

Extrapolation is the conventional way of forecasting, unless we already have indications of substantial changes of trends. One characteristic of recent developments that with some changes in speed but hardly in direction may be expected to continue for some time is the relative decline of the number of industrial workers as a proportion of the total labor force. Data relating to the short period between 1974 and 1978 clearly suggest that this process is universal in the industrial countries of the West, as Table 5 indicates. Altogether the countries of the European Economic Community (E.E.C.) lost during this period some 2.5 million industrial jobs and gained 3 million service jobs. The latter then represented 53 percent of total employment.

That a party exclusively identified with the proletariat could not obtain government control by democratic means was recognized as early as the

Table 5.
Industrial Workers as a Percentage of the Total Labor Force.

| | Percent of population working in industry | |
Country	1974	1978
Belgium	41.2	36.7
Holland	35.6	32.5
Luxemburg	47.1	43.5
France	39.6	37.1
Denmark	32.3	30.3
Germany	47.3	45.1
Italy	39.4	38.3
Ireland	31.4	30.9
United Kingdom	42.3	39.7

Source. *The Economist*, Sept. 16–21, 1979, 54.

1920s by the Austrian Social Democrats, a party then profoundly committed to the Marxian analysis of the social and political situation. The famous Austro-Marxists, led by the great theoretician Otto Bauer, tried to solve the contradiction—attainment of a parliamentary majority and preservation of the party's identification with the proletariat—by redefining the concept of the working class.[1] He included "small peasants, small businessmen and trades-men, skilled craftsmen, and intellectuals—traditionally referred to as 'petty bourgeoisie'—as comprising the 'totality of those who live by the sale of their labor power.' "[2] In another version Bauer returned to a narrower definition of working class but advocated an alliance between the latter and the "petty bourgeoisie." Thus at the party conference of 1926, which adopted the fa-mous Linz program, the quintessence of what has come to be known as Austro-Marxism, he said: "Democracy permits the class struggle to be de-cided by the ballot, by the vote of the majority of the voters, the majority of the people. . . . Here we stand, proletariat and bourgeoisie, struggling for the majority. . . . [The bourgeoisie] struggles for the middle strata who belong neither to the bourgeoisie nor the proletariat. . . . The task of Social Democ-racy becomes increasingly not only to unite the entire working class within itself but to attract the exploited strata of the petty bourgeoisie, the small peasantry and the intelligentsia, to gain for the working class the allies it needs to win a majority."[3]

Thus recognition of the problem goes back half a century. What was missing is the identification of the ideological adaptations that the strategy recommended by Bauer required. The necessary changes go much farther than Bauer and other Marxian Socialists indicated. For in the new version the tie between labor and Socialism is at the least weakened, especially when labor is defined as no more than the industrial working class. This also implies that the class struggle of the workers is not the only force that moves society beyond the institutions of capitalism. This has been recognized, as we have seen in the new formula of the Godesberg program that makes Marxism only one of the many motivations of the advance of Socialism. As events devel-oped, Marxian ideas came to rank rather low on the list of these motivations. Indeed, the trend has been distinctly away from theoretical constructs and long-term views in the direction of day-to-day practice. Even parties like the German and Austrian Social Democrats, renowned in the past for their ability to combine practice and theory, though sometimes with little success, have almost completely abandoned their search for theoretical foundations of their practical work.

It is obvious that these changes require a tremendous amount of adjust-ment on the part of the Western labor movements, as far as both organization and ideology are concerned. The sense of forming a class in which the common interests and a common frame of reference prevailed over the un-avoidable diversities no longer exists. The element of cohesion that presided over the formative period of the movement and that was the basis of class solidarity—more on the continent than in Britain—is weak, if it exists at all. While in the United Kingdom it was governmental policy in the nineteenth century that, by offering sharply circumscribed reforms, split the working class into groups of diversified status, rights, and interest, continental societies, by officially assigning lesser status to the workers in general, forged a bond among all or almost all of them, especially the manual workers, that was stronger than the undeniably existing differences among them. This bond has now only the force of tradition and is getting increasingly weaker as the evolution creates a labor force of highly diversified status, education, income, life-style, and interest. Not only is the working class becoming more and more diversified, but the importance of work is declining in the life of the worker. It takes up less of his time and by reducing, for many, the skill requirements of the job, technology reduces also its meaning for the worker. The extent to which labor organizations will be capable of adjusting themselves to this phenomenon of an internally less and less cohesive labor force less involved in its job is likely to be a decisive factor in labor's ability to absorb new elements in the working population.[4]

This will involve not only tremendous organizational changes but also great adaptations of ideology and appeal. The rapidly growing numbers of white-collar workers and salaried professionals—those whom C. Wright Mills called the "new middle class"—have shown a greater willingness to support the Socialist party than to join unions.[5] To find new ways of attracting and holding these groups is the most important task of the Western unions, the more so as the more highly educated people participate more frequently in elections and exert greater intellectual leadership than any other social grouping.[6] One of the reasons for the relatively high electoral standing of German and Austrian Socialists and—until most recently—of the French Communists is precisely their ability to bring out the white-collar vote. The unions have as yet far less success in recruiting new middle-class people. There is, first of all, tremendous diversity in the social and economic status of white-collar workers: they range from clerical assistants to managerial personnel. Their interests are consequently quite diverse. Most often—though not always—they lack any class consciousness and solidarity with the blue-collar workers. It is precisely the effort to bring at least some of these groups into the ranks of the Socialist parties that has forced these parties to stress their character as people's rather than class parties.

While this is an old trend, there is a new element: a substantial change in the response of the movement to this evolution. In the first place, there has been a steady blurring of the boundaries between the classes and a consequent weakening of class consciousness and class solidarity. The mainstay of class solidarity—social and political discrimination against manual workers—has been changed to the point that a subproletariat of foreign workers has become the main victim of discrimination while native workers have acquired relatively high status in most industrial societies. Even in the absence of full employment, which attracted foreign workers by the millions into the developed countries of the West, a return to the former highly structured forms of class societies is hard to conceive. Labor has so far shown a limited ability to handle the problem of the guest workers, even though some labor organizations have shown a remarkable sense of solidarity with such workers.

A second difference in labor's reaction to the changing social structure, contrasting sharply with that of the interwar period, is a clear diminution of its distrust of the democratic loyalty of other social groups, a feeling that most of these reciprocate. One expression of this new state of affairs has been the almost total disappearance among non-Communists of any principled opposition to coalition governments with non-Socialist parties, an issue hotly disputed prior to world War II.[7] On the trade union side, the concept of the "social partners" has been widely accepted, and all indications are that the new terminology and the implied rejection of the ideas of a Marxian class struggle is a permanent feature of the Europe social scene.[8]

All this has been accompanied by a decreasing intensity of political and ideological emotions, which tends to make political conflict more civilized but also far less interesting and attractive for youth than in the past.[9] There is little reason to assume that a reversal of this trend is probable in the near future, except possibly in so far as international problems are concerned. The main enemy of democracy, it is believed in most Western countries, is no longer on the right as in the days of the Weimar Republic but on the left, in the form of international Communism. This is increasingly regarded as an external threat, and that only in moderation.

Of the traditional long-term objectives of Western European labor, none seems likely to arouse again the passionate concern that prevailed in the early stages of the movement. Nationalization has had far less impact upon the life of the workers than the Marxian theory or even the more moderate pronouncements of the British Fabians implied.

It is instructive to contrast earlier statements of labor's objectives with those of the Godesberg program. "All socialists were united in proclaiming the moral and historical necessity of some form of common ownership of the means of production, distribution and exchange. Indeed, this became the accepted definition of socialism."[10] The modern version emphasizes management rather than ownership and codetermination instead of expropriation. Bailing out failing enterprises with public funds maintains private management and is thus regarded as compatible with mixed economies.[11] A further spread of codetermination, on the other hand, seems likely. It corresponds to the tendency in industrial relations to follow foreign models regarded as successful. There is, apart from France, no trend in the direction of further substantial nationalization of industries. Sporadic references to nationalization measures in other countries betray a praiseworthy loyalty to tradition rather than a more desirable willingness to learn from experience. While it is unlikely that there will be a wholesale return of nationalized enterprises to private property, it is equally doubtful that there will be a radical shift to public ownership in most Western European societies. Full employment, rising living standards, shorter and flexible working periods appear attainable without further major shifts in property arrangements; reasonable price stability, however, appears far more difficult to achieve. Only if future economic development should refute these assumptions based upon the experience of the three decades following World War II might there be an incentive to search for new social and economic institutions. This possibility cannot be excluded—three decades are too short a period from which to extrapolate for very long—but for the time being John Maynard Keynes or some variation of his theory has won out over Karl Marx in most Western labor movements.[12] A mixed, predominantly capitalistic, society is likely to persist for a long time to come.

The desire for continued economic expansion has profoundly affected the meaning of another traditional Socialist objective—equality. As the total elimination or perhaps even a substantial reduction of material incentives is likely to affect productivity, equality has come to mean equal opportunities rather than equal incomes or wealth. Confronted with the choice between equality in the latter sense and economic efficiency, the great majority of labor's supporters are likely to choose economic growth.[13]

The main instrument for achieving equality of opportunity has been education rather than the redistribution of wealth and the narrowing of income differentials. A case can be made that it is Europe's antiquated educational system that is the main block on the road toward achieving equality of opportunity. Progressive income taxes and heavy inheritance taxes tend to make income and wealth differentials perhaps less insuperable hurdles than educational discrimination for the social advancement of the children of the working classes.

"Today's [educational] system is basically the same as at its creation in the nineteenth century. It is based on the distinction between primary education, which is universal, and secondary education, which was usually reserved for children of the wealthy. In some countries, secondary education is divided into two or three streams, only one of which leads to the university, a goal reserved in practice, if not in theory, for the culturally or economically privileged."[14] It is true that there has been a tremendous expansion of the university student body and of the number and size of higher educational facilities. But the nature and content of education have undergone only modest changes, falling far behind the rapid pace of change in the economic, social, and political systems for which education is intended to prepare the students. And the background of the university students, although also changing, has failed to reflect the need for easier access to higher education for students of working-class backgrounds. Thus, while in France the student population doubled between 1961 and 1967, the proportion of students whose fathers were businessmen, civil servants, or members of the liberal professions fell only from 64 percent to 62.4 percent. The proportion of students from working-class or rural families rose during the same period from 21.4 percent to 26.2 percent.[15] Equally important: "The content, teaching methods, and structure of today's education system mirror yesterday's society."[16] The main change that has occurred is an expansion but not a real readaptation of the system. One of the most regrettable by-products of this lateral expansion has been the almost unbelieveable waste of human talent and effort that has resulted. The most serious criticism of this educational system is that instead of reforming itself, it has merely grown. And this does not assure "that graduates will be able to find their places in rapidly changing societies with more and more sophisticated economies."[17]

Equality of opportunity thus requires far more substantial and basic changes in Europe's educational system than have so far occurred. For democratic Socialists this may turn out to be one of their most urgent assignments.

It is, of course, a matter of dispute whether equality of opportunity, when achieved, would change other aspects of society or, on the contrary, extend their life span. A meritocracy may deprive the lower social groups of the leaders they would need to help them out of the oppressive conditions in which they find themselves. The reasoning shows the multiplicity of meanings of the term equality and the inner contradictions of some forms of it.

More important still is the issue of whether a higher degree of equality of opportunity, especially as regards access to higher education, would tend to lead to greater equality in other respects, such as income, wealth, and perhaps status. Indeed, a meritocracy, even if founded on educational achievement rather than on inheritance, may be no less burdensome and far more difficult to modify than earlier forms of a hierarchical society. The social mobility produced by greater equality of access to higher learning leads to the result that ascending movements along the social ladder are less likely to occur than descending ones. This is the inevitable consequence of the shape of the social pyramid that narrows toward the top.[18] In other words, a more democratic educational system may increase upward social mobility less than movement in the opposite direction. The hopes for education as an instrument for achieving greater equality may thus have been mistaken, much as a more democratic system for admission to higher education may be desirable on other grounds. Changes in the occupational hierarchy and corresponding changes in the system of compensation may be useful approaches to pursue.

In the absence of an actual and long-term decline of real wages—a perspective that the actions of the Organization of Petroleum Exporting Countries (O.P.E.C.) and the possible reality of a declining branch of the Kondratieff cycle may well present—the main emphasis of worker demands may undergo an important shift. Signs for this appeared already in the 1970s. Thus "the quality of working life"[19] and a "meaningful participation in the determination of the conditions of work" have become sharply accentuated issues, supplementing at the workplace the well-advanced campaign for some form of codetermination at the top level of the enterprise and in national institutions. Shorter working hours—difficult to obtain against the resistance of employers concerned with high overhead costs—or longer vacations have emerged as burning issues. Even though some of the intensity of these demands resulted from unemployment or fear of unemployment, they also correspond to long-term trends in industrial relations in the West. "The work force of tomorrow will be better educated and will be making more demands for interesting and meaningful jobs that satisfy their requirements for challenge, growth, and self-fulfillment; many will become disaffected because too few fulfilling jobs will be available. These problems seem to be deeply rooted in the structure of technologically advanced societies. Although the more pressing problems of inflation and unemployment may push the issue of worker dissatisfaction off the front page, this problem seems destined to be a major concern of developed societies for the indefinite future."[20]

Industrial conflict has been another major concern in many Western societies, even though the problem has been of significance in only two or three countries of Western Europe. It is particularly the strike, and especially the sudden, unforeseen strike, that has called forth public protest. It is obvious that strikes are only one form among several that express the conflict of interests among the partners of the industrial relations system. Indeed, some of the other forms such as sabotage, slow down, or absenteeism may have more serious consequences for the public and the enterprise. Still, strikes draw most public attention and the desire for industrial harmony and peace is widespread.

Apart from England, Italy, and, intermittently, France, strikes have not been numerous or burdensome in most of Western Europe. While it is perhaps easy to demonstrate that a strike is not necessarily the most intelligent way of settling disputes, it should be recognized that conflict is inherent in an industrial relations system that combines antagonism among its partners with a community of interest. The most obvious methods of suppressing the open confrontation of the partners are likely to be far worse than the evil they aim to eliminate. A dictatorship may, by the use of force, prevent strikes (though not necessarily other forms of industrial conflict) as part of the destruction of freedom. Alternatively, in a grotesque parody of syndicalism, a coalition of employers and unions may eliminate conflict by making each other liberal concessions that have to be paid for by the public. Neither the totalitarian nor the quasisyndicalist solution holds out much appeal and chances are that neither will be applied on a large scale, in spite of public grumbling, in the foreseeable future in Western Europe. Yet the ability of a system to manage conflict in a socially tolerable way will continue to be regarded as one criterion of its success.[21]

In that respect, the United Kingdom and Italy are likely to continue to be the least successful of the Western countries. Unless the rate of economic growth in Great Britain improves considerably, it will be difficult to satisfy, even in a modest way, the aspirations of the workers, and the union leaders will continue to be under extreme pressure. The danger that effective control of their members will rest with the shop stewards and the resulting diffusion of power and conflict will continue to loom large. In Italy political and administrative chaos remains the main problem of a country with astonishing vitality. Against this background the industrial relations system remains difficult to manage and offers favorable conditions for the growth and the activities of terrorist groups. The bulk of the members of the latter do not appear to come out of working-class ranks, but they find in the acuity of industrial conflicts fertile soil for spreading terroristic activities. There are no indications that this is likely to change in the near future.

Perhaps the most significant development that is likely to influence labor's evolution far into the rest of this century is the change in the character of collective bargaining. One factor determining this change is a high level of employment, which may or may not materialize in the next two decades. The other is the institutionalization of collective bargaining, which has turned union and management leaders into what the Austrians and Germans call "social partners." These two factors point in the same direction. Full employment threatens the foundation of the traditional idea of collective bargaining as a private arrangement between labor and management, a concept that always had less validity on the continent than in England and the United States. The institutionalization of collective bargaining, the view of this process as an agreement among partners rather than an expression of the class struggle, further emphasizes the integration of the European working class into the existing social order and enhances the likelihood of syndicalist or corporate solutions.

However, there are different degrees of integration and in particular widely differing degrees of understanding of its implications. The contrast is most clearly perceived in the role of the British unions and even more the shop stewards when compared with the German or the Austrian unions. The issue dividing the two types of union behavior is the degree to which they concern themselves with more than their narrowly defined short-term interests. This may be ideologically determined: unions devoted to a Socialist ideal, distant and ill-defined as it may be, or to supporting a political party from which they expect services in return, may be more willing to consider the impact of their actions upon the community at large than others not so inspired. The structure and authority of the union confederation may be even more relevant. Where the central confederation exerts a good deal of control over the affiliated unions as in Austria, Sweden, or, to a decreasing extent, West Germany, union policy may be influenced by considerations of a general nature that may not matter or not be applicable to an individual union. This runs counter to the desire to make unions as democratic as possible, in the sense of bringing them close to the rank and file. The more decentralized collective bargaining is, the readier the group is to use the strike; the more direct union democracy is, the greater the likelihood that the union or its subgroup will limit its concerns to those of fractional groups of employees. This will often pit one group against another and even more frequently against the interests of the labor movement as a whole or the community at large. It is not true, as is often said, that in this way no one can win. Small groups can improve their relative standing at the expense of others. What is not possible for large numbers such as the working class as a whole—unless the social and economic system is radically changed—can be achieved by a small group or by individuals. It follows that in the same degree to which class solidarity is weakened, small groups may succeed in improving their real incomes and, by way of pattern bargaining or competitive spirit, stimulate a wave of wage increases. They may well end up by being monetary rather than real increases, but those who were among the first in the queue may for some time enjoy a real advantage until the rest of the group has caught up with them and prices have risen correspondingly. There is thus a painful choice to be made. As Otto Kahn-Freund put it: "The strike as a social institution—once considered as the supreme example of working class solidarity—may have been dialectically transmuted into its opposite: action of groups of workers seeking advantage at the expense of others."[22] All this does not mean that no further and important social changes are due to occur in the foreseeable future. But they are not likely to follow any preconceived program and will correspond to pragmatic needs of the moment, and a large part will consist of the adjustment of tradition-bound movements to a radically changed world. Whether all of them can do so remains to be seen.

An example of a failure to see the signs of the times is the draft of a new basic program that the West-German trade union confederation (D.G.B.) submitted to its members and the public in general toward the end of 1979. This document was to be discussed during 1980 and was to be voted on at an extraordinary congress early in 1981. In spite of its size and the broad coverage of issues—from workers' rights to art and culture—it is difficult to discern any basic concepts. Instead, the document appears to be a lengthy list of hardly connected and rather general demands, reminding the reader of an American election manifesto, widely at variance with the philosophically founded early programs of the German labor movement but also with a pragmatic orientation toward the needs of the time. The main difference between this program and that of an American union—if it had a long-term program—

is the scope of interests that the German union pursues, far beyond the confines of the employment relationship. Obviously, even for the German unions the latter is the center of their concerns, but tradition in thought and institutions requires that they express their interests on a wide range of issues, the more so as work appears, as was pointed out earlier, to be a less dominant aspect of the workers' lives than in the past. Yet no view of a better society appears in the program, but rather disconnected demands for change.

A most significant feature of labor movements from their modern beginnings has been the search for a model. Models have traditionally exerted tremendous influence on the behavior of European labor movements. Prior to 1914 it was the German Social Democratic party and its associate trade unions, the so-called free trade union movement, that inspired the rising labor movements in almost all except the Latin countries. Even V. I. Lenin, at the time, was enthusiastic in his praise of the German left. After 1918 the British took over the role of model for the non-Communist movements of Europe but with less success than their German predecessors and with far less desire to play this role.

After World War II, the U.S. trade unions, both the American Federation of Labor and the Congress of Industrial Organizations, made a deliberate and large-scale effort to influence the reconstructed movements of the continent to restrict trade union activities to the defense of the short-term interests of their members without any attempt at consciously changing the structure of the society in which they were operating, to become pragmatic and nonideological.[23] To accept a reformed capitalism was to be the new vision of Western European trade unionism. While, in this view, they were to widen their distance from the Socialist parties, the European representatives of U.S. labor went fairly far in conceding that in that respect European unions might have to behave differently from their transatlantic colleagues. Their attitude seemed to be that while U.S. labor would not show any sympathy for Socialist ideas, they were willing to defend the right of their—perhaps misguided—European associates to pursue Socialist objectives and speak the language of Socialism, as long as it was not that of Communism.

With the revival of the European economies, the glamor surrounding American labor and consequently its influence began to decline. German *Ostpolitik,* the attempt of the non-Communist left to make life less burdensome in Central Europe, marked the end of U.S. predominance on the European labor scene. The British, less concerned with proselytizing, made no special effort to succeed the Americans in their role as model. Once again, the Germans, especially under Willy Brandt's leadership, took over the role of ideological model. In the trade union area the startling success of the West German economy, often ascribed to the German system of codetermination, gave the latter the status of an international model.[24] In various forms codetermination or comanagement became one of the main objectives of Western

European labor.[25] The idea of labor representation on company boards in many variants was widely discussed.[26] There are, in addition, submodels, presenting an example in one or two limited areas. Thus Swedish labor market policy has had considerable influence beyond Scandinavia. Sweden has also had an impact on the discussion of codetermination by integrating it into the collective bargaining system. The special role that Italian unions have assigned to themselves in dealing with economic and political issues far beyond the normal range of collective bargaining and the cooperation among ideologically divided union confederations have given Italian labor prestige and influence in a number of Latin countries. Whether any of these models can long survive the developing crisis of the 1980s remains to be seen.

One final word may be devoted to the most recent developments of Euro-Communism. Euro-Communism, which appeared dying or dead after the breakdown of the French leftist alliance in 1978–79, has been somewhat revived by the events in Afghanistan and even more by those in Poland. The glamor of the earlier period when Euro-Communism was a new departure full of promise has turned pale, but a movement of some significance and—perhaps—promise still exists. It may be better to speak of revival than of continued existence, and the unintentional agent of the renaissance was Moscow.

After the collapse of the French Leftist coalition and the failure of the Italian Communist party in its efforts to achieve a "historic compromise" to enter the government in coalition with the Christian Democrats, the Euro-Communist movement was dormant or, as some observers saw it, dead. The Soviet Communist party thought the time had come for a final attack on the heretic brethren. In a speech in Moscow B. Ponomariov, responsible in the Soviet central committee for "relations with brother parties," accused the Euro-Communists of being "under the direct influence of socialdemocratic and bourgeois concepts."[27]

The three then existing main centers of Euro-Communism, Rome, Madrid, and Paris, reacted sharply. *Unita,* the Italian Communist daily, responded with the blunt statement: "We are no comrades of Ponomariov; we do not agree with him and similar people."[28] In Spain the Communist reaction was a proposal to revive "after a period of stagnation" the conversations among Rome-Paris-Madrid.

The Euro-Communist protest was sharpened by the sentences in Prague against spokesmen of "Charter 77," the outspoken anti-Moscow group. Spanish Communist papers called the sentence an "offence against Socialism." In Paris the divided left rallied in a common demonstration near the Czechoslovakian embassy. Even the tiny Communist parties of England, Switzerland, and Belgium, otherwise not known for their Euro-Communist views, suddenly proclaimed their support for these victims of Moscow. And *Unita* told Ponomariov that "Euro-Communism is not dead." The protest against Andrei

Sakharov's exile, however, was rather weak, indicating the disarray among the Euro-Communists.

Still, the Italian Communist party does not appear any nearer to a historic compromise with the Christian Democrats that could propel it into the government. French unity was forced upon the reluctant Communist party leadership by the rank and file. And the Portuguese Communist party still clings to its unconditional loyalty to Moscow. The future of Euro-Communism remains uncertain, though logic would lead to the conclusion that it is "the wave of the future," given the relative stability of the social systems in the West.

Once again, the country in which Euro-Communism asserted itself most clearly on the occasion of the Polish events was Italy. The break between Moscow and the Italian Communist party was never before as sharp and as openly expressed as upon the occasion of the attack upon the Polish unions. It is perhaps no longer in doubt that the Italian party is heading for a position in which a merger with the Socialists becomes a distinct possibility. That this would not remain without consequences on the union side appears almost inevitable.

In summary, the main issues confronting Western European labor are those of adjustment of organizations now a century or more in existence. The most important challenges are summarized below.

1. The rapid change of the structure of the labor force in the direction of services, white-collar work, and rising educational standards, the decline of the labor force in agriculture, the stable or diminishing proportion of labor in industry, the decline of the proportion of unskilled workers, and the slight decline of semiskilled workers all require the unions to make organizational and ideological changes.

2. Union-party relations have been greatly affected by the changes of labor force structure. Since a party of the industrial workers alone can hardly aspire any more to majority control of a democratic nation, the parties of the non-Communist left have transformed themselves into people's parties, recruiting their members not only in their traditional areas but also among middle-class people, service workers, and professionals. This, too, has involved considerable changes in ideology, electoral appeal, and organization. Many of these changes are still underway. Whether all of them can be successfully implemented is highly uncertain, given their sometimes contradictory character.

3. Independently of this evolution, though reinforced by it, the non-Communist labor movements, in both their political and trade union form, have accepted the existence of a mixed economy, though some programs for further nationalization measures are being put forward in a few countries. Codetermination in various forms, greatly inspired by the West German example, is more and more frequently advanced as an objective of the move-

ment. In order to avoid what appears the danger of unions being on "both sides of the bargaining table," some movements have preferred other solutions to the representation of labor or company boards. Thus, the extension of the scope of collective bargaining to subject matters up to now regarded as a "managerial prerogative"—such as investment or plant location—has been put forward as a new form of codetermination.

4. Full employment continues to be in the forefront of labor's demands. Indeed, in many, if not most countries of the West, it is the number one objective of the trade unions and has an equally high rank or runs a close second to price stability in the lists of some of the labor parties' priorities. However, the full implications of a long-run state of full employment or of stagflation for other institutions of the industrial relations system have not yet been understood by the movements in general. Nor has the economics profession to any appreciable extent assisted labor in this regard.

5. Adjustments in the collective bargaining system are nevertheless slowly getting underway. There is in some countries a trend toward the determination of a bargaining framework at a very high level, frequently with the participation of the government and experts, in addition to the social partners. At the same time there is a growing recognition that, in order to be relevant to the workers, the unions have to be active in the workplace. Bargaining shifts, therefore, not only toward top levels but also toward the plant. Whether oligarchy or democracy will emerge as the stronger of these contradictory tendencies is still unclear.

6. Increasing emphasis is being placed on nonmonetary aspects of the working relationship. Under various slogans (such as the "humanization of industrial work") more and more attention is being paid to changes in the organization of industrial work in order to make it more responsive to the workers' personality and their wish for self-expression in their work and to eliminate or at least reduce dangers to the workers' safety and health.

There is, of course, the threat of catastrophic events that would make this list beside the point or even ridiculous. A further sharpening of the oil crisis, increased tension or even hostilities between the superpowers, a long period of economic stagnation or decline—these and the unlimited list of unforeseeable crises may present the world and the labor movement with entirely new problems. But these possibilities are beyond the reach of the historian as well as the planner.

Neither in the short nor in the long run are the labor movements in the industrialized countries of the West likely to pursue their time-honored ways much longer. In the short run stagflation presents new problems of a kind that labor has not encountered in the last three decades, if ever. Stagflation forces upon organized labor a decision of priorities: to continue its traditional policy of pushing for improvements in wages and working conditions, at the risk of higher unemployment, or to make concessions in order to reduce prices and the rate of inflation, to increase the demand for goods and services, and to make their countries more competitive on the world markets, but at the price of abandoning hard-won advantages and reversing the traditional role of the labor movement. Since the seniority principle plays a much smaller role in lay-offs in European industrial relations, the burden of unemployment is distributed over much larger portions of the labor force by way of short hours and similar devices than in the United States. Making concessions would thus be somewhat easier for organized labor to accept in Europe than in the United States. Still, how far labor can go without endangering internal discipline and the size of its membership is uncertain. The alternative—going on as if the process of continuing economic expansion and full employment still prevailed—would turn labor into the guardian of the privileges of a fraction of the labor force, that is, those workers not threatened by unemployment. Another group of workers would become foes of the labor organizations, and that group would include the younger workers deprived, as they would see it, by the unions of a chance to join the ranks of the employed. Thus, the short run does not offer organized labor favorable prospects unless the economy—with or without union or party assistance—is turned around and stagflation is replaced by a new forward march.

In the long run, even this favorable prospect may not offer splendid opportunities for the unions, although perhaps slightly better ones are available for the non-Communist left in general. Given the past and future changes of the structure of the labor force, the chances for a substantial expansion, indeed even for the preservation of the present union membership, are not good, even if the hard core of unionists maintains its loyalty to organized labor. Thus unions would be fortunate if they could maintain their hold on the presently organized proportion of the labor force.

While this alone might be an important factor in limiting or even reducing the impact of unionism in Western societies, the increasing internal diversity of the organized part of the labor force is likely to be a further weakening element. There will be some common objectives uniting the movement, and a few of these, such as attaining and maintaining full employment, will be of vital importance. A well-developed social security system may be another such objective, although there some differences between blue- and white-collar workers and younger and older members of the labor force may develop. But beyond these elementary union demands—most of which are already achieved and widely regarded in Western Europe as matters of course—differences and cleavages may become increasingly manifest.

For example, in Sweden the interests of professional groups such as those organized in the T.C.O. (the white-collar union confederation) and S.A.C.O. (which represents academically trained managerial employees) are not identical with those of the bulk of the members in the L.O. (an organization of primarily manual workers); perhaps their diverse interests are not even easily compatible with each other. Nor are the employers likely to forego the opportunity to weaken the cohesion of the unions. As early as 1962, T. L. Johnston in his study of Swedish industrial relations pointed out this strategy of S.A.F. (the employers' organization). "S.A.F.'s policy is to favor individual differentiation of salary for all salaried employees, a policy accepted by the union of Clerical and Technical Employees."[29] Opportunities for such disintegrating maneuvers should multiply as the internal differentiation of the labor force increases. A wide distance separates the computer programmer and the managerial employee from the factory sweeper.

Somewhat similar problems confront the parties "left of center," though they seem perhaps a bit more manageable. Most of the former labor parties have made the transformation to people's parties. This is probably irrevocable and in their long-term interests, since a revival of the trends in the labor force structure is highly unlikely. What is, perhaps, of less certain value for them is their adoption of moderate and highly pragmatic policies. Some tension over certain aspects of this change have manifested themselves already in the German S.P.D. and in other Socialist parties. These were mainly over issues that concern the environment, the development of nuclear energy, or the installation of nuclear weapons, all problems of tremendous importance for the young and the environmentalists and of lesser significance for the industrial workers. Sharp disputes have developed for instance between Willy Brandt, chairman of the S.P.D., and a group around Annemarie Renger, widow of Kurt Schumacher and leader of a party wing that wishes a clear separation from those, colloquially called the "greens," whose main concerns are regarded as tangential to the principal mission of the party.

Somewhat similar conflicts have contributed to the split in the British Labour party. Unilateral nuclear disarmament was one of the issues underlying the breakaway of the Social Democrats from Labour.

While the internal conflicts are of considerable importance by themselves, an even more threatening issue looms on the horizon. The adjustment of the movements to the post–World War II environment was clearly related to the wave of prosperity that made possible most of the reforms and working-class advances characteristic of that period. If, however, the economic slow-down since the mid-1970s were to introduce a long period of stagnation and unemployment or even a reduction of living standards, then this belated adjustment to prosperity may prove to be a source of lasting weakness to the movements "left of center." A much more active and fundamental opposition to the existing social order would then better reflect the mood of the large numbers of people threatened by the economic decline or by the measures used, for example, in Great Britain, to shift the burden of the economic loss to the lower income groups and to undo the social reforms of the last half century. Such a development could indeed upset the internal balance and change the entire direction of the movement and move the left further away from the center.

NOTES

1. Kurt L. Shell, *The Transformation of Austrian Socialism* (Albany: State University of New York Press, 1962), esp. 45. This study illuminates a great many difficult problems of post–World War II Socialism, although its interpretation of the party's attitude toward democracy in the interwar period does not render full justice to the party's profound democratic convictions.

2. *Ibid.*

3. *Ibid.*, quoting from the proceedings of the Austrian party congress of 1926. This is a paraphrase of the text adopted at the congress.

4. Jean-Daniel Reynaud made some penetrating remarks about the lessened importance of work for the worker. See his presidential address to the Congress of the Internaional Industrial Relations Association, reprinted in the *British Journal of Industrial Relations*, XVIII (1979), 3.

5. For France, data are given in Richard F. Hamilton, *Affluence and the French Worker in the French Republic* (Princeton: Princeton University Press, 1967). Moderate parties do get a large part of the support of the new middle class while the old middle class—urban small businessmen, artisans, and farmers (in Europe perhaps just peasants) tend to vote for conservative parties in Germany, France, and Britain.

6. There are sharply contrasting views on the social role of white-collar workers. While there are factual data to demonstrate their relative reluctance to organize in unions, it would appear that in West Germany they play a significant part in politics and fail to do so in France. On the first, see Adolf Sturmthal, ed., *White-Collar Trade Unions: Contemporary Developments in Industrialized Societies* (Urbana: University of Illinois Press, 1966); political activism and inertia are discussed in the literature quoted by Hamilton, *Affluence and the French Worker,* 49, esp. the works of C. Wright Mills and Juan Linz.

7. In the Austro-Marxian version of the interwar period a "balance of class forces" would create the danger of a Fascist movement. Since 1945, however, this same situation would be regarded by most non-Communist labor movements as the precondition for successful cooperation among different political parties and unions and management.

8. The British rejection of coalition governments, sometimes observed more in form rather than in substance, has its foundation in the British electoral system rather than in any theoretical considerations of the Marxian type.

9. S. M. Lipset in his *Introduction to Political Man: The Social Bases of Politics* (Garden City, N.Y.: Doubleday, 1963), xxxiii, states: "I trust it will be clear that I do not favor a decline in political interest or in reform movements, but rather that I have attempted to analyze the sources of an actual phenomenon. Agreement with this point of view has recently come from a surprising source, Richard Crossman of the *New Statesman,* who writes of Western Europe and America: 'The truth is that *"we are all conservatives now,"* that liberalism and socialism, which even

thirty years ago were still doctrines of social revolution, have become necessities for conserving national independence and personal freedom.' [Richard Crossman, *op. cit.*, p. 7. (Emphasis mine. SML)]."

10. Socialist Union, *Socialism—A New Statement of Principles* (London: Lincoln-Prager Press, Ltd., 1952), 14–15.

11. Indeed, in the United States salvaging private enterprises with public funds has been accepted as in line with the official ideology of "free private enterprise." The Meidner plan in Sweden, which aimed at using union-administered social security funds to buy shares of private companies, did not imply nationalization in the strict sense of the term. See Rudolf Meidner, *Employee Investment Funds. An Approach to Collective Capital Formation* (London: George Allen and Unwin, 1978).

12. Even the confidence in Keynes has been shaken by the recent experience of inflation accompanied by unemployment, leaving the labor movement in doubt about the meager remnants of its theoretical foundations.

13. As against R. H. S. Crossman's views accepting lower efficiency as the price he was willing to pay for greater equality; see R. H. S. Crossman, ed., *New Fabian Essays* (London, 1952).

14. Raymond Georis, "Europe's Antiquated Educational Systems," *European Community*, 154 (Mar. 1972), 20.

15. *Ibid.*

16. *Ibid.*

17. Raymond Boudon, *L'inégalité des chances. La Mobilité Sociale dans les Sociétés industrielles* (Paris: Armand Colin, 1973), 190. I owe this reference to a suggestion of my friend, Jean-Daniel Reynaud. The French author derives his conclusions from studies in England and France.

18. Proofs of this proposition can be found not only in mathematical logic but also in empirical studies in a number of countries including the United States, Denmark, and Germany, in addition to the British and French investigations referred to in the previous note.

19. This term has at least three meanings relating to the conditions of work and the workplace, consumption, and environment. The extent to which advances in these three areas are compatible with the growth of the national product as conventionally measured is a matter of intense dispute, as is the issue of which should be given precedence, if there is a contradiction. In which way could people express their preferences, for instance, between working less or earning more? See Bernard Cazes, "Europe: International Dimensions and Factors of Economic Growth," in Wolfgang Michalski, ed., *The Future of Industrial Societies. Problems—Prospects—Solutions* (Alphen an den Rijn: Rightoff, 1978), 30–32.

20. Willis W. Harman and F. Lloyd Lewis, "United States: Growth, Decline or Metamorphosis," in Michalski, ed., *Future of Industrial Societies,* 7.

21. *"The only effective restraint on the power of the dominant class is counterpower.* The primary weapons of the lower strata, of the exploited classes, are the ability to organize, to strike, to demonstrate, and to vote rulers out of office. In any given society at any given time in history, the lower classes may not use these weapons effectively, they may not recognize their interests, but there is no other

way. Hence a society which denies the masses such rights is not only undemocratic politically, it also fosters the increased privileges of the ruling groups. As Milovan Djilas and many others have demonstrated, Communist dictatorship has meant the creation of a New Class more exploitative than the ruling classes of Western capitalism. The distribution of rewards in the Soviet Union is much more unequal than it is in most other industrialized nations. And it is primarily the fear of the potentially revolutionary masses that has, since 1953, led the rulers of the Eastern European states to make concessions to alleviate the standard of living of the workers and peasants." Lipset, *Introduction to Political Man,* xxiii.

22. *Labour Relations: Heritage and Adjustment* (London: O.V.P., 1979).

23. Obviously, the underlying assumption was that acceptance of the existing social institutions was nonideological.

24. The Spanish Socialist leader, Felipe Gonzalez, has expressly referred to Social Democracy as his model.

25. Indeed, even one or two U.S. unions, though remaining uncommitted, demonstrated considerable interest in German industrial relations and especially codetermination.

26. Wolfgang Lecher and Ulrike Sieling-Wendeling, "New Developments in the Discussion of Co-determination in Europe," *Labor and Society,* 4 (Jan. 1979), 80–98. This article was first published in German in *Das Mitbestimmungsgespräch,* nos. 11 and 12 (1977).

27. There seems to have been some disagreement about the appropriateness of this attack among the Soviet leaders. In a repeat transmission of the Soviet news agency TASS, the attacks on Euro-Communism were mysteriously missing. *Zukunft,* Dec. 1979, 7. Conceivably Ponomariov's attack was just a trial balloon to test reaction from abroad.

28. Author's translation of the report in *ibid.*

29. T. L. Johnston, *Collective Bargaining in Sweden. A Study of the Labor Market and Its Institutions* (Cambridge, Mass.: Harvard University Press, 1962), 254. In German codetermination, a similar strategy was successful.

Index

A Note on the Author

Adolf Sturmthal is professor emeritus of Labor and Industrial Relations at the University of Illinois at Urbana-Champaign. Born in Vienna, Austria, he came to the United States in 1938, having received his doctorate at the University of Vienna. Before his arrival at the University of Illinois in 1960, Mr. Sturmthal had also taught at Bard College, Columbia University (1940–55) and at Roosevelt University (1955–60). He has also served as a consultant to various U.S. government agencies and business and labor organizations. He has several publications in the area of industrial relations, including *The Tragedy of European Labor, 1918–1939*, *White-Collar Trade Unions,* and, with James G. Scoville, *The International Labor Movement in Transition.*